Guns, Polls,
and
Democracy

Americans want Congress to enact sensible gun laws.

Congress refuses.

Is that how American democracy is supposed to work?

Gary Reed

Top Quark Publishing Co.

Copyright © 2020 D. Gary Reed

All rights reserved.

ISBN-13: 979864986270

ASIN: B089J4CFYQ

Top Quark Publishing Company
Union, Kentucky 41091

The reader who needs legal advice should consult an attorney who is licensed in the relevant state and has experience in gun law matters.

No part of this book may be reproduced, or stored in a retrieval system, or transmitted in any form or by any means, electronic, mechanical, photocopying, recording, or otherwise, without express written permission of the publisher.

Cover design by Kelly A. Martin

Cover Images: DepositPhotos: rolffimages

GPD062221

Contents

Introduction 1
The Polling Data 11
PART ONE: TAKING AIM AT GUN VIOLENCE.............................25
1. Guns: The Terrible Toll 27
2. Guns: How Many of Us Own Them?.................................. 41
3. The Second Amendment: *Heller* and *McDonald* 60
PART TWO: WHICH GUN LAWS DO AMERICANS WANT?............73
4. Should We Require Universal Background Checks? 75
5. Can We Not Sell Guns to Terrorists, Please? 98
6. Should We Close the "Boyfriend" Loophole?........................109
7. Should We Close The "Emergency Order" Loophole?...............121
8. Should Violent Offenders Get to Keep Their Guns?..................129
9. Should We Enact "Red Flag" Laws?......................................138
10. Should We License Gun Owners? 159
11. Should We Register and Track Guns?.................................167
12. Should We Ban Assault Weapons? 178
13. Should Teenagers Have Assault Weapons? 204
14. Should We Ban Large-Capacity Magazines? 221
15. Should We Ban Bump Stocks? 243
16. Should We Require Gun Owners to Secure Their Guns? 259
17. Should We Repeal the Second Amendment and Ban Guns?...275
PART THREE: GUNS *vs.* DEMOCRACY 283
18. What We Want *vs.* What We're Getting 285
19. Why Does Congress Refuse What Most Americans Want? ... 296
20. What Can We Do? 306
Conclusion 311

APPENDICES	317
–Federal Age Limits for Possession, Sale, and Purchase	319
–The Gun Policy Polls	320
–The Public Opinion Polls	325
–The Gun Ownership Polls	348
ENDNOTES	357
SELECTED BIBLIOGRAPHY	411
INDEX	419
ACKNOWLEDGMENTS	420
AUTHOR	421

"Is this how American democracy is supposed to work?"

Justice Elena Kagan dissenting in <u>Rucho</u> v. <u>Common Cause</u>, 588 U.S. _, _, 139 S. Ct. 2484, 2519 (June 27, 2019)

Introduction

We think of proposals to reduce our country's gun violence as hugely controversial, and at least in the abstract, any suggestion that we should "do something" about gun violence *is* controversial. But polls consistently show that while deeply divided on the rhetoric of guns and gun violence, Americans—being practical people—mostly agree on a broad range of specific policy proposals.

In June 2017, J. Baxter Oliphant, a researcher at the Pew Research Center, put it this way:

> Republicans and Democrats find rare common ground on some gun policy proposals ... Large majorities in both parties continue to favor preventing people with mental illnesses from buying guns, barring gun purchases by people on federal no-fly or watch lists, and background checks for private gun sales and sales at gun shows.[1]

After a May 2019 poll, Tim Malloy, Assistant Director of polling at Quinnipiac University, summed things up this way:

> A nation with more guns than people and a history of horrifying mass shootings continues to call—or cry—for tighter gun regulation.[2]

After the spree of mass shootings in late summer 2019, Dr. Lee Miringoff, Director of The Marist College Institute for Public Opinion, wrote:

> You'd be hard-pressed to find something where the gap between public sentiment and legislative action or inaction is wider because you've got a clear consensus across party lines.

The gap is huge, and the congressional crowd is very much out of step with where public opinion is on this. And therein lies the frustration [of many Americans], as the frequency of these shootings increases.[3]

This book gathers data from public opinion polls to better understand the extent to which there is consensus on steps we could take to address our country's gun violence. In other words, this book asks: *On which proposals is there a consensus? And how much of a consensus?*

Most of us recognize that the United States has a gun violence problem—one that is far worse than in other developed, democratic countries. Our gun fatality rate, 12.15 per 100,000 persons in 2018, was about five times higher than Canada's, eleven times higher than Australia's, and 175 times higher than Japan's.

Because our gun violence problem is multifaceted, thoughtful people have put forward a mixture of proposals, most designed to chip away at some aspect or another of the problem. The proposals range from pinpoint attacks on narrow issues, like prohibiting gun sales to known and suspected terrorists, to broader measures aimed at reducing the illegal gun trafficking that makes possible so much of our inner-city gun violence.

The proposals are varied. We could, for example, require background checks on *all* gun sales, including private sales. We could get serious about disarming violent domestic abusers. We could prohibit individuals with violent misdemeanor convictions from owning guns, at least for some time. We could allow law enforcement and families to petition courts for "red flag" or "extreme risk" orders that authorize the police to disarm someone whose behavior indicates they are an imminent danger to themselves or others.

To keep guns out of the wrong hands and to reduce the black market in guns, we could license gun owners and establish a tracking system for gun transfers. To reduce the number of mass shootings, or at least reduce the number of victims, we could ban "assault weapons" and large-capacity magazines. Or, if that's a bridge too far, we could require individuals to be at least twenty-one-years old before they can buy weapons of war.

We could require gun owners to secure their guns when not in use, so their kids don't find them and kill themselves or someone else. And we could make gun owners legally responsible when they leave a loaded gun where a child can get it, and the child uses it to kill himself or some-one else.

Opinion polls by well-respected polling organizations show that majorities of voters—often substantial majorities—want Congress and our state legislatures to enact most of those measures.[4] Republicans, Independents, and Democrats, gun owners and non-gun owners, and individuals at every educational level, overwhelmingly agree on universal background checks, not selling guns to terrorists, and several other measures that might help reduce the carnage. Other measures—banning "assault weapons" and large-capacity magazines, for example—are more divisive.

But a vast chasm separates what the American public wants and what its elected representatives in Congress are willing or able to enact. *And that is what this book is about*—the sharp divergence between the gun laws most Americans want, as measured by respected public opinion polls, and what their elected representatives are willing (or able) to deliver. The point is hardly a new one, but this book marshals the results of polls so that readers can judge for themselves just how wide that chasm is.

To be clear: Not all politicians refuse to support policies that might reduce our country's gun violence. But pro-gun—mainly Republican[5]—members of Congress and our state legislatures, funded by gun manufacturers, armed with gun lobby talking points, and buoyed by Second Amendment absolutists, too often stand in the way of enacting the very modest measures most Americans want.

This book argues that such a stark division between what most Americans want and what Congress is willing to deliver cannot be healthy for representative democracy in this country.

This Book Is Intended For the Lay Reader Who Wants to Know More about Gun Policy

Most of us are interested, but not deeply immersed in gun-violence-prevention and gun-rights issues. And many of us—on both sides of the debate—harbor some serious misconceptions. With that in mind, this book provides the reader some background both on the dimensions of our gun violence problem and on the specific proposals this book discusses.

General readers may find the background information eye-opening, or at least helpful, but for some, the detailed polling data may be of less interest. If you find that to be the case, the brief recap that follows the detailed polling data may be enough to satisfy your appetite for polling data.

At the opposite end of the spectrum, gun-violence-prevention advocates and researchers are well-versed in the size and contours of our gun violence problem. For them, the introductory material may be familiar territory. But unlike some general readers, they may find the polling data of most interest. They may also wish to consider using the rich data polling organizations have in their own research projects.

The folks who do polling may be interested mainly in how their poll results stack up against others' results—and bristle at the one suggestion I make. They would be justified in pointing out that they know far more about polling than I do.

And finally, I hope that those who hold public office, or are thinking of running for office, find the book especially useful—even if the public doubts that most politicians read books.

Whatever your background, the chapter titles and subheadings should guide you to the material that interest you most.

How This Book Is Organized

Chapters 1 through 3 provide background for the discussion that follows:

Chapter 1 discusses the size and contours of our gun violence problem. It will be tragically familiar to anyone who follows the issue closely, but it may contain some surprises for those who don't.

Chapter 2 discusses how many Americans own guns or live in households where there is a gun. It also discusses some long-term trends in the types of guns we own. And it looks at some misperceptions—held by those on both sides of the gun-violence-prevention debate—about how many of us own guns.

Chapter 3 briefly summarizes the Supreme Court's *Heller* and *McDonald* decisions, the pair of decisions that changed the legal landscape for gun regulation. This book, however, does not weigh in on the controversy surrounding those decisions, the original intent of the Second Amendment, or whether the Second Amendment still makes sense today. Library bookshelves already sag under the weight of volumes devoted to those topics.

The central chapters in this book are Chapters 4 through 17. Each discusses a different gun-violence-prevention proposal and proceeds as follows:

The Issue. People come to these discussions with varying levels of understanding and often with misunderstandings, both about current law and about specific proposals. This section, which appears in each chapter, explains what the proposal entails. The aim of this section is simply to level set and focus the discussion.

What We Want. Under this heading, each chapter discusses the extent to which the public supports or opposes the proposal—as measured by publicly available opinion polls. This is the heart of the book. The point is to assess the level of public support—and opposition—the proposal generates. Where the necessary polling data are available, this section also indicates whether Republicans and gun owners support or oppose the proposal. The assumption is that Republican and other pro-gun legislators care, or at least *should* care, what their fellow Republicans and fellow gun owners think.

What We're Getting Instead. This section briefly explains what Congress has (or has not) done with the proposal. When appropriate, this section will also mention what states have done, but not in the detail the topic deserves.

As we'll see, year in and year out, congressional Republicans and other pro-gun legislators oppose the gun-violence-prevention measures that most Americans—often supermajorities of Americans—want. This book, by the way, considers a "supermajority" to be 66% or higher.

Perhaps even more troubling, Republican and other pro-gun legislators block even the gun-violence-prevention proposals their fellow Republicans and most gun owners want.

Chapter 18 pulls together the separate discussions and makes this point: The American public wants action on gun violence, but their representatives in Congress, particularly in the Senate, are determined to keep Americans from getting what they want.

Chapter 19 briefly discusses why that might be so.

Chapter 20 offers a few suggestions about how we might close the rift between most Americans and our representatives in Congress.

The Public Opinion Polls Appendix has more information about these polls and in the digital version of this book, links to the data.

Districts and States Elect Members of Congress and Senators

Based on the data presented in Chapters 4 through 16, this book draws the obvious conclusion: Congress refuses to enact the gun-violence-prevention measures most of us want it to adopt.

But it is worth noting that this book focuses on national polls, which show where the country as a whole stands. Members of Congress, however, represent congressional districts, and Senators represent individual states. The country as a whole doesn't elect them.

When House Members and Senators vote against what the great majority of Americans want, they may claim that they are merely doing what voters in their home district or state prefer. House Members and Senators, for example, may argue that most people in their home district or state come down solidly in favor of guns everywhere, all the time—the cost to society be damned.

Those Representatives and Senators may claim that the fine, hardworking people in their districts or states believe that we *should* keep the "private sale" exception to background checks that fuels our country's black market in guns. They may even argue that their constituents insist that, *Yes, we should allow gun dealers to sell guns and ammunition to known and suspected terrorists.*

They may also claim that the God-fearing folks in their districts or states believe that violent domestic abusers *should* be allowed to "keep and bear Arms" against their spouses and dating partners. They may even insist that the people in their districts or states believe the Second Amendment includes the right to keep a loaded handgun where a toddler can find it and kill himself or someone else.

Without seeing their private polls, it is impossible to know if they are correct. There simply aren't enough publicly available state-level or congressional-district-level polls to be able to assess that. And even if there were, there aren't enough pages in this book—or in any book anyone would read—to address all fifty states, let alone all 435 congressional districts.

But given the size of the majorities in favor of some of the issues discussed in this book, it is difficult to believe that most congressional districts or states are like that. Indeed, it's hard to fathom how that math might work: If 90% of us want universal background checks, how could the majority in each—or even most—of the fifty states oppose that measure?

An Important Limitation on the Scope of this Book

This book stresses that our gun violence problem is multifaceted and that different solutions may be appropriate for different types of gun violence. But, like media coverage of gun violence in general, polls tend to focus on mass shootings, or at least on those shootings that involve white, suburban students or adults.

This book compiles polling data. Because polling data do not reach the full range of potential solutions to issues like suicide, inner-city gun violence, domestic abuse and domestic terrorism, this book does not cover everything that needs to be done to address our gun violence problem. There is no shortage of other books, reports, studies, and articles that do.

This Book Is Not an Attack on Gun Owners

Another of the major themes in this book is that gun owners are not a distinct species or subset of the population that doesn't care about gun violence and the lives it takes.

Most gun owners and *nearly* everyone else agree that we should try *most* of the proposals discussed in this book. If we did, we would see soon enough if these measures reduce gun violence and save lives. I emphasize "most" and "nearly" because neither *all* gun owners nor *all* non-gun owners agree on all the proposals discussed in this book—or this being America, on anything. In fact, as discussed in Chapter 17, most Americans and most gun owners do not favor banning all guns, or even all handguns.

The Second Amendment Absolutists

This book draws a distinction between most gun owners and the Second Amendment absolutists (the folks who believe the Second Amendment does not permit *any* regulation of guns). Gun owners may find it reassuring to learn that most Americans, including gun owners like themselves, support many common-sense proposals to reduce our country's horrific gun carnage.

But I suspect that Second Amendment absolutists, if they could somehow be persuaded to read this book, would object to the conclusion that they are a distinct minority. The data, however, are clear.

Second Amendment absolutists and "2A" folks may also object to the notion that in a representative democracy, supermajorities of Americans should usually get the legislation they want (as long that doesn't violate the Constitution). Even so, I sincerely hope Second Amendment absolutists and "2A" folks will read this book anyway, so that they can get a better grasp of where the rest of us are coming from.

But a couple of caveats about the concerns of Second Amendment absolutists and other dogmatic gun-rights advocates are worth mentioning. They tend to respond to every plea that we need to do something about gun violence as an attack on gun owners. They point out, correctly, that there are millions of gun owners who are law-abiding and have never shot anyone. It's essential, therefore, to acknowledge that most gun owners *are* responsible. And to stress that this book is not an attack on gun owners. It is also not an attack on the rights of law-abiding adults, who are not disqualified by prior bad behavior or mental illness, to own a gun.

But Second Amendment absolutists and strident gun-rights advocates do make some assumptions that overstate their case.

Unspoken Assumption #1

For starters, their protests equate all gun owners with Second Amendment absolutists and gun rights dogmatists like themselves. That is neither accurate nor fair. Gun owners, as a group, are more conservative than most, and they are more likely to be Republicans. But they don't want to see their kid or grandkid gunned down at school, in church, or in a cineplex any more than their neighbors who don't own guns. To say the same thing differently: Most gun owners are mainstream Americans, who share their neighbors' concerns about our country's horrific gun violence.

Public opinion polls sometimes break out gun owners or, more often, those who live in households where there is a gun ("gun householders"). When they do, healthy majorities of gun owners and gun householders usually support whatever gun-violence-prevention measure is under discussion. The notable exceptions are banning assault weapons and large-capacity magazines.

Colleen Barry, Ph.D., the lead author of a 2018 study on public support for and opposition to gun-violence-prevention, wrote:

> Widespread claims that a chasm separates gun owners from non-gun owners in their support for gun safety policies distracts attention from many areas of genuine agreement—areas that can lead to policy solutions and result in the prevention of gun violence.[6]

Her survey and most of the polls cited in this book show that there are indeed several measures on which majorities of both gun owners and non-gun owners agree.

Clifford Young is the president of U.S. Ipsos Public Affairs, a major polling organization. His organization collaborated with BuzzFeed News to figure out where gun owners' heads were on gun-violence-prevention issues. "We found," he wrote, "that most gun owners are terribly similar to the rest of Americans."

He elaborated.[7]

They believe gun ownership should not be taken lightly and are supportive of more stringent background checks and limitations on firearm accessories. Gun owners might be less supportive of outright bans and worry about broader gun restrictions; [but] they are not completely opposed to any gun control measures. Confirming Americans, even gun owners, are a sensible, pragmatic people.

As we will see, surveys by other polling organizations bear out his conclusion.

Unspoken Assumption #2

When they rage against any suggestion that we should try to reduce our horrific gun violence, Second Amendment absolutists often make a second unspoken assumption—namely, that not just other gun owners, but indeed that most Americans think just like they do. That's a natural assumption, as most of us tend to surround ourselves with others who share our own interests, attitudes, and beliefs.[8]

Gun rights advocates go hunting or target shooting or grab a beer with friends who share their interests in guns and gun rights. And they often immerse themselves in America's toxic gun culture: They read gun magazines and posts on gun rights websites. They watch videos and webcasts put out by the NRA and other gun rights organizations. They may attend the meetings of their local NRA or other gun rights organization. As a result, they come to assume that most people, or at least most white men in their part of the country, are just like themselves and share their beliefs.[9]

But as the polls discussed in this book make clear, gun rights activists, "2A" people, and others who oppose any and all proposals to reduce gun violence are actually a relatively small minority—maybe only 7% of Americans and probably no more than 12%.[10] Of course, on particular issues, others join with the hardliners in opposition.

The Polling Data

Before beginning work on this book, like most Americans, I was generally aware that for the last quarter-century, Congress has largely refused or been unable to do anything constructive about our nation's gun violence. I assumed that our representatives in Congress refused or were unable to act because the public was deeply divided on what to do.

But while researching polling data for a different project, I stumbled onto something that surprised me: The American public actually supports a wide range of gun-violence-prevention measures—and has for quite some time. The issue is largely not one that divides most Americans. Instead, it's part of the larger disconnect between most Americans and their representatives in Congress.

In this book, I collect the polling data that back up—or, for some policy proposals, constrain—that observation. In doing so, I present data only from legitimate polls by respected polling organizations that make their data available to the public and disclose their methodology. I do not include "polls," like those seen on some gun-rights websites, in which people who actively oppose proposals to restrict access to guns are urged to weigh in.

The Gun Policy Polls Appendix contains a list of the polls cited in connection with the proposals discussed in Chapters 4-16. The Public Opinion Polls section in the Appendix has more information on those and the other polls cited in the text. The digital version of this book also has links to those polls.

Time Frame

For the most part, this book gathers polls since the Las Vegas Strip shooting on October 1, 2017, through the end of 2019.[11] That's both to make this book current (when published in 2020) and to keep it somewhat manageable in size.

The longer-term trend has been in the direction of more support for doing something about our gun violence problem, with a bump up in support after each headline-grabbing mass shooting, and a reversion to-ward the longer-term trendline between those events.

Events That May Have Influenced the Polls

During the period that is the focus of this book, several seismic events have prompted polling organizations to conduct new polls. Those events may have also influenced the opinions those polls measured.

The Las Vegas Strip Shooting

On the evening of October 1, 2017, from a suite high up in the Man-dalay Bay Resort and Casino on the Las Vegas Strip, 64-year-old Stephen Paddock opened fire on the country music fans attending the Route 91 Harvest Music Festival. In a ten-minute shooting spree, Paddock killed 58 and left a total of 868 injured—413 with gunshot or shrapnel wounds and the rest with injuries incurred while trying to escape. It was the deadliest mass shooting in the country's history.

Congress, controlled at the time by Republicans, did not hold a hear-ing to examine whether the country needed new laws to prevent more such massacres. In fact, during eight years of Republican control, Con-gress did not hold *any* hearings on gun-violence-prevention legislation. Shortly after President Trump assumed office, however, it did hold hearings on and passed legislation making it easier for the severely mentally ill receiving Social Security disability benefits to buy guns. President Trump signed that legislation into law.[12]

In the midst of a suicide epidemic among veterans, the House also approved, on a largely party line vote, The Veterans 2nd Amendment Pro-tection Act.[13] That bill provided that "a person who is mentally incapac-itated, deemed mentally incompetent, or experiencing an extended loss of consciousness shall not be considered" ineligible to buy a gun. The Senate never acted on that legislation.

The Parkland School Shooting

On Valentine's Day, February 14, 2018, Nikolas Cruz, armed with an AR-15-style semi-automatic rifle and multiple magazines, entered Marjorie Stoneman Douglas High School in Parkland, Florida, and pulled a fire alarm.[14] Students were expecting an active-shooter drill and promptly filed out of their classrooms. As they did, Cruz opened fire, killing 17 students and staff members and wounding 17 more. The shooting was the worst high school shooting, but not the worst school shooting in the country's history.

The #NeverAgain Movement

After school shootings and other high-profile mass shootings, Congressional leaders and pro-gun advocates routinely declare that it is too soon to discuss how to prevent the next mass shooting. After the tears and funerals and speeches, the public moves on. As other events fill the news cycle, pressure on legislators to do something about gun violence eases.

But after the massacre of their fellow students at the Stoneman Douglas High School, a remarkable thing happened. David Hogg, Emma González, and other student leaders at the Parkland, Florida, high school reacted by calling for real reform. They said students of their generation were tired of being killed by losers with guns because legislators were unwilling to stand up to the gun lobby.

Some of the Parkland students, along with victims of other mass shootings, met with President Trump, who came out on Twitter in favor of comprehensive background checks, keeping guns out of the hands of the mentally ill, raising the minimum age for gun purchases to 21, and banning bump stocks.[15] Other Parkland students appeared on a televised CNN Town Hall. They and the audience excoriated Senator—and gun lobby supporter—Marco Rubio.

To remember the 17 killed and 17 wounded in the Stoneman Douglas High School shooting, the Women's March Network organized a nationwide 17-minute school walkout on March 14, 2018.[16]

The students and others also organized rallies to demand legislative action. Working with Everytown for Gun Safety, the students organized a massive march in Washington, D.C., and smaller rallies around the country, collectively called the "March for Our Lives." That took place on March 24, 2018, and garnered a huge amount of media coverage.[17] Their pleas struck a responsive note with other students around the country and with parents.

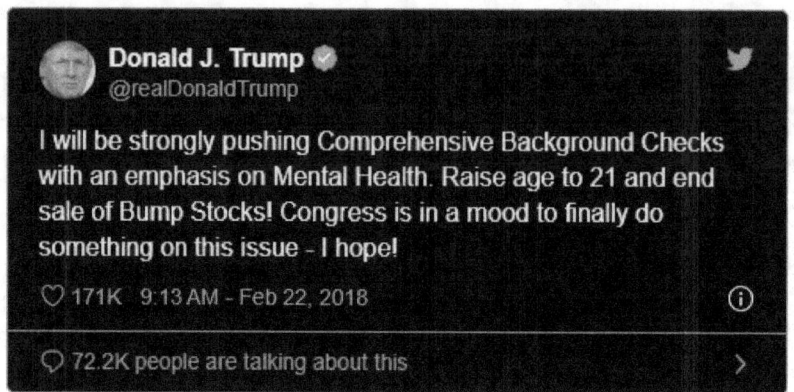

Second Amendment absolutists, however, responded as they usually do—with rote talking points, paranoid conspiracy theories, and threats. Some claimed, with no evidence, that the Parkland shooting was a "false flag" operation staged by anti-gun activists. Others accused the student leaders of being "crisis actors" flown in for the occasion—even though their teachers and fellow students knew them well. Still others admitted that, *yes, the student leaders were Stoneman Douglas students*, but claimed the students were not at school on the day of the shooting. Others threatened to kill the student leaders.

Ignoring the threats, the students responded by launching the #NeverAgain movement. They bluntly told politicians they needed to take action, or voters would replace them. In the "Gunshine" state of Florida, which had been a laboratory for NRA proposals, the legislature quickly passed a number of laws restricting violent and impulsive individuals' access to guns.

Republicans in Congress, however, refused to budge. In November 2018, voters made good on the students' promise: Voters replaced 40 pro-gun Members of the House of Representatives, giving Democrats control of the House. (Voters rejected Republican House candidates for a variety of reasons, not just gun issues. Most of those reasons had to do with President Trump and with Republicans' efforts to strip them of their health insurance.[18]) Republicans kept control of the Senate, where voters from low-population, gun-friendly rural states are overrepresented.

Gilroy, El Paso, Dayton

In late summer of 2019, a string of high-profile mass shootings once again drew attention to gun violence.

On Sunday, July 28, as the annual Garlic Festival in Gilroy, California was drawing to a close, a gunman killed three people, including a six-year-old boy, and injured a dozen more. After police shot and wounded the gunman, he turned his gun on himself.

The following weekend, on Saturday, August 3, a gunman killed 22 people and injured 24 others in a Walmart in El Paso. The gunman specifically targeted Mexicans and Mexican Americans. Later, in the early hours of Sunday morning, August 4, a gunman in an entertainment district in Dayton, Ohio, began shooting. Police killed the gunman about 30 seconds into his shooting spree. But in that 30 seconds, the gunman killed nine and injured 27.

And then, at the end of August, a gunman led police on a chase through Odessa and Midland, Texas, that left seven dead and 25 injured. The police killed the gunman in a shootout.[19]

Polling Averages and Bias

This book stresses the averages of the available polls. Averages smooth the effects of the occasional outlier poll. As famed polling authority Nate Silver notes, "Polling averages are more accurate than individual polls. The average isn't foolproof—it doesn't help when all the polls miss in the same direction—but you're usually better off taking your chances with [an average] than with individual surveys."[20]

Media reports often refer to public opinion surveys as a "Fox" or "CNN" or "NPR" poll. That may raise concerns about bias. News organizations, however, don't do their own polling. They hire professional polling organizations to conduct surveys and compile the results. Politico, for example, retains the polling organization Morning Consult to conduct polls on topical issues. CNN contracts with SSRS, and so on.

Adults, Voters, and Other Technical Matters

Polls vary in the size of their representative samples of the population and in the way they select those representative samples. They also vary in the way they obtain respondents' views and in the way they present data. This book isn't about those technical matters, but it may be useful to flag a few things readers should be aware of.

Some of the polls at the heart of this book chose a representative sample of "adults," *i.e.*, individuals eighteen-years-old or older. Others chose a representative sample of "registered voters." And a few polls targeted "adults" but also broke out results for the portion of their samples who were registered voters.

The differences are obvious. In this country, many individuals are ineligible to register to vote. Others are eligible but don't bother. Given that there are more adults than voters, it's a bit easier for polling organizations to reach adults. Our elected representatives, however, may care more about the opinions of those who do register and vote.

Sample size is important. Most of the polls discussed in this book have about 1,500 respondents, but some have as few as 800, and others have far more than the usual 1,500. Everything else being equal, polls with larger numbers of respondents tend to be more accurate and have smaller margins of error.

Some polls use the "gold standard" of live telephone interviews—and there's a whole science, which we'll ignore, about whether there are differences between people with landlines and people who have only cell phones. Other polling organizations ask the individuals they select to respond online. Some polling organizations offer respondents the opportunity to respond in Spanish, and others don't.

With one exception, this book simply assumes that polling organizations know their stuff and get the technical details right. That exception has to do with the percentage of gun owners or gun householders in the sample. (A "gun householder" is someone who lives in a household in which someone keeps a gun.) Although polling organizations make statistical adjustments for quite a few demographic factors, they do not control for or make adjustments for the percentage of gun owners or gun householders in their sample—even when their samples include lopsided numbers of gun owners or gun householders.

Polling organizations are reluctant to go there because there is no accepted reference for the percentages of the public who personally own guns or who live in a household where someone does. That issue bedevils researchers as well. (When conducting studies at the state level, research-ers often use the rate of gun suicides in a state as a proxy for gun owner-ship, because the gun suicide rate correlates closely with the gun ownership rate. Others use the numbers of FBI background checks, hunting licenses, or some combination of all three. For more on how many of us own guns, see chapter 2.)

This book asks, but doesn't answer, if including far more gun owners than expected tilts the outcome of those polls toward more opposition to gun-violence-prevention proposals.

Another issue, discussed at greater length in the Appendix, has to do with the sponsored YouGov polls (*e.g.*, the Economist polls). Those polls use an "opt-in" or volunteer panel and have other issues.[21] They are, therefore, not included in the polls that measure where the public stands on the gun-violence-prevention policy proposals discussed in chapters 4-17, except where few or no other polls are available.

When presenting polling data, I show the percentages of those who favored and those who opposed the proposal. For simplicity, I omit the percentages who said they didn't have an opinion or declined to answer that question. If 90% approve a proposal and 7% oppose it, the reader may safely assume that the remaining 3% took no position.

Crosstabs

Some polling organizations publish cross-tabulated data ("cross-tabs") that breakout results for various demographic groups. Not all polling organizations publish crosstabs, and the ones that do sometimes vary the demographic groups for which they report data.

Generally speaking, strong majorities of some groups, including Democrats and women, support every measure discussed in this book except repeal of the Second Amendment and gun confiscation. But Democrats and women are not the ones blocking legislation to reduce gun violence. For the most part, it is a subset of white men without college degrees and Republican politicians who oppose any measure that would make it harder for criminals and other dangerous individuals to access guns.

With that in mind, when crosstab data are available, this volume will focus on the opinions of Republicans and gun owners or gun householders. The assumption is that what Republicans and gun owners/householders want is, or should be, important to Republican and pro-gun politicians. For the same reason, this volume also presents data on the opinions of those earning $100,000 or more[22]—traditionally, a key constituency for Republican politicians.

When the data are available, this volume also breaks out how Americans with various levels of educational attainment view things. But on that score, there's an important detail readers need to know.

Some of the polls cited in this book break out individuals with and without college degrees. Some also break out those with post-graduate (Masters degrees, Ph.D.'s, etc.) or professional degrees (doctors, lawyers and so on). More specifically, polling organizations break out those *with* and *without* Bachelor's degrees (the traditional four-year college degree). Accordingly, when this book refers to those with or without college educations or degrees, it means individuals with or without a Bachelor's degree or more.

That's not to disparage those with Associate degrees or individuals who got some college but left before getting a degree. It's just how polling organizations collect data and report the results of their polls. (Bill Gates, who created Microsoft, is one of those who left college, in his case Harvard, before graduating, to pursue other opportunities.)

To put those groups in perspective, over the period 2014-2018, the Census Bureau estimates that **87.7%** of individuals twenty-five-years old or older had *at least* a high school diploma. About 19.5% had a Bachelor's degree (but not a higher degree). And some 12.1% had a graduate or professional degree. Altogether, **31.5%** of individuals twenty-five-years old or older had a Bachelor's degree or more.[23]

One final note about methodology: Some polls simply ask if the respondent favors or opposes the proposal in question. Others ask if the respondent "strongly" or "somewhat" favors or opposes the proposal. To reduce the amount of data, I've combined the "strongly" and "somewhat" figures into net approve and disapprove figures.

This Book Is Not About Why Some People Own Guns and Others Don't

Some people own guns, and others don't. Except in rural areas, most people who owned guns in the 1970s and earlier did so primarily for hunting, target shooting, and the like. Today, most gun owners cite personal protection. Of course, many other factors figure into why some folks own guns and others don't. Military service is a big factor. So is learning about guns from one's father.

Sociologists point to the important roles that gender and race play in gun ownership and in carrying a concealed handgun. Although gun manufacturers and others have made efforts in recent years to interest women in guns, our culture has historically made guns "man things." Even now, despite more women serving in the military and in law enforcement, and despite other societal changes, far more men than women own and carry guns. Some scholars argue that, at least for some men, owning or carrying a gun is a "manhood act" that demonstrates or bolsters their confidence in their own masculinity.[24]

In this country, whites—and white men in particular—have for decades had higher rates of gun ownership than other races or ethnic groups. As we'll see in Chapter 2, that trend persists. Non-Hispanic whites, especially white males without college degrees, are also more opposed to laws that restrict unstable and antisocial individuals' access to guns. Notably, white males have also been responsible for most of our school, workplace, church, and other high-profile mass shootings.[25]

With that in mind, I've broken out gender and race (and specifically, non-Hispanic white males) in a few chapters where the differences in opinions are especially stark. I don't include those breakouts in other chapters, mainly because when eighty or ninety percent of us agree on something, gender and racial differences are compressed and often near the polls' margins of error. Limited availability of crosstab data and the length of this book were also factors.

I don't argue, however, that the polling data in this book "prove" or "disprove" any particular theory about why so many white men without college degrees feel they need guns or why they are more likely to object to gun-violence-prevention legislation.

Deaths of Despair

While researching this book, I was struck by the fact that, as a group, white males without college degrees are in crisis. That demographic is experiencing high rates of suicides in general and suicides by gun in particular. (*See* Chapter 1.) Non-whites without college degrees are also experiencing high rates of alcohol-induced deaths.[26] And, in some parts of the country, they have been experiencing high rates of fatal drug overdoses, mainly of opioids.[27]

As I was putting the finishing touches on this volume, economists Ann Case and Angus Deacon released an extraordinary book that makes this point in detail.[28] They call these deaths "deaths of despair." Importantly, they demonstrate that this despair is to a large extent the result of our country's economic policies, which for decades have kept after-inflation wages for blue and pink collar workers stagnant.

Since the "Reagan Revolution" in 1980, those policies have also shifted wealth from the poor and middle class to big corporations and the wealthy. Of course, as Professors Case and Deaton show, other things, like automation, globalization and our broken health care system, factor into the equation as well.

The polling data in this book do not explain why middle-aged whites are dying in alarming numbers in "deaths of despair." You'll have to read Case and Deaton for that. But it is hard to ignore the fact that the same segment of population that is experiencing epidemics of suicide, alcohol-induced deaths, and substance-abuse deaths, find guns (and opposition to new gun laws) so important. It is hard not to wonder if the underlying explanations for both phenomena are the same.

Our society clearly is not devoting enough attention or resources to dealing with those deaths of despair and their causes.

More Strict? Less Strict?

Polling organizations insist on asking people whether they believe our gun laws should be "more strict" or "less strict." Those questions elicit responses that are more tribal than meaningful.

I say that because pollsters usually follow up the "more strict" or "less strict" question by asking respondents if they favor or oppose several *specific* changes to our gun laws. Inevitably, people who just said they believe we should *relax* our gun laws or leave them as they are do something very interesting: They say, *Yes, we should adopt some or all of the suggested changes to make our gun laws more restrictive.*

There is another reason, besides tribalism, for the disconnect between the responses to the "more strict" or "less strict" question and the responses to specific policy prescriptions. Some people misunderstand what laws are on the books now.

Federal law, for example, currently requires a background check before a licensed gun dealer sells a gun to a retail customer. Federal law, however, generally does not require a background check before an *unlicensed* seller sells a gun to someone in a so-called "private sale." Those "private sales" probably account for more than 20% of gun sales. They also account for a disproportionate share of "crime guns" and feed the country's black market in guns. (*See* Chapter 4.)

Gun-violence-prevention advocates argue that we should have "comprehensive" or "universal" background check laws. Those laws, which some states have enacted, require background checks before *all* retail gun sales, including private sales. (Again, see Chapter 4.)

In a 2016 study, only **53%** said they wanted gun laws that were more strict, but **77%** favored requiring universal background checks.[29] Researchers wondered if people mistakenly thought that universal background checks were already the law. When they surveyed on the issue, **41%** *incorrectly* said that federal law already required universal background checks. Only **47%** *correctly* answered that federal law requires background checks for some, but not all gun purchases. Consistent with the notion that some of us may not be familiar with current gun law, another **12%** *incorrectly* said that federal law currently does *not* require background checks at all.

It is undoubtedly true that a good many of us misapprehend what current law does—and does not—require. But that is not the only possible explanation for that *specific* discrepancy. In my own experience, many gun-rights advocates insist that the country already has "universal background checks"—*unless* the question or statement to which they are responding specifically mentions "private sales" or "gun shows."

Those individuals typically know the law but routinely respond as if "universal background checks" refers to the background checks that licensed firearm dealers must perform before most retail sales of firearms. The reason for that is unclear, but it may be that many gun-rights enthusiasts don't follow the mainstream media and are unfamiliar with the gun-violence-prevention literature. The news media and that literature use "comprehensive background checks" or "universal background checks" to refer to background checks for *all* gun sales, including so-called private sales.

So, for all those reasons, this book ignores the "more strict" or "less strict" questions and looks instead at how people respond to specific proposals.

"2A" Mantra: If the Data Don't Support What I Think, Then the Data Are Fake!

Here's one final note about the polling data. Dogmatic gun-rights advocates will likely refuse to believe the polling data collected here. They will, I suspect, continue to insist that only "libtards" or "snowflakes" or "gun grabbers" favor measures to restrict dangerous individuals' access to guns. And in any event, they will almost certainly continue to insist that most people, or most people in their part of the country, or most people they know, hold the same views they do.

Consider, for example, Scott Brian Haven, the 54-year-old Utah man federal agents recently arrested. The charging documents allege Haven made more than two thousand calls over three years to threaten members of Congress. In one call, Haven told an unnamed Senate staffer that there are "far more Second Amendment people than whiny, crying liberals."[30]

Haven is white, middle-aged, conservative, and vociferously pro-gun. Without suggesting that Haven is otherwise typical of "Second Amendment people,"[31] many of those folks do seem to share Haven's belief that most people share their dogmatic views and that only a small minority of "whiny, crying liberals" favor measures to reduce America's horrific gun violence. As we will see, what everyday Americans, including most gun owners, tell polling organizations reveals a different—and more nuanced—story.

On social media, some strident gun advocates take a different tack. They argue that polls cannot be trusted because "polls" said Hillary Clinton was going to win the 2016 election. The truth, of course, is that polls do not make predictions. They measure public opinion at the time of the survey.

A more accurate statement would be this: Most polls showed Ms. Clinton leading and even widening her lead in the final weeks leading up to the election. But on October 28, 2016, just days before the election, FBI Director James Comey announced that the FBI was reopening its investigation into Ms. Clinton's emails. The Trump campaign and Russian disinformation agents immediately pounced on and amplified Director Comey's announcement. As they did, polls tracked a precipitous decline in support for Ms. Clinton's candidacy. Ms. Clinton herself has given a painful account of seeing the election slip away after Comey made his unusual election-eve announcement.[32]

Even so, Ms. Clinton won the popular vote by almost three million votes. In short, the 2016 pre-election polls are not a convincing argument that all polls are entirely unreliable and should be ignored.

PART ONE: TAKING AIM AT GUN VIOLENCE

1. Guns: The Terrible Toll

Each year in late summer, our kids or grandkids, our nieces and nephews, and our friends' and neighbors' kids head back to school. As they do, they have something on their minds that never occurred to kids in my generation: They wonder if this year will be the year their school has a mass shooting. To prepare for that possibility, they attend "active shooter" drills. And as they do, they speculate about whether this or that misfit will be the shooter. They wonder if their friends, their teachers, or they themselves will be among the dead.

But while high-profile mass shootings in our schools, churches, workplaces, and elsewhere grab media attention and worry our young people and their parents, those shootings account for less than one percent of the country's gun carnage.

That carnage took **39,740** lives in 2018, the last year for which the Centers for Disease Control and Prevention ("CDC") has released data. In 2018, the unadjusted or "crude" rate for the country as a whole was 12.15 firearm fatalities per 100,000. The age-adjusted rate was 11.85.[33] Mississippi, Alabama, and Wyoming had the highest rates of gun deaths. Rhode Island, Massachusetts, and Hawaii had the lowest.

Gun suicides took the most lives—**24,432** or about **61%** of all gun fatalities. In 2018, about 91% of firearm suicides were whites, and 86% were males. They disproportionately lived in states with high levels of gun ownership and lax gun laws.[34] At the intersection of those groups are the very folks—white males in states with high levels of gun ownership and lax gun laws—who are *both* the most resistant to any efforts to deal with our gun suicide epidemic *and* the most likely to kill themselves with a gun.

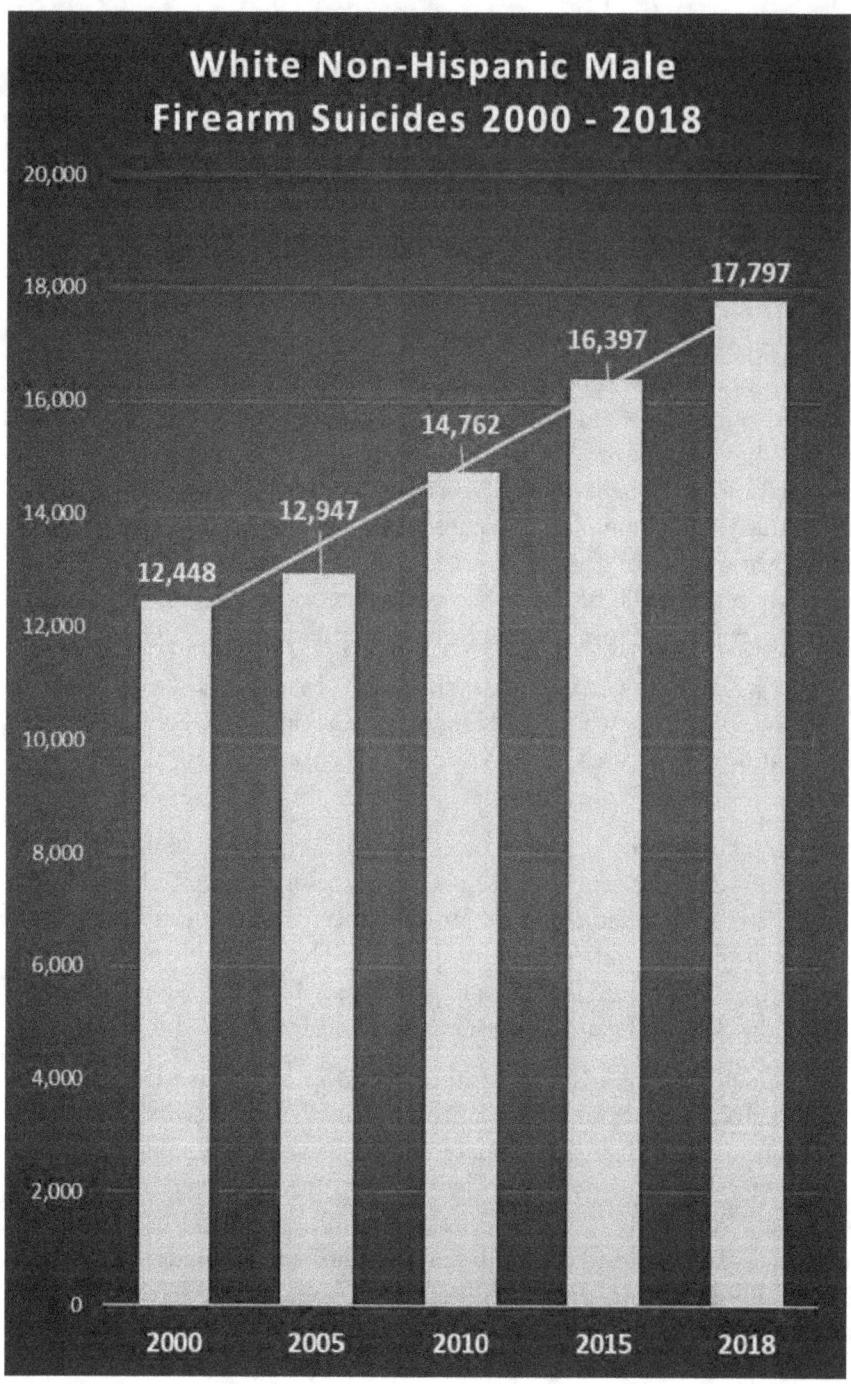

Domestic abusers with guns inflict their own measure of violence—on spouses, former spouses, dating partners, and their children. There are also inner-city shootings, mainly among young men of color. And there are "road rage" and "retail rage" shootings. In total, gun homicides account for about **37%** of gun fatalities.

Unintentional shootings, often involving a toddler who finds a gun a parent left loaded and unsecured, also contribute to the overall total. The child picks up the gun to play with it and without meaning to, shoots himself, a sibling, or a playmate. Or his parent.

It's harder to get a handle on the number of individuals with nonfatal gunshot wounds, but the Gun Archive, which collects data from news reports and other sources, probably has the best available tally. For 2018, it indicates gunshots and shrapnel injured about **28,244** individuals.

The U.S. Has Far More Gun Violence Than Other High-Income Countries

Gun-violence-prevention researchers Erin Grinshteyn and David Hemenway recently compared the rates of violent gun deaths in the United States with the rates of violent gun deaths in other countries. For their study, they used data from the CDC for the United States and data from the World Health Organization for other populous, high-income countries (in both cases for the year 2015). The peer-reviewed medical journal Preventive Medicine published their study in 2019.[35]

After crunching the data, Grinshteyn and Hemenway found:

- The firearm **suicide** rate in the United States was **9.8** times higher than in other high-income countries.
- The firearm **homicide** rate in the United States was **24.9** times higher than in other high-income countries.

In their data set, 83.7% of all firearm deaths occurred in the United States. Even more alarming, 91.6% of the women and 96.7% of the chil-dren aged 0-to-4 killed by firearms were in the United States.

Grinshteyn and Hemenway also compared firearm-homicide rates in high- and low-gun ownership states in the United States with the firearm-homicide rates in those other high-income countries. Again using 2015 data, they found that the combined firearm-homicide rate in

high-gun-ownership states in the U.S. was **36 times higher** than the combined firearm-homicide rate for other high-income countries. In **lower gun-ownership U.S. states**, the firearm-homicide rate was **13.5 times higher** than the combined rate in those other high-income countries.

Gun rights enthusiasts often blame gun violence in the United States primarily on inner-city blacks. Given that, it is noteworthy that Grinshteyn and Hemenway found, "The firearm homicide rate among the US white population was **12 times higher** than the firearm homicide rate in other high-income countries."[32] [Emphasis added.]

In short, while guns by themselves, without human intervention, may not kill people, where there are more guns, there are more gun deaths. That's largely because an argument, a bout of depression, or a careless act is far more likely to end in something tragic when a gun is available.

Firearm Mortality in the United States and Other Highly Developed Countries (JAMA 2018)

A different study, this one published in the Journal of the American Medical Association in August 2018,[36] used the 2016 firearm mortality rates for the eleven nations ranked highest in the Human Development Index in 2016.[37] (Why eleven nations instead of the usual top ten? The United States and Canada tied for 10th place in the Human Development Index.)

Once again, the United States stood out against its peers for its remarkable level of gun deaths. (See chart.) The main determinants were each country's rate of gun ownership and the strength of its gun laws. Note Switzerland and Canada on the chart. Both nations have much lower gun ownership than the United States, but higher levels of gun ownership than the other nations that scored high on the Human Development Index. Both Switzerland and Canada have much lower firearm fatality rates than the U.S. but higher rates than their other peers.

State-to-State Comparisons

Writing an editor's note in the Journal of the American Medical Association, Robert Steinbrook, M.D., observed that even within the

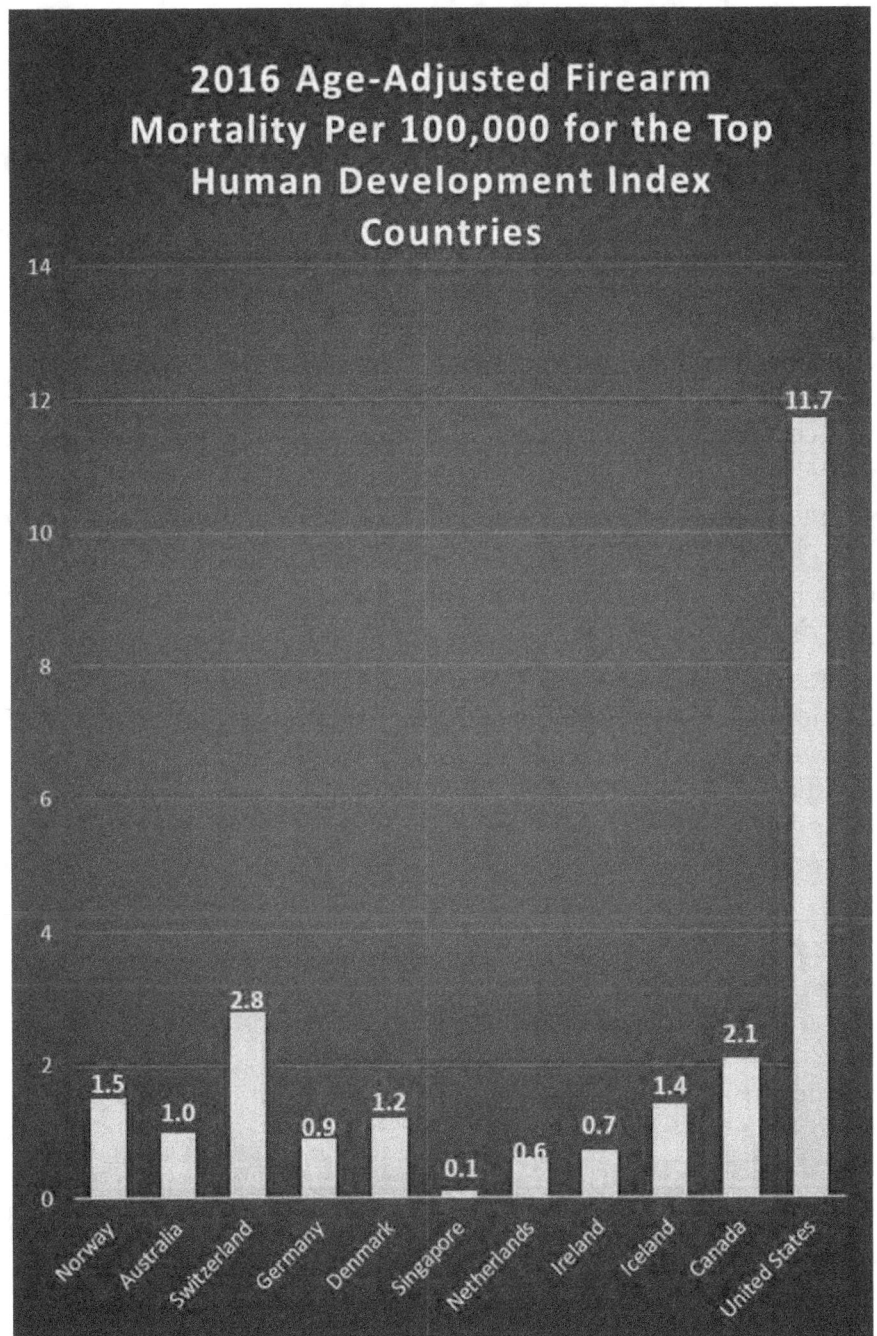

United States, the rates at which firearm deaths occurred—measured by deaths per 100,000 persons in 2015—varied considerably from state to state, depending on the rate of gun ownership, the strength of the state's gun laws, and other factors.[38]

To illustrate the point, Dr. Steinbrook contrasted Massachusetts, which in 2015 had the *lowest* firearm-fatality rate in the country, with Kentucky, which had the *highest* firearm-fatality rate in the contiguous 48 states. Massachusetts had relatively low gun ownership and tough gun laws. Its firearm mortality rate in 2015 was **3.1 deaths per 100,000**. In contrast, Kentucky had high gun ownership and lax gun laws. It had a firearm-fatality rate of **20.4 deaths per 100,000**. For the country as a whole, the 2015 rate was **11.3 gun deaths** per 100,000.

I've updated his figures to show the tally for 2018, the most recent year for which the CDC has made data available. In 2018, the age-adjusted firearm fatality rate for the country as a whole was **11.9 gun deaths per 100,000**.

Rhode Island had the lowest age-adjusted firearm fatality rate, 3.2 firearm deaths per 100,000.[39] Mississippi, with high gun ownership and weak gun laws, had the highest age-adjusted firearm fatality rate, **22.5** firearm deaths per 100,000.[40] Mississippi's firearm fatality rate was seven times higher than Rhode Island's rate. (See chart, "2018 Age-Adjusted Firearm Rates."

In the same issue of JAMA, Elinore J. Kaufman, MD, MSHP, and colleagues took the analysis further. They found that strong gun laws in a state were associated with lower **firearm suicide rates**. They also found lower **overall suicide rates** (all means of suicide in the states with strong gun laws. That means individuals contemplating suicide did not simply substitute another means of committing suicide when a gun was not available.

The Gun Violence Archive

The Gun Violence Archive collects information on shootings from media reports and other sources. Its data serves as an informal cross check for the CDC numbers and are also more current. The Gun Violence Archive reported 15,416 firearm fatalities in 2019, not counting sui-cides. For 2018, the comparable figure was 14,848.[41]

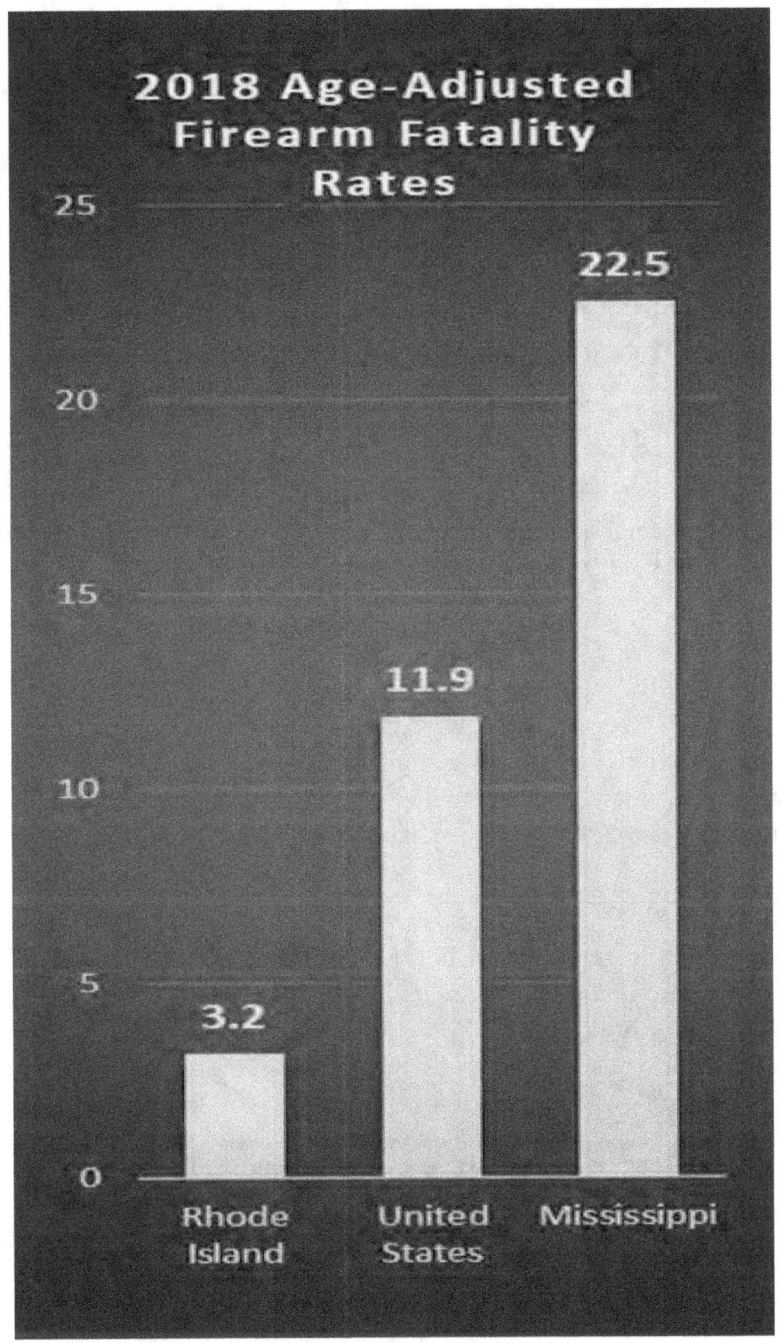

The CDC hasn't released 2019 numbers yet. In 2018 it counted 13,958 deaths from gun assaults. That figure didn't include unintentional firearm fatalities, which the CDC put at 458. Including those (13,958 + 458=14,416) would nudge the CDC's estimate close to the Gun Archive's 2018 figure of 14,848.

Gun Violence Is Dragging Down Life Expectancy

Our gun violence is so severe, it is dragging down life expectancy in the U.S., especially for African-Americans. Researchers analyzed CDC data from 2000 to 2016 and found that gun fatalities took about 2.23 years off the life expectancy of whites and 4.14 years of blacks.[42] Whites had a far higher *rate* of suicides. Blacks, who make up a smaller percentage of the population, experienced a far higher *rate* of gun homicides. But suicides are more prevalent in middle age and later. Gun assault fatalities occur more often at younger ages and therefore have a greater impact on lost life expectancy.

The Financial Price Tag

With all that carnage comes a financial price tag. Researchers at Stan-ford University Medical School crunched the numbers for inpatient stays nationwide as a result of gunshot wounds.[43] They found that for the years 2010 through 2015, the *average annual* cost for gun injury inpatient care was $911 million. The government paid for 45% of that—through Medicaid and, to a lesser extent, Medicare, and other public insurance programs.

Importantly, that $911 million-per-year estimate only included inpatient services. In other words, it did not include rehabilitation, home health care, physician fees, or prescription drug costs. That figure also did not include lost wages and other expenses associated with what, for some, will be a lifetime of disability.

The Psychological Toll

There is also a psychological toll. A domestic abuser with a gun doesn't have to pull the trigger to induce stress in his or her spouse. Abuse aside, family members in households with children report higher levels of stress when the gun owner in the household keeps his gun loaded and easily accessible.[44]

Some kids who live through school shootings experience Post Traumatic Syndrome Disorder-like symptoms. Many others experience anxiety and stress. In fact, a recent study found that in the twenty-four months after a fatal school shooting, nearby mental health care providers prescribed antidepressants to young people at a rate 21% higher than before the shooting.[45]

Some children, especially very young schoolchildren, are traumatized by school lockdowns even when it turns out that—this time —there was no shooter.[46] In early 2020, the two largest teacher unions, the American Federation of Teachers and the National Education Association, called for an end to *unannounced* active shooter drills and life-like simulations, pointing to the traumatic effects on students.[47]

How Many Young People Are Affected?

In a 2018 survey, the American Psychological Association (APA) assessed the stress levels of Americans and what drives those stress levels.[48] It found that gun violence was a huge factor for young people. The APA refers to people who were between the ages of 15 and 21 in 2018 as "Generation Z." Among those in Generation Z, 75% reported mass shootings as a significant source of stress, and nearly as many, 72%, said the same about school shootings. School shootings were also a top concern for 74% of parents.

The Parkland student leaders called that generation the "Columbine Generation"– young people born after the 1999 Columbine High School shooting. More recently, they have referred to their generation as the "Lockdown Generation." That cohort has grown up with the ever-present threat of school shootings and other mass shootings. It has also grown up with the knowledge that Congress refuses to do anything to protect their generation—or any other —from gun violence.

In late 2018, SocialSphere conducted an extensive poll of young people, ages 14-29.[49] Responding to its pollsters, 68% in that age group said school shootings were the most important issue facing the country.[50]

School shootings were the top issue for female, white, black, Hispanic, urban and suburban youth, and they were in the top three for male, Republican, and rural youth.

Della Volpe, CEO of SocialSphere and director of polling at the Institute of Politics within the Harvard Kennedy School, told Axios, "The issue connects with young Americans unlike anything in the last 20 years except 9/11."[51]

Steve LeVine, an Axios editor, echoed Volpe's assessment. He wrote: "To a degree not entirely fathomable to older Americans, the de-fining issue for today's youth aged 14–29—crossing race, age, gender, and political affiliation, whether rural or urban—is the long wave of deadly school shootings."[52]

Not Just Young People

It's not just young people who are stressed by the risk that someone with a gun will start shooting. Consider this incident, as reported by The Baltimore Sun:[53] In November 2018, during a performance of "Fiddler on the Roof" in Baltimore, a man who had too much to drink stood up and shouted, "Heil Hitler! Heil Trump!" Immediately, audience members ran for cover. "I'll be honest, I was waiting to hear a gunshot," one theatergoer said. "I thought, 'Here we go.'"

In August 2019, after the shootings in El Paso and Dayton, a dirt bike backfired near Times Square. Hundreds of tourists and others fled down alleys and into businesses and Broadway theaters. The New York Times quoted a Long Islander who explained, "I think that we all, as Americans, sort of know the drill."[54]

We Underestimate How Many Die in Gun Violence

There's an odd twist to this. Even though gun violence concerns us, quite a few of us underestimate just how many people in this country die each year from gun violence. In an exceptionally large poll that explored some of the misconceptions Americans harbor about gun violence, Ipsos asked: "To the best of your knowledge, how many people die from gun fatalities each year in the United States?" [55] It offered four choices – 300, 3,000, 30,000, and 300,000 gun fatalities per year.

The low ball estimate of 300 gun fatalities a year was the choice of 7% of respondents—6% of Democrats and 8% of Republicans. Another low-ball answer—3,000 per year—sounded right to 24%. Specifically, 20% of Democrats and 27% of Republicans chose that answer. Combining those re-sponses, 26% of Dem-ocrats and 35% of Republicans underestimated the number of gun fatalities.

For this study, the researchers pegged the number of gun fatalities at 30,000. Only **38%** chose that number, including 46% of Democrats and 35% of Republicans. (That number itself underestimates the death toll. As we've seen, in 2018, the actual figure was almost 40,000.)

Democrats were a little more likely to pick the

Ds	Rs	Gun Fatalities Per Year
6%	8%	300 gun fatalities
20%	27%	3,000 gun fatalities
46%	35%	30,000 gun fatalities
10%	7%	300,000 gun fatalities

answer that overshot the mark by a mile: "300,000 gun fatalities" per year. Some 10% of Dem-ocrats and 7% of Republicans chose that response. "Don't know" was the choice of 15% of Democrats and 24% of Republicans.

The differences between Democrats and Republicans were not large, but Republicans were a little more likely than Democrats to downplay the toll gun violence takes (+9%) or to say they didn't know (another +9%). Conversely, 10% of Democrats and 7% of Republicans had a greatly exaggerated notion of how many die each year in gun violence.

Those numbers suggest cognitive bias may be at work in both groups. Republicans as a group are more favorably disposed to gun rights. They were more likely to underestimate or be unaware of the toll guns take. Democrats, as a group, were more likely to support gun-violence-prevention measures and were a little (+3%) more likely than Republicans to overestimate the toll. Still, even among Democrats, 26% underestimated the gun fatality rate.

What Accounts for the Most Firearm Fatalities?

In 2018, the CDC indicates there were **39,773** firearm fatalities in the U.S. Of those, suicides by gun (**24,432**) accounted for about **61%**. Next, homicides (**13,958**) made up about **35%**. Legal Intervention, Unintentional, and Undetermined were each about **1%**.

But when AMP Research Lab asked in July 2019 which accounted for the most gun deaths, a plurality, **33%**, chose homicides. Only **27%** correctly chose suicides. Reflecting the disproportionate media attention they attract, a remarkable **25%** thought mass shootings caused the most firearm fatalities.[56]

On this topic, gun owners were a little more knowledgeable than non-gun owners. About **30%** of gun owners knew or correctly guessed that gun suicides account for the most gun deaths. Among people who did not own a gun or live in a household where someone else did, only **20%** picked suicides. Some **19%** of gun owners chose mass shootings as causing the most deaths; a startling **30%** of non-gun owners also chose mass shootings. In fact, mass shootings account for only about 1% of gun deaths each year.

Those misperceptions may influence how individuals prioritize solutions to gun violence.

We Think Things Are Worse Now Than They Used to Be

The NRA has been preaching for years that the world is an increasingly dangerous place. Whether for that reason or simply because our minds place more emphasis on recent events, Americans tend to think gun violence is worse today than 25 years ago. The reality is that gun homicides peaked in the US in 1993, when, during the cocaine wars, there were **7.0** gun homicides per 100,000. By 2018, the gun-homicide toll had dropped to **4.3** gun homicides per 100,000. The 2018 rate was **39% less** than what it was in 1993.

The October 2017 Ipsos "misconceptions" poll[57] asked if it was true or false that the rate of gun homicides in the United States has **declined** since the 1980s. Only **20%** (correctly) thought the statement was true; **61%** thought it false. In other words, only one in five correctly thought the rate of gun homicides had gone down since the 1980s. Among Democrats, only 17% (correctly) thought the statement was true; 70% thought it was false. Among Republicans, 26% (correctly) thought the statement was true; 54% thought it false.

An NPR/PBS poll[58] in February 2019 also asked how the gun murder rate now compared to 25 years ago. It gave respondents three choices—the gun murder rate was higher, lower, or about the same as 25 years ago. Among adults, only **12%** (correctly) thought the gun murder rate was lower now. A surprising **59%** (incorrectly) thought the gun murder rate was higher now. Some **23%** opted (incorrectly) for the about-the-same answer.

Among Democrats, **73%** (incorrectly) thought the gun murder rate was higher now than 25 years ago. Only **8%** of Democrats (correctly) thought it was lower, with **15%** opting for about the same. Among Republicans, **52%** (incorrectly) thought the gun murder rate was higher now, **9%** (correctly) thought it was lower, and **34%** chose about the same. That represented a 21-percentage-point gap between Democrats and Republicans who thought things are worse now.

But the biggest gap was the gender gap: **47%** of men and **71%** of women incorrectly thought the gun murder rate is higher now. That was a 24 percentage point difference.

Conclusion

Gun violence in the United States is dramatically higher than in other high-income countries, all of which have lower levels of gun ownership and more restrictive gun laws. Gun violence is also higher in states with more guns and weaker gun laws than in states with fewer guns and more restrictive laws. Those facts convince most of us that we need to do a better job of keeping guns from violent and impulsive individuals.

But quite a few of us believe there is far less gun violence each year than there actually is. That may make those individuals less inclined to believe we need to address gun violence. In other words, someone who thinks there are only 300 gun fatalities in the U.S. each year may be less inclined to believe that we need to address gun violence than someone who knows the actual number is almost 40,000 firearm fatalities.

Mistakenly thinking that gun violence is worse now than 25 years ago is a mixed bag. It convinces some that we need to take steps to rein in gun violence. But that misapprehension convinces others that the gun measures adopted in the last quarter-century haven't worked and therefore, more legislation won't help. Or that, as the NRA falsely claims, the country is becoming increasingly dangerous, and therefore, now more than ever, we need to arm ourselves.

2. Guns: How Many of Us Own Them?

During the coronavirus pandemic, an astonishing number of individuals—some responding to attacks on Asian Americans, others fearing an imminent breakdown of society—engaged in panic buying of guns. That almost certainly created an uptick in the percentages of Americans who personally own a gun or live in a household where someone else does. When this book was published, reliable figures on the impact of gun purchases during the pandemic were not yet available. This chapter reports what was known before the pandemic began.

Americans often greatly overestimate how many of us own guns. That may influence how politicians, political parties, and the rest of us size up the debate over gun-violence-prevention policy.

Professors Donald P. Haider-Markel and Mark R. Joslyn of Kansas University are co-authors of a study recently published in the journal *Politics & Policy*.[59] Their study examined the results of a 2016 nationally representative survey of 1,290 American adults. Among other things, the survey asked people to give their "best guess" of what percentage of Americans owned firearms.

According to Professors Haider-Markel and Joslyn, the percentage of U.S. individuals who own guns is roughly 25%. In response to their survey, however, more than 75% overestimated how many of us own guns. Almost one-in-five respondents estimated the gun owner population was 70% or higher. The most common estimate was 50%. Only a tiny minority of 2% underestimated the number of gun owners.

How Many of Us Own Guns?

Are the professors' estimates of gun ownership accurate?

Professors Haider-Markel and Joslyn relied on the General Social Survey, a huge government-sponsored survey conducted every two years. The 2014 General Social Survey pegged personal gun ownership in 2014 at **22%**.[60] (Unfortunately, the surveys in 2016 and 2018 did not ask about personal gun ownership, and the 2020-survey results aren't available yet.)

The professors also looked at data from prior General Social Surveys. They found that personal gun ownership "fell from an average of 27.4% in the 1980s to 27.0% in the 1990s, 24.6% in 2000-2004, and 21.9% in 2006-2012 for a net decline of 5.5 points."[61]

The General Social Survey is important, but the 2015 National Firearms Survey is more recent.[62] Like the General Social Survey, it found that **22%** of Americans age 18 and older own guns.[63]

Public opinion polls, which draw on much smaller numbers of respondents, vary a bit in their results.[64] Over the last few years, YouGov has surveyed on gun ownership more than any public polling organization. Its polling shows 20% to 24% of Americans personally own guns, with the average being 22%—the same as the larger studies.

Gun Owner?	Polling Dates	Sponsor/Pollster
22%	10/2-3/17	Huff Post/YouGov
22%	11/12-14/17	Economist/YouGov
24%	2/18-20/18	Economist/YouGov
22%	2/25-27/18	Economist/YouGov
20%	3/4-6/18	Economist/YouGov
20%	3/25-27/18	Economist/YouGov
24%	11/4-6/18	Economist/YouGov
24%	11/11-13/18	Economist/YouGov
22%	3/17-19/19	Economist/YouGov
23%	4/13-16/19	Economist/YouGov
22%	7/29-31/19	Economist/YouGov
24%	8/3-6/19	Economist/YouGov
21%	8/10-13/19	Economist/YouGov

Gun Owner? Polling Dates   Sponsor/Pollster
22%   9/14-17/19   Economist/YouGov

Averages: Gun Owners? 22%. Range: 20% - 24%

Other public opinion polls have larger percentages of gun owners in their samples. In an October 2017 poll, for example, Ipsos found that **26%** of us personally own one or more guns.[65] And in a January 2019 poll, Ipsos found personal gun ownership to be **28%**.[66] In July 2019, SSRS conducted a survey for APM. It put gun ownership at **29%**.[67] Monmouth polls in March 2018 and August 2019 pegged the percentage at **34%**.[68]

That puts the professors' estimate of 25% gun ownership higher than the 2014 National Firearms Survey (22%, the 2015 National Firearms Survey (22%, and the average of the YouGov polls (22%, but lower than the Ipsos (26% and 28%) and APM/SSRS (29%) polls.[69]

Polling organizations make adjustments to be sure their polls don't underweight or overweight a variety of demographic groups—gender, political party, age group, and so on. But they don't adjust for gun ownership, even though (as a group) gun owners tend to be less supportive/more resistant to gun-violence-prevention measures than non-gun owners. As a result, the polls with disproportionate percentages of gun owners may tell us more about the accuracy of those polls' results than they do about the actual level of gun ownership. (The same is true of polls with disproportionate percentages of gun householders, the topic to which we turn to next.)

How Many of Us Live in Gun Households?

Instead of asking if the respondent owns a gun, pollsters often ask if there is a gun in the household—in other words, if anyone in the household owns a gun. That's because there are more gun householders than gun owners; thus, it takes fewer attempts to reach the desired mix of survey respondents.

Professors Haider-Markel and Joslyn estimated that about 33%-40% of U.S. households have at least one gun in the home.

Are they right?

The General Social Surveys showed the percent of households with guns declining from a high of **54%** in 1977 to a low of **32%** in 2010, 2014, and 2016.[70] The 2018 survey pegged the percentage of U.S. homes in which someone owned a gun at **35%**.[71]

The Behavioral Risk Factor Surveillance System is a different government survey. Its 2002 survey included an enormous 240,735 adults from randomly selected households with telephones in the 50 states and the District of Columbia.[72] (That's a huge number of respondents. Most of the commercial polls cited in this book have 800 to 1,500 respondents.) Its data indicated that **33%** of adults had firearms in or around their home in 2002.[73]

Several commercial opinion polls also asked if anyone in the home had a gun. Once again, in our time frame, YouGov has surveyed on this issue (percentage of gun householders) far more often than other polling organizations:

Yes	*No*	*Polling Dates*	*Sponsor/Pollster*
36%	55%	10/2-3/17	Huff Post/YouGov
36%	54%	11/12-14/17	Economist/YouGov
34%	53%	2/18-20/18	Economist/YouGov
37%	55%	2/25-27/18	Economist/YouGov
34%	55%	3/4-6/18	Economist/YouGov
34%	55%	3/25-27/18	Economist/YouGov
40%	52%	11/4-6/18	Economist/YouGov
41%	51%	11/11-13/18	Economist/YouGov
36%	55%	3/17-19/19	Economist/YouGov
37%	53%	4/13-16/19	Economist/YouGov
37%	54%	7/29-31/19	Economist/YouGov
30%	52%	8/3-6/19	Economist/YouGov
37%	56%	8/10-13/19	Economist/YouGov
37%	51%	9/14-17/19	Economist/YouGov

Gun Household? Averages: Yes 36%. No 54%.

On average, these YouGov surveys put the percentage of gun households at **36%**. That's three percentage points more than the Behavioral Risk Factor Surveillance System's **33%** (2002 data) and one point more than the 2018 General Social Survey (**35%**. Given the polls' margins of error, these figures are quite close but may indicate a small uptick in gun households from 2002 to 2019 (*i.e.*, from 33% to 36%.

Other pollsters have also surveyed on this topic, but their results—as might be expected given their relatively small sample sizes—are less consistent.

Yes	*No*	*Polling Dates*	*Poll*
38%	62%	10/5-9/17	Morning Consult
46%	_	10/5-10/17	Quinnipiac[74]
43%	55%	10/5-11/17	Gallup[75]
45%	_	11/7-13/17	Quinnipiac
44%	53%	2/20-24/18	Suffolk/USA
41%	_	2/23-26/18	Quinnipiac
41%	59%	2/22-26/18	Morning Consult
46%	47%	3/2-5/19	Monmouth
44%	_	3/3-5/18	Quinnipiac
35%	59%	3/14-19/18	AP-NORC
40%	60%	3/29-4/1/18	Morning Consult
47%	_	4/6-9/18	Quinnipiac
47%	53%	4/10-13/18	NPR/PBS
41%	_	5/16-20/18	Quinnipiac
39%	61%	8/2-6/18	Morning Consult
46%	53%	10/1-10/18	Gallup
44%	_	1/9-13/19	Quinnipiac
41%	59%	1/11-28/19	Ipsos/Reuter
46%	_	3/2-5/19	Monmouth
37%	60%	7/16-21/19	APM (SSRS)
36%	64%	8/05-07/19	Morning Consult
46%	49%	8/10-14/19	NBC/WaPo
44%	51%	8/16-20/19	Monmouth
50%	46%	8/20-25/19	Suffolk/USA

Averages: Gun Households: **43%**. *Range: 35% - 50%.*

These commercial polls report slightly—and sometimes much—higher percentages of gun householders than the government surveys. That may be, at least in part, because the commercial polls have much smaller sample sizes than the large government-sponsored polls and, therefore, may be a bit less exact. But it may also mean that some polling organizations select samples in a manner that recruits disproportionate numbers of gun householders. With that in mind, the Appendix shows the same polls arranged by the percentage of gun households.

Does Not Controlling for Gun Ownership Skew Poll Results?

As we just saw, in some polls, gun owners and gun householders make up disproportionate shares of the sample population. As we'll see in later chapters, those polls also seem to show the least support and most opposition to gun-violence-prevention proposals. That raises an important question: *Does over-representation of gun owners or gun householders bias those polls' results? In other words, do polls with more gun owners or gun householders than expected result in those polls showing less support for and more opposition to gun-violence-prevention measures than they should?*

The September 2019 NPR/PBS/Marist poll had an astonishingly high level of **personal gun ownership** in its sample (**42%** of registered voters *vs.* the expected 22%).[76] The poll showed five percentage points *less* support than the average for universal background checks and four points *more* opposition. When the poll asked about "red flag" laws, it found the lowest level of support of all the polls to address that topic (seven points *below* the average level of support, and eight points *above* the average level of opposition among adults). On banning large-capacity magazines, the poll found six percentage points *less* support than the average and a remarkable 12 points *more* opposition.

Of all the polls discussed in this book, the August 2019 Suffolk/USA Today poll[77] had the highest level of respondents who lived in a household where someone owned a gun. Some **50%** of the respondents in its sample lived in **gun households** instead of the expected 35% or so. The poll didn't ask about most of the issues discussed in this book, but it did ask about banning large-capacity magazines. (*See* Chapter 14.) Suffolk found nine percentage points *less* support than the average of the fourteen polls that addressed the issue and twelve percentage points more opposition. That was the lowest level of support for (and the highest level of opposition to) banning large-capacity magazines of the fourteen polls that asked about such a ban.[78]

All that said, I cannot make more than an anecdotal showing that failure to control for gun ownership skews (or doesn't skew) the results of polls with high levels of gun owners or gun householders. That's due in part to the fact that some polls ask about personal gun ownership, and others ask about household gun ownership. Still others don't ask about gun ownership at all. Or they asked but didn't disclose the results.

It's also because the polls discussed in this book don't all cover the same topics. As a result, one is left without enough polls that show personal or household gun ownership *and* address one or more topics to make a convincing analysis one way or the other. (One would also need the ability to do the sort of sophisticated statistical analyses polling firms routinely perform.)

The Percentage of Americans Who Own Guns Has Declined, But Unevenly

The percentage of Americans who own guns has been on a long-term decline. Most of us don't realize that. That's according to the Ipsos "mis-conceptions" poll.[79] Ipsos asked if this statement was true or false:

> The percentage of Americans who own a gun has increased over the last twenty years.

In response, 78% *incorrectly* said the statement was true. Only 10% *correctly* labeled it false.

Professors Haider-Markel and Joslyn reached the same conclusion. In their study, they found that most of us believe that gun ownership is expanding. That belief was especially strong among gun owners.

The professors point out that if a politician believes, incorrectly, that most people own guns and that gun ownership is growing, he or she may be reluctant to support laws that gun-rights organizations oppose. Conversely, if a politician understands that only a shrinking 22% of the population owns guns, he or she may be more willing to support gun-violence-prevention measures.

There is an important caveat: Famed statistician and polling expert Nate Silver has pointed out that while gun ownership is declining, it's not declining evenly across all demographics. "Gun ownership has declined over the past 40 years," he wrote, "but almost all of the decrease has come from Democrats."[80] He noted that the General Social Survey put gun ownership in 1973 at **55%** among Republican households and **46%** among Democratic households. By 2010, gun ownership in Republican households had fallen only a little, to **50%**, but had dropped to **22%** among Democrats.[81]

What Nate Silver didn't mention (in that column) was that there was also a remarkable political realignment during that period: Before the 1960s, the Democratic Party included a Southern or "Dixiecrat" wing dominated by segregationists and white supremacists. In the late 1960s, Democratic President Lyndon Johnson signed landmark civil rights leg-islation that ended *de jure* segregation in the South and banned racial dis-crimination in housing and employment. Senator Barry Goldwater, Rich-ard Nixon, Ronald Reagan, and George H.W. Bush responded with the "Southern Strategy" of using code words and "dog whistle" appeals to racism and racial resentment.[82]

White southerners and others unhappy with the end of segregation and the passage of civil rights legislation responded by moving from the Democratic Party to the Republican Party. When they did, they evidently took their guns with them.

Who Owns Guns?

While the percentage of Americans who own guns is smaller than it was in earlier decades, still, roughly 22% of adults, and maybe more, own guns. By any measure, that's a large number of individuals.

Here are two more categorical generalizations that are true:

People in **every** demographic group tracked by polling organizations own guns—just not to the same extent. For example, according to sur-veys Gallup conducted in the last decade, 64% of married men in the South owned guns; so did 10% of unmarried women from outside the South.

People in **every** state and geographic environment—urban, suburban, and rural—own guns. Again, just not to the same extent. A 2013 survey pegged gun ownership at a high of 62% in Alaska and a low of 5% in Delaware.[83] Not coincidentally, in 2013, the age-adjusted gun fatality rate in Alaska, 19.8 per 100,000, was also the highest in the nation. Delaware ranked 19th at 10.3 gun fatalities per 100,000, just under the (then) national rate of 10.4.[84]

But with those caveats in mind, is there a "typical" gun owner? Or phrased better, is there a demographic group in which gun ownership is noticeably more prevalent?

The National Firearms Survey conducted in 2015 found that "gun owners overall are disproportionately male, white, older, non-urban, and from the South."[85] Thirty percent of conservatives were gun owners, compared with only 14% of liberals. The historical racial disparities in overall gun ownership remained in place: **25%** of white Americans said they personally owned a gun, compared with **16%** of Hispanics and **14%** of African Americans. But the strongest predictor of gun ownership was military service, with 44% of veterans owning a firearm.

The 2018 General Social Survey showed the Midwest catching up with the South in **household gun ownership**, with 41% in the Midwest reporting a gun in the home versus 40% in the South.[86] (That difference was well within the survey's margin of error.) The survey put household gun ownership among whites at **42%**, among blacks at **22%**, and **15%** among "others." Household gun ownership increased with age. Among those 18 - 34 years old, household gun ownership was **30%**; among those 35 - 49, it was **35%**; among those 50 - 64, it was **38%**; and among those 65 and older, it was **43%**. Those findings were consistent with the 2015 National Firearms Survey.

Although household gun ownership has been in a long term decline across all education levels, it has plummeted among those who did not graduate from high school.[87] As recently as 1980, when the country elected Ronald Reagan president, 51% of those over age 25 without a high school education lived in a home where there was a gun. Gun ownership steadily declined in that group until 2000, when it stood at **26%**.[88]

After the terrorist attack on September 11, 2001, household gun ownership among individuals with less than a high school diploma briefly jumped to **41%**.[89] Apparently, quite a few men without high school diplomas imagined themselves the NRA's "good guy with a gun," who stops a terrorist or a mass shooter. But by 2004, household gun ownership among those without high school diplomas dropped to **35%**. And in 2006, as the country headed into the Great Recession, it plunged to **24%**. In 2018, only **21%** of those without a high school education lived in a home where there was a gun. The reason for the decline likely has more to do with financial concerns than with beliefs about the utility of gun ownership.

The core group of gun owners appears to be white men without college educations. These are generally men who graduated from high school and may or may not have some college. Their education (or the traits that kept them from dropping out of high school) qualify them for better jobs than those without a high school diploma. That gives them the financial wherewithal to afford a gun or guns, as well as ammunition, practice shooting, and so on.

Focusing on who owns guns, Gallup did an analysis in 2013 of its polling from 2007 through 2012.[90] "Men are three times more likely than women to personally own guns," it reported, "representing one of the largest demographic differences in gun ownership." There were also considerable regional variations, with gun ownership highest in the South. Gun owners were also more likely to be married.

Gallup found other factors were also prominent:

- Non-Hispanic **whites** were significantly more likely (33%) than nonwhites (22%) to own guns. Twenty-one percent (21%) of blacks owned a gun. Hispanics (18%) had below-average gun ownership.
- Younger Americans (20%) were *less* likely to own guns than older Americans.
- Gun ownership was much higher among those who are politically conservative (39%) than among those who are politically liberal (17%).

Based on its own, more recent polling, Pew Research Center also found that gun ownership was *higher* among white men without Bachelor's degrees, and *lower* among minorities, women, and the college-educated.[91] (Its analysis, *America's Complex Relationship with Guns*, is well worth the read.)

But just to be clear: College-educated men also own firearms. Think of former Vice President Dick Cheney, who peppered a fellow hunter with buckshot, or of Supreme Court Justice Antonin Scalia, who died in his sleep while vacationing at an upscale hunting resort. But statistically, smaller percentages of men (and women) with college degrees own guns than do those who do not have college degrees.

How Many Guns Do Americans Own?

Although the percentage of Americans who own guns is in a long-term decline, paradoxically, the absolute number of guns that Americans (collectively) own is increasing. The long-term trend has been toward a smaller percentage of Americans owning more and more guns.

The 2015 National Firearms Survey estimated that Americans owned about 265 million guns. That worked out to about **88 guns for every 100 persons**. Although most gun owners had only one or two guns, a small group of gun owners had ten or more. As a result, about 3% of American adults collectively owned 130 million firearms, half of the nation's total stock of civilian guns.[92]

Let's drill down on that last statistic. In the researchers' own words:[93]

> Put another way, half of the [U.S.] gun stock (approximately 130 million guns) is owned by approximately 86 percent of gun owners, and the other half is owned by 14 percent (14 percent of gun owners equals 7.6 million adults, or 3 percent of the adult U.S. population).

On average, those in that 3% owned about 17 guns per person. As with any average, that doesn't mean each of the 7.6 million individuals who make up that 3% owns 17 guns. Some owned more; some owned fewer.

Most reports refer to gun owners in that 3% as "super owners."[94] Some of those super owners are well-vetted, licensed gun collectors. In 2017, there were 54,729 federally licensed collectors (about 0.7% of the U.S. population).[95] But most of the 3% were individuals whose identities are wrapped up in guns and the gun culture.[96] They tend not to have college degrees. Some researchers describe them as men "who are anxious about their ability to protect their families, insecure about their place in the job market, and beset by racial fears."[97] Researchers also describe them as men who feel they need to demonstrate their masculinity.

At least one commentator suggests that the gun industry has seized upon feeding those insecurities as a solution to the declining percentage of Americans interested in owning a gun:[98]

> The gun industry has clearly figured out how to make a lot of money convincing a small number of Americans to own a whole bunch of guns. Unfortunately, the result is a subculture of gun fanatics whose combination of masculine insecurities, paranoia, and hostility to their fellow Americans make ... the people you least want to be around, armed and dangerous.

Of course, one suspects that the "gun fanatics" she describes would almost certainly put *her* in the category of folks *they* would least want to be around.

At the fringes of that 3%, some super owners—studies don't tell us how many—are white men stockpiling guns against what they imagine is an imminent breakdown of society or imminent race war.[99] Some—maybe as many as 20,000 to 60,000—are the "angry white guys with guns"[100] who belong to rightwing militias.[101] As one writer put it, "There is no shortage of heavily armed militiamen in rural America with large basement arsenals, itchy trigger fingers, and a hatred of the government."[102]

And then there are the anti-government crackpots who call themselves "sovereign citizens." There may be 100,000 of them,[103] and they're responsible for killing a remarkable number of police officers.[104] Others are violent white supremacists engaged in trafficking guns and drugs, usually crystal methamphetamine ("meth").[105] And still others belong to a variety of other antigovernment groups.[106] Collectively, they're some of the gun industry's best customers and most ardent supporters.

In several of its polls, YouGov asked the gun householders how many guns there were in their homes. Some 4% to 9% of gun householders (about **1.4%** to **3.3%** of adults) said there were ten or more guns in their homes. And about 1% of gun householders said there were ninety to one hundred guns in their homes. (*See*: Appendix, "The Economist/YouGov Polls and 'Super Owners.'") Those results line up remarkably well with the much larger government-sponsored surveys.

We Underestimate How Many Guns Americans Own

Although most Americans overestimate the percentage who own guns, many underestimate how many guns Americans (collectively) own. That, too, may skew how politicians and the rest of us feel about gun-violence-prevention measures.

In its "misconceptions" poll, Ipsos asked: "To the best of your knowledge, how many guns are there in the United States per 100 people?" About 10% opted for the low-ball "8 guns per 100 people" answer, and 29% chose the "32 guns per 100 people" answer. That's

Ds	Rs	How Many Guns in US?
11%	10%	**8 guns per 100 people**
26%	33%	**32 guns per 100 people**
27%	18%	**88 guns per 100 people**
15%	11%	**175 guns per 100 people**
21%	28%	**Don't Know**

a total of 39% who underestimated the number of guns per 100 people. Only 21% chose the correct answer, "88 guns per 100 people." Some 14% chose the high answer, "175 guns per 100 people." The rest admitted they didn't know.[107]

The results varied some between self-identified Democrats, who were a little less likely to underestimate the number of guns, and Republicans, who were a little more likely to do so. Among Democrats, 37% underestimated the number of guns per 100 people; so did 43% of Republicans. Among Democrats, only 27% correctly chose 88 guns per 100 people, as did an even smaller 18% of Republicans.

Ipsos also asked if this statement was true or false: "About half of all civilian-owned guns in the world are in the United States." Sixty-two percent (62%) correctly answered "True," but again, there were party differences: 70% of Democrats correctly thought the statement was true; so did a smaller, but still robust, 55% of Republicans.

Those differences are not terribly large, but Republicans were a little more likely to downplay just how many guns Americans own. And, as we saw in the last chapter, Republicans were also a little more likely to underestimate the toll gun violence takes or to say they didn't know. That suggests cognitive bias may be at work in both groups, but on these specific issues, a bit stronger among Republicans.

But if there is a bottom line, it may be what Mayor Pete Buttigieg said during a Democratic presidential debate: "If more guns made us safer, we'd be the safest country on earth."[108]

Changes in the Types of Guns We Own
More Handguns

As the reason for owning a gun shifted from hunting and trap shooting to personal protection, there was a shift toward more handgun ownership.

A recent study, for example, pointed out that while the percentage of Americans who own guns is declining, the percentage of white, non-Hispanic families *with young children* who own handguns has increased.[109] In 1976, about 50% of white families with young children, ages 1 to 5, owned firearms. That fell to 29% in 2002. Then the NRA and the gun industry went to work to convince whites that they needed guns to protect against home intruders and other threats. By 2016, 45% of white families with young children at home owned a firearm.

Handgun ownership played a key role in this. In 1976, 49% of white firearm owners with a young child at home had a handgun. By 2016, an enormous 72% of white firearm owners with a young child at home had a handgun. (That's 72% of the 45% of white families with young children who owned guns; in other words, about 32% of white families with young children had one or more handguns in the home.)

Increased handgun ownership in that demographic came at a terrible price. Child deaths from firearms peaked in the late 1970s and early 1980s and were on the decline until 2001. But as handgun ownership increased, the rates of child deaths from firearms climbed, nearly doubling from **0.36** per 100,000 children, ages 1 to 4, in 2006 to **0.63** child deaths from guns per 100,000 in 2016.[110]

There are obvious reasons for the correlation between handgun ownership in families with young children and child deaths. Someone who owns a handgun to deal with the threat of an intruder is more likely to keep the gun loaded and easily accessible. It's also easier for a toddler to shoot himself with a handgun than with a shotgun or rifle. Chapter 16 discusses whether the public supports mandating safe gun-storage practices for gun owners with young children.

Larger Caliber Bullets

In addition to more handguns, there has also been a shift toward larger caliber bullets—*i.e.*, away from "Saturday night specials" and .22 caliber bullets to .40 and .45 caliber bullets. The larger bullets are more deadly than smaller caliber bullets.[111] The unusually high ratio of fatalities-to-injured in the Virginia Beach shooting in 2019 may well be because the shooter used .45 caliber bullets.

Semi-Automatics, "Assault Weapons," and Large-Capacity Magazines

In recent decades, many owners of long guns have shifted to semi-automatic rifles and large-capacity magazines.

The history of semi-automatic rifles, including the AR-15-style rifle, is an oft-told story.[112] Armalite, a small-arms company, developed the AR-15 rifle for use by the military. Armalite saw in the AR-15 an answer to the Soviet bloc AK-47 ("Kalashnikov") rifle used by North Vietnamese and Viet Cong soldiers in the Vietnam War. "AR" stood for Armalite Rifle. When Armalite failed to convince the military to buy the gun, it sold the rights to the design to Colt, which had more success—the gun became the M-16 rifle, long the U.S. military's standard weapon.

The military version of the AR-15 was capable of both automatic and semi-automatic fire. For non-gun enthusiasts, here's the difference: With an *automatic* weapon, the shooter can pull and hold the trigger, and the weapon will continue to fire until the shooter releases the trigger or the gun runs out of ammunition. With a *semi-automatic*, the shooter needs to pull the trigger again for each shot.

As we discuss in Chapter 12, both federal law and many state laws ban automatic weapons. To sell the AR-15 to civilians, Colt modified it to eliminate the ability to fire like an automatic. Colt's initial marketing efforts had scant success. And then Patrick Edward Purdy, 26, a drifter and bigot with guerrilla-warfare fantasies, entered the picture. He used an AK-47 semi-automatic rifle to kill five young school children and wound 32 others in a playground in Stockton, California, in 1989.[113] His victims were mainly children of Southeast Asian refugees.

The shooting prompted calls for regulation of AK-47 and AR-15-style weapons. *Time* magazine, for example, asked, "Why could Purdy, an alcoholic who had been arrested for such offenses as selling weapons and attempted robbery, walk into a gun shop in Sandy, Oregon, and leave with an AK-47 under his arm?" *Time* added, "The easy availability of weapons like this, which have no purpose other than killing human beings, can all too readily turn the delusions of sick gunmen into tragic nightmares."[114]

As calls for regulation multiplied, sales of the AR-15 (the American answer to the weapon Purdy used) soared—at least until the assault weapons ban (from 1994—2004).[115] During the assault weapon ban, gun manufacturers designed around the ban and continued selling as many of the guns as before the ban.[116]

In 2004, there were enough pro-gun votes in Congress to prevent renewal of the ban. Gun manufacturers were once again able to include the combat-related features that distinguish an "assault rifle" from an ordinary semi-automatic rifle, and sales increased. After that, each new high-profile mass shooting and the attendant calls for a renewed ban on assault weapons have led to new boosts in sales.[117]

Barack Obama became president in January 2009. Several mass shootings forced his Administration to focus on gun violence. That, in turn, gave rise to persistent rumors—likely spread by gun dealers—that his Administration was going to ban assault weapons or even confiscate all guns. The shootings and the rumors of a new ban doubled sales of AR-15-style rifles.[118]

Over this same general timeframe, gun manufacturers also began marketing semi-automatic pistols. AR-15 rifles may be the weapon of choice for school shooters and other high-profile mass murderers, but semi-automatic pistols play a much more significant role in street crime.

The 2015 National Firearms Survey reported:[119]

> Of the estimated 265 million guns in civilian hands in the United States, approximately four in ten (42 percent) are handguns; the remainder primarily (53 percent) long guns; (4 percent are "other" guns). Among handguns, the majority are semiautomatic pistols (62 percent) and revolvers (29 percent); the remainder are described by respondents as "other" handguns.

If 42% of our 265 million guns were handguns, and 62% of those were semi-automatics, then by 2015 American civilians owned more than 69 million semi-automatic handguns. In short, semi-automatic rifles and pistols have dramatically changed the gun landscape.

Concealed Carry

As handgun ownership has gone up, so too have the number of Americans who have concealed carry permits. The Crime Prevention Research Center is an organization that promotes research and books by controversial pro-gun researcher John Lott. It reported that 11.1 million Americans held concealed carry permits in 2014, which was up from an estimated 4.6 million in 2007.

In 2015, the CPRC boasted, "Since President Obama's election the number of concealed handgun permits has soared, growing from 4.6 million in 2007 to over 12.8 million this year." In its July 2016 report, CPRC claimed: "During President Obama's administration, the number of concealed handgun permits soared to over 16.36 million—a 256% increase since 2007."[120]

Announcing its 2019 report, CPRC said, "Last year, the number of permit holders continued to grow by about 1.4 million. Despite expectations that increases in permits were primarily driven by fears of Democratic presidencies, the growth has continued at a similar pace after the

November 2016 election." CPRC put the total number of concealed carry permit holders in 2019 at 18.66 million.

Making those numbers even more remarkable, a growing number of states—16 according to CPRC—now allow their residents to carry concealed handguns without a permit—what CPRC and other gun rights advocates call "Constitutional Carry."

Whether the increase in concealed carry permits and "Constitutional Carry" laws has led to increased incidents of road rage and retail rage in which someone brandishes—or uses—a gun is a hotly contested issue. In fact, gun rights advocates argue that all those people carrying guns make us safer.

On the other side of that debate, the Violence Policy Center maintains a "Concealed Carry Killers" database "that includes hundreds of examples of non-self-defense killings since May 2007 by private citizens with permits to carry concealed, loaded handguns. Those incidents include homicides, suicides, mass shootings, murder-suicides, lethal attacks on law enforcement officers, and unintentional deaths."[121]

That argument is outside the scope of this book.

Conclusion

A smaller percentage of Americans own guns than in past decades, but collectively, those who do own guns own more guns than ever. That's due mainly to "super owners"—the roughly 3% of Americans who own ten or more guns.

The mix of guns that today's gun owners own are a different mix than the guns Americans owned in the 1970s and earlier. A larger percentage are handguns, and those handguns often fire larger caliber rounds than in the 1970s. Those rounds are more deadly.

More of today's guns, both long guns and handguns, are semi-automatics, including those controversially called "assault weapons."

And more Americans than ever have concealed carry permits or live in the growing number of states that allow anyone permitted to own a gun to carry a concealed weapon.

Gun-rights advocates argue that these trends are positive; because more guns make us safer. We just have to learn not to get upset when kids use their parents' guns to shoot their classmates or commit suicide, or when a toddler finds a loaded gun and kills himself or a sibling.

Gun-violence-prevention advocates, on the other hand, see those trends, if they could be reversed, as opportunities to reduce our country's gun carnage.

In short, in one view of the world, shootings are going to happen. Empathy is the problem. In the other view, dead children and the rest of our gun carnage are the problem.

3. The Second Amendment: *Heller* and *McDonald*

It is a bedrock principle of our democracy that Congress may not, even at the urging of a majority of voters, enact legislation that tramples on the constitutionally protected rights of the minority. That thought brings us to the Second Amendment and the two recent Supreme Court decisions that establish its contemporary import.

The Constitution and the Militia

As most of us learned in high school, the American Revolutionary War effectively ended with the British surrender at Yorktown, Virginia, in October 1781. A formal treaty officially resolved the conflict on September 3, 1783.

Soon thereafter, it became clear that the Articles of Confederation, which treated the original thirteen states as a confederation of independent nation-states, wasn't working. The states selected delegates and charged them with revising the Articles of Confederation. The delegates got together in Philadelphia, and after much debate, instead wrote a completely new constitution. The delegates signed the proposed new constitution on September 17, 1787. The Confederation Congress approved it on September 28, 1787.

What many of us may have forgotten, or only dimly recall, is that after hammering out the new constitution and getting the Continental Congress to approve it, the work of the delegates to the convention in Philadelphia wasn't over. They had to go back to their respective states and convince their fellow citizens to ratify the new constitution. As they left Philadelphia, their success in that endeavor was by no means certain.

James Madison, for example, had to convince the important Virginia convention to ratify the proposed constitution. When he presented the document, a fierce debate ensued between the federalists, who favored ratification, and the anti-federalists, who opposed it. If Virginia rejected the constitution, the effort to create a new nation might have come to naught.

As constitutional scholar and law school professor Carl Bogus explains, George Mason and Patrick Henry raised a series of objections to the proposed constitution.[122] Mason was the intellectual leader of the anti-federalists, and Henry was Virginia's governor. Henry—of "Give me liberty or give death!" fame—was also a powerful orator.

Among other things, Mason and Henry expressed concern about the authority the proposed Constitution gave the federal government over state militias.[123] Specifically, Article I, Section 8 of the Constitution provided that Congress would have the power:

> [15:] To provide for calling forth the Militia to execute the Laws of the Union, suppress Insurrections and repel Invasions;
>
> [16:] To provide for organizing, arming, and disciplining, the Militia, and for governing such Part of them as may be employed in the Service of the United States, reserving to the States respectively, the Appointment of the Officers, and the Authority of training the Militia according to the discipline prescribed by Congress[.][124]

The proposed constitution also stipulated, in Article II, that "The President shall be Commander in Chief of the Army and Navy of the United States, and of the Militia of the several states, when called into the actual Service of the United States."[125]

Like most white southerners, Mason and Henry saw state militias as essential in putting down slave rebellions. They expressed concern that the national government might abuse its powers over state militias and weaken them as a back door means of making slavery untenable. "Slavery is detested," Henry warned the Virginia convention. "The majority of Congress is to the North, and the slaves are to the South."

Madison promised to draft an amendment to address their concern, and in the end, the Virginia convention ratified the Constitution.

The Second Amendment

Madison won election to the new Congress, where he kept his word and drafted what—after some revision—became the Second Amendment.

Madison's proposal, as adopted by the House Select Committee on July 28, 1789, read:[126]

> A well-regulated militia, composed of the body of the people, being the best security of a free State, the right of the people to keep and bear arms shall not be infringed, but no person religously scrupulous shall be compelled to bear arms.

During the debate, Congress streamlined the wording and stripped out the religious exemption to military service. As finally approved by Congress in 1789, the Second Amendment read:

> A well regulated Militia, being necessary to the security of a free State, the right of the people to keep and bear Arms, shall not be infringed.

The states ratified the amendment, making it part of the Constitution on December 15, 1791.[127]

In recent decades, scholars and political partisans have waged scholarly and polemical wars over the original meaning of that unhappy word salad. *Was the Second Amendment meant to protect a state's right to keep a well-regulated militia (with which it might put down a slave rebellion or other insurrection)? Or was the Second Amendment, as the NRA and gun rights advocates insist, in-tended to protect an individual right to own a firearm, both for personal protection and so that the people, or some of them, might launch an armed insurrection against any administration they consider tyrannical?*

Scholars and political partisans have also clashed on a related question: *Whatever the original intent, should our contemporary understanding of the Second Amendment take into account the fact that the world has changed a great deal since 1789 when Congress proposed the Second Amendment? Or should we pretend the world hasn't changed and focus on the original intent?*

The militia system in place when Congress approved the Second Amendment consisted of calling upon free, white males of a certain age to serve in a local or state militia, with each citizen supplying his own musket. In the mythology of Second Amendment absolutists, those militias were essential to Americans winning the revolutionary war against Great Britain.

To be sure, those militias were effective in getting the colonies into a shooting war with Great Britain. But after Bunker Hill, militias proved to be no match for Great Britain's well-trained professional army. Moreover, in the Midland and Appalachian regions, the militias—some aligned with the British, some with the revolution—mainly fought each other. And the southern states, for the most part, refused to send their militias to fight the British for fear that while the militia was away, slaves would seize the opportunity to revolt. It was the national army that General George Washington commanded and the French navy that won the war.[128]

When pushing for ratification of the Second Amendment, its proponents in the slave states did not highlight the contentious issue of putting down slave rebellions. Doing so would have stirred up opposition in the northern states. Instead, slave-state proponents of the Second Amendment argued, as did their northern anti-federalist counterparts, that a standing army would inevitably lead to tyranny. Therefore, they argued, it was best not to have a standing army except in times of war. Better, they contended, to rely instead on the militia to "execute the Laws of the Union" and "suppress Insurrections."

Along with other considerations, those oft-cited statements about the dangers of a standing army have led some to conclude that the Second Amendment was about *collective* defense—*i.e.*, making sure state and local militias would be ready and sufficiently armed when needed. Those same statements about the evils of a standing army—again, along with other considerations—have led others to conclude that the intent was to protect an individual right to own a gun or guns. In the latter view, the reference to a "well regulated militia" was merely prefatory and largely superfluous.

Gun Owners Protect Us from Tyranny. If You Doubt It, Just Ask a "2A" Absolutist.

Some dogmatic gun-rights advocates go further. They argue that the Constitution was never intended to ensure that the federal government would be able to call upon state militias to "to execute the Laws of the Union [and] suppress Insurrections"—as the Constitution itself states.[129]

On the contrary, they argue, when the Founding Fathers added the Second Amendment to the Constitution, they intended to guarantee that the people would be able to launch an armed insurrection against the government if they believed it had become tyrannical—in other words, to launch a modern-day Whiskey Rebellion. In their social media posts, "freedom" appears to mean being able to own and carry a gun; conversely, "tyranny" seems to refer to a government that registers or confiscates civilian guns. "Democracy" is defined as "mob rule."

In this view, gun owners heroically preserve freedom in this country by owning guns and by putting the federal government on notice, mainly through social media, that they stand ready to resist "tyranny." This viewpoint is repeated endlessly by gun rights advocates on social media sites like Quora, where they debate such pressing topics as whether gun owners, faced with "a gun registration/confiscation scheme," would actually shoot police officers who tried to enforce such a law, and whether gun owners could defeat the U.S. military.

This is standard fare for that genre:

> I can 100 percent guarantee you there will be a war if a democrat [sic] gets elected here in the US and attempts gun bans. It won't be pretty and about half the population of the US will die in it.

> Go ahead, try and ban and confiscate fire arms [sic]. I seriously doubt the police will make it [to] the first door before people show up at the doors of politicians killing them [sic] who passed such a law. It's long over due [sic] anyway.[130]

One such gun-rights advocate had a more nuanced view. He made the point that "guns already protect us from tyranny each and every day":

> I harbor no delusions that armed civilians could beat a legitimate military in an outright war, but you shouldn't harbor any delusions that wide ranging confiscation would be anything other than a horrific and bloody mess, and for that reason it will never happen. We the people don't have to be able to win in some kind of hypothetical war, we just have to be able to make the idea of confiscation so incredibly unpalatable that it will never be attempted, and we're already there, so guns are currently protecting us from tyranny.[131]

In short, simply by owning guns and posting threats of insurrection on social media, "2A" folks protect the rest of us from "tyranny."

But just to be sure our elected representatives get the message, from time-to-time, some of those "2A" folks show up in our state capitals dressed in camouflage fatigues, boots, and tactical gear, and when permitted, carrying assault rifles.

Okay, most of us know those folks exist, but they're not the typical gun owner. Let's be realistic. Just how many of those people are there?

In March 2018, Monmouth asked gun owners why they owned guns. About one in four (**23%**) said that defending against government tyranny was a major reason why they own a gun.[132] (In that poll, 34% said they personally owned a gun. That figure may be rather high, but if we use it, then 23% of that 34%, or about **7.8%** of American adults, say they have a gun—or an arsenal of them—at least in part to fend off tyranny.)

Interesting as those arguments may be, they are outside the scope of this book. For our purposes, a pair of Supreme Court decisions, *Heller* and *McDonald*, tell us what, for present purposes and for the present time, we need to know.

Heller *v.* District of Columbia (2008)

Until this century, the last substantive word from the U.S. Supreme Court on the proper application of the Second Amendment was a decision in 1939, *United States v. Miller*.[133] In that case, the defendant argued that the National Firearms Act's ban on short-barreled shotguns violated the Second Amendment. The court rejected the argument, holding that there was no evidence that owning a short-barreled shotgun had "some reasonable relationship to the preservation or efficiency of a well regulated militia."

In 2008, in *District of Columbia v. Heller*,[134] the Supreme Court took up the meaning of the Second Amendment again. In a five-to-four decision, it held that the Second Amendment protects an individual right to possess a firearm unconnected with service in a militia and to use that firearm for traditionally lawful purposes, such as self-defense within the home.

The *Heller* decision concerned a pair of District of Columbia ordinances. The first required all handguns to be registered. The second prohibited registration of handguns kept in the home. The net effect was to outlaw keeping a handgun in the home. Because they made it illegal to keep a handgun in the home for self-protection, the court struck down the ordinances. In so doing, the Supreme Court held that the Second Amendment protected an *individual* right to "keep and bear Arms."

Justice Antonin Scalia wrote for the majority. His opinion did not adopt the absolutist position that the Second Amendment tolerates no restrictions whatsoever on an individual's right to have a firearm. Instead, he stressed that, "Like most rights, the right secured by the Second Amendment is not unlimited." He cautioned that:

> … nothing in our opinion should be taken to cast doubt on longstanding prohibitions on the possession of firearms by felons and the mentally ill, or laws forbidding the carrying of firearms in sensitive places such as schools and government buildings, or laws imposing conditions and qualifications on the commercial sale of arms.

Justice Scalia added one more caveat, which is crucial to the debate over assault weapons and large-capacity magazines: "We also recognize another important limitation on the right to keep and carry arms." That limitation, he wrote, restricted the right to "keep and bear Arms" to the sorts of weapons "in common use at the time."

McDonald *v.* City of Chicago (2010)

When ratified in 1791, the common understanding was that the first ten amendments to the Constitution, *i.e.,* the "Bill of Rights," applied only to legislation enacted by the federal government and not to legislation enacted by the states. The First Amendment, for example, begins, "Congress shall make no law respecting an establishment of religion ..."

The Fourteenth Amendment, adopted after the Civil War, changed that. With remarkable brevity, it said:

> No state shall make or enforce any law which shall abridge the privileges or immunities of citizens of the United States; nor shall any state deprive any person of life, liberty, or property, without due process of law; nor deny to any person within its jurisdiction the equal protection of the laws.

Congress intended the amendment to protect the rights enshrined in the Bill of Rights from infringement by the States—and in particular, to protect the rights of those who until recently had been enslaved. But throughout much of the Jim Crow era, the Supreme Court refused to interpret the Fourteenth Amendment as protecting those rights against state action.

A key event in that history was the Colfax Massacre on Easter Sunday, April 13, 1873.[135] A large band of armed white supremacists, upset over a bitterly contested gubernatorial election, descended on a Louisiana town populated by freed blacks. The white mob captured and then massacred at least several dozen—and maybe as many as 150—black men.

Federal prosecutors won convictions of a number of the white participants for violating an early Civil Rights law, which a Reconstruction-era Congress enacted to protect the constitutional rights of black citizens. Three of the men who participated in the massacre appealed. The Supreme Court accepted the appeal and overturned the convictions. Justice Morrison Remick Waite, a racist of the first order, wrote the decision for the court. *United States v. Cruikshank*, 92 U. S. 542 (1876).

The court premised its decision on the odd proposition that the federal Civil Rights Act could apply only to rights *created* by the Constitution and not to rights merely *protected* by the Constitution. There was no logical reason for that premise, and the court did not offer one.

The indictment charged, among other things, that the white mob violated the black citizens' right of peaceful assembly. The court held that the First Amendment did not create a right of freedom of assembly. That right "derives its source from those laws whose authority is acknowl-edged by civilized man throughout the world."[136] In other words, the right to assemble and petition the government arose from Natural Law. Because Congress did not create that right, the court held, Congress had no power to protect citizens from infringement of that right by the states.

Similarly, the court held that the Second Amendment did not create a right of "bearing arms for a lawful purpose," as alleged in the indictment. "This is not a right granted by the Constitution," Justice Waite wrote. "Neither is it in any manner dependent upon that instrument for its existence." It was, apparently, like freedom of assembly, a right that "derives its source from those laws whose authority is acknowledged by civilized man throughout the world."

On the same grounds, the court also dismissed the counts in the indictment that alleged that the mob violated the murdered blacks' Fourth Amendment right to be secure in their persons.

In so doing, the court stripped the Fourteenth Amendment of its meaning and purpose. In essence, the *Cruikshank* court held that the rights protected by the Bill of Rights were not "privileges or immunities of citizens of the United States," and Congress, therefore, had no ability to protect citizens of the United States against infringement of those rights by the states.

The court also held that the Second Amendment did not, in any event, apply to the states. "The second amendment declares that it [*i.e.*, the right "to keep and bear Arms"] shall not be infringed," Justice Waite wrote, "but this ... means no more than that it shall not be infringed by Congress."

Thus, the Court concluded, the slaughtered black men did not have a constitutional right to freedom of assembly, or to keep and bear arms, or to be secure in their persons; moreover, the federal government was powerless to prevent the states from infringing the Second Amendment.[137]

A decade later, in *Presser v. Illinois*, 116 U.S. 252 (1886), the Supreme Court rejected the argument that the Second Amendment rendered an Illinois gun law unconstitutional. Citing *Cruikshank*, the court again held that the Second Amendment "is a limitation only upon the power of con-gress and the national government, and not upon that of the state."

Beginning in the 1930s, the Supreme Court reversed course and, in a series of decisions held that, like the federal government, the states may not infringe the rights protected by the Bill of Rights. But it did so painstakingly, one amendment at a time. The Supreme Court never directly overruled *Cruikshank*. Instead, it relied on the due process clause of the Fourteenth Amendment.

Before the Supreme Court decided *Heller*, it had never reconsidered whether the Fourteenth Amendment protected the right to "keep and bear Arms" from infringement by the states. The issue simply didn't arise as long as the Supreme Court treated the Second Amendment as protecting only a collective right, *i.e.,* the right of the states to maintain a militia. The *Heller* court didn't address whether the Second Amendment applied to the states because the District of Columbia is a federal enclave, not a state, and so the issue was not before the court. In short, when the Supreme Court decided *Heller*, it left that issue undecided.[138]

But not for long.

In 2010, in *McDonald v. City of Chicago*, the Supreme Court considered a pair of Chicago ordinances that were essentially the same as those the court struck down in *Heller*—*i.e.,* they required handguns to be registered, but prohibited the registration of handguns kept in the home, thus making it illegal to keep handguns in the home. To no one's surprise, the Supreme Court held that the Fourteenth Amendment made the Second Amendment applicable to state action. In other words, states and their political subdivisions, *e.g.,* the City of Chicago, may not infringe the individual right recognized in *Heller*. Because the Chicago ordinances effectively prohibited keeping a gun in the home for personal protection, the court declared them unconstitutional.[139]

As a result of *McDonald*, the states and their political subdivisions may not infringe the constitutional right recognized in *Heller*. That's true no matter what a majority may think about the matter—unless sentiment were to become so strong that citizens convince Congress and the states to amend the Constitution to repeal the Second Amendment or to limit it to protecting the right of the states to maintain militias. As we discuss in chapter 17, at present, there isn't much sentiment in the country in favor of that.

There is, however, room to argue about the full contours of the right recognized in *Heller*. As noted above, the court indicated that the right applied only to guns "in common use at the time." As we discuss in Chapter 12, some people would like to ban AR-15-style rifles and other "assault weapons." Opponents of a ban on assault weapons argue that AR-15-style firearms are the most popular rifle in the country and therefore are "in common use" today. Thus, they insist, the Second Amendment protects the right to own an AR-15 or AK-47 style rifle. Or an arsenal of them.

Proponents of a ban counter that most of us don't own assault rifles; indeed, even most gun owners don't own assault rifles. And hardly anyone owns an assault weapon for defense in the home against an intruder. Therefore, they argue, assault rifles are not "in common use" for self-defense in the home at the present time. Thus, they conclude, the Second Amendment, as interpreted by *Heller*, does not protect a gun buyer's desire to own an assault rifle from federal or state legislation restricting their sale or possession.

Five U.S. courts of appeal have upheld state and local bans on assault weapons (again, see Chapter 12). But the Supreme Court, which has the final say, has not yet ruled on this contentious issue. Proponents of a ban on assault weapons hope that the unbroken string of Circuit Court decisions upholding bans may make the Supreme Court reluctant to intervene, lest it look openly partisan. Opponents of a ban hope that the partisan, pro-gun-rights justices President Trump appointed to the Supreme Court will provide the votes necessary for the court to declare assault weapon bans unconstitutional. (The same concerns apply to bans on large-capacity magazines, discussed in Chapter 14.)

Putting aside bans of assault weapons and large-capacity magazines, none of the other issues discussed in this book come anywhere close to infringing the right recognized in *Heller* and *McDonald*.

***

With those introductory notes, we turn now to the core of this book, the dozen or so proposals that have been the subject of opinion polls.

We start with the most popular proposal, universal background checks, and end with the least popular, repealing the Second Amendment and banning civilians from owning guns.

PART TWO: WHICH GUN LAWS DO AMERICANS WANT?

4. Should We Require Universal Background Checks?

Item: *July 16, 2012: Tavares Donnell Colbert bought a gun in Kansas City and was on his way to sell it to someone in the parking lot of an Oklahoma City convenience store. Near the store, he decided to pull into a parking lot and check to make sure the gun worked. When he removed the gun from its case, it discharged and shot him in the genitals. The police arrested Colbert, but not for recklessly discharging the gun or even because he planned to sell the gun to someone in the parking lot of a convenience store without a background check. In most states, private sales of guns without background checks are not against the law. The police arrested Colbert because he was a convicted felon. Federal and state law barred him from having a gun.*[140]

Item: *Zina Daniel Haughton obtained a restraining order, barring her estranged husband, Radcliffe Haughton, from threatening her. The order also barred him from having a firearm. That meant Radcliffe Houghton wouldn't be able to pass a background check. So, he logged onto Armslist.com, a website dedicated to sales of firearms, gun parts, and ammunition. Houghton chose the option that allowed him to bypass ads by licensed dealers, who would be required to perform a background check, and arranged to buy a Glock .40 semi-automatic pistol for $500 in a private transaction in a McDonald's parking lot.*

The next day, October 21, 2012, Haughton went to the Azana Salon & Spa in Brookfield, Wisconsin, where Zina worked. He forced the women there to lie on the floor and then proceeded to shoot them execution-style. Haughton killed three, including his wife, and wounded four. When he had to reload the gun, the new magazine jammed, and one woman escaped. Haughton then killed himself.[141]

The victims' families sued Armslist.com, alleging that it facilitated Haughton's rampage by making it easy for prohibited persons to get guns. In April 2019, the Wisconsin Supreme Court held that the federal Communications Decency Act, 47

U.S.C. § 230(c)(1), made Armslist immune from suit.¹⁴² The U.S. Supreme Court declined to hear the case.¹⁴³

Item: *March 27, 2018.* The student leaders from the Marjory Stoneman Douglas High School in Parkland, Florida, led the March for Our Lives in March 2018. Shortly after that, Public Policy Polling (PPP) surveyed people across the country on gun-related issues. Its poll showed that 87% supported background checks for all gun purchases, compared to only 8% of voters who were opposed. Universal background checks had the backing of 89% of Democrats and 85% of Republicans and Independents. "It's hard to find anything 87% of Americans agree on," Dean Debnam, PPP's President, said. "In fact, in this same poll, we found that only 81% think the sky is blue with 11% disputing that notion."¹⁴⁴

Item: *On August 31, 2019,* Seth Ator killed seven and injured more than 20 others in a West Texas shooting spree. Before his murderous rampage, he had failed a background check due to his history of mental illness. So, he purchased his AR-15 style rifle in a private sale.¹⁴⁵

Under current law, *federally licensed firearm dealers* handle most retail gun sales. Federal law requires those dealers to run background checks before selling a gun to most retail customers. Those background checks use the National Instant Criminal Background Check System (NICS). They are designed to alert the dealer if federal law bars the would-be purchaser from having a gun, *e.g.*, because he or she is a felon, has been involuntarily committed to a mental institution, has been convicted of domestic abuse, and so on.

But there's an enormous loophole. It is legal for an individual who is not a licensed gun dealer to sell a gun in a "private sale" without asking for identification, arranging for a background check, or even keeping a record of the sale.¹⁴⁶ Less controversially, individuals may also inherit guns without a background check.

Researchers from Northeastern and Harvard Universities did an online survey in 2015 of 1,613 adult gun owners.¹⁴⁷ Among gun owners who obtained their most recent gun within the previous two years:

- 22% *overall* said they obtained the guns without a background check. (Some of those may have been gifts or inheritances.)

- 13% who *purchased* firearms said they did so without a background check.

Some states go further than federal law and require background checks for all gun purchases, eliminating the "private sale" loophole. Of those who purchased their most recent firearm within the previous two years in a private purchase:

- 26% of those who lived in states that required a background check for a private sale bought the firearm without a background check.

- 57% of those who lived in states that did not require a background check bought the firearm without undergoing a background check.

And quite a few claimed they couldn't remember or refused to answer.

It's those private purchases without background checks that are worrisome. For the convicted felon, mentally ill person, or spouse abuser barred by federal law from buying a gun, the private sale loophole makes it easy to buy a gun. They can find the gun they want on Armslist.com or a similar site and arrange to meet the seller in a mall or convenience store parking lot, where they can complete the purchase, no questions asked. The seller, in turn, may get a better price than a legal purchaser would pay.

Most Americans part company with their representatives in Congress on an important question: *Should federal law allow unlicensed individuals to sell firearms, including "assault rifles" and semi-automatic handguns, to strangers, with no background check and no recordkeeping?* The public overwhelmingly says, "Of course, not." Congress, or at least congressional Republicans, disagree, essentially saying, "Well, if that's what the NRA wants."

The Issue

Should Congress require background checks before *all* gun sales, including private sales?

The National Instant Criminal Background Check System (NICS) is the system Congress put in place for determining at the point-of-sale if a prospective buyer is among those the law prohibits from having a firearm. The Brady Handgun Violence Prevention Act of 1993[148] mandated the NICS. The Federal Bureau of Investigation (FBI) made it operational in 1998.

One hears talk of the "gun show" and "internet" loopholes.[149] To a large extent, those terms are misnomers. Often used loosely, they refer to a gap in our gun laws that, subject to the limitations discussed below, allows gun sales by unlicensed[150] sellers to private[151] purchasers.

Those "private sales" may occur at or on the periphery of a gun show[152] or in face-to-face sales arranged through the internet. But "private sales" also include sales between unlicensed sellers and buyers arranged through other means. Thus, it is more accurate to refer to the "private sale" exception to background checks.

Federal law does not require a private seller to arrange for a licensed dealer to perform a background check on a buyer.[153] Federal law also does not require unlicensed individuals to ask for identification or to make a record of the sale.

The usual justification for the private sale loophole is to allow someone to give or sell a gun they no longer want to a family member or friend. Gun-rights advocates typically offer the example of a father giving a gun to his son or daughter. The loophole, however, is far broader than that. It also covers unlicensed individuals who sell guns to strangers in transactions arranged through sites like Armslist.com, to strangers at gun shows, in bars or convenience store parking lots, and so on.

There are some important qualifications:

Importantly, the private sale exception does not authorize someone to go into the business of selling or trafficking in guns.[154] Thus, it does not protect the street hustler, like the unfortunate Tavares Colbert, who frequently buys and sells guns in convenience store parking lots or in sales arranged over the internet. Nonetheless, the private sales exception does create an opportunity for a gun owner to sell a gun in a private sale without realizing, or perhaps not caring, that the buyer is someone who may not legally buy or possess a gun—as in the private sales that enabled the Azana Spa and the Odessa shootings highlighted at the beginning of this chapter.

Some other qualifications and caveats:

Felons and other purchasers who are barred by federal law from owning a gun may not legally buy a firearm in a private sale.[155] That's why the police were able to arrest Colbert. But, as his case indicates, that doesn't stop prohibited persons from doing so. To discourage such purchases, federal law says the seller may not complete the sale or transfer of a firearm if he or she *knows* or *has reason to know* that federal law prohibits the buyer from buying a gun (*e.g.*, because the buyer is a convicted felon).[156] That, of course, gives "Don't ask, Don't tell" a new life.

Private sellers may only sell guns to residents of the same state, and even then, federal law permits the sale only if state or local law does not prohibit it.[157] Thus, states may enact laws that require background checks for private sales. That sort of law is generally called "comprehensive," or more recently, "universal" background check legislation.

Do Universal Background Check Laws Save Lives?

Some states have enacted universal background check laws, and others haven't. That allows researchers to assess the impact of universal background check laws by comparing the rates of firearm fatalities in the states that have enacted universal background check laws and those that haven't.

Michael Siegel and Claire Boine analyzed the effectiveness of various gun laws for the Rockefeller Institute of Government. Their study, published in March 2019, found that states with universal background check laws have about 12.9% lower gun-homicide rates than states that don't. They also have lower overall homicide rates, indicating that people who could not buy a gun did not simply use another weapon instead.[158]

In January 2017, L. K. Lee and colleagues analyzed the peer-reviewed research published from 1970 to 2016 that addressed the relationship between firearm laws and firearm homicide.[159] They found that states that required background checks for all gun sales had significantly lower gun homicide and gun suicide rates.

An important study by Bindu Kalesan and colleagues, published in The Lancet in 2016, examined a variety of gun laws enacted by the states.[160] It concluded that state laws that required background checks for *all* gun sales were strongly associated with lower rates of gun fatalities. State laws that required background checks for ammunition purchases also had significantly lower rates of gun deaths. And so did state laws that required purchasers to show identification.

The authors projected those reductions in gun mortality rate across the nation and estimated that if Congress were to enact universal background checks, it could reduce the national-firearm mortality from 10.35 deaths per 100,000 persons to 4.46 deaths (using 2014 data). Adding universal background checks for ammunition would reduce gun mortality to 1.99 per 100,000. And adding a requirement that purchasers show identification would reduce firearm mortality still further to 1.8 per 100,000. (That's about the same rate as New Zealand.)

Dr. Kalesan and her colleagues concluded, "Implementation of universal background checks for the purchase of firearms or ammunition, and firearm identification nationally could substantially reduce firearm mortality in the USA." No other measure discussed in this book would have anywhere near as large an impact.

As if to drive home the point, in 2016, California voters passed an initiative, Proposition 63, that required gun owners to show identification and undergo a background check before they could buy ammunition. The purpose was to screen out felons and others attempting to buy ammunition for illegal firearms. Litigation delayed putting the law into effect, but in 2019, in advance of the delayed effective date, gun owners swarmed gun dealers to buy ammunition.

It's likely that many of those California gun owners desperate to buy ammunition were felons or others who knew they were not allowed to own guns and therefore would not be able to buy ammunition once the new state law went into effect. "Most people know about the deadline. They are running scared," Mike Hein of Ade's Gun Shop in Orange County told the Los Angeles Times.[161]

A different study[162] looked at regulation of gun dealers and offered suggestions to reduce the number of guns sold *illegally* by a small number of licensed gun dealers. "Bad apple" gun dealers aside, the authors noted: "Federal law permits private sellers to transfer their firearms with no background check or other paperwork. This is a crucial omission. Police recovered 85% of crime guns from someone who was not the original retail purchaser."

Private Sales in Practice

Most private sales probably begin with an internet ad, typically on a site like Armslist, followed by a meeting in a mutually convenient mall parking lot or in a bar.[163] Naturally, there is some concern about how strictly two strangers observe legal requirements when they meet in a parking lot or bar, in a transaction in which the seller is not required to ask for identification, arrange for a background check, or even make a record of the sale.

As noted in the introduction to this chapter, Seth Ator, the West Texas shooter who killed seven and injured at least twenty more, bought his AR-15-style rifle in a private sale after failing a background check. Here's another, more typical, example of the problem with no-background-check private gun sales:

In April 2018, the U.S. Attorney for the Northern District of Illinois (Chicago) announced the arrest of three men on gun-trafficking charges. According to the 72-page criminal complaint,[164] two of the men, Christopher Henderson and John "JoJo" L. Phillips, bought firearms in Kentucky, which has very lax gun laws. They arranged these purchases through Armslist.com. Henderson and Phillips would then transport the guns to Chicago, where they worked with the third man, Jaiqail Wright, to re-sell them, mainly to gang members and drug dealers.

Phillips and Wright allegedly had ties to the "Coco and Cornell" faction of the Conservative Vice Lords, a street gang on Chicago's west side. When the guns arrived in Chicago, Wright would use Facebook and other means to advertise the weapons. At least three of the guns the trio sold later figured in homicides.[165]

Federal authorities charged the three men with dealing in firearms without a license. They also charged Phillips, who had a prior felony-firearm conviction, with possession of a firearm by a felon. But neither the Feds nor state law enforcement authorities announced any charges against the gun owners who sold the guns to Phillips and Wright in Kentucky. If those sellers did not engage in multiple gun sales and did not know that Phillips was a felon, the sales would have been perfectly legal *for the sellers* under the private sale exception.

And that's the problem. There will always be bad guys willing to traffic in guns. But in many cases, the sellers are—presumably—just regular gun owners, not hardened criminals, looking to sell a gun they no longer want or need. If the seller had to arrange for a federally licensed firearm dealer to run a background check before he could complete the sale, far fewer guns would be sold to felons or leak into the black market. Would that be a perfect, 100% solution? No, of course not. No law ever is.

But if "private sales" in mall and convenience-store parking lots between strangers, with no identification, no background checks, and no recordkeeping were not the law, websites like Armslist.com would likely not exist, or at least would not flourish to the extent that they do now.

Street gangs and drug dealers need guns, and they often need new guns because they used their current guns in crimes and needed to ditch them, or because the police seized the guns they had. Gangs and drug dealers, therefore, are an important, albeit indirect, source of revenue for gun manufacturers and gun dealers. By resisting universal background checks, legislators protect that revenue stream.

In short, when legislators vote against or refuse to allow a vote on universal background checks, they enable gun trafficking. Bluntly, they make it easier for criminal gangs and drug dealers to get guns. Sadly, that may not be just an unfortunate and unexpected consequence of the private sale exception. It may well be the reason the private sale exception still exists in federal law.

What We Want

Polls by major, well-known polling organizations demonstrate that Americans overwhelmingly believe we *should* require background checks for *all* gun purchases, including private sales. Summing up the polls, The New York Times concluded that background checks are the most popular gun control measure.[166] The famed (and very conservative) Gallup organization said Americans favor background checks for all gun sales "with near unanimity."[167] In fact, after an in-depth review of its past polling results, the Gallup organization concluded in June 2016, "Large majorities of Americans support almost all proposals that deal with increased or more thorough background checks before guns can be purchased."[168]

Two nights after that Gallup analysis, CBS News reported on a new survey, in which nine in ten Americans supported background checks for all gun buyers.[169] In its poll, 92% of Republicans wanted legislation that requires background checks on all potential gun buyers; 97% of Democrats agreed. Those are truly remarkable numbers.

Public Policy Polling (PPP) also surveyed registered voters in December 2016.[170] PPP's cross-tabulated data from that poll indicated **96%** of Hillary Clinton voters supported universal background checks, as did **81%** of Donald Trump voters. Only **14%** of Trump voters objected to finding out if the purchaser was a felon, a threat to his family, or otherwise banned from buying guns before he could buy a gun. (On an unrelated note: **14%** of Trump voters also told PPP that they believed Hillary Clinton ran a child-sex ring out of the basement of a popular Washington, D.C. pizzeria.[171])

In June 2017, Quinnipiac University surveyed registered voters and concluded that American voters supported background checks for all gun buyers **94%** to **5%**. An amazing **98%** of Democrats and **98%** of women favored universal background checks, and so did **96%** of college graduates. Even **92%** of voters in households where there was a gun supported universal background checks. But since then, as discussed in the introduction, several seismic events have prompted polling organizations to conduct new polls.

Polling Results

The tables below compile the results of the polls since the Las Vegas Strip shooting that have asked about universal background checks. Bear in mind that some polling organizations survey only registered voters ("Voters"). Others surveyed adults, whether or not the adult was registered to vote or even eligible to register to vote ("Adults"). The appendix contains more information about these and the other polls (and in the digital version of this book, links to the poll results).

Registered Voters

Favor	*Oppose*	*Polling Dates*	*Poll*
88%	7%	10/5-9/17	Morning Consult
94%	5%	10/5-10/17	Quinnipiac

Favor	Oppose	Polling Dates	Poll
95%	4%	11/7-13/17	Quinnipiac
97%	2%	2/16-19/18	Quinnipiac
88%	6%	2/22-26/18	Morning Consult
90%	5%	3/29/4/1/18	Morning Consult
91%	7%	3/18-21/18	Fox News
87%	8%	3/23-25/18	PPP
86%	8%	6/8-10/18	PPP
92%	5%	8/2-6/18	Morning Consult
92%	6%	1/9-13/19	Quinnipiac
93%	6%	3/1-4/19	Quinnipiac
94%	4%	5/16-20/19	Quinnipiac
90%	5%	8/5-7/19	Morning Consult
90%	7%	8/11-13/19	Fox News
90%	8%	8/20-25/19	USA/Suffolk
93%	6%	8/21-26/19	Quinnipiac
91%	8%	9/2-5/19	ABC/WaPo

Voters: **91%** vs. **6%**. *Ratio: 15 to 1.*

Adults

Favor	Oppose	Polling Dates	Poll
96%	4%	10/5-11/17	Gallup
92%	7%	12/3-10/17	CBS/SSRS
94%	6%	2/27-28/18	NPR/Ipsos
83%	16%	3/2-5/18	Monmouth
92%	7%	3/5-11/18	Gallup
84%	7%	3/14-19/18	AP/NORC
85%	14%	9/24-10/7/18	Pew
84%	16%	1/11-28/19	Ipsos
89%	9%	7/15-17/19	NPR/PBS
89%	10%	8/10-14/19	NBC/WSJ
83%	13%	8/16-20/19	Monmouth
83%	14%	9/5-8/19	NPR/PBS

Favor	Oppose	Polling Dates	Poll
87%	11%	9/3-15/19	Pew

Adults: **88%** *vs.* **10%**. *Ratio: 9 to 1.*

Combined Averages: **90%** *vs.* **8%**. *Ratio: 12 to 1.*

To find so many polls that, when averaged, show support for proposed legislation at the 90% level, with only 6% - 10% opposed, is extraordinary.

There is a small difference between the results for registered voters and for adults. That is usually the case for the breakouts in this book, which *suggests* that this small difference is real—in other words, that registered voters really are a little more in favor of gun-violence-reduction measures than nonvoters. Even so, those differences *may be* the result of some other factor. For example, polling organizations that survey "adults" may do something else that inadvertently tips their results (*e.g.*, they may include more gun owners in their samples).

A few additional comments: Shortly after the shooting at the Stoneman Douglas High School in Parkland, Florida, Quinnipiac University did a separate poll of Floridians.[173] In that poll, 96% of Florida voters wanted universal background checks. New Miami Times managing editor Tim Elfrink wrote: "Ninety-six percent! You couldn't get 96 percent of Floridians to agree that the Atlantic Ocean is real."[174]

Fox News commissioned a poll in March 2018, around the time of the #NeverAgain protests. The poll is of interest more for the way Fox News reported its results than the results themselves, which were in line with other polls. In its coverage, Fox News acknowledged that voters favored several gun measures, but stressed that voters did not believe Congress would act.

Fox News told its viewers that voters considered protecting against gun violence more important than protecting gun rights by a 13-point margin.[174] Fox did not mention that voters favored universal background checks by an 84-point margin. But Fox may be right that the real story was that Americans had lost faith in Congress.

In July 2019, Quinnipiac surveyed **Ohio** voters and found that they favored universal background checks **90%** to **8%**. Ohio Republicans favored universal background checks **89%** to **10%**, and Democrats **95%** to

3%. Gun households were in favor **89%** to **9%**, and gun owners **87%** to **11%**.[175] That year, Ohio's Republican-dominated legislature refused to pass a universal background check law and instead passed pro-gun legislation.

Crosstab Data

We start our analysis of crosstab data with what polls reveal about where self-identified Republicans stand on universal background checks.

Republicans

Favor	Oppose	Polling Dates	Poll
87%	10%	10/5-9/17	Morning Consult
93%	6%	10/5-10/17	Quinnipiac
92%	7%	11/16-19/18	Quinnipiac
88%	10%	12/3-10/17	CBS/SRRS
97%	2%	2/16-19/18	Quinnipiac
88%	8%	2/22-26/18	Morning Consult
89%	11%	2/27-28/18	NPR/Ipsos
72%	26%	3/2-5/18	Monmouth
89%	9%	3/18-21/18	Fox Poll
85%	10%	3/23-25/18	Public Policy Polling
91%	5%	3/28 -1/18	Morning Consult
75%	15%	6/8-10/18	Public Policy Polling
89%	6%	8/2-6/18	Morning Consult
89%	9%	1/9-13/19	Quinnipiac
78%	21%	1/11-28/19	Ipsos/Reuters
89%	10%	3/1-4/19	Quinnipiac
94%	3%	5/16-20/19	Quinnipiac
84%	14%	7/15-17/19	NPR/PBS
90%	7%	8/5-7/19	Morning Consult
89%	8%	8/11-13/19	Fox News Poll
72%	24%	8/16-20/19	Monmouth
89%	11%	8/21-26/19	Quinnipiac
83%	15%	9/2-5/19	ABC/WaPo

Favor	Oppose	Polling Dates	Poll
72%	23%	9/5-8/19	NPR/PBS

*Averages: **86%** vs. **11%**. Ratio: 8 to 1.*

On average, 86% of Republicans supported universal background checks. Republican lawmakers who refused to enact universal background check laws stood in the way of what all but a small minority of their fellow Republicans want.

Trump 2016 Voters

Some polling organizations broke out those who voted for Donald Trump or Hillary Clinton in the 2016 election. Except for two outlier polls, Trump voters varied little from Republican voters:

Favor	Oppose	Polling Dates	Poll
88%	10%	10/5-9/17	Morning Consult
87%	10%	2/22-26/18	Morning Consult
91%	5%	3/28- 4/1/18	Morning Consult
90%	8%	3/18-21/18	Fox News
76%	15%	6/8-10/18	Public Policy Polling
82%	15%	7/15-17/19	NPR/PBS/Marist
90%	7%	8/2-6/18	Morning Consult
90%	6%	8/5-7/19	Morning Consult
90%	8%	8/11-13/19	Fox News
72%	25%	9/5-8/19	NPR/PBS/Marist

*Averages: **86%** vs. **11%**. Ratio: 7.9 to 1.*

On this issue, Trump voters were in line with Republicans and only a little less supportive than the population as a whole.

The June 2018 Public Policy Polling (PPP) poll and the September 2019 NPR/PBS/Marist poll were outliers. The PPP poll surveyed only 679 respondents, by far the smallest of all the polls discussed in this book. It did not disclose how many in its sample population were gun owners. In the NPR/ PBS/Marist poll, which showed the lowest level of support, 42% of voters (*vs.* the expected ~22%) were gun owners.

Gun Owners

Several polls provided crosstab data for gun owners or for households in which someone owned a gun. Let's look at gun owners first:

Favor	Oppose	Polling Dates	Sponsor/Pollster
87%	12%	3/1-4/19	Quinnipiac
90%	9%	5/16-20/19	Quinnipiac
93%	7%	8/21-26/19	Quinnipiac
77%	21%	9/5-8/19	NPR/PBS

Averages: **87%** *vs.* **12%**. *Ratio: 7.1 to 1.*

Gun Households

Favor	Oppose	Polling Dates	Sponsor/Pollster
86%	11%	10/5-9/17	Morning Consult
93%	6%	10/5-10/17	Quinnipiac
94%	5%	11/16-19/17	Quinnipiac
97%	3%	2/16-19/18	Quinnipiac
92%	8%	2/27-28/18	NPR/Ipsos/
90%	9%	3/18-21/18	Fox
90%	5%	3/28- 4/1/18	Morning Consult
90%	8%	8/2-6/18	Morning Consult
90%	10%	3/1-4/19	Quinnipiac
92%	7%	5/16-20/19	Quinnipiac
91%	7%	8/5-7/19	Morning Consult
93%	6%	8/11-13/19	Fox News
94%	5%	8/21-26/19	Quinnipiac
88%	11%	9/2-5/19	ABC/WaPo

Average **91%** *vs* **7%**. *Ratio: 12 to 1.*

That's a high level of support for universal background checks among both gun owners and gun householders.

In the ABC/Washington Post Poll conducted September 2-5, 2019, support among individuals in homes in which no one owned a gun ran 91% in favor and 7% against universal background checks.[176]

Education

Large majorities at every educational level support legislation requiring background checks for all gun purchases, but slightly larger percentages of those with Bachelor degrees support this measure.

Less than College Degree

All Races

Favor	Oppose	Polling Dates	Poll
87%	7%	10/5-9/17	Morning Consult
86%	7%	2/22-26/18	Morning Consult
81%	17%	3/2-5/18	Monmouth
88%	5%	3/28- 4/1/18	Morning Consult
89%	6%	8/2-6/18	Morning Consult
89%	6%	8/5-7/19	Morning Consult
81%	13%	8/16-20/19	Monmouth
79%	17%	9/5-8/19	NPR/PBS

Averages: **85%** vs. **10%**. *Ratio: 8.5 to 1.*

Whites

Favor	Oppose	Polling Dates	Poll
93%	6%	1/9-13/19	Quinnipiac
93%	6%	3/1-4/19	Quinnipiac
92%	7%	5/16-20/19	Quinnipiac
87%	12%	7/15-17/19	NPR/PBS
90%	7%	8/11-13/19	Fox News
81%	15%	8/16-20/19	Monmouth
96%	4%	8/21-26/19	Quinnipiac
82%	16%	9/5-8/19	NPR/PBS

Averages: **89%** vs. **9%**. *Ratio: 9.8 to 1.*

Bachelor Degree or More *All Races*

Favor	Oppose	Polling Dates	Poll
91%	6%	10/5-9/17	Morning Consult
91%	3%	2/22-26/18	Morning Consult
87%	11%	3/2-5/18	Monmouth
93%	4%	3/28- 4/1/18	Morning Consult
97%	2%	8/2-6/18	Morning Consult
94%	4%	8/5-7/19	Morning Consult
86%	13%	8/16-20/19	Monmouth
92%	7%	9/2-5/19	WaPo/ABC

Averages: **91%** *to* **6%**. *Ratio: 14.6 to 1.*

Whites

Favor	Oppose	Polling Dates	Poll
95%	5%	1/9-13/19	Quinnipiac
94%	6%	3/1-4/19	Quinnipiac
92%	7%	5/16-20/19	Quinnipiac
91%	8%	7/15-17/19	NPR/PBS
84%	14%	8/16-20/19	Monmouth
94%	5%	8/11-13/19	Fox News
94%	6%	8/21-26/19	Quinnipiac
89%	10%	9/5-8/19	NPR/PBS

Averages: **92%** *to* **8%**. *Ratio: 12 to 1.*

In each of these polls, both non-college grads and college grads supported universal background checks at extremely high levels, but college graduates were a tiny bit more supportive.

Annual Income Over $100,000

Census data indicate that 8.5% of the income-earning, non-student population in the United States makes over $100,000.[177] Those high-income individuals are, or at least used to be, a critical demographic for the

Republican Party. Folks at that income level overwhelmingly support universal background checks.

Favor	Oppose	Polling Dates	Poll
91%	6%	10/5-9/17	Morning Consult
94%	3%	2/22-26/18	Morning Consult
97%	3%	3/28-4/1/18	Morning Consult
95%	2%	8/2-6/18	Morning Consult
95%	2%	8/5-7/19	Morning Consult
84%	16%	8/16-20/19	Monmouth
89%	11%	9/2-5/19	WaPo/ABC

*Averages: **92%** vs. **6%**. Ratio: 15 to 1.*

Support was only slightly less in the lower-income brackets. For example, in the August 2019 Morning Consult poll, support was **89%** among those with incomes below $50,000 and **92%** among those in the $50,000-to-$100,000 bracket. In the Washington Post/ABC poll, support in the less than $50,000 income bracket was **89%**. In the $50-$100,000 bracket, it was **90%**.

Polling Wrap Up

In the national polls that have asked about this issue since the Las Vegas Strip shooting, *on average*, Americans favored requiring background checks for all gun sales **90%** to **8%**, or about 12 to 1.

It is hard to find a topic on which 90% of Americans agree, but some topics come close. In a Public Policy Polling poll, **89%** of Americans said they have an *unfavorable* opinion of Neo-Nazis, and **87%** said they have an *unfavorable* opinion of white supremacists.[178] In the same poll, **86%** said they had a *favorable* opinion of the Statue of Liberty.

To put the roughly 8% opposed to universal background checks in perspective, 7% percent of voters say the government faked the moon landings, and 9% say the government adds fluoride to the water supply for some nefarious, conspiratorial reason.[179] After President Trump disparaged Canada, 5% of registered voters and 7% of Republicans said the U.S. should punish Canada for its role in the War of 1812.[180] In other words, as opinion polls go, when only about 8% support or oppose something, we are talking about folks whose views are outside the mainstream.

The more significant point is that Americans—including Republicans, Trump voters, and gun owners—overwhelmingly support background checks for *all* gun sales. That raises the central question posed by this book: If 86% of Republicans, 86% of Trump voters, and 87% of gun owners support universal background checks, why do congressional Republicans adamantly oppose universal background checks?

What We're Getting Instead

Democrats in Congress have repeatedly introduced legislation to extend NICS background checks to private gun sales, but the gun lobby and its captive legislators in Congress have successfully resisted every attempt.[181] Here are a few of the key events:

The Senate

On December 14, 2012, Adam Lanza shot his mother in the face, killing her. He then went to Sandy Hook Elementary School, where he shot to death twenty 6- and 7-year-olds and six adults. Police found his own body in the school, dead from an apparent suicide.

Five months later, on April 17, 2013, the Senate rejected a proposal to expand background checks to all gun sales. The Senate also rejected a ban on assault weapons and a ban on large-capacity gun magazines.[182] More than fifty of the one hundred senators voted in favor of universal background checks, but the bill needed sixty votes to get past Republican procedural roadblocks.

When the clerk announced the vote tally, family members of some of those killed at Sandy Hook shouted from the gallery, "Shame on you." Later, President Obama made a statement from the Rose Garden. Surrounded by victims and family members of the victims of several mass shootings, he called it "a pretty shameful day for Washington."[183]

On Wednesday, December 2, 2015, Syed Rizwan Farook, 28, and his wife, Tashfeen Malik, 29, both heavily armed and wearing tactical gear, entered a Christmas party in San Bernardino, California, and began shooting. When their shooting spree ended, the pair had killed fourteen and wounded seventeen. They, in turn, died in a shootout with police.[184]

The next day, before families could bury their dead, the Senate again rejected proposals to expand background checks to private sales. The Senate also blocked a ban on gun sales to persons on the terrorist watch-list. The vote on the expanded-background-check amendment was 48 - 50, and the vote on the ban on sales to suspected terrorists failed 45 – 50.[185] Both votes were mostly along party lines, with almost a   nocrats voting for the measures, and nearly all Republicans voting against them.

On June 12, 2016, Omar Mateen, 29, killed 49 people and wounded 53 others in a mass shooting inside Pulse, a gay nightclub in Orlando, Florida. Eight days later, on June 20, 2016, the Senate again rejected, mainly along party lines, amendments to require background checks for private gun sales and to block people on the federal terrorism watch list from buying guns.[186]

The House

In the House, then-Speaker Paul Ryan (R. Wis.) and his leadership team refused to bring the issue to the floor for a vote. Speaker Ryan took the Orwellian position that allowing a vote on a measure the American public wanted would be "undemocratic."[187]

Trump Administration

With substantial backing from the NRA, real estate magnate and reality television star Donald J. Trump won the presidency in November 2016. He assumed office on January 20, 2017, promising not to let the NRA down. A test of his commitment to the gun lobby came early in his administration.

Federal law prohibits the sale of any firearm or ammunition to someone who "is a fugitive from justice."[188] An audit of the NICS system, covering the period Nov. 30, 1998, through Dec. 31, 2014, determined that the FBI had denied gun sales to fugitives 127,949 times. That accounted for almost 11% of all NICS denials.[189]

The FBI and ATF, however, disagreed about how to apply the ban and therefore disagreed about what information should be fed into the NICS. The FBI, which generally reflects the point of view of law enforcement, argued that the law should be interpreted to mean any fugitive from justice. The ATF, which generally reflects the point of view of the NRA and the gun industry, argued that the ban should be applied only when there was evidence that a fugitive from justice had fled across a state line into another state.

The FBI position meant fewer fugitives would be able to buy guns, and potentially, fewer police officers would die trying to arrest armed fugitives. The ATF position would allow gun manufacturers and gun dealers to sell more guns and generate more revenue.

The Trump administration sided with the ATF. Press reports at the time put the number of fugitives who were immediately able to buy guns at about 518,670.[190] In the months immediately following the change in interpretation, the NICS blocked 80% *fewer* sales on the grounds that the would-be buyer was a fugitive.

Due to congressionally imposed limits on what information the FBI may keep, no one knows how many fugitives have been allowed to buy guns after passing NICS checks, let alone how many of those have gone on to kill police officers or others.

U.S. Voters Put Democrats in Charge in the House

When Democrats gained control of the House of Representatives in early 2019 (after winning a majority in the fall 2018 election, one of their top priorities was to pass legislation, H.R. 8, requiring universal background checks. The House approved the measure on February 27, 2019. The vote was 240 to 190. Eight Republicans voted for the bill, and 188 voted against it. Among Democrats, 232 voted for H.R. 8, and only two voted against it.

Quinnipiac University released a poll in early March 2019, shortly after the House passed H.R. 8. Quinnipiac summed up its findings this way: "U.S. voters support 86–12 percent, including 80–17 percent among Republicans and 76–20 percent among gun owners, a bill passed by the U.S. House of Representatives requiring background checks for all gun purchases, including at gun shows and online purchases."[191] In September 2019, Quinnipiac reprised its earlier question on this topic and got essentially the same result (83% in favor, 14% opposed).[192]

That seemingly put Republican and other pro-gun Senators in a bind: Should they side with the overwhelming majority of Americans who want universal background checks? Or should they side with the gun lobby, its money, and its extremist followers?

To avoid putting Republican senators in the position of having to vote against legislation most Americans wanted, but the gun lobby opposed, Senate Majority Leader Mitch McConnell refused to allow a vote on the bill in the Senate.

Gilroy, El Paso, and Dayton

That's where things stood when the shootings in Gilroy, California; El Paso, Texas; and Dayton, Ohio, grabbed headlines in late summer 2019.

The El Paso shooter posted a bigoted diatribe before his shooting spree, echoing President Trump's anti-immigrant and anti-Mexican rhetoric. After his arrest, the shooter admitted he targeted Mexicans and Mexican Americans. The media pointed to President Trump's role in encouraging white supremacy and fear of immigrants, particularly those from Central America.

President Trump responded by once again endorsing universal or expanded background checks. He said, "I think background checks are important. I don't want to put guns into the hands of mentally unstable or people with rage or hate, sick people. I'm all in favor of it." He didn't mention his threatened veto of the universal background check bill the House had already passed.

Acknowledging that previous attempts to get universal background legislation through Congress had failed, President Trump said, "But there's never been a president like President Trump." He also said he had spoken with Senator McConnell, and the senator was "100% on board" with background checks. Trump said McConnell would allow the issue to come to a vote after the August recess. Senator McConnell's spokesperson promptly issued a denial.

The NRA's controversial chief executive officer, Wayne LaPierre, contacted Trump and reminded him that the NRA opposed universal background checks. After that discussion, Trump tweeted that the NRA's views should be "respected." He did not explain why the NRA's views should be respected, but not the views of 90% of Americans.

After more conversations with LaPierre and gun rights advocates, Trump walked back his support altogether. He said that we already have "a lot of background checks."[193] The Trace, an independent, nonprofit online news organization, noted, "The president's apparent reversal is similar to what happened after the Parkland shooting, [when] Trump also called for gun reforms only to later reverse course at the NRA's behest."[194]

That's where things remained when this book went to press.

The States

In state legislatures, where the Parkland students and their allies did not have to deal with Senator Mitch McConnell, they got results. The Giffords Law Center notes that in 2018, six states added a background check requirement or improved an existing background check law. *See*: Florida S.B. 7026, Louisiana S.B. 231, New Jersey AB 2757, Oregon HB 4145, Tennessee S.B. 834, and Vermont S.B. 55.[195]

The impact of the #NeverAgain movement continued to ripple through the states in 2019. On February 15, 2019, Nevada's Governor Steve Sisolak signed a universal background check law (S.B. 143). The law passed on a party-line vote in the legislature, with Republicans voting against the measure.[196] The background check law replaced a law passed by voters, which the previous governor and attorney general, both Republicans, refused to implement.

In March 2019, New Mexico Governor Michelle Lujan Grisham signed a bill (S.B. 8), expanding background checks to most private gun sales in her state. Republican lawmakers vowed to repeal the legislation. Twenty-five of the state's 33 counties passed "Second Amendment sanctuary county" resolutions, claiming they would not enforce the new measures.[197]

New York (S.B. 2374 and AB 1213 and Washington (HB 1465 enhanced their background check laws in 2019.[198]

In 2020, the Virginia legislature passed, and on April 10, 2020, Governor Ralph Northam signed into law universal background check legislation.[199]

Altogether, however, only twenty-two states and the District of Columbia require point-of-sale background checks when the seller is a private party.[200] Meanwhile, the private sale loophole allows guns to bleed into the black market in this country and across the border to Mexican drug cartels.

Conclusion

About 90% of Americans favor universal background checks, but Senator Majority Mitch McConnell refuses to allow H.R. 8 to come to the floor of the Senate for debate and a vote. A president deeply dependent on NRA support Tweets support for comprehensive background checks after high-profile mass shootings but retreats when the NRA tugs on his leash.

In a different context, Justice Elena Kagan recently asked: "Is this how American democracy is supposed to work?"[201]

5. Can We Not Sell Guns to Terrorists, Please?

Item: *August 2015. Georgia militia members Terry Eugene Peace, Brian Edward Cannon, and Corey Robert Williamson plotted to start an "active revolution against the government" by targeting law enforcement agencies and sabotaging power grids, transfer stations, and water treatment facilities. They hoped the attacks would prompt the government to declare martial law, sparking an uprising by like-minded militiamen. Instead, the FBI arrested them. After they pled guilty to conspiracy charges, a federal judge sentenced each of them to twelve years in prison.*[202]

Item: *November 2015. Richmond-area white supremacists got together at the home of one of their members in September 2015 to plan a reign of terror—shooting or bombing the occupants of black churches and Jewish synagogues," robbing jewelers and armored cars, and "conducting acts of violence against persons of the Jewish faith." In a conversation recorded by the FBI, one of the men said he wanted to use the proceeds to "purchase land, stockpile weapons, and train for the coming race war." The FBI alleged in an affidavit that the men were part of a "white supremacy extremist version of the Ásatrú [neo-pagan] faith."*[203]

Item: *October 12, 2017. An operation dubbed "To the Dirt" resulted in indictments for drug and firearms trafficking against 70 individuals, most of whom belonged to white supremacist groups in Arkansas. During the two-year investigation, law enforcement officials made 59 controlled purchases of methamphetamine. They also seized more than 25 pounds of methamphetamine and 69 firearms, including AR-15-style rifles. The investigation began with the New Aryan Empire, an Arkansas-based white supremacist group, but also led to arrests of members of the White Aryan Resistance, a neo-Nazi white-supremacist organization.*[204]

Item: *April 30, 2018. Law enforcement officials in Texas charged 57 members of white supremacist groups, including the Aryan Circle, the Aryan Brotherhood of*

Texas, the Aryan Brotherhood, and the Dirty White Boys, with drug and gun trafficking and with kidnapping conspiracies. During the investigation, officials seized more than 126 pounds of methamphetamine, 31 firearms, and $376,587 in cash. "Not only do white supremacist gangs subscribe to a repugnant, hateful ideology, they also engage in significant organized and violent criminal activity," Attorney General Jeff Sessions said in a statement. "The quantities of drugs, guns, and money seized in this case are staggering."

Item: November 15, 2018. In the Tampa Bay area, Bureau of Alcohol, Tobacco, Firearms and Explosives (ATF) agents and Pasco County Sheriff's office personnel arrested 39 people affiliated with two major white supremacist gangs, the Unforgiven and the United Aryan Brotherhood. The arresting officers caught the groups with crystal methamphetamine, fentanyl, and 110 illegal weapons including guns, pipe bombs, and a rocket launcher.[205]

Item: November 19, 2018. In "Operation Vanilla Gorilla," federal agents in Georgia arrested 43 Ghost Face gangsters. Officials accused the white supremacist group of drug offenses, possessing counterfeit money, and illegally altered weapons, including a sawed-off rifle and a weapon with an obliterated serial number. The government won convictions of all 43.[206]

Item: February 12, 2019. Federal agents arrested 54 white supremacists, members of the New Aryan Empire, in the Russellville, Ark, area on drug and gun trafficking, murder, maiming, and witness intimidation charges.[207]

Item: February 5, 2020. In testimony before the House Judiciary Committee, FBI Director Christopher Wray announced that the FBI had raised its assessment of the threat posed by racially motivated violent extremists in the U.S. to a "national threat priority." Wray said the FBI put the risk of violence from those groups "on the same footing" as the threats posed by foreign terrorist organizations. "Not only is the terror threat diverse," Wray said, "it's unrelenting."[208]

The FBI's Terrorist Screening Center compiles a central terrorist database for the federal government. Officially, this database is the Terrorist Screening Database (TSDB), but the media and nearly everyone else calls it the "terrorist watch list."

Two primary sources feed into the TSDB: (1) International terrorist information from the Terrorist Identities Datamart Environment, a central database of known or suspected *international* terrorists maintained by the National Counterterrorism Center (NCTC); and (2) the FBI itself. The FBI provides the names of known and suspected *domestic* terrorists.

Multiple agencies use the TSDB to compile their own watch lists and for screening. Of importance for this chapter, the National Counterterrorism Center uses a subset of the TSDB data for its "No Fly" list.[209]

The Issue

Should Congress enact legislation prohibiting the terrorists and suspected terrorists on the "terrorist watch" or "No Fly" lists from buying assault rifles, semi-automatic handguns, and other guns?

Federal law does not prohibit licensed gun dealers from selling guns to individuals on the "terrorist watch" or "No Fly" lists. Therefore, federal law does not require or authorize the FBI to add their names to the National Instant Criminal Background Check System (NICS). Attention focused on this omission when the Los Angeles Times revealed that Oman Mateen, the Pulse nightclub killer, had been on the terrorist watch list for ten months and had still been able to buy the assault rifle and handgun he used in his terrorist attack.[210]

To be fair, the FBI investigated Mateen from May 2013 to March 2014, but closed its investigation and removed Mateen from the watch list after concluding, "there was nothing there."[211] The FBI believed Mateen was just a hothead who made false and contradictory claims about belonging to rival terrorist groups. Mateen purchased the weapons he used in the Pulse nightclub *after* the FBI removed his name from the terrorist watch list. Thus, including persons on the terrorist watch list or the No-Fly list would not have prevented the Pulse nightclub shooting.

Nonetheless, the incident drew renewed attention to the fact that federal law does not prohibit licensed firearms dealers from selling guns to known and suspected terrorists. That, as we discuss below, struck most people as wrongheaded.

What's less well known is that the FBI *does* run the names of gun buyers against the TSDB or terrorist watch list. If there is a hit, the FBI can delay the sale up to 72 hours to investigate further (unless state law permits a longer timeframe). But if the FBI cannot find a prohibiting factor, *e.g.*, a felony conviction or an involuntary commitment to a mental institution, the sale can go forward. The NICS section, however, may continue to investigate for up to ninety days, but then must destroy any records relating to the transaction.

Between February 2004, when the FBI began checking against the watch list, through 2015, it was able to deny 212 sales to suspected terrorists for reasons other than the fact that the would-be buyer was a suspected terrorist. But it had to allow some 2,265 sales of guns or explosives to proceed. Assuming that rate has remained more or less the same since 2015, the FBI has had to stand down while gun dealers made something like 3,000 sales of guns, ammo, or explosives to suspected terrorists.

There have not been news media reports that someone was on the terrorist watch list when he or she bought a gun and used it to kill or injure someone in a terrorist attack. One could argue that if suspected terrorists have bought guns roughly 3,000 times since 2005, the terrorist watch list must be too inclusive.

Unfortunately, we simply don't know how many of those suspected terrorists *did* buy guns and used them to commit acts of terrorism or other violent crimes. We also don't know how many of those suspected terrorists law enforcement officials arrested before they could commit an act of terrorism. The government simply hasn't reported that information, probably because it is not allowed to keep records of transactions it allows.

But what we do know is this: Each such sale increases the odds that a suspected terrorist will use a gun or explosive device to kill or injure Americans.[212]

Federal Firearm Law: There Are No Domestic Terrorists

Because of the large number of guns and related paraphernalia they purchase and their hostility to gun-violence-prevention measures, the folks preparing for what they believe is a coming race war or civil war ("preppers"), white supremacists, and other anti-government folks are important NRA constituencies. The NRA was concerned that some future administration would label them domestic terrorists and add them to the NICS, with the result that licensed gun dealers would no longer be permitted to sell to them.

That may sound like a cheap shot, but consider this: Our primary gun law, 18 U.S.C. §§ 921 *et seq.*, carefully limits "terrorism" to certain defined activities "committed by an individual who is not a national or permanent resident alien of the United States."[213] In other words, for purposes of the federal gun law, only foreigners who are not resident aliens can commit an act of "terrorism."

Obscure provisions like that don't get into a statute by accident. Lobbyists and lawyers draft these provisions and give them to friendly legislators to insert into legislation. In this case, the definition of terrorism entered our gun laws as part of a bill that made it harder for prosecutors to convict individuals who sell guns without a license. The bill required the government to show that the seller had a profit motive. Legislators concerned about terrorism got an exception to the profit motive for gun transfers between terrorists. As a result, prosecutors must show that the unlicensed gun dealer had a profit motive *unless* he or she was supplying guns to fellow terrorists.

That exception alarmed the gun industry. It apparently feared that someday federal prosecutors would go after groups like the Aryan Brotherhood as unlicensed gun dealers and domestic terrorists. To prevent that, lobbyists came up with language that defined "terrorism" to exclude domestic terrorists like all those white supremacists participating in the Aryan Brotherhood, White Aryan Resistance, Dirty White Boys, and similar organizations. Congress evidently agreed because it incorporated that language into our gun law.

What We Want

Politicians have a shorthand name for legislation that makes it illegal for gun dealers or others to sell guns to persons on the U.S. government's No-Fly list. They call it "No Fly, No Buy." As we'll see, the public strongly favors "No Fly, No Buy." In other words, the public wants known and suspected terrorists flagged in the National Instant Criminal Background Check System, so that gun dealers won't sell to them.

Pew Research Center

In a lengthy analysis in June 2017, the Pew Research Center discussed survey results that showed close agreement among gun owners *and* non-gun owners on "No Fly, No Buy" legislation.[214] Pew reported:

> Solid majorities of both gun owners and non-owners favor limiting access to guns for people with mental illnesses and individuals who are on the federal no-fly or watch lists (82% or higher favor among each group).

More specifically, in its poll, 82% of non-gun owners and 84% of gun owners believed Congress should ban gun sales to individuals on the No-Fly or terrorist watch list.

Overall Results

Polling on this issue became less frequent after Republicans blocked "No Fly, No Buy" legislation in 2016, so this chapter will include polling from 2016. In each of the polls since then that have included this issue, 80% or more favored adding the names on the "No Fly" list to the NICS:

Favor	*Oppose*	*Polling Dates*	*Poll*
84%	8%	12/6-7/16	Public Policy Polling
86%	13%	6/20-23/16	ABC/Wash. Post[215]
86%	12%	6/21-27/16	Quinnipiac
85%	14%	6/16-19/16	CNN/ORC
83%	16%	3/13-27/17	Pew
82%	10%	10/5-9/17	Morning Consult
82%	10%	2/22-26/18	Morning Consult
84%	4%	3/29- 4/1/18	Morning Consult
83%	8%	8/2-6/18	Morning Consult
84%	15%	9/24-10/7/18	Pew
84%	17%	1/11-28/19	Ipsos/Reuters

Averages: **84%** vs. **12%**. *Ratio 7.3 to 1.*

Averaging those results suggests that, consistent with the Pew analysis, Americans favor this commonsense step about 84% to 12%. The percentages opposed to "No Fly, No Buy" ranged from a low of 4% to a high of 17%.

Republicans

In these polls,[216] Republicans, like the rest of the country, wanted Congress to ban people on the No-Fly list from being able to buy guns.

Favor	*Oppose*	*Polling Dates*	*Poll*
85%	12%	6/21-27/16	Quinnipiac
90%	8%	6/16-19/16	CNN/ORC[217]
78%	12%	12/6-7/16	Public Policy Polling[218]
83%	11%	10/5-9/17	Morning Consult
82%	9%	2/22-26/18	Morning Consult
87%	8%	3/29- 4/1/18	Morning Consult
85%	6%	8/2-6/18	Morning Consult
85%	15%	1/11-28/19	Ipsos/Reuters

*Average: **84%** vs. **10%**. Ratio: 8.3 to 1.*

In short, if Republican House members and Senators were responsive to what the American people want, or even to what Republicans want, they would be leading the charge to enact legislation banning people on the No-Fly list from buying guns.

Trump 2016 Voters

The folks who voted for Mr. Trump in the 2016 presidential election also endorse "No Fly, No Buy."

Favor	*Oppose*	*Polling Dates*	*Poll*
82%	11%	10/5-9/17	Morning Consult
81%	9%	2/22-26/18	Morning Consult
85%	8%	3/29-4/1/18	Morning Consult
85%	8%	8/2-6/18	Morning Consult

*Average: **83%** vs. **9%**. Ratio: 9 to 1.*

Gun Households

Most of us who live in gun households agree that individuals the FBI won't let board a plane for fear they will highjack it shouldn't be allowed to buy guns, ammunition, or explosives.

Favor	Oppose	Polling Dates	Poll
81%	13%	10/5-9/17	Morning Consult
86%	9%	3/29- 4/1/18	Morning Consult
84%	9%	8/2-6/18	Morning Consult

*Averages: **84%** vs. **19%**. Ratio: 8 to 1.*

Annual Income Over $100,000

Individuals earning $100,000 or more, long a key Republican demographic, don't want suspected terrorists to be able to buy a gun, ammunition, or explosives.

Favor	Oppose	Polling Dates	Poll
86%	8%	10/5-9/17	Morning Consult
90%	5%	2/22-26/18	Morning Consult
87%	6%	3/29- 4/1/18	Morning Consult
90%	6%	8/2-6/18	Morning Consult

*Averages: **88%** vs. **6%**. Ratio: 14 to 1.*

Polling Wrap Up

When we average these polls, the American public supported "No Fly, No Buy" **84%** to **12%**, or more than 7 to 1. For Republicans, the margin was 84% to 10%, or 9 to 1. For Trump voters, it was essentially the same, 83% to 9%. In gun households, the averages were 84% to 10%, or 8.4 to 1 in favor of No Fly, No Buy. Among individuals with annual incomes of $100,000 or more, support ran just a little higher: 88% to 6% or 14 to 1.

Those results are remarkably consistent and indicate that the American public solidly supports legislation barring those on the No-Fly list from being able to buy guns, ammo, or explosives until the FBI or CIA can resolve their status or a court determines that they do not, in fact, belong on the list.

What We're Getting Instead

As mentioned in the last chapter, on the day after the December 2015 San Bernardino office-party shooting, the Senate voted down a proposal to ban gun sales to persons on the No-Fly list. Fifty (50) senators voted for the ban; only forty-three (43) senators voted against it, but the measure failed because the fifty-vote majority fell short of the sixty votes needed to overcome Republican procedural roadblocks.[219] Senators voted mainly along party lines, with almost all Democratic senators voting for the measure, and almost all Republican senators voting against it.[220]

The Pulse nightclub massacre occurred on June 12, 2016. Eight days later, on June 20, 2016, the Senate again rejected, once more mainly along party lines, amendments to require background checks for private gun sales and to block people on the federal No-Fly list from buying guns.[221]

That was the Senate. Meanwhile, in the House, on June 22–23, 2016, Civil Rights icon and longtime Georgia Congressman John Lewis led an overnight sit-in on the floor of Congress in an unsuccessful effort to embarrass House Speaker Paul Ryan and Congressional Republicans into allowing a vote on prohibiting gun sales to suspected terrorists.

The demonstration won support from 170 lawmakers, galvanized social media, and riveted the nation's attention on the issue, but failed to convince House Speaker Ryan to allow a vote on the issue. As noted previously, in a strangely Orwellian moment, Speaker Ryan criticized the Democrats' effort to get Congress to vote on legislation the American public wanted as a threat to "democracy."

More substantively, Republicans argued that adding the names of known and suspected terrorists to the NICS "No Buy" database would violate the affected individuals' due process rights to fair notice and a hearing. (Paradoxically, they did not believe denying the vote to people purged from voter rolls required notice and a hearing before citizens could be disenfranchised.)

In fact, federal law allows individuals to challenge their inclusion in the NICS database, but only *after* the FBI adds them to the list. If the individual can show that the information is wrong, he or she can obtain an order requiring the information to be corrected in the NICS and in the records of any state or city that provided the information. The individual may also obtain a court order allowing the gun sale and an award of attorney fees.[222]

Republicans insisted that was not good enough. Senator John Cornyn, for example, argued that it was unfair to add known and suspected terrorists to the list of people who could not buy assault weapons or explosives without giving them due process *first*. In other words, he and other Republicans insisted that the government hold a hearing and prove that an individual was a terrorist *before* the FBI or CIA could add his or her name to the NICS. While that process played itself out, they argued, the suspected terrorist should be allowed to buy all the guns, ammunition, and explosives he or she wants.

The American public, understandably, didn't agree. Neither did President Trump. During a televised meeting with several legislators on February 28, 2018, he said, "I like taking guns away early. Take the guns first, go through due process second."

In February 2018, after the Stoneman Douglas High School shooting in Parkland, Florida, Senator Susan Collins (R. Maine and a handful of "moderate" Republican Senators re-introduced the "Terrorist Firearms Prevention Act" in the Senate, so that they could tell their constituents they tried to do the right thing. The Republican-dominated Senate Judiciary Committee ignored the bill, and its co-sponsors quickly moved onto other issues—like confirming pro-gun-rights individuals to lifetime appointments as federal judges.[223]

President Trump and "No Fly, No Buy"

During his 2016 campaign, Mr. Trump said he would consider backing "No Fly, No Buy" legislation. He said he would meet with the National Rifle Association to discuss it.[224] The NRA opposed "No Fly, No Buy" legislation and evidently refused to give Mr. Trump permission to endorse the legislation. Mr. Trump walked back his support, saying he "understands exactly" the organization's position. He didn't share his understanding of the NRA's position with the American public.

But the reason the NRA opposes banning sales to suspected terrorists is clear: The Aryan Brotherhood, Neo-Nazis, and other domestic terrorists buy lots of guns. The gun manufacturers and the gun dealers the NRA represents don't want to risk losing sales to members of those groups.

In Congress, or at least in the Republican congressional caucus, gun sales to domestic terrorists count for more than the opinions—and lives—of law-abiding Americans.

6. Should We Close the "Boyfriend" Loophole?

Item: *July 4, 2018. Donald Hairston spent the July 4 Independence Day holiday in jail, awaiting sentencing for the murder of an ex-girlfriend, Stephanie Goodloe, of Washington, D.C. Two years earlier, Ms. Goodloe, a church youth minister, had broken up with Hairston. He responded by slashing her tires, pounding on her front door during the night, stealing her house keys, stalking, and threatening to kill her. Ms. Goodloe obtained a restraining order, prohibiting Hairston from continuing to harass her. That didn't stop Hairston, and so the court scheduled a hearing on Monday, June 20, 2016, to address the continuing problems.*

Despite the restraining order and Hairston's threats to kill Ms. Goodloe, neither federal nor D.C. law prohibited Hairston from buying a gun, and neither federal nor D.C. law required him to surrender his firearms to law enforcement. Neither federal nor D.C. law required law enforcement to seize Hairston's guns, even temporarily. That's because Hairston and Goodloe had dated but had not married or had a child.

On Friday, June 17, Ms. Goodloe complained to the police that Hairston had violated the restraining order, calling her twice to threaten her and to tell her he didn't care if he went to jail. Early the next morning, Saturday, June 18, Hairston got into Goodloe's home, went to her bedroom, and shot her five times as she slept in bed. Her 11-year-old daughter heard the shots, saw Hairston flee, and found her mother dead.[225]

Prosecutors pursued murder charges against Hairston, and in May 2018, won a conviction. On July 20, 2018, a judge sentenced Hairston to forty-nine-and-a-half years in prison for the murder of Ms. Goodloe. That was a stiff sentence, but it didn't restore Ms. Goodloe to life or give her daughter her mother back.[225]

"This country witnesses more than a million acts of domestic violence, and hundreds of deaths from domestic violence each year." So noted the Supreme Court in *United States v. Castleman*, 572 U.S. 157 (2014.

Firearms are the most commonly used weapons in domestic homicides. In our country, someone uses a gun to kill an intimate partner or "ex" every sixteen hours.[226] "The number of U.S. women alive today who have had an intimate partner use a gun against them is substantial: About 4.5 million have had an intimate partner threaten them with a gun, and nearly one million have been shot or shot at by an intimate partner."[227] After a long term decline beginning in the early 1990s, researchers noticed an uptick in domestic violence homicides between 2015 and 2017.[228] (That's also when dramatically more individuals, mainly men, began getting concealed carry permits.

Congress addressed the problem of domestic violence and guns in 1996 in what is commonly known as the "Lautenberg Amendment," after its sponsor, the late Frank Lautenberg (D-NJ.[229] The Lautenberg Amendment did two things. First, it made it a crime for an individual to possess or receive a gun if he or she is subject to a *final* domestic violence restraining order.[230] Second, the Lautenberg Amendment made it a crime for an individual to possess or receive a gun if he or she has been convicted in any court of a misdemeanor crime of domestic violence.[231] (Federal law already made it a crime for anyone who has been convicted of a felony to possess or receive a gun.[232]

To reiterate: There are *two* domestic violence disqualifiers: (1 a *final* domestic violence restraining order issued in a civil proceeding, and (2 *conviction* of domestic violence crime.

The Problems with the Federal Law

On the plus side, the federal statute makes it a crime for someone to buy or possess a gun if he or she is the subject of a final domestic violence restraining order (DVRO or has a violent domestic abuse conviction. If the state feeds information about the restraining order or conviction into the NICS, the background check system should preclude the individual from buying a new gun or ammunition from a licensed gun dealer. But there are several well-documented problems with the federal statute. Perhaps the most important is the so-called "boyfriend" loophole.

Federal law does not apply to abuse or violence directed at a current or former romantic or dating partner. Viewers who follow Samantha Bee's television show, Full Frontal, may recall her scathing review of the issue.[233] In the situation highlighted at the beginning of this chapter, federal law did not prohibit Hairston from having a gun because Ms. Goodloe was his former girlfriend. That—and the fact that the law did not require Hairston to surrender his gun—cost Ms. Goodloe her life.

Ms. Goodloe was by no means an unfortunate exception. The Associated Press (AP analyzed crime data from 49 states (excluding Florida for the years 2006 through 2014. Its reporters found that during that period, on average, boyfriends fatally shot more than 210 women each year—1,953 women altogether over the nine years.[234] Also, on average, dating partners shot to death more than 50 men each year—488 over the nine years covered by the study. And yet, year-after-year, Congress chooses to leave dating relationships out of the law.

A second problem is this: The time of highest risk for the abused party is the brief period between the issuance of an emergency restraining order, shortly after the victim files for protection, and the issuance, after a hearing, of a final order. The federal statute does not apply to emergency DVROs; it applies only to final orders. It offers no protection during the period when the victim is at the greatest risk.

Finally, while federal law makes it a crime for an abuser to buy, receive, or have a gun after a final DVRO or a criminal conviction for domestic violence, it does not require the abuser to surrender his or her gun. Federal law and most state laws also do not require law enforcement to remove the abuser's gun if the abuser fails to turn it into the police or sell it.

This chapter provides an overview of the federal gun law's domestic violence provisions. It then delves a little deeper into the "boyfriend" or "dating partner" omission. Chapter 7 discusses the emergency DVRO exception. There is no polling on the federal statute's omission of proactive measures to make sure abusers don't keep their guns. The discussion, therefore, will not include that issue.

The Issue

Should the federal prohibition on gun possession by subjects of domestic violence restraining orders and domestic violence convictions apply to those who violently abuse dating partners?

The gun law provisions addressing violent domestic abuse have more qualifications than some tax code provisions.

Consider this hypothetical: After a hearing and weighing the evidence, a court issues a final domestic relations violence restraining order (DVRO) against Joe Blow. Mr. Blow, who has anger management issues, is furious. Immediately after the hearing, Mr. Blow heads to a gun store, where he buys a gun before the information about the order makes its way into the NICS. ATF agents somehow learn about the purchase, find Mr. Blow, and ask to see his gun, which he shows them.[235] The agents arrest Mr. Blow for possession of a firearm in violation of the federal statute.[236]

To prove the violation, a federal prosecutor must present evidence establishing issuance of the restraining order and purchase or possession of the gun. No surprise there.

The prosecutor must also prove that Mr. Blow had actual notice of and an opportunity to participate in the hearing that led to the issuance of the restraining order.[237] Among other things, that means the order could not have been an *ex parte* order—an emergency order issued based on the representations of one party or the police. The next chapter discusses that issue.

The federal prosecutor also must prove that the order restrained the defendant:

> from harassing, stalking, or threatening an intimate partner of such person or child of such intimate partner or person, or engaging in other conduct that would place an intimate partner in reasonable fear of bodily injury to the partner or child;[238]

Also, the prosecutor must prove either:

> (i) the order included a finding that the defendant represents a credible threat to the physical safety of the intimate partner or her/his child; or
>
> (ii) the order explicitly prohibited the use, attempted use, or threatened use of physical force of the sort "that would reasonably be expected to cause bodily injury."[239]

If the busy state court judge who issued the domestic violence order, or the lawyer who prepared the order for the judge's signature, missed any of those particulars, the prosecution for possessing a gun in violation of the federal statute fails.

But wait, there's more!

The federal prosecutor must also prove that the gun or ammunition was "in or affecting commerce" or was "shipped or transported in interstate or foreign commerce."

In fact, to get a conviction on the gun possession charge, the federal prosecutor must prove *all* of those elements beyond a reasonable doubt. Plus, the prosecutor must also prove, again beyond a reasonable doubt, that the individual violated the statute "knowingly."

Upon conviction, the court may fine Mr. Blow, send him to prison for up to ten years, or both. The same penalty, by the way, applies to individuals convicted of gun possession after a domestic violence misdemeanor conviction.

The Dating Partner Omission

For a domestic abuse restraining order or misdemeanor conviction to limit an individual's right to own guns under the federal statute, the offender must have abused an "intimate partner." The statute defines that term as follows:

> The term "intimate partner" means, with respect to a person, the spouse of the person, a former spouse of the person, an individual who is a parent of a child of the person, and an individual who cohabitates or has cohabited with the person.[240]

Thus, an "intimate partner" may be: (i) a spouse; (ii) a former spouse; (iii) the other parent of the abuser's child or children; or (iv) an individual who "cohabitates" (lives with) or has cohabited with (lived with) the abuser.

Importantly, the definition does not include someone with whom the abuser was romantically involved if they did not have a child or "cohabit." Thus, a state court misdemeanor conviction for domestic violence against a dating partner, or even a series of misdemeanor convictions for violent abuse against several dating partners, would not trigger the federal statute. Neither would a restraining order directing an abuser to stop threatening and harassing a former dating partner. Critics refer to this as the "boyfriend loophole."

State Law Plays A Crucial Role

If a woman learns that her ex has a gun and has been drinking and is on his way to her house, or hears him outside her home banging on her door and demanding to be let in, she isn't going to call the ATF or even the FBI. She's going to call 9-1-1 and ask for the local police.

When deciding what charges, if any, to bring, state and local police look to state law. Some state laws merely replicate federal law or are weaker than federal law. Other states fill in at least some gaps in federal law.

What We Want

What do opinion polls say about all this? Do we want Congress and our state legislatures to prohibit those who violently abuse dating partners from owning a gun? Or do we think that a man who holds a gun to his current or former girlfriend's head and tells her he's going to kill her should be allowed to keep his gun?

YouGov /Huffington Post
July 24, 2014

In 2014, YouGov surveyed public opinion for Huffington Post on whether lawmakers should close the dating-partner loophole:

> Do you support or oppose expanding the definition of

"domestic violence" under federal gun laws so that couples who are dating, but not married or living together, are included in the category of domestic abusers who can be prohibited from owning a gun?

In response, **66%** said they supported expanding the definition to include dating couples and **22%** opposed. Support was robust across all demographic groups.

On April 4, 2019, the U.S. House of Representatives took up consideration of H.R. 1585, which proposed reauthorizing the Violence Against Women Act. The bill contained provisions closing the "boyfriend loophole" and extending protection against stalkers. The NRA, which objects to any proposal that might reduce gun sales, objected to the proposed new provisions.

Privately, Republican House of Representative Members complained about having to choose between the NRA and protecting women, but in the end, most House Republicans chose to side with the NRA and violent abusers.[241] The vote was 263—158. Some 33 Republicans broke ranks and voted for the bill. Only one Democrat voted against it.

A few days later, in an exceptionally large survey, YouGov asked whether those surveyed favored or opposed renewing the Violence Against Women and extending its terms to include dating partners.[242] Here's the text:

> The House recently passed legislation to reauthorize the Violence Against Women Act and added a provision to prevent people convicted of stalking or abusing dating partners from buying a gun. Do you support or oppose this decision?

Responding to the survey, **73%** of adults favored reauthorizing the Violence Against Women Act and tweaking it to include dating partners. Only **10%** opposed.

YouGov made some crosstab data available:

	Favor	Oppose
Men	67%	15%
Women	78%	6%

	Favor	Oppose
Republicans	64%	18%
Democrats	86%	4%
>$80,000 family income	78%	11%

Clear majorities in every demographic group for which YouGov collected data approved renewing the Violence Against Women and extending it to include dating partners. But there were noticeable differences between men and women (11 percentage points) and between Republicans and Democrats (22 percentage points).

What We're Getting Instead

Senate Majority Leader Mitch McConnell refused to allow renewal of the Violence Against Women Act to come to a vote in the Senate. Democrats lacked the votes to overcome his refusal.[243] Meanwhile, gun manufacturers and gun dealers continued to sell guns and ammunition to violent abusers who stalked and threatened dating partners. Women, children, and police officers, whose lives might have been spared, continued to die.

State Law

The Giffords Law Center has detailed information on its website about domestic violence laws that restrict access to guns.[244] What follows borrows heavily from its site; the reader interested in up-to-date details, including state-specific information, should check the Giffords website.

By way of a general overview, some states prohibit domestic violence misdemeanants who abuse dating partners from buying or possessing guns or ammunition, but most do not.[245] The same is also true of emergency DVROs. According to the Giffords Law Center analysis, about half the states allow a former or current dating partner to seek a protective order prohibiting the abuser from purchasing or possessing firearms.

2017-2018

In 2017 and 2018, several states—some in response to the #NeverAgain movement—changed their gun laws to include dating partners.

Louisiana added "dating partners" to the categories of violent abusers banned from owning guns. *See* HB 776, HB 896, and S.B. 231.

Ohio HB 1 extended domestic violence protection orders to dating partners. For anyone who doesn't know what a "dating relationship" is, the legislation explained: "'Dating relationship' means a relationship between individuals who have, or have had, a relationship of a romantic or intimate nature." Ohio's solons felt compelled to clarify: "'Dating relationship' does not include a casual acquaintanceship or ordinary fraternization in a business or social context"[246]—not that anyone thought it did.[247] For the Ohio law to apply, both the abuser and the abused in a dating relationship must be adults. Even though they are frequent targets of domestic violence, teenage girls have to fend for themselves.

Oregon HB 4145 expanded the prohibition on possession of firearms and ammunition to include DVROs and domestic violence convictions involving certain dating partners.[248] It changed the term "intimate partner" to "family or household member," but specified that the term "family or household member" included persons who have cohabited with each other or have had a sexually intimate relationship. As in Ohio, legislators worried that domestic violence restraining orders and gun prohibitions might somehow apply to men who violently abused women in business or casual relationships. The legislation included language to make completely certain that men who did that would *not* be barred from buying guns.

2018

In 2018, several other states adopted new laws or amendments to existing laws that brought their states in line with where federal law was in 1996. Or at least closer.

Kansas HB 2145 amended the state's illegal use of weapons law to include persons who are subject to a final domestic violence restraining order and to persons convicted within the last five years of a violent misdemeanor. That caught Kansas law up to the 1996 Lautenberg amendment. The bill also added a violent misdemeanor provision. (For more about violent misdemeanor laws, see Chapter 8.)

Utah S.B. 27 almost caught Utah law up with the 1996 Lautenberg Amendment. It banned the subjects of *final* domestic violence orders and anyone convicted of misdemeanor domestic assault from *acquiring* guns. But barring some other disqualifier, abusers could keep the guns they already owned. (It would still be a felony under federal law for an abuser subject to a DVRO or domestic violence conviction to keep his guns. Even so, Utah's legislators weren't willing to require violent domestic abusers to give up guns they already owned.)

Vermont HB 422 *allowed* officers to seize firearms at the scene of domestic violence under certain conditions. It also authorized—but did not require—a court to condition an abuser's release from jail on relinquishment of his or her firearms.

Washington S.B. 6298 added domestic abuse to the list of crimes for which a person becomes ineligible to own firearms. For the statute to apply, however, the victim had to be a family or household member, not a dating partner.

2019

In 2019, six more states enacted or strengthened laws intended to keep firearms away from domestic abusers: Arkansas HB 1851, California AB 164, Louisiana HB 279, New Mexico S.B. 328, Oregon HB 2013, and Washington HB 1225, HB 1517, and HB 1786.[249]

California already made it a crime for an individual who is subject to a DVRO issued by a California court to keep or acquire a firearm. Assembly Bill 164 expanded its law to include persons subject to DVROs issued by courts in other states.[250]

Arkansas H.B. 1851 tightened the language of Arkansas Code § 9-15-207(b).[251]

Louisiana HB 279 tightened the language of existing law, mainly to make sure the respondent surrenders any firearm he may have.[252]

New Mexico Gov. Michelle Lujan Grisham signed S.B. 328 into law on April 4, 2019.[253] It requires New Mexico courts, when they enter DVROs, to determine if the individual represents a credible threat. If the court determines the individual is a credible threat, the court must order him to relinquish his gun or destructive device (*e.g.*, a bomb) to one of the authorized recipients *within 48 hours*. S.B. 328 also requires the abuser to refrain from purchasing, receiving, possessing, or attempting to purchase, receive, or possess any firearm while the order of protection is in effect.[254]

Oregon enacted legislation in 2015 that barred people convicted of a domestic violence crime or subject to a domestic violence restraining order from possessing firearms. HB 2013 went a giant step further and required abusers to turn in their guns to law enforcement, a federally licensed firearm dealer, or a sworn third party.[255] HB 2013 also spelled out how that is supposed to happen.[256]

Governor Kate Brown testified in favor of House Bill 2013.

Washington HB 1225 tightened existing law by requiring persons subject to DVROs to surrender their weapons "immediately."[257] It also required the individual to surrender any concealed pistol license he or she had. And it changed the statutory terminology from "intimate partner" to "protected person." Governor Jay Inslee signed the bill into law on May 7, 2019.

Conclusion

Congress enacted legislation in 1996 that prohibits violent domestic abusers from owning or buying guns. The prohibition, however, does not apply to violent, abusive dating partners. To apply, the abuser and the abused must have married, lived together, or had a child. Research shows that this omission—the "boyfriend loophole"—costs lives.

The recent uptick in men (and some women killing dating partners has pushed this issue back on the table. So has research showing that misogyny and domestic violence are frequently associated with mass shootings.[258]

Polling on this issue is scant, but what there is suggests that the public—by a wide margin—supports closing the "boyfriend loophole." Women are especially supportive.

In early 2019, the U.S. House of Representatives passed a bill to renew the Violence Against Women Act and to expand its terms to include dating partners. Senate Majority Leader Mitch McConnell and Senate Republicans refused to allow the House-passed measure to come to the floor for a vote. Meanwhile, federal law allows those who violently abuse dating partners to continue to buy and own guns.

In most states, state laws similarly protect gun sales to those who violently abuse dating partners. As a result, women, children, and the police officers called to deal with domestic violence continue to die at the hands of violent domestic abusers.

7. Should We Close The "Emergency Order" Loophole?

Item: *Donna R. Brown, 45, wanted to end her ten-year long romantic relationship with Dennis Haggin, 62, but Haggin wasn't having it. He threatened to kill Ms. Brown. On Friday, July 19, 2019, Ms. Brown went to the Montgomery County, Ohio, courthouse to request a domestic violence restraining order. On the way, Haggin tried to force Brown's car off the road. The court issued the temporary domestic violence restraining order. Among other things, the order required Haggin to relinquish any firearms he had. A Montgomery County sheriff's officer served the temporary restraining order on Haggin the same day but did not seize Haggin's gun. The sheriff's office considered it Haggin's responsibility to make an appointment with the local police department to turn in any firearms he had. On Sunday afternoon, July 21, 2019, Haggin found Ms. Brown leaving a Family Dollar store in Dayton, Ohio, and shot her to death. He then turned his gun on himself.*[259]

Item: *In April 2015, Regina Annas, 33, obtained a temporary domestic violence protective order against her husband, David Annas, 40. The order required Mr. Annas to leave the couple's home in Prairie Ridge, Washington, and prohibited him from having a firearm. A prior assault conviction also precluded David Annas from having a gun. Before leaving the couple's home, David Annas asked the deputies who served the order to return his gun to him, which the deputies did. That evening, David Annas returned to the home and used the gun to shoot and kill his wife. He also shot, but not a fatally, Rachel Holland, a friend of his wife. He then killed himself. Regina Annas' Estate and her son, Dylan Kinney, sued Pierce County. So did Rachel Holland. In December 2019, Pierce County settled the litigation.*[260]

In the last chapter, we discussed the "boyfriend" exception to federal gun law. A second problem with the federal statute is that it prohibits domestic abusers from having guns only after a court has issued a final order. This assures the respondent gets a chance to be heard before giving up his guns, even temporarily. But the abused spouse, dating partner, or ex-partner seeking the order is at greatest danger during the time between the issuance of an emergency or *ex parte* order and the issuance, after a hearing, of the final order. That's the time when the spouse abuser is in a frenzy over his loss of control of his spouse or girlfriend.

The Issue

Should our laws prohibit domestic violence offenders who are subject to *emergency* domestic violence restraining orders from having guns while the order is in effect?

A request for a domestic violence restraining order (DVRO often starts as an emergency request to the local state court with jurisdiction over domestic relations matters. Typically, a sworn statement from the victim accompanies the request and explains why, from the perspective of the victim, the court should issue an emergency restraining order. In other words, the affidavit explains what the alleged abuser has done or threatened to do and why the situation is an emergency.

These requests are usually made without notice to the abuser out of concern that if the abuser knew that his wife, girlfriend, or "ex" was going to court, he might physically attack or kill her first.[261] Lawyers and courts call any order issued in response to an emergency request without notice to the other side an *"ex parte"* order. (I will use "emergency" and *"ex parte"* interchangeably, not because they mean the same thing but because, in this context, courts generally issue *ex parte* orders only in an emergency.

When a court issues an emergency domestic violence restraining order, it schedules a hearing at which both sides have notice and an opportunity to participate, *i.e.,* to present evidence and arguments. After that hearing, if the court determines that an order is warranted, the court issues a final restraining order prohibiting the subject from threatening or harassing the other party. If, on the other hand, the court doesn't believe an order is warranted, it will not issue a final domestic violence restraining order and instead will dismiss the case. In a state where the accused abuser must surrender any firearms he owns after an emergency order, he can then retrieve his gun or guns.

Based on mountains of anecdotal evidence, the period of greatest danger for the woman seeking the order is the time between the request for an emergency order and issuance of the final restraining order. This brief period is when the abuser is reacting to the loss of control of the other party. Scholarly research confirms what common experience tells us: "[V]ictims who had restraining orders against the perpetrator were more likely to have a weapon used against them in a domestic violence incident."[262]

As we've already noted, the federal statute does not prohibit the abuser from buying or possessing firearms unless and until the court issues a final order, after a hearing in which the abuser has the opportunity to be heard. The gun lobby's argument for this is simple: We should not deprive the alleged abuser of his or her Second Amendment right to bear arms without first affording him or her the due process rights of notice and the opportunity to be heard. Taking guns away and then holding a hearing to see if the guns should be returned isn't good enough.

The argument gun-violence-prevention advocates would make is this: If the abuser is allowed to keep his gun, then the woman may not live to make it to the hearing. To deal with situations where irreparable harm may occur, courts routinely issue temporary restraining orders, followed by a hearing, usually within a week or ten days. No matter what gun rights hardliners may believe, courts do not consider temporary restraining orders a violation of due process.

What We Want

Where does the American public stand on this issue? Do we want Congress and our state legislatures to close the "murder window" between the issuance of an emergency restraining order and the issuance of a final restraining order? Or, like pro-gun legislators in Congress, are we more concerned about the Second Amendment "right" of violent abusers to "bear arms" against abused women?

Only one of the usual high-quality opinion polls since the Las Vegas Strip shooting has addressed emergency domestic violence restraining orders.

Quinnipiac University Poll
March 3-5, 2018[263]

In a March 2018 poll, Quinnipiac asked:

> Do you support or oppose banning the possession or purchase of a gun if an individual has had a restraining order filed against them for stalking or domestic, sexual, or repeat violence?

Quinnipiac found 91% support for banning the possession or purchase of a gun if an individual has had a restraining order filed against him or her under these circumstances. Only 6% said they were opposed. Obviously, 91% is a very high degree of consensus, even if the usual 6%, who oppose any effort to reduce gun violence, show up again.

Given that level of consensus, the usual breakouts were about what one would expect:

	Support:	Oppose:
Overall Results:	**91%**	**6%**
Men:	88%	10%
Women:	96%	2%
Republicans:	89%	6%
Gun Households:	89%	7%
Whites, College Degree:	93%	5%
Whites, No College Degree:	92%	6%

Of note, women are practically unanimous on this issue (96% *vs.* 2%). Men, Republicans, and gun owners are just a little less so. Only a small percentage of men (10%), Republicans (6%), and gun householders (7%) think we *should* let violent abusers keep their guns until the court can hold a contested hearing *or* the abuser shoots the woman seeking the court's protection, whichever comes first. (Actually, there's another alternative, at least for some women, and it's the one the NRA likes: They can buy a gun and attempt to shoot the abuser, either preemptively or defensively. Those scenarios, however, almost never end well for the woman.)

Unfortunately, Quinnipiac's question did not explicitly distinguish between *emergency* and *final* restraining orders. But the two polls discussed next *did* make the distinction between *emergency* and *final* restraining orders in their questions. Their results suggest that the public doesn't attach much importance to that distinction.

YouGov/Huffington Post
July 2014

A YouGov/Huffington Post poll[264] conducted July 24-25, 2014, probed issues surrounding domestic abuse more deeply than any other survey in recent memory.[265]

The survey began by testing support for prohibiting gun possession by those subject to final or "permanent" domestic violence restraining orders, the orders to which the federal gun ban applies:

> Do you support or oppose banning people who have been issued a permanent restraining order for domestic violence by a judge, but have not been convicted of a crime, from possessing guns?

When phrased this way, **68%** supported current federal law, and **21%** opposed it. By any measure, 68% in favor and only 21% opposed is strong support for not allowing those who are subject to final DVROs to have guns. But it's not nearly as high as the level of support the Quinnipiac poll found four years later—after the media began to focus on the link between domestic abuse and many of the shooters involved in high-profile mass shootings.[266]

Every demographic group supported this measure by wide margins. Except for the gender difference, these discrepancies were modest and generally within or close to the poll's margin of error.

In its next question, the YouGov poll went beyond where federal law is currently (in early 2020). It specifically asked if we should also prohibit individuals subject to *temporary* restraining orders from having guns while the order is in place. The poll asked:

Do you support or oppose banning people who have been issued temporary restraining orders for domestic violence, but have not been convicted of a crime, from possessing guns for the duration of the order?

Support for this measure was the same as for permanent restraining orders (68% in favor, 21% opposed). Women (49%) were about twice as likely as men (26%) to *support* this measure "strongly." Only a small percentage of men opposed this measure, but men were about twice as likely as women to "strongly" oppose disarming violent abusers.

In sum, the available data from polling organizations, while thin, suggests that most of us don't want abusers to keep their guns during the period between the issuance of an *emergency* order and the issuance of a *final* order—the time when the woman is most at risk. Only about 21% of us believe that abusers should be able to keep their guns pending a final order, even if that means more women and kids will die.[267]

Barry et al. 2017

Colleen L. Barry, Ph.D., and her colleagues at the Johns Hopkins Center for Gun Policy and Research sponsored a national public opinion survey in January 2017 to compare support among gun owners and non-gun owners for twenty-four gun policies. In their survey, **81%** favored temporary gun prohibitions on persons subject to *temporary* domes-tic violence restraining orders.[268]

The higher level of support in this survey, as opposed to that found in the mid-2014 YouGov survey (69%), may reflect a growing awareness of the connection between domestic violence and mass shootings. Or it may merely reflect the way You.Gov worded its questions ("but have not been convicted of a crime").

What We're Getting Instead

According to the Giffords Law Center, some states ban abusers from having guns while an emergency order remains in effect. California, Illinois, Massachusetts, Texas, and West Virginia, for example, go beyond federal law and prohibit firearm purchases and possession by individuals subject to domestic violence restraining orders issued before a full hearing. The bans are temporary and are lifted if, after a hearing, the court decides a DVRO is not warranted.

Other states require, or at least authorize, judges to prohibit gun access by people subject to *emergency* protective orders. Massachusetts, for example, requires a court issuing an *emergency* DVRO to order the immediate suspension and surrender of any license to carry firearms (the firearms identification card). The court must order the defendant to surrender all firearms and ammunition that he or she possesses to the appropriate law enforcement official.

Still other states, however, simply follow federal law or have even weaker laws.

Conclusion

When federal and state legislators consider whether to strengthen their state's gun laws, they choose between protecting the revenues and profits of gun manufacturers and dealers *or* protecting the lives of abused women and their children.

Gun manufacturers and gun dealers, their lobbyists, and organizations like the NRA provide both campaign contributions and independent expenditures on behalf of gun-friendly legislators. And they are not shy about recruiting primary challengers to run against legislators who don't toe the gun lobby line.

Dead women and children, on the other hand, don't make campaign contributions, hire lobbyists, or vote. So, for many legislators, the decision is easy. They vote to protect the Second Amendment "right" of violent abusers to bear arms against their current and former spouses and dating partners, at least until a court issues a final DVRO. Until then, they leave abused women and children to fend for themselves.

If that seems unfair, the NRA has a ready answer: It urges abused and threatened women to buy guns.[269] *Gosh, what better way to settle domestic violence than by a shootout?*

At least two-thirds of Americans, and probably as many as 80%, believe that Congress and our state legislatures should close this loophole. But until recently, neither Congress nor most of our state legislatures were willing to stand up to the gun lobby and give the American public the legislation it wants.

After the November 2018 mid-term election, in which Democrats took control of the House, that chamber passed legislation to fix the "boyfriend" and emergency order loopholes. But despite public support for action, Senator Mitch McConnell and the Republican majority in the Senate refused to allow the House-passed bill to go to the Senate floor for a vote. A cartoon image of McConnell with the caption "Murder Turtle" made its way around social media.

Meanwhile, women and teenage girls continued to be shot to death by former boyfriends and by men who were subject to temporary restraining orders.

8. Should Violent Offenders Get to Keep Their Guns?

Item: August 31, 2019. Seth Ator, the Odessa-Midland shooter, fatally shot seven and injured twenty-five during his rampage. He had prior convictions for trespass and public intoxication, which are not a violent misdemeanors, and resisting arrest, which is. According to press reports, he also had a history of angry, impulsive behavior and mental health issues. Fifteen minutes before his shooting spree, his employer fired him for showing up at work angry and out-of-control.[270]

Item: April 29, 2019. Joseph A. Brown, 38, of Grafton, New Hampshire, and Jason Marandos, 46, also of Grafton, got into a road rage altercation. Brown allegedly tailgated the slower driving Marandos, then sped around him, only to stop suddenly, causing Marandos to crash into the rear end of Brown's Ford Flex SUV. During the argument that ensued, Marandos swung at and hit Brown. In response, Brown pulled a pistol from his waistband and shot Marandos in the abdomen.

The state charged Brown with two counts of first-degree assault. Brown's attorney asked the court to dismiss the charges, arguing that Brown was the victim and shot in self-defense. That's when the prosecutor revealed seven prior incidents, between July 2017 and April 27, 2019, of Brown engaging in the same tailgating, passing, and suddenly stopping that led to the incident with Marandos.[271] (As of this writing, the case against Brown has not gone to trial, and he has not been convicted of anything.

Item: The nonprofit Gun Violence Archive tracks fatal and nonfatal shootings, as well as disputes in which someone brandished a gun. After analyzing the Archive, The Trace reported that road-rage altercations involving guns had increased dramatically in the United States, more than doubling from 241 in 2014 to 623 in 2016. In the first six months of 2017, there were at least 325 incidents.[272]

Previous chapters explained that federal law bars most persons convicted of felonies from having a gun. We've also discussed laws that ban gun possession by persons who have domestic violence misde-

-meanors on their records or are the subject of domestic violence restraining orders. This chapter considers laws that take a broader view of the violent offender problem. Those laws prohibit gun possession by individuals who have one or more convictions of *any* violent misdemeanor—not just domestic violence misdemeanors.

The thinking behind "violent misdemeanor" laws goes something like this: Some people have anger management issues or poor impulse control. This may exhibit itself in any number of ways. They may, for example, engage in domestic violence, child abuse, or elder abuse. Or they may get involved in "road rage" or "retail rage" incidents, drunken outbursts, or fights. They may have problems with alcohol or drugs. They often have frequent job changes, broken marriages, DUI arrests, and so on. Putting a gun in the hands of someone who frequently exhibits poor anger management or impulse control ("loses it") puts the rest of us in danger.

In a 2015 study,[273] a surprising number of individuals self-reported *both* engaging in a pattern of impulsive, angry behavior *and* possessing firearms at home (8.9%) or carrying a gun outside the home (1.5%).

Very few of those angry, impulsive individuals will ever be involuntarily hospitalized for mental illness, and most mentally ill people don't threaten anyone with guns or shoot people. Research-ers, therefore, suggest that an approach based on *behavior* rather than *mental health* might be more effective in reducing gun violence. Instead of disarming everyone with a mental health issue, they argue, it would be more effective to prohibit gun ownership by persons with impulse control and anger management issues.

It's not feasible to obtain a detailed personal history and do psychological testing on everyone who wants to buy a gun. There is, however, a rough but effective way of identifying people whose impulse-control problems are severe enough to make any reasonable person question letting them have a gun: Do they have an arrest record for one or more *violent* misdemeanors?

With that in mind, some states have gone beyond the federal ban on persons with felony or domestic violence convictions and have enacted "violent misdemeanor" laws. Those laws prohibit gun possession by per-sons who have a history of convictions for violent misdemeanors. The ban usually lasts only for a specified time—*typically* five years after the individual's most recent violent misdemeanor conviction.

Some might argue that it's unfair to take away someone's right to have a gun for several years based on one unfortunate incident. But in a 2001 study,[274] male handgun purchasers with a single violent-misdemeanor conviction were eight times more likely to be charged with a later gun crime or violent crime. Among those with multiple convictions, the rate was only a little higher—tenfold that of someone without a prior violent misdemeanor conviction.

Just as someone who repeatedly drives drunk is more likely to have a DUI arrest on his or her record than someone who has only driven under the influence once, so too with people with impulse control or anger management issues: They almost certainly offend more often than their arrest records show.

Misdemeanor *vs.* Felony

A word about "misdemeanor" *versus* "felony." Generally, our laws designate less serious crimes as misdemeanors and more serious crimes as felonies. In the discussion above, I used the usual shorthand and said that federal law prohibits gun possession by persons with "felony" con-victions. That is close, but not a technically accurate description of fed-eral law.

More accurately, federal law prohibits gun and ammunition sales *to* and purchases or possession of a gun or ammunition *by* a person who is "under indictment for, or has been convicted of, a crime punishable by imprisonment for a term exceeding one year."[275] Traditionally, crimes punishable by more than a year in prison were felonies; hence, the short-hand version. But in some states, certain misdemeanors are also punish-able by more than a year in prison, so the shorthand is not entirely cor-rect.

The federal statute, moreover, has its own explanation of "crimes punishable by imprisonment for a term exceeding one year." The provision, 18 U.S.C. § 921(a)(20), is not a definition in the usual sense. Instead, it *excludes* three categories of offenses that might otherwise fall within the ban. The first excludes antitrust or similar crimes:

> (20) The term "crime punishable by imprisonment for a term exceeding one year" does not include –
>
> (A) any Federal or State offenses pertaining to antitrust violations, unfair trade practices, restraints of trade, or other similar offenses relating to the regulation of business practices ...

Persons who commit antitrust crimes, *e.g.*, price-fixing, are more likely to be corporate executives than the usual folks arrested for felonies—robbery, drug distribution, and so on. Antitrust violators are probably less likely to engage in violent crimes. Besides, business executives are a crucial constituency of the Republican party. The antitrust exception might be explainable on those grounds alone.

But the statute applies not just to "persons" in the usual sense. It also applies to corporations and other legal entities. Thus, without this loophole, a gun manufacturer or retailer convicted of price-fixing or another antitrust crime would no longer be able to manufacture or sell guns. That, apparently, was a huge issue for gun manufacturers and, therefore, for the NRA.

The second exception or loophole is more relevant to the present discussion. It provides:

> (20) The term "crime punishable by imprisonment for a term exceeding one year" does not include ...
>
> (B) any state offense classified by the laws of the state as a misdemeanor and punishable by a term of imprisonment of two years or less.

Under this exception, a crime punishable by two years in prison is not a "crime punishable by imprisonment for a term exceeding one year" if the state statute classifies the crime as a misdemeanor. That likely allows many thousands of gang members, drug dealers, and others, who would otherwise have been barred from owning guns, to continue to be able to buy guns—and, thus, to produce revenues and profits for gun manufacturers and gun dealers.

The statute contains one more loophole:

> Any conviction which has been expunged, or set aside or for which a person has been pardoned or has had civil rights restored shall not be considered a conviction for purposes of this chapter, unless such pardon, expungement, or restoration of civil rights expressly provides that the person may not ship, transport, possess, or receive firearms.

Expungement of convictions has become quite popular in state courts. This practice allows many people who would otherwise be prohibited from buying and owning guns to patronize their local gun dealers once again.

The Issue

Should we ban the sale of firearms to people who have one or more convictions for violent misdemeanors in the last five years?

"Violent Misdemeanor" statutes typically ban an individual from having a gun for some time, *e.g.*, for five or ten years after their last conviction for a violent misdemeanor. As the name implies, these laws do not apply to all misdemeanors, but only to *violent* misdemeanors. If in state X, shoplifting is a misdemeanor punishable by less than two years in prison, a person could have a long string of shoplifting convictions and still be allowed to buy a gun. But a person who has one or more convictions for assault would be banned from buying or possessing a gun for several years.

A substantial body of research links alcohol and substance abuse with unsafe behavior with guns.[276] The short version is this: A drunk with a gun is a formula for disaster, both for the drunken gun owner himself and for those around him. Some violent misdemeanor laws, therefore, include individuals with a history of drunk driving charges.

What We Want

Morning Consult and Quinnipiac University included questions about violent misdemeanor laws in several polls. Morning Consult asked:

"Do you support or oppose each of the following?—Preventing sales of all firearms to people who have been convicted of violent misdemeanors?" Quinnipiac's question was less specific: "Do you support or oppose a nationwide ban on the sale of guns to people who have been convicted of violent crimes?"

Overall Results

Favor	Oppose	Polling Dates	Poll
82%	11%	10/5-9/17	Morning Consult
86%	12%	10/5-10/17	Quinnipiac
91%	8%	11/7-13/17	Quinnipiac
84%	9%	2/22-26/18	Morning Consult
86%	7%	3/31-4/1/18	Morning Consult
80%	13%	8/2-6/18	Morning Consult
84%	9%	8/5-7/19	Morning Consult

Averages: **85%** vs. **10%**. *Ratio: 8.5 to 1.*

Throughout this period, support was at the 80% level or higher. The chronological listing suggests a bump up in support after the Las Vegas Strip shooting, returning to baseline by late summer 2018.

On average, an overwhelming 85% supported this measure. But the interesting thing may be the roughly 10% who opposed it. As discussed earlier, research suggests that about 9% of adults in the U.S. self-reported both a history of angry, impulsive behavior and access to guns.[277] That's not to say that the folks who oppose this measure all have violent misdemeanor convictions on their record or even that they all have anger-management issues. But it would be interesting to know how many of the small minority of individuals who object to this measure *do* have misdemeanor convictions or serious anger-management problems.

Republicans

Republicans were in step with the rest of America on this issue. By wide margins, they favored a ban on the sale of guns to individuals with violent misdemeanor convictions.

Favor	Oppose	Polling Dates	Poll
82%	13%	10/5-9/17	Morning Consult
87%	12%	10/5-10/17	Quinnipiac
91%	8%	11/7-13/17	Quinnipiac
87%	7%	2/22-26/18	Morning Consult
89%	7%	3/31-4/1/18	Morning Consult
78%	13%	8/2-6/18	Morning Consult
85%	9%	8/5-7/19	Morning Consult

Averages: **86%** vs. **10%**. *Ratio: 8.6 to 1.*

Trump 2016 Voters

Like the rest of the nation and Republicans generally, Trump voters favored banning gun sales to individuals convicted of violent crimes, including misdemeanors.

Favor	Oppose	Polling Dates	Poll
84%	13%	10/5-9/17	Morning Consult
85%	10%	2/22-26/18	Morning Consult
88%	7%	3/31-4/1/18	Morning Consult
79%	15%	8/2-6/18	Morning Consult
83%	10%	8/5-7/19	Morning Consult

Averages: **84%** vs. **11%**. *Ratio: 7.6 to 1.*

Gun Households

Gun households showed the highest level of support for prohibiting gun sales to violent criminals.

Favor	Oppose	Polling Dates	Poll
85%	8%	10/5-9/17	Morning Consult
88%	11%	10/5-10/17	Quinnipiac
91%	7%	11/7-13/17	Quinnipiac
89%	10%	3/31-4/1/18	Morning Consult
80%	15%	8/2-6/18	Morning Consult
82%	13%	8/5-7/19	Morning Consult

Averages: **86%** vs. **11%**. *Ratio: 7.8 to 1.*

Education

Less Than a Bachelor Degree

People without college degrees agreed that we should prohibit gun sales to violent criminals. Their support waned a bit between high-profile mass shootings but returned to high levels after each new massacre.

Favor	*Oppose*	*Polling Dates*	*Poll*
81%	12%	10/5-9/17	Morning Consult
86%	13%	10/5-10/17	Quinnipiac
92%	6%	11/7-13/17	Quinnipiac
82%	10%	2/22-26/18	Morning Consult
83%	9%	3/31-4/1/18	Morning Consult
75%	15%	8/2-6/18	Morning Consult
81%	11%	8/5-7/19	Morning Consult

Averages: **83%** vs. **11%**. *Ratio: 7.5 to 1.*

Bachelor Degree or More

People with a Bachelor's degree or more showed an even higher level of support and the least drop off. On average, nine-in-ten college-educated individuals supported violent misdemeanor laws.

Favor	*Oppose*	*Polling Dates*	*Poll*
91%	8%	10/5-10/17	Quinnipiac
95%	4%	11/7-13/17	Quinnipiac
87%	9%	10/5-19/17	Morning Consult
88%	9%	2/22-26/18	Morning Consult
91%	5%	3/31-4/1/18	Morning Consult
88%	10%	8/2-6/18	Morning Consult
89%	8%	8/5-7/19	Morning Consult

Averages: **90%** vs. **8%**. *Ratio: 12 to 1.*

This level of support, including support from Republicans, Trump voters, and people with and without college degrees, is extraordinary. *So, Congress is all over this, right?*

What We're Getting Instead

Despite strong public support for violent misdemeanor laws, Congress has not amended federal law to bar those with violent misdemeanor convictions from buying or possessing guns. Research suggests that doing so would save lives, but it would also cut into the revenues and profits of gun manufacturers and gun dealers. The gun lobby contributes millions of dollars to congressional campaigns and political action committees (PACs);[278] fatal gunshot victims, not so much.

The same phenomenon plays out in our state legislatures, where the gun lobby has been able until recently to prevent the enactment of new violent misdemeanor laws since 2003. Researchers[279] have identified five states with longstanding violent misdemeanor laws on the books, all of which became effective fifteen or more years ago: New York (pre-1984), California (01/01/91), Illinois (01/01/95), Maryland (10/01/03), and Minnesota (10/01/03). Kansas enacted a violent misdemeanor law in 2018.

Meanwhile, year-after-year, angry, impulsive individuals with violent convictions on their records buy guns and use them to threaten, injure, and kill.

9. Should We Enact "Red Flag" Laws?

Item: *April 16, 2007. Before Seung-Hui Cho shot and killed 32 and wounded 17 more at Virginia Tech, he had a long history of mental illness. Privacy laws kept much of that history secret. Campus police warned Cho twice about stalking co-eds. Cho's instant messages and Facebook postings were so disturbing that the father of another co-ed reported him to the campus police. An English professor was so concerned about Cho, she refused to have him in her classroom and threatened to resign if the university didn't transfer him out of her class.*

A clinical social worker determined that Cho was mentally ill and a danger to himself and others. After a commitment hearing, a justice ruled that Cho was mentally ill and posed a danger to himself but required only outpatient treatment, not involuntary hospitalization. Cho attended one session and chose not to go back. Instead, Cho began buying firearms and ammunition. In a video he sent to NBC News, he said, "You had a hundred billion chances and ways to have avoided today."[280]

Item: *In 2014, the parents of Elliot Rodger warned police that their son was disturbed, wanted to hurt others, and was armed. The final "red flags" were: (1) a manifesto he posted online complaining that he had been lonely for years and that attractive women were not interested in him; and (2) a video he posted on YouTube in which he outlined his plan to kill as many attractive young men and women as he could. But without a "red flag" law, police told his parents they couldn't do anything until their son committed a crime.*

Rodger obliged by going on a murder spree in the Isla Vista area of Santa Barbara, California, killing six people and injuring fourteen others. He thus became California's poster boy for a law allowing preventative gun seizures from legal gun owners in crisis.[281]

Rodger is also one of several "incel"—involuntarily celibate—killers.²⁸²

Item: July 2019. After the Steak 'n Shake restaurant in St. Petersburg, Fla., fired 26-year-old Zachary Walls, he sent a former co-worker a text that talked about, "just walking in there and killing everyone then shooting myself." Using Florida's new red flag law, police obtained a "risk protection order" that required Walls to surrender his guns. Walls turned in an AR-15 style rifle and multiple magazines and got help. There was no mass shooting.²⁸³

Item: When Moms Demand Action for Gun Sense in America representatives showed up to testify in the Vermont House of Representatives in support of a "red flag" bill, male Republicans on the legislative panel wore strings of pearls. According to a report in The Washington Post, a Moms Demand Action representative said the implication was clear: "These politicians thought gun-control activists were 'clutching their pearls' in overwrought and self-righteous outrage—and, specifically, female outrage."²⁸⁴

Nickolas Cruz

Nikolas Cruz, the 19-year-old who killed seventeen and injured seventeen more at Marjory Stoneman Douglas High School in Parkland, Florida, had a history of torturing and killing animals.²⁸⁵ He picked fights with other kids, vandalized property, and stole things. A woman caught him peeping in her window. Neighbors and even his mother called the police on him frequently. The school suspended him repeatedly.

After his mother died of pneumonia in November 2017, Cruz's conduct deteriorated to the point where it was clear he was in crisis. He became so weird and threatening the school kicked him out, and what few friends he had largely stayed away from him. He made videos of his plans to return to Stoneman Douglas and become the next school shooter.

Tim Elfrink, writing for the Miami New Times, put it this way:²⁸⁶

> Everyone knew Nikolas Cruz was deeply disturbed. He'd been in and out of mental health treatment. He'd been kicked out of school. His Instagram page was full of photos of dead animals and weapons. He was so frightening to teachers that he'd been banned from even carrying a backpack into school.

In short, Cruz put up more red flags than the Red Army. Or as Senator Lindsey Graham put it, "He did everything but take an ad out in the paper saying, 'I'm going to kill people.'"

Speaking for many of us, Elfrink asked:

> So how does a guy like that get his hands on a military-style weapon capable of pumping dozens of rounds into innocent victims without even reloading?

Elfrink answered his own question this way: "Well, this is Florida, so he just walks into a gun shop and buys one."

At the time, gun-friendly Florida had no "red flag" law that would have enabled the police, if they could get a court to authorize it, to separate Cruz and his guns until he got help and his situation stabilized. Florida also had no law that would have allowed the police to preclude Cruz, even temporarily, from purchasing a gun. As a result, Cruz, who wasn't allowed to bring a backpack to school, was able to buy an assault rifle.

Ian Howard

In Lafayette, Louisiana, 28-year-old Ian Howard was in crisis. Police found him running around in front of a store in an agitated state. He complained that the FBI wanted to kill him and that white vans followed him wherever he went.

The police took Howard to a nearby hospital, where a psychiatrist certified him a danger to himself or others. The hospital, however, released Howard a couple of days later, apparently believing the immediate crisis had passed. Emergency commitments for observation and evaluation often end in quick releases. In other cases, mental health professionals convince the individual to commit himself voluntarily for treatment. Neither outcome makes the person ineligible to buy or own guns under federal law; only an extended involuntary commitment does.

Louisiana is another "gun-friendly" state. It did not have a red flag law that might have enabled the police to get a court order authorizing the temporary seizure of any guns Howard owned. The police also had no way to prevent him from buying a gun. So, three days after his release from the psych ward, Howard bought an AR-15 semi-automatic rifle, the favorite of mass murderers. Two or three weeks later, he bought a Smith & Wesson pistol.

About then, the restaurant where Howard worked fired him, and he didn't handle it well. Howard repeatedly threatened the supervisor who fired him and sent him a picture of someone whose brains a gun had blown out. Howard warned the restaurant's employees about going into the restaurant's parking lot alone at night.

The restaurant complained to the police, and they telephoned Howard and told him to knock it off. That worked after a fashion. Howard stopped harassing the restaurant manager and staff. Instead, he used the Smith & Wesson pistol and another gun to shoot two convenience store employees. When a police officer responded to the shootings, Howard shot him too. The convenience store employees survived; the policeman did not.[287]

Travis Reinking

Before the 2018 Waffle House shooting in Nashville, Travis Reinking had a history of paranoid delusions and bizarre behavior.[288]

In May 2016, sheriff's deputies in Tazewell County in central Illinois responded to a call that Reinking was having a meltdown in the parking lot of a drugstore. When the deputies arrived, Reinking complained that singer-songwriter Taylor Swift was stalking him and hacking his Netflix account. The police report noted: "Travis is hostile toward police and does not recognize police authority. Travis also possesses several firearms."

In 2017, Reinking lived in an apartment above his father's crane rental business in Tremont, Illinois. In June, an employee of the business called the police, saying Reinking had come downstairs wearing a pink dress and carrying a rifle, used an expletive, tossed the rifle into the trunk of his car, and left. On another occasion around the same time, a public pool director called the police to report that Reinking had come to the pool in a "pink women's housecoat" and exposed himself to lifeguards.[289]

In July 2017, the U.S. Secret Service arrested Reinking near the White House after he crossed a barrier and refused to leave. The Secret Service said Reinking "wanted to set up a meeting with the president."[290] The report also noted that Reinking claimed to be a "sovereign citizen."[291] Secret Service officers charged him with unlawful entry, a misdemeanor.

Following Reinking's arrest, Illinois authorities revoked his state firearms authorization and seized his weapons—the AR-15 later used in the Nashville shooting, two other rifles, and a handgun.[292] Reinking's father held a valid Illinois Firearm Owners ID card and asked the Sheriff's Deputies if he could keep the guns. He assured them, "he would keep them secure and away from" his son. Without a red-flag law to authorize the gun seizure, the Deputies agreed.[293]

In the autumn of 2017, Reinking moved to the Nashville area where he worked as a crane and construction worker from January to April 2018. The construction company fired Reinking on April 3, 2018, over his frequent complaints that people, including other employees, were "after him."[294]

On April 22, 2018, Reinking parked his pickup truck in the parking lot of a Nashville Waffle House. When he left the truck, he was naked except for a green camo jacket. But even if he couldn't find his pants, he had his AR-15-style rifle. Reinking shot and killed two people outside the Waffle House. He entered the restaurant and shot two more, killing one instantly and fatally injuring the other.

When Reinking stopped shooting to reload, a customer, 29-year-old James Shaw Jr., rushed Reinking and wrestled the rifle away. Reinking fled on foot, leaving behind his rifle and ammunition. Shaw suffered a bullet graze wound. In addition to those shot, flying glass injured two more.

Both the Nashville police chief and the Tazewell County Sheriff believed that Reinking's father returned the guns to his son sometime before the Waffle House shooting.[295]

Tennessee's legislators praised the courage of Shaw, the man who took Reinking's gun away, but they lacked the courage to buck the NRA and pass a "red flag" or "extreme risk" law.

"Red Flag" or "Extreme Risk" Laws

Those incidents and others like them have prompted gun violence opponents to press for "red flag" or "extreme risk" gun seizure laws.

Those laws focus on individuals who are in crisis—making threats, acting bizarrely, and so on. They allow the individual's family or the police to go to a judge and make a showing that the individual is a danger to himself or others. If the court agrees, it issues an order that authorizes the police to seize the individual's guns temporarily until the crisis passes, while still affording due process guarantees.

"Red flag" or "extreme risk" laws focus on the conduct of an individual who is an immediate threat to himself or others, rather than a class of potential gun owners. These laws allow courts to consider domestic violence and other violent misdemeanor convictions, alcoholism, and mental health. Thus, they draw on the lessons learned from the measures discussed in other chapters.

Red flag laws give the police another tool to use when, for example, a 19-year-old posts on social media that tomorrow he's going back to his former high school or place of work and kill as many people as he can. Or someone a good deal older wants to kill his neighbor because he believes the neighbor is a shapeshifter.[296] Or is obsessed with "hypersexual Martians who disguise themselves as humans but really look like giant green frogs with proboscises on the top of their heads."[297] Or is a senior with dementia who refuses to give up his guns and makes threats against the mailman.

The Issue

Should we have "red flag" or "extreme risk" gun seizure laws that authorize the temporary removal of guns from persons determined by a court to be at serious risk of harming themselves or others?

"Red flag" or "extreme risk" laws[298] allow law enforcement and families to ask a court for an order authorizing the police to remove guns from an individual they believe may be about to harm himself or someone else.[299] *If* the evidence presented convinces the court that the individual is indeed a danger to himself or others, the court issues an order that allows the police to take the individual's gun or guns away temporarily and bars the individual from buying guns while the order is in effect.

After the order issues, the individual may request a hearing, usually within two or three weeks, to argue for the return of his guns. Based on the evidence presented, the court determines if it's safe to do so.

Although red flag or extreme risk laws vary a bit from state-to-state, they are civil proceedings that focus on the individual's *behavior*, including threats, drug use, and the like. The idea is to target risky behavior. Unlike a civil commitment proceeding, in which the court may order the individual confined to a psychiatric hospital, a red flag or extreme risk gun-seizure order simply authorizes police to seize his (or, less often, her) guns.

A red flag or extreme risk gun seizure order is far less intrusive than locking someone up in a psychiatric facility. And, unlike a brief mental health commitment, a red flag order takes the individual's guns away, at least temporarily.

In short, red flag or extreme risk gun seizures avoid the intrusiveness, stigma, and expense associated with involuntary mental health commitments, but still attempt to keep individuals in crisis from killing themselves or others. As Allison Anderman, managing attorney at the Giffords Law Center, explained, "The whole point of these laws is to disarm someone without subjecting them to the stigma of involuntary commitment."[300]

Proponents argue that police need this tool when someone posts a message on social media announcing that tomorrow, he is going to become the next school or workplace shooter, or otherwise makes it clear he is an immediate threat to himself or others. Or a husband tells his wife that he has been laid off from work and is going to take his gun to the lake, get drunk, and kill himself.

Opponents of these laws argue that the police have no business intervening unless and until the individual—the would-be school shooter, or more often, the husband who intimates he's going to kill himself—actually kills some school kids or himself. Or at least until a court can hold an adversarial hearing.

Opponents also argue that temporary restraining orders, issued without notice to the gun owner and without an adversarial hearing before the order issues, are unconstitutional violations of due process. They offer no authority for this other than their own opinion. Courts, however, routinely issue temporary restraining orders without notice and without an adversarial hearing first, when doing so could lead to irreparable harm. *See, e.g.,* Rule 65(b), Federal Rules of Civil Procedure. A prompt hearing after the temporary order issues satisfies due process. This is something every first-year law student learns.

At least one pro-gun organization has trafficked in the fevered fantasy that a future liberal administration might use a federal red flag law to confiscate guns from conservatives.[301] The same organization beefed up its attack with an article penned by Congressman Thomas Massie (R., Ky.) and controversial gun-policy researcher John R. Lott, Jr.[302] They compare red flag laws to the movie *Minority Report.*[303]

As discussed below, by overwhelming majorities, most of us think the courts and police *should* be authorized to intervene before there are dead bodies on the ground.

Gun Suicides

Before the Stoneman Douglas High School shooting in Parkland, Florida, only five states had "red flag" laws. Connecticut was the first, joined later by Indiana, California, Washington, and Oregon. Since the Parkland shooting, more states have enacted these laws. In practice, families and police have used those laws mainly to prevent suicides.

The Second Amendment crowd—*i.e.,* those most stridently opposed to almost any effort to reduce our country's gun violence—dismiss gun suicides out of hand as not part of our gun violence problem. In their view, aside from the headline-grabbing mass shootings, our gun problem consists almost entirely of home intrusions, black-on-black violence, and gang shootings. Everything else, they'll tell you, is a mental health or a personal responsibility problem that no constraint on who can have guns will reduce.

According to a CDC report, there were about 45,000 suicides (by all means, not just guns) in the United States in 2016.[304] That was more than double the number of homicides that year. Suicide rates in the United States have risen nearly 30% since 1999 and are continuing to rise. In 2016, suicide decedents were predominantly non-Hispanic whites (83.6%) and males (76.8%).

The highest *rates* of suicide occurred in rural states with high levels of gun ownership, drug use, and economic hardship—states like Alaska, Oklahoma, Montana, and Wyoming. The highest *increases in the rates* of suicide also occurred in mostly rural, famously gun-friendly states—Vermont, New Hampshire, and North Dakota.

The CDC report also analyzed suicides in the twenty-seven states for which data about the mental health status of the suicide decedents were available. In those states, in 2015, there were 11,039 suicides among individuals with no known mental health condition (54%) and 9,407 with known mental health conditions (46%). Those without known mental illness were often experiencing relationship problems and other life stressors such as criminal/legal matters or eviction/loss of home.

In just about half of all suicides (48.5%), the decedent used a gun. Individuals *without* any known mental condition used a gun more often than not—55.3%. Those *with* known mental conditions used guns somewhat less—40.6%. Suicide decedents *without* any known mental health condition were almost three times as likely to commit murder-suicide—typically, the individual kills a spouse, former spouse, or dating partner, and maybe their kids, before killing himself.

Even when the person committing suicide doesn't kill someone else first, gun suicides are particularly gruesome for the survivors, who have to clean up the bloody mess gun suicides leave behind.[305] And, unlike other methods, gun-suicide attempts are almost always fatal.

What We Want

What do we, the American public, think about this? Do we want our legislators to enact "red flag" or "extreme risk" laws? Or do we think it's better to allow someone who is obviously in crisis to keep his guns until he kills himself or shoots someone else?

Johns Hopkins Survey Finds 79% Support for Red Flag Laws

Barry *et al.*, AJPH - 2018

In early 2017, well before the Las Vegas Strip and Stoneman Douglas shootings, a team of researchers from the Johns Hopkins Center for Gun

Policy and Research arranged for a poll to assess public support for a variety of gun issues. In the survey, **79%** of adults favored, "Allowing family members to ask the court to temporarily remove guns from a relative who they believe is at risk of harming himself or others."[306]

Since then, quite a few polls have come up with similar results.

Overall Results

Registered Voters

Favor	*Oppose*	*Polling Dates*	*Poll*
89%	8%	3/3-5/18	Quinnipiac
85%	12%	4/8-11/18	ABC/WaPo*
81%	13%	8/11-13/19	Fox News
73%	21%	8/16-20/19	Monmouth*
80%	15%	8/21-26/19	Quinnipiac
86%	12%	9/2-5/19	ABC/WaPo*
73%	23%	9/5-8/19	NPR/PBS*

Registered Voter Averages: **81%** vs. **15%**. *Ratio: 5.5 to 1.*

Adults

Favor	*Oppose*	*Polling Dates*	*Poll*
78%	11%	3/14-19/18	AP-NORC
79%	12%	4/8-11/18	ABC/WaPo*
77%	21%	7/16-21/19	AMP (SSRS)
76%	22%	8/10-14/19	NBC/WSJ
75%	20%	8/16-20/19	Monmouth*
86%	12%	9/2-5/19	ABC/WaPo*
72%	23%	9/5-8/19	NPR/PBS*

Adult Averages: **78%** vs. **17%**. *Ratio: 4.5 to 1*

Combined Averages: **79%** vs. **16%**. *Ratio: 4.9 to 1.*

* *Note: The ABC/Washington Post, NPR/PBS/Marist, and Monmouth surveys reported results for both adults and registered voters. The NPR/PBS/Marist poll had an unexpectedly large percentage of gun owners (40% of adults, 42% of voters), likely skewing its result toward less support and more opposition.*

Averaging these polls, **81%** of registered voters and **78%** of adults supported taking guns away from individuals if a judge determines they are a danger to themselves or others; on average, **15%** of registered voters and **17%** of adults opposed acting until the individual in crisis kills himself or someone else.

Crosstab Data

Only some of these surveys published crosstab data.

Republicans

Favor	Oppose	Polling Dates	Poll
89%	9%	3/3-5/18	Quinnipiac
70%	27%	7/16-21/19	AMP
75%	19%	8/11-13/19	Fox
72%	25%	8/21-26/19	Quinnipiac
85%	14%	9/2-5/19	ABC/WaPo
57%	36%	9/5-8/19	NPR/PBS

Averages: **75%** *vs.* **22%***. Ratio: 3.4 to 1.*

Democrats

Favor	Oppose	Polling Dates	Sponsor or Pollster
94%	4%	3/3-5/18	Quinnipiac
85%	13%	7/16-21/19	APM/SSRS
88%	7%	8/11-13/19	Fox
89%	6%	8/21-26/19	Quinnipiac
94%	5%	9/2-5/19	ABC/WaPo
93%	5%	9/5-8/19	NPR/PBS

Averages: **91%** *vs.* **7%***. Ratio: 13.6 to 1.*

Gun Owners/Households

Only two polls broke out gun owners, but in those polls, gun owners favored red flag/extreme risk laws by a margin of two to one:

Favor	Oppose	Polling Dates	Poll
67%	30%	7/16-21/19	AMP/SSRS[307]

Favor	Oppose	Polling Dates	Poll
62%	34%	9/5-8/19	NPR/PBS

Averages: **64.5%** *vs.* **32%**. *Ratio: 2 to 1.*

Households in which one or more individuals owned a gun overwhelmingly supported enactment of red flag laws:

Favor	Oppose	Polling Dates	Poll
87%	9%	3/3-5/18	Quinnipiac
78%	18%	7/16-21/19	AMP (SSRS)
79%	17%	8/21-26/19	Quinnipiac
77%	17%	8/11-13/19	Fox News
82%	16%	9/2-5/19	ABC/WaPo

Averages: **81%** *vs.* **15%**. *Ratio: 5.2 to 1.*

Note: Most polls do not break out what people who live in "no gun" households think. The September 2019 ABC/Washington Post poll is an exception. In that poll, among those in households where no one owned a gun, support ran **91%** in favor and **6%** opposed.[308] About 60% of us live in "no gun" households.

Education

We start with a look at the impact a college education has, without regard to race.

Less Than A College (Bachelor) Degree

Favor	Oppose	Polling Dates	Poll (Target)
88%	9%	3/3-5/18	Quinnipiac (Whites)
81%	15%	8/21-26/19	Quinnipiac (Whites)
69%	25%	9/5-8/19	NPR/PBS (Whites)

Averages: **79%** *vs.* **16%**. *Ratio: 4.9 to 1.*

College (Bachelor) Degree or More

Favor	Oppose	Polling Dates	Poll (Target)
91%	7%	3/3-5/18	Quinnipiac (Whites)
82%	16%	7/16-21/19	AMP/SSRS (All)

82%	13%	8/21-26/19	Quinnipiac (Whites)
74%	22%	9/5-8/19	NPR/PBS (Whites)

*Averages: **82%** vs. **15%**. Ratio: 5.7 to 1.*

The September 2019 NPR/PBS NewsHour/Marist poll made available crosstabs that cut deeper and allow us to factor in race and gender as well.

White Non-College Graduates

	Favor	Oppose
➡ **White Men**	**59%**	**36%**
White Women	78%	15%

White College Graduates

	Favor	Oppose
White Men	72%	25%
White Women	76%	20%

In each of these breakouts, majorities of whites—non-college grads and grads, males and females—supported red flag laws. But white men who were not college graduates were clearly out of step with whites in the other categories—and thus even further out of step with the country as a whole.

White men without college degrees are more likely to own guns than other demographic groups.[309] They are also more likely to carry a concealed gun.[310] As we saw in Chapter 2, white men are also committing suicides with guns at much higher rates than other demographic groups. This and other factors suggest that whites without college educations, and especially white males without college degrees, are experiencing a crisis. The NPR/PBS NewsHour/Marist poll tells us that white men without college degrees are also more likely to object to laws that authorize the police to take guns away from those who may be about to kill themselves.

But these polls, by themselves, don't explain why any of that is so.

Polling Wrap Up

On average, voters favored red flag laws about **81%** to **15%**. Adults were in favor **78%** to **17%**.

Republicans were in favor **75%** to **22%**, and Democrats favored red flag laws by an overwhelming **91%** to **7%**. In two polls, gun owners supported red flag laws, on average, **65%** to **32%**. Gun households supported red flag laws **81%** to **15%**. Non-college grads split **79%** in favor and **16%** against. College grads split **82%** to **15%**.

White men without college degrees were the outliers, with only **59%** in favor of red flag laws and **36%** opposed. Nonetheless, even in that demographic, a majority favored red flag laws.

What We're Getting Instead

The NRA Pretends to Endorse Extreme Risk Legislation

In March 2018, shortly after the Stoneman Douglas High School shooting, the National Rifle Association expressed carefully cribbed support for red flag laws, which it calls "extreme risk" legislation. Chris Cox, the then longtime executive director of the NRA's Institute for Legislative Action, conceded, "We need to stop dangerous people before they act. So, Congress should provide funding for states to adopt risk protection orders."[311]

Everytown for Gun Safety noted:

> While this could be an important reversal from an organization that has spent years advocating against these policies, the NRA has already issued a lengthy list of conditions any Red Flag bill would need to meet to win its support."[312]

Everytown noted that "the question remains whether this is a sincere effort from the NRA, or an attempt to deflect."

Everytown added:

> If the NRA is serious about supporting these important bills, it can make that clear by backing Red Flag proposals pending in 21 states: Alaska, Alabama, Delaware, Hawaii, Iowa, Illinois, Kansas, Kentucky, Louisiana, Massachusetts, Maryland, Michigan, Minnesota, Missouri, North Carolina, New Jersey, New York, Pennsylvania, Rhode Island, Tennessee, Vermont and the District of Columbia.

The NRA did not support any of those bills; in fact, in some states, its opposition was critical in killing "extreme risk" legislation.

In 2019, a series of revelations about lavish spending and self-dealing by the NRA's executive director, Wayne LaPierre, rocked the NRA.[313] Its board closed ranks behind LaPierre and forced out its ceremonial president, Oliver North, after he called for reforms. Several board members who objected to the lavish spending also left or were pushed out. Eventually, the NRA forced out Chris Cox, its number two man and chief lobbyist. It was Cox who had crafted the NRA's strategy of deflecting criticism by pretending to endorse extreme risk laws.

After the August 2019 shootings in El Paso, Texas, and Dayton, Ohio, President Trump endorsed red flag laws once again, as he had after the Parkland shooting. The NRA's embattled executive director, Wayne LaPierre, spoke with Trump and warned him that the NRA's members opposed red flag laws. Trump vacillated and said the NRA's views should be "respected." As we've seen, after Trump gave in to NRA pressure, support for red flag laws dropped a bit, especially among white males without college educations.

If there was confusion about where the NRA stood, there was no question about where the National Association of Gun Rights (NAGR stood. NAGR, which is even more extreme than the NRA, objects to red flag laws.[314] In 2019, it greeted visitors to its website with a red and black banner spread against a photograph of SWAT team officers pointing their guns ominously. The banner read:

STOP RED FLAG GUN CONFISCATION.

Substantively, NAGR condemns red flag orders as violations of due process. It refuses to acknowledge that, where giving notice may lead to irreparable injury, courts routinely issue temporary restraining orders without advance notice to the subject party—and then hold a hearing. Unlike NAGR, courts and legal scholars do not consider that a violation of due process.

The Federal Commission on School Safety

In March 2018, in response to the school shooting in Parkland, Florida, and the March for Our Lives, President Trump appointed The Federal Commission on School Safety to study school shootings. To head the Commission, the president appointed Education Secretary Betsy DeVos, who famously argued during her confirmation hearing that schools should have guns to protect against grizzly bear attacks.[315]

The Commission released its final report just before Christmas 2018 and offered the reader chapters like "Curating a Healthier and Safer Approach." The report addressed "extreme risk" laws in Chapter 10. That chapter explained what these laws are and noted that thirteen states had a red flag law in effect, including eight states that enacted red flag laws after the Parkland shooting. The report contained a helpful table listing the laws and providing citations and brief summaries of their essential elements.

After noting that President Trump had pronounced himself in favor of extreme risk laws, the report recommended that states *should* adopt extreme risk protection laws. But echoing the NRA, it cautioned that those laws should require high levels of proof. They should also provide for automatic hearings after *ex parte* orders, rather than requiring a hearing only if the individual affected actually wanted one. Echoing the NRA, the Commission also discussed safeguards against people maliciously filing requests for extreme risk protection orders, as if that were a real problem.

The report did not mention the critical importance of law enforcement acting promptly on red flag orders by removing guns from the person found to be an imminent danger to himself or others. Instead, it stressed that law enforcement should promptly return the individual's guns when the order expires.

Congressional Action and Inaction

As we've seen, supermajorities of Americans support the enactment of red flag/extreme risk laws. After reviewing the empirical literature, President Trump's Commission concluded that red flag laws work and recommended that states should enact them. As a result, one might expect that Congress and most states have enacted federal and state red flag laws. But that is not the case.

At the federal level, in the aftermath of the Parkland shooting, Senators Graham (R. S.C.) and Blumenthal (D. Conn.) introduced a federal red flag bill that would have given federal courts jurisdiction to issue temporary gun seizure orders that would be effective across state lines.[316] Their bill did not even get a hearing in Majority Leader Mitch McConnell's Senate.

Senators Marco Rubio (R. Fla.) and Bill Nelson (D. Fla.) introduced a different bill. They wrote their proposal to meet precisely the NRA's recommendation that any federal legislation provide federal grants to help states and local governments implement red flag laws—if they can pass those laws in the face of gun lobby opposition.[317] The Senate didn't consider their bill either.

Some States Act…

Before the Parkland shooting and the student leaders there began the #NeverAgain campaign, only five states had "red flag" laws: California, Connecticut, Indiana, Oregon, and Washington.[318] Since the shooting at Stoneman Douglas High School, several states have enacted red flag laws:[319]

- **Florida:** Under pressure from students and their parents, Florida's legislature enacted a red flag law as part of the "Marjory Stoneman Douglas High School Public Safety Act."
- **Maryland:** Republican Governor Larry Hogan signed a red flag bill, H.B. 1302, into law on April 9, 2018.
- **Vermont:** The legislature passed a red flag bill without a single dissenting vote. The bill, however, is the narrowest in the country. It only permits a state's Attorney or the Office of the Attorney General to request a risk protection order from a court. (Signed into law April 11, 2018.)

- **Rhode Island:** Democratic Governor Gina Raimondo signed a red flag bill into law on June 1, 2018.
- **New Jersey:** Democratic Governor Philip Murphy signed a red flag bill into law on June 13, 2018.
- **Delaware**: Democratic Governor John Carney signed House Substitute for H.B. 222 into law on June 27, 2018.
- **Massachusetts:** Republican Governor Charlie Baker signed H.B. 467 into law on July 3, 2018.
- **Illinois:** Republican Governor Bruce Rauner signed a red flag bill into law on July 16, 2018.
- **New York.** On Feb 25, 2019, when New York Governor Mario Cuomo signed S.B. 2451, New York's red flag law, Speaker of the House Nancy Pelosi showed up to witness the signing and congratulate him.[320]
- **Colorado:** Democratic Governor Jared Polis signed HB 1177 into law on April 12, 2019, making Colorado the fifteenth state to adopt an extreme risk protection law.[321] (Outraged that the government might take guns away from mentally ill, suicidal, and other folks in imminent danger of killing themselves or others, gun rights activists in Colorado mounted a campaign to recall the state legislator who introduced the red flag bill.[322] The campaign failed.)
- **Indiana**: On May 6, 2019, Indiana enacted HB 165, updating its first-in-the-nation extreme risk protection law.[323]
- **Washington:** On May 7, 2019, Democratic Governor Jay Inslee signed into law Washington S.B. 5027, which updated its 2016 extreme risk protection law.[324] The bill allows for Extreme Risk Protection Orders (ERPOs) for individuals under the age of 18. If a court believes an ERPO is necessary, the order will prohibit the minor from purchasing, possessing, or receiving a gun.
- **Nevada:** Nevada became the sixteenth state to adopt a red flag law, when Democratic Governor Steve Sisolak signed AB291, the so-called "1 October Bill," into law on June 14, 2019.[325]
- **Hawaii:** Hawaii became the seventeenth state. Democratic Governor David Ige signed S.B. 1466 into law on June 26, 2019.[326]
- **California**: California expanded who may invoke its red flag law, allowing employers, co-workers, and teachers to ask a judge to

disarm dangerous individuals.[327] Democratic Governor Gavin Newsom signed Senate Bill 61 into law on October 11, 2019.
- **New Mexico:** On February 25, 2020, flanked by gun violence survivors, Democratic Governor Michelle Lujan Grisham put her signature on a red flag bill, making New Mexico the eighteenth state to enact a red flag law.[328]
- **Virginia:** Governor Ralph Northam signed extreme risk protection legislation into law on April 10, 2020.[329]

Washington, D.C., also enacted a red flag law.[330]

... But Most States Don't

In 2018, after the Parkland shooting, state legislators introduced red flag laws in these states, but didn't succeed in getting their legislatures to pass their bills: Alabama (H.B. 478), Alaska (H.B. 75), Arizona (S.B. 1347), Iowa (H.F. 2180), Kansas (H.B. 2769), Kentucky (H.B. 544), Louisiana (H.B. 448), Maine (L.D. 1884), Minnesota (HF 4360), Missouri (S.B. 1101), New York (A11148), North Carolina (H.B. 723), Tennessee (H.B. 961), and Utah (H.B. 483).[331] In 2019, however, New York reversed course and enacted a red flag law.

In sum, in recent years, about as many states have refused to pass red flag laws as have enacted them. In most of these states, Republican legislators kept red flag bills from coming to the floor for a vote. That way, they did not have to go on record as voting against a commonsense measure most Americans wanted.

Texas fell into that category. In May 2018, 17-year-old Dimitrios Pagourtzis, who had posted on his Facebook page a photo of himself in a "Born to Kill" shirt,[332] killed 10 and wounded 13 at a high school in Santa Fe, Texas. Governor Greg Abbott said that Pagourtzis "advertised his intentions but somehow slipped through the cracks." Abbott briefly suggested he was open to a red flag law.

Lest anyone get the mistaken impression that Republican leaders in the state were actually open to the idea of protecting the state's schoolchildren, legislative leaders quickly squelched talk of enacting a red flag law. They made it clear that they were not interested in removing guns from someone like Dimitrios "Born to Kill" Pagourtzis, Nikolas Cruz, Travis Reinking, Ian Howard, or ... well, anyone, no matter how disturbed or threatening.[333] Despite widespread public support in the state for a red flag law, they refused to enact one.[334]

Kentucky also fell into the category of states where legislators introduced a red flag bill, but Republican leadership refused to give the bill a hearing. In January 2018, just three weeks before the Parkland shooting, Kentucky experienced a shooting in a high school in rural Benton, Kentucky. The state also had a racially motivated shooting outside a grocery store near Louisville (the shooter wanted to kill blacks in a nearby church, but the church was closed and locked). Kentucky also had at least two near misses in 2018.[335]

The Kentucky legislature was still in session when the Benton and Parkland school shootings occurred but refused to allow a vote on a red flag law or any other legislation aimed at stopping school shootings or mass firearm violence.[336] Instead, the Kentucky legislature enacted legislation to allow concealed carry without a license, making it likely that Kentucky's already high homicide rate would increase.

Mike DeWine, Ohio's new Republican Governor, said he supported weakening gun laws but also said he intended to push for a red flag law that met the NRA's "due process" criteria—if he could find a version that Republicans in the state legislature would support.[337] Evidently, that wasn't possible because, for a time at least, Governor DeWine no longer talked of pushing for a "red flag" law.

But Governor DeWine did keep his campaign promise to put the gun industry ahead of Ohio's citizens. The first bill DeWine signed into law, H.B. 228, barred local governments from enacting gun-violence-prevention measures—shutting the door on attempts by Cleveland, Columbus, and Cincinnati to curtail gun violence. H.B. 228 also shifted the burden of proof in self-defense cases from the shooter to prosecutors, overturning—at least in Ohio—what had been the law since the country's founding.

After the shooting in Dayton, Ohio, Governor DeWine attempted to speak at a vigil for the victims. The crowd drowned him out with a chant of "Do something." Two days later, DeWine once again spoke of trying to work with legislators to pass a red flag bill. As this book went to press, legislators from Ohio's rural areas weren't interested in supporting his effort.[338]

Conclusion

The day-to-day experience of the states that have enacted red flag laws demonstrates that they save lives.[339] On average, registered voters supported red flag laws 81% to 15% or about five to 1. Among adults, the split was 77% to 18% or about four to 1.

President Trump's school violence commission endorsed red flag laws. President Trump himself endorsed red flag laws when it made him look good in front of television cameras but retreated when the NRA pressured him.[340]

Despite what the American people want and despite President Trump's on-again, off-again support, Congress and most states still refuse to enact red flag laws.

10. Should We License Gun Owners?

Item: *Illinois requires a Firearm Owner Identification (FOID) card to own a firearm. Due to mental health concerns, police revoked Donald Garrity's Firearm Owners Identification card in 2015, and Garrity turned his Glock 17 into the police. Subsequently, the police allowed Garrity's fiancé to have the weapon. Months later, Garrity used the gun to commit suicide.*[341]

Item: *After Jeffrey Reinking engaged in a string of bizarre acts, including breaching the White House grounds, the Sheriff's office in Tazewell County, Illinois, revoked Reinking's FOID card. The Sheriff's office also seized Reinking's Bushmaster AR-15-style rifle but later entrusted it to Reinking's father, who promised not to let his son have it back. Reinking responded by moving to Tennessee, which does not require a permit to buy or own a gun. There he showed up at a Waffle House with the Bushmaster AR-15-style rifle, killed four, and injured two others. But for a customer who rushed Reinking and wrestled away his rifle, the death toll would have been worse.*

Item: *In January 2019, Illinois partially closed the omission that allowed Garrity and Reinking to get their weapons back. That's when a law took effect prohibiting gun transfers to someone at the same address as someone whose FOID card the police have revoked.*[342]

Every state requires its citizens to get drivers' licenses before they are permitted to drive a motor vehicle. Every state also suspends or revokes a driver's license if the driver accumulates too many convictions for driving under the influence or other infractions. Similarly, some states require individuals to obtain a license *to own or possess* a gun. Others require a permit *to purchase* a gun. For simplicity, this chapter discusses licenses to have a gun and permits-to-purchase a gun together.

Most states do not require gun owners to obtain a license or permit-to-purchase. In those that do, licensing and permit-to-purchase laws vary from state to state.[343] Some are in addition to background checks at the point-of-sale; others give the holder a pass on background checks. Some apply only to handguns; others apply to any gun. Individuals in active military service and law enforcement typically do not need to have a license or permit for weapons they personally own.

The process for obtaining a license or permit-to-purchase also varies from state to state. Most states require the applicant to take a course on gun safety and the state's gun laws. Generally, the applicant must also make an in-person trip to the county sheriff's office or some other local law enforcement office, where the police take fingerprints and photo-graph the applicant. And that, advocates say, is one of the law's strengths: Showing up in person at a law enforcement office dis-courages the "lie and try" attempts that are frequent occurrences at gun dealers.

Law enforcement officers do a background check before issuing or denying a gun license or permit. When necessary to investigate the individual's background, law enforcement may spend significantly longer than the three days allowed for a NICS background check. That's another strength, advocates say.

In some states, these licensing laws allow law enforcement to use judgment and experience in dealing with applications from people they know are unstable, violent, or trouble, but who have not yet been convicted of a felony or involuntarily committed to a mental institution. From prior run-ins, local law enforcement officers often know folks like a Jeffrey Reinking or a Nikolas Cruz and will refuse to issue, or will revoke, a license or permit to someone who is unstable and obviously des-tined for trouble.

In other states, lobbyists and gun-friendly legislators have incorporated language into their states' laws that requires law enforcement to issue ("shall issue") a license if no disqualifying facts, *e.g.,* felony convictions or involuntary mental health commitments, turn up—guaranteeing that a Jeffrey Reinking or a Nikolas Cruz can get a gun (or a concealed carry permit).

This chapter began with an analogy to driver's licenses. Gun rights advocates object to that analogy. The Constitution protects the right to bear arms, they argue, but it does not protect the right to drive an automobile or truck. The argument is not entirely specious, but it is mostly beside the point.

As every first-year law student learns, the government may regulate the exercise of a constitutional right so long as it does not unduly burden that right. The First Amendment, for example, protects freedom of speech, but we require television and radio stations to obtain broadcast licenses from the Federal Communications Commission (FCC). We just don't allow the FCC to deny or terminate broadcast licenses because it (or the president) doesn't like the political content of what the station broadcasts. We also allow the police to put certain restrictions on where demonstrators may protest, so long as those restrictions are not excessive or driven by the political leanings of the protestors. The Sixth Amendment protects the right to counsel, but we still require attorneys to have licenses. And so on.

States require licenses to protect public health and safety. States, or at least some of them, have licensed cosmetologists, interior designers, dog trainers, casket sellers, hair shampooers, animal massage practitioners, and faith healers. If we can protect the public from the likes of untrained hair shampooers and animal massage practitioners, surely, proponents argue, we can protect the public from mentally unstable and dangerous would-be gun owners.

The Issue

Should we require individuals to obtain a permit from the Bureau of Alcohol, Tobacco, Firearms and Explosives or from local law enforcement to own or buy a firearm or ammunition?

Gun owner licensing laws serve much the same purpose as the federal background check law. Unfortunately, ATF and other federal law enforcement officials rarely prosecute prohibited individuals who "lie and try" to buy guns.[344] State licensing laws require individuals seeking a firearm license or permit to go to a local law enforcement office, where they are photographed and fingerprinted. This discourages bad actors who would be willing to try their luck with a background check at a gun store. And as mentioned above, these laws also typically allow more time for a thorough investigation.

Gun licensing laws also help to fill a gap in federal law. As we've noted elsewhere, federal law requires background checks for purchases from federally licensed gun dealers but allows private sales between strangers with no background check and no record keeping.[345] States that prohibit a sale to anyone without a license or permit-to-purchase give an honest seller a way to make sure he or she isn't selling a gun to a criminal or fugitive: The seller can ask to see the buyer's FOID or "gun card." (There is anecdotal evidence that in states that do not license gun owners, *some* sellers ask to see a concealed-carry permit as a substitute for a gun card.[346])

Federal law exempts certain gun license holders from the national background check system, provided the license or permit was issued not more than five years before the gun purchase or transfer.[347] As of May 10, 2017, ATF recognized gun licenses from only a handful of states.[348] Additionally, ATF recognized concealed-carry permits from some states as exempting purchasers from the NICS.

Although the Giffords Law Center praises the virtues of licensing gun owners and permits to purchase guns, it expresses concern about skipping the NICS background check at the point of sale for individuals who may have obtained a license up to five years earlier.[349]

> While these requirements ensure that a background check has been conducted at some point, a person may fall within a prohibited category after the license or permit is issued but before the time the person attempts to purchase a firearm. **As a result, licensing laws do not necessarily prevent prohibited people from accessing firearms as effectively as point-of-transfer background checks.** [Emphasis in original.]

But it doesn't have to be that way. In Massachusetts, for example, someone wanting to buy a gun must go to his or her local police department and obtain a permit to purchase first. Before the police issue a permit, they do a background check. And the gun purchase is logged into a database—even private transfers must be registered. That system may be the reason Massachusetts consistently has one of the lowest gun fatality rates in the country.[350]

A very recent and impressively thorough study suggested that "fire-arm purchaser or ownership licensing with fingerprinting reduce the risk of fatal mass shootings in addition to firearm homicides more broadly."[351]

What We Want

Polling on how the public feels about gun-owner licensing laws is thin and mostly from 2019. That which is available, however, suggests that the public, including gun owners, support licensing gun owners.

Barry *et al.* (2017)

In their January 2017 in-depth polling on gun violence prevention measures, Colleen L. Barry and her colleagues[352] in the Johns Hopkins Center for Gun Policy and Research asked if the survey respondents supported or opposed:

> Requiring a person to obtain a license from a local law enforcement agency before buying a gun to verify their identity and ensure that they are not legally prohibited from having a gun?

Overall, **77%** supported this idea. Both gun owners and non-gun owners were supportive, but not at the same level. Some **81%** of non-gun owners supported licensing gun owners. A lower, but still robust, **63%** of gun owners agreed.

Overall Results

Three polls since October 1, 2017, asked about licensing gun owners:

Favor	*Oppose*	*Polling Dates*	*Poll*
77%	19%	5/16-20/19	Quinnipiac
82%	16%	8/21-26/19	Quinnipiac
72%	25%	9/5-8/19	NPR/PBS/Marist

Average: **77%** *vs.* **20%**. *Ratio: 3.9 to 1.*

The main takeaway is that a supermajority of Americans supports licensing gun owners.

Republicans

Favor	Oppose	Polling Dates	Poll
65%	31%	5/16-20/19	Quinnipiac
69%	28%	8/21-26/19	Quinnipiac
58%	37%	9/5-8/19	NPR/PBS

*Average: **64%** vs. **32%**. Ratio: 2 to 1.*

Again, the headline is that a majority of Republicans supported licensing gun owners. But, not surprisingly, more Republicans than the public in general opposed requiring gun owners to get a license or permit.

On a technical note, the September 2019 NPR/PBS poll, which had far more gun owners in its survey than expected, showed lower support (about nine percentage points less than the average of the other two polls) and more opposition (about +7.5 points).

Gun Owners

What do gun owners think about licensing gun owners?

Favor	Oppose	Polling Dates	Poll
60%	35%	5/16-20/19	Quinnipiac
72%	25%	8/21-26/19	Quinnipiac
57%	40%	9/5-8/19	NPR/PBS

*Averages: **63%** in favor and **33%** opposed. Ratio: 1.9 to 1.*

Education

Less Than A Bachelor Degree

Favor	Oppose	Polling Dates	Poll
72%	23%	5/16-20/2019	Quinnipiac (Whites)
81%	17%	8/21-26/19	Quinnipiac (Whites)
68%	27%	9/5-8/19	NPR/PBS

*Average: **74%** favor, **22%** oppose. Ratio: 3.4 to 1.*

Bachelor Degree or More

Favor	Oppose	Polling Dates	Poll
82%	15%	5/16-20/2019	Quinnipiac (Whites)
80%	17%	8/21-26/19	Quinnipiac (Whites)
80%	18%	9/5-8/19	NPR/PBS

*Average: **81%** favor, **17%** oppose. Ratio: 4.8 to 1.*

As these tables indicate, supermajorities of those with and without college degrees favored licensing gun owners. And, as usual, support for doing something about gun violence was a little higher (+7 percentage points) among college graduates.

The two Quinnipiac polls provided another look. They broke out white men and white women:

Quinnipiac	**May 2019**	**Aug. 2019**
White Men	68%/28%	70%/28%
White Women	85%/10%	90%/6%

The 17- and 20-point gaps in support between white men and white women are striking. The September NPR/PBS News Hour/Marist poll went even deeper. It broke out white men and women who did and did not graduate from college with a Bachelor's degree:

NPR/PBS/Marist (Sept. 2019)

White Men and Women	*Favor*	*Oppose*
Men Non-College Grad	58%	37%
Women Non-College Grad	78%	17%
Men College Grad	76%	23%
Women College Grad	85%	13%

Once again, white men without college degrees were clear outliers.

Polling Wrap Up

On average, polls of the public at large show 77% in favor of licensing gun owners and 20% opposed, or almost four to one in favor. Among Republicans that drops, on average, to 64% in favor and 32% against, but that's still two-to-one in favor. The tally is essentially the same among gun owners, 63% in favor and 33% opposed.

As we've seen throughout, support rose modestly with education. Those without Bachelor's degrees supported licensing gun owners 74% to 22%. Those with a Bachelor's degree or more, on average, favored licensing gun owners 81% to 17%. That's +7 points in support and -5 points opposition.

Race, gender, and education all affected the percentages that supported and opposed licensing gun owners. But the big takeaway is this: The minority who were least supportive/most opposed to licensing were white males who didn't graduate from college. That's consistent with what we've seen previously.

What We're Getting Instead

If polls tell us that the public, including Republicans and gun owners, support licensing, then Congress and our state legislators are all over this, right?

Ah, not exactly.

Congress has not enacted legislation that would require gun owners, or handgun owners, or even assault-weapon owners, to obtain licenses. Federal law, therefore, does not require gun owners to get a license or permit from the ATF or from local law enforcement to buy or own a gun, even an assault weapon.

The situation is only a little better at the state level. A small minority of states require gun owners to obtain a license or permit to purchase. But the easy availability of guns from nearby states that do not require licensing undermine their efforts and allow guns to flood in.

11. Should We Register and Track Guns?

Item: When detectives request a "trace" on a crime gun, they hope to find out where and when the first retail purchaser bought the gun. On its website, The Bureau of Alcohol, Tobacco, Firearms and Explosives (ATF) informs visitors: "A key component of ATF's enforcement mission is the tracing of firearms on behalf of thousands of local, state, federal and international law enforcement agencies. Firearms trace data is critically important information developed by ATF."

Item: "Time-to-crime" refers to how long passes between a gun's purchase from a retail seller and its recovery at a crime scene. If police recover a gun at a crime scene less than twelve months from the retail sale, it suggests that the gun may have been bought for criminal purposes or illegally trafficked. The Trace's Daniel Nass and Alex Yablon used aggregated ATF trace data to find the source and destination states with the highest numbers of traced guns with a time-to-crime of under a year. At the top of the list? Guns moving from Nevada to California and from Alabama to Illinois.[353]

Item: Santino William Legan was one of those to transport a short time-to-crime gun from Nevada to California. Legan bought a WASR-10 semi-automatic rifle with a detachable magazine at Big Mikes Gun and Ammo in Fallon, Nevada, on July 9, 2019. The AK-47-style rifle is legal in Nevada but banned in California. Legan illegally transported the rifle into California, where, on July 29, 2019, he used the gun in a shooting rampage at the Garlic Festival in Gilroy, California.

When police officers in this country find a gun at a crime scene or take a gun from a suspect, they may contact the ATF's National Tracing Center (NTC) to learn the gun's provenance. In its most recent Fact Sheet, the

National Tracing Center says it processed more than 440,000 trace requests in fiscal year 2018.[354]

With one exception (discussed below), Congress forbids the ATF or its National Tracing Center from recording or keeping gun sale or gun owner data. Thus, the National Tracing Center may not keep gun-sale or gun-ownership information in a database or on a computer.[355] Instead, federal law requires gun manufacturers, importers, dealers, and collectors (collectively, federal firearms licensees or FFLs) to keep records of sales.

As a result, when it receives a request from a local police department for a gun trace, the National Tracing Center contacts the gun manufac-turer or importer. That entity culls through its records to determine which licensed gun dealer bought the gun. ATF then contacts the gun dealer and asks it to search its records to determine the identity of the retail customer who bought the gun.

Except in a handful of states that require gun registration, that's the end of the trail. If the original retail purchaser resold the gun, ATF and the policeman with a crime to solve might never learn who owned the gun when it was used to commit the crime.

In its most recent Fact Sheet, ATF says, "The goal of the NTC is to complete traces classified as 'Urgent' in less than 24 hours. Traces classi-fied as 'Routine' are completed within nine days on average. The law enforcement agency submitting the trace request determines [if the request is urgent or routine]."[356] If Congress would authorize the National Trac-ing Center to keep records of gun sales and store them in a database, most of those searches that now take nine days or more could be done in minutes.

The Issue

Should Congress authorize a national database with information about each gun sale or transfer?

This chapter discusses whether Congress should change the law to authorize ATF or its National Tracing Center to track gun sales and other transfers of ownership. To accomplish that, gun manufacturers, gun dealers, and gun owners would need to provide information to ATF on every gun sale or transfer. Gun owners would probably need to register their guns.

For ATF to handle gun traces quickly and efficiently, Congress would also need to allow ATF to store information about gun sales and other transfers of ownership electronically, *i.e.*, in a database. At present, Congress prohibits both, ostensibly to keep the federal government from confiscating the nation's privately held guns.

The Firearm Owners' Protection Act

The backstory begins with The Firearms Owners' Protection Act, which made the gun lobby's wish list the law.

President Ronald Reagan signed the Firearms Owners' Protection Act (FOPA into law on May 19, 1986.[357] Drafted by the NRA, the Act's sponsors argued that the legislation was necessary to protect gun owners' Second Amendment rights and perhaps more to the point, to protect licensed gun dealers from "harassment" by "heavy-handed" federal agents.

Among other things, the Firearms Owners' Protection Act (FOPA made it more difficult for law enforcement to convict *unlicensed* dealers of engaging in the business of selling guns without a license. (We're talking about folks like the unfortunate Tavares Colbert mentioned in Chapter 4. Under the Act, the government has to prove, beyond a reasonable doubt, that the individual "devotes time, attention, and labor" to dealing in firearms "with the principal objective of livelihood and profit" through "the repetitive purchase and sale of firearms," and is not someone "who makes occasional sales, exchanges, or purchases of firearms ..."[358] That provision, alone, was an invitation for the creation of a thriving black market in guns.

The Firearms Owners' Protection Act also made it more difficult for ATF to crack down on *licensed* dealers who sold guns illegally. The Act limited ATF to one inspection of a gun dealer each year. For any other inspection, it required ATF to obtain a search warrant after showing probable cause a crime had been committed.

Under the law, ATF may revoke a dealer's license only if it can prove that the dealer "willfully" violated gun laws and regulations.[359] The Firearms Owners' Protection Act also precluded ATF from revoking a dealer's license if the government prosecuted the dealer criminally and failed to prove its case beyond a reasonable doubt. In every other area of the law, civil proceedings, which require only proof by a predominance of the evidence, are permitted despite a failed criminal prosecution.[360]

The Act left intact a requirement that gun manufacturers, dealers, and other FFLs keep records of sales, but stipulated that the government could not require those records or their contents to "be recorded at or transferred to a facility owned, managed, or controlled by the United States, or any State or any political subdivision thereof …"[361] The Act also mandated that the federal government may not establish "any system of registration of firearms, firearms owners, or firearms transactions or disposition."[362]

Congress authorized one important exception. When a gun dealer goes out of business, it must transfer its sales records to ATF, or more precisely, to the National Tracing Center, where the paper records add to the mountains of similar records in its warehouses.[363] As noted above, the Firearm Owners' Protection Act effectively prohibited ATF from putting the data contained in those records into an electronic database.

In 2005, Congress relented slightly. It authorized the NTC to microfilm the defunct dealers' paper records, many of which were decaying. From time-to-time, mainly during Democratic Admini-strations, the National Tracing Center invites media outlets to see what it has to deal with when conducting a search for a defunct dealer's records. The result is a flurry of "You can't believe how bad it is" stories.[364]

What We Want

This chapter has the most surprising polling data in this book. Despite decades of fear-mongering by gun rights organizations about government confiscation of guns, polls show strong support for allowing the federal government, *i.e.,* ATF, to create a database that tracks all gun sales, so that the police can do their jobs of solving crimes and arresting bad guys.

In several polls since the Las Vegas Strip massacre, Morning Consult has asked registered voters: "Do you support or oppose each of the following ... Creating a national database with information about each gun sale?" After the Las Vegas Strip massacre, Ipsos asked about "Creating a federal government database to track all gun sales."[365] Pew queried about support for (and opposition to "Creating a federal government database to track all gun sales?"[366] Gallup asked if respondents favored or opposed, "Requiring all privately-owned guns to be registered with the police?"[367]

The results showed overwhelming support for tracking gun sales and for using a database—in other words, a computer—instead of using paper or microfilm records. As Monmouth put it,

> The vast majority of Americans support comprehensive background checks and a national registry for gun purchases. But there is a stark difference of opinion among gun owners on these policies depending on their affiliation with the National Rifle Association. NRA members are particularly worried that a national gun registry would be used to monitor other activities.[368]

These polls don't tell us whether gun owners were distrustful of the government even before they joined the NRA or became that way after marinating in NRA propaganda.

Overall Results

Favor	*Oppose*	*Polling Dates*	*Poll*
70%	29%	10/5-10/17	Gallup
77%	18%	10/5-9/17	Morning Consult
80%	20%	10/10-11/17	Ipsos/NPR
78%	16%	2/22-26/18	Morning Consult
77%	17%	3/29-4/1/18	Morning Consult
65%	28%	3/8/18	Monmouth[369]
77%	15%	8/2-6/18	Morning Consult
74%	25%	9/24-10/7/18	Pew
80%	20%	1/11-28/19	Ipsos/Reuters

Averages: **75%** *vs.* **21%**. *Ratio: 3.6 to 1.*

On average, **76%** believed that law enforcement should create a database tracking each gun sale; only **21%** opposed allowing law enforcement to do so.[370] Those who favored giving law enforcement this tool outnumbered those who disagreed by almost four-to-one.

Both men and women supported creating a database that tracked all gun sales, but there was a noticeable gender gap.

Men	*Women*	*Polling Dates*	*Poll*
72%/22%	80%/13%	10/5-9/17	Morning Consult
73%/22%	80%/12%	2/22-26/18	Morning Consult
52%/45%	77%/20%	3/2-5/18	Monmouth
70%/22%	81%/12%	3/29-4/18	Morning Consult
71%/22%	81%/9%	8/2-6/18	Morning Consult

Men: **68%** *in favor vs.* **27%** *opposed. Ratio: 2.5 to 1*

Women: **80%** *in favor vs.* **13%** *opposed. Ratio: 6 to 1*

The remarkable thing here is not that men were less supportive than women. That is the case for every gun-violence-prevention measure discussed in this book. The remarkable thing is that about 68% of men supported a national database that would track each gun sale, with only 27% opposed. That's roughly a 2.5-to-1 margin.

Republicans

Republicans were only a little less inclined than voters in general to support creating a database that tracks all gun sales:

Favor	*Oppose*	*Polling Dates*	*Poll*
69%	26%	10/5-9/17	Morning Consult
71%	29%	10/10-11/17	Ipsos
71%	24%	2/22-26/18	Morning Consult
55%	52%	3/8/18	Monmouth
68%	28%	3/29-4/1/18	Morning Consult
68%	25%	8/2-6/18	Morning Consult
74%	27%	1/11-28/19	Ipsos/Reuters

Averages: **68%** *vs.* **30%***. Ratio: 2.3 to 1.*

Almost seven in ten Republicans believed that Congress should authorize the federal government to create a database that tracks all gun sales. Even more remarkable, almost half of Republicans, ranging from 44% to 50%, pronounced themselves "strongly" in favor. (In the outlier Monmouth poll, that figure dropped to 30%.

Evidently, only about three-in-ten Republicans cling to the notion that allowing the federal government to track firearm sales will inevitably lead to the confiscation of their guns.

Trump 2016 Voters

Morning Consult broke out Donald Trump and Hillary Clinton voters. Trump voters fell out about the same as Republicans generally—mainly in favor of this measure:

Favor	*Oppose*	*Polling Dates*	*Poll*
69%	26%	10/5-9/17	Morning Consult
70%	26%	2/22-26/18	Morning Consult
65%	28%	3/29-4/18	Morning Consult
69%	27%	8/2-6/18	Morning Consult

Averages: **68%** *vs.* **27%**. *Ratio: 2.6 to 1.*

Averaging these polls, Trump voters favored this measure 68% to 27%. Clinton voters (*not shown*) favored creating a database that tracks gun sales by much larger margins, with about 89% in favor and only single-digit opposition.

Gun Households

Morning Consult provided crosstab data on gun households in three of these polls. The results are essentially the same in all three polls, suggesting little movement over this period:

Favor	*Oppose*	*Polling Dates*	*Poll*
68%	26%	10/5-9/17	Morning Consult
68%	27%	3/29-4/18	Morning Consult
68%	25%	8/2-6/18	Morning Consult

Averages: **68%** *vs.* **26%**. *Ratio: 2.6 to 1.*

As the table shows, those in gun households believe we should allow law enforcement to create a national database that tracks all gun transfers by almost 3-to-1. Those results are about the same as for Republicans and Trump voters.

As usual, households in which no one owned a gun were more supportive, favoring this measure by 81% to 10%, 82% to 10%, and 83% to 9%. It's worth remembering that far more of us—between 60% and 65%—live in households where no one owns a gun.

Monmouth University broke things out differently, showing results for gun owners who were and weren't NRA members. It also broke out non-gun owners.[371] There were remarkable differences in how NRA gun owners, non-NRA gun owners, and non-gun owners view this issue.

Favor	Oppose	Status
31%	68%	Gun Owner, NRA Member
52%	45%	Gun Owner, Not NRA Member
79%	20%	Non Gun Owner, Not NRA

Education

People at every educational level supported creating a national database to track gun transfers. As with most measures to address our gun violence, support rose modestly with more education.

Less Than College Degree

Favor	Oppose	Polling Dates	Poll
75%	18%	10/5-9/17	Morning Consult
76%	17%	2/22-26/18	Morning Consult
62%	34%	3/2-5/18	Monmouth
74%	18%	3/29-4/1/18	Morning Consult
73%	16%	8/2-6/18	Morning Consult

*Average: **72%** vs. **21%** opposed. Ratio: 3.5 to 1.*

Bachelor Degree

Favor	Oppose	Polling Dates	Poll
79%	16%	10/5-9/17	Morning Consult

Favor	Oppose	Polling Dates	Poll
81%	17%	2/22-26/18	Morning Consult
72%	26%	3/2-5/18	Monmouth
77%	18%	3/29-4/18	Morning Consult
82%	15%	8/2-6/18	Morning Consult

*Average: **78%** vs. **18%**. Ratio: 4.25 to 1*

Postgraduate

Favor	Oppose	Polling Dates	Poll
78%	17%	10/5-9/17	Morning Consult
85%	13%	2/22-26/18	Morning Consult
84%	11%	3/29-4/18	Morning Consult
87%	8%	8/2-6/18	Morning Consult

*Average: **84%** vs. **12%**. Ratio: 7 to 1.*

Annual Income Over $100,000

Those with annual incomes over $100,000 overwhelmingly favored creating a tracking system for gun transfers.

Favor	Oppose	Polling Dates	Poll
81%	15%	10/5-9/17	Morning Consult
82%	16%	2/22-26/18	Morning Consult
79%	15%	3/29-4/18	Morning Consult
81%	12%	8/2-6/18	Morning Consult

*Average: **81%** vs. **15%**. Ratio: 5.4 to 1*

Polling Wrap Up

To sum up, since the Las Vegas Strip shooting, polls have found high levels of support for creating a national database that tracks all gun transfers. Among registered voters, support has averaged **75%** to **21%**. That's an astonishing 54-point difference between the majority who support this measure and the minority who oppose it.

As usual, men were less supportive, and so were those without college degrees. Nonetheless, Republicans, Trump voters, and people at every education and income level supported allowing the federal government to track gun sales and allowing it to use a database to do so.

On this issue, NRA members, as a group, voiced more opposition. They are also notoriously more distrustful of the government than the rest of us.

What We're Getting Instead

Polls tell us that the public, including Republicans and gun owners, support allowing the federal government to track gun sales. Congress, however, not only refuses to allow ATF to create a national database to track gun transfers; it explicitly prohibits ATF from doing so. That makes it unnecessarily difficult and time-consuming to trace crime guns. It also makes it more difficult to detect "bad apple" gun dealers who divert guns to the black market and to Central American gun cartels.

The situation is only a little better at the state level, where only a tiny handful of states require gun registration. Hawaii requires all guns to be registered. New York requires handguns to be registered. Massachusetts requires dealers to report all firearm sales and maintains those records. California and Maryland require new residents to register their guns. Several states require registration of assault weapons, including California, Connecticut, Maryland, New Jersey, and New York.

Conversely, several states forbid gun registration or tracking gun sales—Delaware, Florida, Georgia, Idaho, Pennsylvania, South Dakota, and Vermont.[372]

But even in the states that require gun registration, the easy availability of guns from nearby states that do not require gun registration undermines their efforts. The absence of gun registration in nearby states allows untracked guns to come in.

Conclusion

The bottom line is: By a wide margin, the public wants the government to track gun sales. Most of the resistance comes from the minority of gun owners who belong to the NRA and other, even more radical organizations. In the face of pushback from the NRA and its members, Congress and most of our state legislatures refuse to authorize tracking gun sales. Gun-friendly legislators seldom explain their refusal. When they do, they typically claim that they are guarding against gun confiscation by the government.

12. Should We Ban Assault Weapons?

Item: *Shortly after a terrorist shot 50 people in two New Zealand mosques, Prime Minister Jacinda Ardern announced at a news conference: "I can tell you one thing right now. Our gun laws will change."[373] And in short order, they did.*

Item: *In February 2018, a Stoneman Douglas student suggested that we should call AR-15s "Marco Rubios" because "they're so easy to buy."[374]*

Item: *In April 2020, former Georgia Congressman Paul Broun was running to reclaim a seat in Congress. In a campaign video, he promised to raffle off an AR-15 rifle to those who sign up for his email list. "Whether it's looting hordes from Atlanta, or a tyrannical government from Washington," Broun said, "there are few better liberty machines than an AR-15."[375] He lost.*

Item: *"[By] the power of my AR you will know who I am."—Posting by Nikolas Cruz, the 19-year-old who shot 17 to death and wounded 17 others at Stoneman Douglas High School in Parkland, Florida.*

The AR-15 rifle is a civilian version of the U.S. military's M-16, modified so that it does not contravene the ban on automatic weapons. As a result, the shooter must pull the trigger for each round shot. The National Rifle Association says the AR-15-style is the "most popular rifle in America." It estimated that Americans own more than eight million AR-15-style rifles.[376]

Bushmaster and other makers of the AR-15 hyped its military features and linked ownership of the weapon to machismo. As The New York Times noted, Bushmaster "appealed directly to the male egos of its most likely customers."[377] One Bushmaster campaign used the tag line: "Consider your man card reissued."

Others would say that Bushmaster targeted the fragile masculinity of potential buyers.

In the Sandy Hook Elementary School shooting, Adam Lanza used a Bushmaster XM15-E2S rifle to shoot and kill 26 people, including twenty children between six and seven years old.[378] In the aftermath of that horrific incident, Bushmaster pulled the campaign.

Appeals to toxic masculinity may or may not explain why in this country, the AR-15-style semi-automatic rifle is the weapon of choice of mass murderers, but the list of mass shootings in the U.S. in which the shooter used an AR-15-style rifle seems endless. Here are some of the most notable:[379]

- **Aug. 31, 2019.** After police attempted to stop Seth Aaron Ator, 36, in Odessa, Texas, for failing to use a turn signal, he went on a driving-and-shooting spree that left seven dead and twenty-two injured. The victims spread across fifteen crime scenes from Odessa to Midland. According to police, Ator was a Texas native, white, and used an AR-15-style rifle.[380] Media accounts indicated Ator had only a high school education and lived in a corrugated metal shack along a dirt road surrounded by trailers, mobile homes, and oil pump jacks. His employer had fired him that morning.[381]

- **April 27, 2019.** After posting an anti-Semitic screed, a 19-year-old with an AR-15-style rifle[382] went to the Chabad of Poway, an orthodox Jewish synagogue in San Diego County, California, and opened fire. He killed one woman and injured three, including the synagogue's rabbi and an 8-year-old girl. The attack took place on the last day of Passover.[383]

- **Oct. 27, 2018.** Robert Bowers, 46, burst into the Tree of Life Synagogue in Pittsburgh, screaming anti-Semitic slurs and shooting. Armed with a Colt AR-15 rifle and three Glock .357 pistols, Bowers killed three men and eight women, including a 97-year-old woman. He also wounded six, including four police officers hit by bullets or shrapnel during a shootout.[384]

- **Feb. 14, 2018:** Nikolas Cruz, 19, used a Smith & Wesson M&P 15 .223, an AR-15-style rifle, to kill 17 people and wound 17 others at Marjory Stoneman Douglas High School in Parkland, Florida.

- **Nov. 5, 2017:** Devin Kelley, 26, used an AR-15-style Ruger rifle to kill 26 people at a church in Sutherland Springs, Texas.
- **Oct. 1, 2017:** Stephen Paddock, 64, used a stockpile of guns, including AR-15-style rifles, to kill 58 and injure 413 with gunshot or shrapnel wounds at a music festival in Las Vegas.
- **June 12, 2016:** Omar Mateen, 29, used a Sig Sauer MCX rifle and a 9mm Glock semi-automatic pistol to kill 49 people and injure 50 more at an Orlando nightclub. Police eventually engaged Mateen in a gunfight and shot him eight times, killing him. The Sig Sauer rifle has an overall layout similar to the AR-15 and can accept an AR-15 lower receiver.
- **Dec. 2, 2015:** Before they died in a shootout with police, Syed Rizwan Farook, 28, and Tashfeen Malik, 27, used an AR-15-style .223-caliber Remington rifle along with two 9 mm handguns to kill 14 and injure 21 of Farook's co-workers at a holiday party.
- **June 7, 2013:** John Zawahri, 23, used an AR-15-type semi-automatic rifle to kill five and injure four in a rampage through parts of Santa Monica before police shot and killed him.
- **Dec. 14, 2012:** As noted above, Adam Lanza, 20, used an AR-15-style rifle, a .223-caliber Bushmaster, to kill 20 students and six teachers at Sandy Hook Elementary School in Newtown, Connecticut, before killing himself with a Glock pistol.
- **June 20, 2012:** James Eagan Holmes, 24, used an AR-15-style .223-caliber Smith and Wesson rifle with a 100-round magazine plus a 12-gauge Remington shotgun and two .40-caliber Glock semi-automatic pistols to kill 12 and injure 58 at a movie theater in Aurora, Colorado.
- **Oct. 7, 2007:** Tyler Peterson, 20, used an AR-15-style rifle to kill six and injure one at an apartment in Crandon, Wis., before killing himself.[385]

For gun manufacturers, the weapon's popularity among mass murders is a definite bonus. Each high-profile mass shooting prompts a burst of new sales.[386] Fear that the government will restrict sales of assault weapons may prompt most of the new buyers. But among the buyers, there are also the sickos who see the carnage the weapon can inflict, marvel at the notoriety it won the shooter, and say to themselves, "I want some of that."

The Issue

Should Congress ban for civilian use the manufacture, sale, and possession of semi-automatic rifles, such as AR-15 and AK-47-style rifles, that have the additional features that make them "assault weapons" or "assault rifles"?

This book is about gun-violence-prevention measures on which the great majority of Americans agree, but which Congress—or at least the pro-gun, mainly Republican leadership in Congress—refuses to enact. This chapter, arguably, doesn't belong in this book, because it is not clear that American public opinion has coalesced around an answer to the problem of "active shooters" using "assault rifles" to commit, or attempt to commit, mass murder. I discuss the issue mainly because if I didn't, the omission would mystify readers. Additionally, this chapter sets the table for the next chapter.

Let's begin with a semantic issue important to gun rights activists.

"Assault Rifle"/"Assault Weapon"

"Assault weapon" is an informal term for semi-automatic rifles with a detachable magazine and a pistol grip. Statutory definitions vary and sometimes include other features, such as a vertical forward grip and a flash suppressor or barrel shroud.[387]

For those not into guns, a "flash suppressor" reduces the chance of the shooter being temporarily blinded by the gun's "flash" during night combat.[388] A "barrel shroud" is a piece of metal that wraps around the barrel. It protects the shooter from burning himself with a barrel hot from repeated firing, *e.g.,* during combat.[389]

A Wiki article, citing the Associated Press style book, suggests that "assault weapon" is the proper term and that "assault rifle" refers only to fully automatic rifles.[390] But "assault weapon" is confusing because it may also include "assault pistols" (however defined. To avoid that issue, gun-violence-prevention experts, the news media, and the public prefer to use the term "assault rifle" to refer to a semi-automatic rifle with the additional features that make it suitable for combat—and so attractive to some.

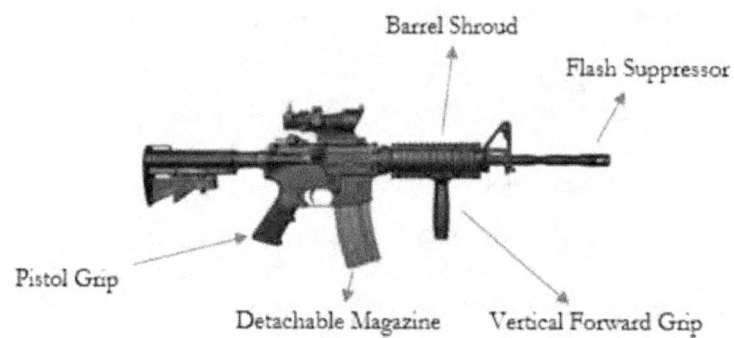

The issue is worth noting because on social media, some gun-rights advocates insist that there is no such thing as an "assault rifle" or "assault weapon." Other gun advocates insist that commenters don't know what they are talking about if they use the term "assault rifle" to refer to anything other than a fully automatic rifle. Both positions give their proponents the smug assurance that they know more than the "idiots" who want to reduce the incidence and lethality of "active shooters" in our schools, workplaces, churches, and entertainment places.

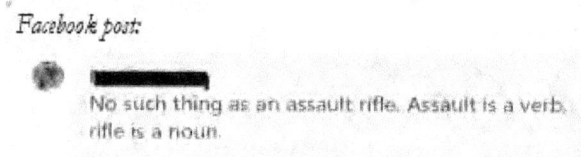

To reiterate, gun-violence-prevention experts, the news media, and the rest of us use the term "assault rifle" to refer to AR-15-style, AK-47-style (Kalashnikov), and similar semi-automatic rifles with a detachable magazine and a pistol grip. Unless quoting someone else, this book uses "assault rifle " and "assault weapon" interchangeably. Some states (and some writers) use the term "assault weapon" to include certain semi-automatic pistols and shotguns as well, but for clarity, this book does not.[391]

The Assault Weapon Ban, 1994—2004

Congress banned the sale—but not the possession of—19 types of "assault weapons" beginning September 13, 1994. The ban, however, ex-empted assault rifles manufactured before that date. At the time the ban went into effect, there were upwards of 1.5 million privately owned such weapons in the U.S.[392] Under pressure from gun manufacturers, gun deal-ers, and the NRA, Congress let the ban expire in September 2004.

Partisans and scholars have spilled much ink on the question of whether the ban was unsuccessful or never serious to begin with. This chapter will not repeat those arguments, except to note that much of the early research measured the impact of the ban on crime rates and overall gun homicide rates.

The ban, however, wasn't intended to impact the overall crime rate or even gun homicide rates. Simply put, no one thought a ban on assault weapons would lower the rates of rapes or robberies or even the homi-cide rate. The ban was intended to reduce the incidence of mass shoot-ings and the number of victims per mass shooting. Proponents also hoped it would reduce the number of police officers outgunned and mur-dered in the line of duty, but that was largely seen as a potential bonus.

More recent research indicates there were fewer mass shootings dur-ing the ban and fewer victims per incident. Since the ban ended, mass shootings have increased dramatically, and so has the number of victims per incident.[393]

For the reader interested in knowing more about that debate, there is a large body of work on the topic. *Rampage Nation* by Louis Klaveras is a good place to start.

Who Owns Assault Weapons?

The Violence Research Center at the University of California-Davis surveyed gun owners in California and turned up something interesting about who owned assault rifles in the state.[394] As Alex Yablon of The

Trace put it, "a small contingent of hardcore collectors own the vast majority of ARs and other so-called assault rifles."[395]

Overall, the survey found that 14% of California adults, or roughly 4.2 million individuals, personally owned one or more firearms. The majority of gun owners (54%) said they have just one or two firearms, but 10% of gun owners owned ten or more firearms. That 10% accounted for roughly half of all civilian-owned firearms in the state. For clarity, that's 10% of the 14% who own guns. Thus, about 1.4% of Californian adults owned roughly half of the civilian firearms in the state.

That 1.4% also owned four out of five "assault rifles." In other words, assuming that pattern isn't unique to California, it's the so-called super-owners who are fueling the demand for AR-15s and similar guns, not the public at large.

California bans the sale of new assault rifles and requires gun owners to register all existing ones with the state's Department of Justice. It has an elaborate definition of an "assault rifle." Gun manufacturers have designed around the restrictions and sell "California legal" guns that are not subject to the ban. The survey counted them as assault rifles anyway. Even with that inclusive definition, only 5% of the firearms that Californians owned were rifles of the type most people call "assault rifles" or "assault weapons" such as AR-, AK- and SKS-rifles. Other long guns (rifles and shotguns) comprised 50%, and the remaining 45% were handguns.

Of note, California is one of our most ethnically diverse states. And yet 67% percent of those who owned assault weapons were white; 69% were over 45 years old; and 84% percent were male.

The Debate Over Assault Weapons

Proponents for restricting or banning civilian access to assault rifles argue that those rifles have acquired a certain allure or mystique that makes the notion of going out in a blaze of infamy seem more attractive to a loser contemplating a mass shooting. As Nikolas Cruz wrote in a post before his murderous shooting spree at the Stoneman Douglas High School, "[By] the power of my AR, you will know who I am." That mystique may give, or help give, a loser intent on a mass shooting the courage to carry out his sick fantasy.

Those who want to restrict or ban assault rifles also argue that a shooter armed with one of those weapons may hit more victims than a shooter with a more conventional gun. Gun enthusiasts scoff at that idea, arguing that a semi-automatic is a semi-automatic, whether or not it has the combat features that make it an "assault weapon." Some gun enthusiasts also argue that it's silly to ban assault rifles because, in the confines of a classroom, a semi-automatic pistol would be a more suitable weapon.

Researchers have studied mass shootings and counted the bodies. On the whole, there were fewer mass shootings during the ten-year federal assault weapons ban.[396] And in the mass shootings that did occur, shooters with assault weapons killed and wounded more victims than those without assault weapons.[397]

But aside from reducing the number of high-profile mass shootings and their body count, there is a larger question: What kind of society do we want? Do we want to be the America that is, or was, the envy of the world? Do we want to be a country where kids don't wonder if some unhappy current or former student will mow them down with bullets sprayed by an assault rifle? Or would we rather our country be like Mogadishu during the 1990s, a place where seemingly every young male had his own assault rifle or a grenade launcher?[398] Or like Mexico and other parts of Central America now, where criminals with assault weapons battle with the police and military?

What We Want

Except for universal background checks, more polls have asked about banning the AR-15, AW-47, and other "assault weapons" than any other issue discussed in this book.

The initial plan for this section was simply to line up all the polls in chronological order, calculate the averages in favor and opposed, and then proceed to the usual demographic crosstabs. Although I list poll results in chronological order throughout this volume, that approach seemed particularly useful here because there have been several events since the Las Vegas Strip massacre that may have influenced poll results.

But closer analysis revealed a different problem: The various polling organizations did not ask the same question. The differences went beyond how they phrased their questions to more substantive differences. Some, for example, asked about banning assault weapons; others asked about banning the *sale* of assault weapons; and still others about banning the manufacture, sale or possession of assault rifles. Some even asked if we should ban *all* semi-automatic rifles.

Different Questions Elicit Different Responses

Banning Assault Weapons?

Some polls asked exactly what you would expect: *Should we ban assault weapons?* Morning Consult, for example, asked if respondents supported or opposed, "Banning assault-style weapons." So did Ipsos, CBS, and Pew.

Favor	*Oppose*	*Polling Dates*	*Poll*
79%	21%	10/10-11/17	Ipsos/NPR
72%	20%	10/5-9/17	Morning Consult
68%	25%	2/22-26/18	Morning Consult
53%	34%	2/20-23/18	CBS News
72%	28%	2/27-28/18	Ipsos/NPR
67%	23%	3/29-4/1/18	Morning Consult
69%	25%	8/2-6/18	Morning Consult
66%	32%	9/24-10/7/18	Pew
69%	31%	1/11-28/19	Ipsos/Reuters
70%	24%	8/5-7/19	Morning Consult
70%	30%	9/3-15/19	Pew

Average: **68%** *vs.* **27%**. *Ratio: 2.6 to 1.*

Among the several variants, that question evoked the highest percentage of responses in favor of a ban. (*Note:* The Pew polls were exceptionally large, and thus, everything else being equal, would be especially reliable.)

Banning the <u>Sale</u> of Assault Weapons?

The federal assault weapons ban prohibited the *sale* of certain assault weapons but not their *possession*. In other words, the 1994-2004 ban grandfathered in any assault weapon the owner already had.

Perhaps with that in mind, the ABC News/Washington Post poll asked, "Do you support or oppose a nationwide ban on the **sale** of assault weapons?" Similarly, Public Policy Polling asked, "Would you support or oppose banning the **sale** of assault weapons?" Quinnipiac University asked, "Do you support or oppose a nationwide ban on the **sale** of assault weapons?" The NBC News/Wall Street Journal asked about "Banning the **sale** of selective semi-automatic firearms referred to as assault weapons?" In two small polls, Monmouth asked, "Do you support or oppose banning the **future sale** of assault weapons?"

Registered Voters

Favor	*Support*	*Polling Dates*	*Poll*
64%	32%	10/05-10/17	Quinnipiac
65%	31%	11/07-13/17	Quinnipiac
67%	29%	2/16-19/18	Quinnipiac
61%	35%	3/03-05/18	Quinnipiac
64%	26%	3/23-25/18	PPP
60%	29%	6/08-10/18	PPP
63%	33%	5/16-20/19	Quinnipiac
57%	41%	7/15-17/19	NPR/PBS
57%	36%	8/16-20/18	Monmouth
60%	37%	8/20-25/19	USA/Suffolk
60%	36%	8/21-26/19	Quinnipiac)
57%	40%	9/2-5/19	ABC/WaPo
58%	38%	9/5-8/19	NPR/PBS

Voters Average: **61%** vs. **34%**. *Ratio: 1.8 to 1.*

Adults

Favor	*Support*	*Polling Dates*	*Poll*
50%	46%	2/15-18/18	ABC/WaPo

Favor	Support	Polling Dates	Poll
62%	35%	4/08-11/18	ABC/WaPo
57%	41%	7/15-17/19	NPR/PBS
62%	37%	8/10-14/19	NBC/WSJ[399]
56%	38%	8/16-20/19	Monmouth[400]
56%	41%	9/2-5/19	ABC/WaPo
57%	39%	9/5-8/19	NPR/PBS)

Adults Average: **57%** *vs.* **40%**. *Ratio: 1.4 to 1.*

Combined: **60%** *vs.* **36%**. *Ratio: 1.7 to 1.*

As the table shows, on average, a clear majority favored a ban on the sale of assault rifles. But this question elicited less support than questions asking about banning assault weapons altogether. That result is counter-intuitive.

As usual, some polls surveyed registered voters; others surveyed adults. In the polls of registered voters, the averages were **61%** in favor of a ban *vs.* **34%** opposed, or about 1.8 to one in favor of a ban on the sale of assault weapons. The polls that surveyed "adults" averaged **57%** in favor *vs.* **40%** opposed, or about 1.4 to one in favor of a ban. In several cases, the same polling organization conducted polls of adults and voters. Those polls suggest that registered voters may be a little more receptive to measures to address our gun violence problem than adults generally.

Ban Manufacture, Sale, and Possession?

Gallup asked, "Are you for or against a law which would make it illegal to manufacture, sell, or possess semi-automatic guns known as assault rifles?" For CNN, the polling organization SRSS also asked about banning the manufacture, sale, and *possession*, but applied that formula to any "rifles capable of semi-automatic fire, such as the AR-15?" That question could be interpreted to mean a ban on all semi-automatic rifles, not just those deemed to be "assault weapons."

Favor	Oppose	Poll	Polling Dates	Gun Type
48%	*49%*	Gallup	10/5-11/17	Assault rifles
49%	*49%*	CNN	10/12-15/17	Semi-auto
57%	*39%*	CNN	2/20-23/18	Semi-auto
40%	*57%*	Gallup	10/1-10/18	Assault rifles
54%	*45%*	Gallup	8/15-30/19	Assault rifles[401]

Average: **50%** *vs.* **48%** *Ratio: ~1 to 1.*

These questions, which suggested a ban not just on the sale, but on possession as well, got the lowest favorable percentages and the highest level of opposition of the three variants.[402]

All "Assault Weapon" Polls: Chronological Order

Below is the usual listing of all the polls since the Las Vegas Strip massacre that asked about banning assault weapons. This list omits polls that seemed to be asking about banning all semi-automatic rifles.

Favor	Oppose	Polling Dates	Poll
72%	20%	10/5-9/17	Morning Consult
64%	32%	10/5-10/17	Quinnipiac
48%	49%	10/5-11/17	Gallup
79%	21%	10/10-11/17	Ipsos/NPR
65%	31%	11/07-13/17	Quinnipiac
50%	46%	2/15-18/18	ABC/WaPo
67%	29%	2/16-19/18	Quinnipiac
53%	44%	2/20-22/18	CBS News
68%	25%	2/22-26/18	Morning Consult
63%	29%	2/20-24/18	Suffolk
61%	35%	3/03-05/18	Quinnipiac
64%	26%	3/23-25/18	PPP
57%	23%	3/29-4/1/18	Morning Consult
62%	35%	4/8-11/18	ABC/WaPo
69%	25%	8/2-6/18	Morning Consult
66%	32%	9/24-10/7/18	Pew

Favor	Oppose	Polling Dates	Poll
69%	31%	1/11-28/19	Ipsos/Reuters
57%	41%	7/15-17/19	NPR/PBS
70%	24%	8/5-7/19	Morning Consult
62%	37%	8/10-14/19	NBC/WSJ
67%	27%	8/11-13/19	Fox News
60%	30%	8/21-26/19	Quinnipiac
57%	40%	9/2-5/19	ABC/WaPo[403]
58%	38%	9/5-8/19	NPR/PBS

Average: **63%** to **32%**. *Ratio: 2-to-1.*

Taken as a whole, by almost a two-to-one margin, Americans favored banning assault weapons, with no clear trend during the period.

The breakouts that follow include only results from polls that asked about banning assault weapons. They do not include polls that asked if we should ban all semi-automatic rifles. And for obvious reasons, the breakouts include cross tab data only from the polls that made that data available.

Gender Divide

In polls that broke out men and women separately, there was an enormous chasm between the genders on the issue of banning assault weapons. Men are deeply split on the issue. Women overwhelmingly favor a ban.

Men	Women	Polling Dates	Poll
64%/29%	80%/13%	10/5-9/17	Morn. Consult
50%/46%	76%/19%	10/5-10/17	Quinnipiac
52%/44%	77%/18%	11/7-13/17	Quinnipiac
53%/44%	77%/44%	2/16-19/18	Quinnipiac
62%/38%	82%/18%	2/27-28/18	Ipsos/NPR
50%/47%	71%/24%	3/3-5/18	Quinnipiac
55%/33%	72%/19%	3/23-25/18	PPP
60%/30%	75%/16%	3/29-4/1/18	Morn. Consult
59%/36%	77%/16%	8/2-6/18	Morn. Consult

47%/50%	75%/22%	5/16-20/19	Quinnipiac
42%/57%	71%/26%	7/15-17/19	NPR/PBS
61%/32%	77%/16%	8/5-7/19	Morn. Consult
47%/48%	72%/25%	8/21-26/19	Quinnipiac
45%/50%	65%/32%	9/2-5/19	ABC/WaPo
42%/55%	72%/24%	9/5-8/19	NPR/PBS

Men: **53%** *favored,* **43%** *opposed.*
Women: **75%** *favored,* **22%** *opposed.*

On average, about **53%** of men favored a ban on assault weapons, and **43%** opposed a ban. In sharp contrast, **75%** of women favored a ban on assault weapons, and only about **22%** opposed a ban. The overall impression is that while *on average*, majorities of both men and women favor a ban on assault weapons, many more women than men favor a ban. As more and more mass shootings fill our news streams, male support may be eroding.

Republicans

The Republican politicians who control the levers of power in the nation's capital may be more concerned about what other Republicans think than about what voters or adults generally think. If they get too far away from other members of their own party, they may face a primary challenge—the only real threat to reelection in many states and districts.

Here's what polls tell us about where Republicans stood:

Favor	*Oppose*	*Polling Dates*	*Poll*
70%	30%	10/10-11/17	Ipsos/NPR
46%	49%	10/5-10/17	Quinnipiac
46%	49%	11/7-13/17	Quinnipiac
43%	49%	2/16-19/18	Quinnipiac
39%	56%	2/20-22/18	CBS News
40%	51%	2/20-24/18	Suffolk
53%	40%	2/22-26/18	Morn. Consult
58%	42%	2/27-28/18	Ipsos/NPR

Favor	Oppose	Polling Dates	Poll
35%	59%	3/2-5/18	Monmouth
38%	60%	3/3-5/18	Quinnipiac
49%	40%	3/23-25/18	PPP
54%	39%	3/29-1/18	Mor. Consult
46%	51%	4/08-11/18	ABC/WaPo
51%	41%	8/2-6/18	Morn. Consult
39%	57%	5/16-20/18	Quinnipiac
57%	43%	1/11-28/19	Ipsos/Reuters
29%	67%	7/15-17/19	NPR/PBS
54%	38%	8/5-7/19	Morn. Consult
37%	59%	8/21-26/19	Quinnipiac
33%	61%	9/2-5/19	ABC/WaPo
37%	56%	9/5-8/19	NPR/PBS

*Average: **45%** favored, **49%** opposed. Ratio: 0.9 to 1.*

These poll results are wildly inconsistent, but on the whole, they show that Republicans tilt against a ban on assault weapons. These numbers also suggest a downward trend over time in support of a ban and an upsurge in opposition among Republicans. Today's Republican Party has moved far from the staid, establishment party of past generations.

Trump 2016 Voters

On average, individuals who voted for Donald Trump in 2016 split about evenly on an assault weapon ban:

Favor	Oppose	Polling Dates	Poll
52%	41%	2/22-26/18	Morning Consult
46%	46%	3/23-25/18	PPP
54%	38%	3/29-4/1/18	Morning Consult
54%	39%	8/2-6/18	Morning Consult
31%	66%	7/15-17/19	NPR/PBS
54%	38%	8/5-7/19	Morning Consult
34%	61%	9/5-8/19	NPR/PBS

*Average: **46%** vs. **47%**. Ratio: 1 to 1.*

It is not clear why the two NPR/PBS NewsHour/Marist polls show dramatically less support for a ban than the rest of these polls. Gun owners, however, represented a disproportionate share of the September 2019 NPR/PBS/Marist sample—40% of adults and 42% of registered voters in the sample personally owned a gun. The expected share was 22% or thereabouts.

That may have been true in the July poll as well, but Marist didn't disclose the percentage of gun owners in that sample. Earlier Marist surveys, however, also heavily overweighed gun owners. (*See* Appendix, Gun Ownership Polls.)

Gun Households

Favor	*Oppose*	*Polling Dates*	*Poll*
62%	23%	10/5-9/17	Morning Consult[404]
49%	47%	10/5-10/17	Quinnipiac
51%	43%	11/7-13/17	Quinnipiac
53%	42%	2/16-19/18	Quinnipiac
49%	49%	3/3-5/18	Quinnipiac
58%	36%	3/29-4/1/18	Morning Consult[405]
54%	40%	8/2-6/18	Morning Consult[406]
49%	47%	3/3-5/18	Quinnipiac
57%	38%	8/5-7/19	Morning Consult[407]
49%	46%	8/21-26/19	Quinnipiac
43%	53%	9/2-5/19	ABC/WaPo[408]
40%	57%	9/5-8/19	NPR/PBS (owners)

*Average: **51%** support vs. **43%** oppose. Ratio: 1.2 to 1.*

These results are somewhat inconsistent but suggest that those who live in gun households were less supportive of a ban on assault rifles than the American public as a whole. These numbers also suggest a downward trend in support for banning assault weapons.

Education

As education increases, so does support for an assault weapon ban:

Non-College Grads (All Races)

Favor	Oppose	Polling Dates	Poll
64%	27%	2/22-26/18	Morning Consult
53%	26%	3/29-1/18	Morning Consult
68%	32%	2/27-28/18	Ipsos/NPR
63%	29%	8/2-6/18	Morning Consult
53%	45%	7/15-17/19	NPR/PBS/Marist
53%	45%	7/15-17/19	NPR/PBS/Marist
64%	27%	8/5-7/19	Morning Consult
50%	32%	8/16-20/19	Monmouth
51%	45%	9/2-5/19	ABC/WaPo
51%	45%	9/5-8/19	NPR/PBS/Marist

Non-College Grad (All Races): **57%** *vs.* **35%**. *Ratio: 1.6 to 1*

Non-College Grads (Whites)

Favor	Oppose	Polling Dates	Poll
56%	38%	10/5-10/17	Quinnipiac
61%	34%	11/7-13/17	Quinnipiac
63%	32%	2/16-19/18	Quinnipiac
51%	43%	3/3-5/18	Quinnipiac
52%	44%	5/16-20/19	Quinnipiac
50%	47%	7/15-17/19	NPR/PBS
49%	44%	8/16-20/19	Monmouth
58%	38%	8/21-26/19	Quinnipiac
55%	41%	9/5-8/19	NPR/PBS

White Non-College Grad Averages: **55%** *vs.* **40%**. *Ratio: 1.4 to 1*

College Grads

College grads support banning assault weapons by a wide margin, with only a slight difference between college grads generally and white college grads. We start with the polls that broke out college grads without regard to race.

College Grads (All Races)

Favor	Oppose	Polling Dates	Poll
73%	24%	2/22-26/18	Morning Consult
78%	22%	2/27-28/18	Ipsos/NPR
73%	24%	3/29-1/18	Morning Consult
64%	35%	7/15-17/19	NPR/PBS
77%	19%	8/2-6/18	Morning Consult
75%	19%	8/5-7/19	Morning Consult
69%	28%	8/16-20/19	Monmouth
62%	35%	9/2-5/19	ABC/WaPo
62%	35%	9/5-8/19	NPR/PBS

All Races with Bachelor Degrees: **70%** *vs.* **27%**. *Ratio: 2.6 to 1.*

College Grads (Whites Only)

Favor	Oppose	Polling Dates	Poll
66%	31%	10/5-10/17	Quinnipiac
69%	29%	11/7-13/17	Quinnipiac
69%	26%	2/16-19/18	Quinnipiac
72%	26%	3/3-5/18	Quinnipiac
71%	26%	5/16-20/19	Quinnipiac
64%	33%	7/15-17/19	NPR/PBS
68%	28%	8/16-20/19	Monmouth
61%	36%	8/21-26/19	Quinnipiac
63%	35%	9/2-5/19	ABC/WaPo
67%	30%	9/5-8/19	NPR/PBS

Whites with Bachelor Degrees: **67%** *vs.* **30%**. *Ratio: 2.2 to 1.*

Post-College Education

Favor	Oppose	Polling Dates	Poll
79%	16%	2/22-26/18	Morning Consult
82%	18%	3/29-1/18	Morning Consult
83%	19%	8/2-6/18	Morning Consult

Favor	Oppose	Polling Dates	Poll
79%	16%	2/22-26/18	Morning Consult
81%	16%	8/5-7/19	Morning Consult
72%	26%	9/2-5/19	ABC/WaPo

Average: **79%** *favored,* **19%** *opposed. Ratio: 4.2 to 1.*

As we have seen repeatedly, as education increases, so does support for measures to curb gun violence. Attitudes toward banning assault weapons followed that pattern, but the differences are more pronounced than usual—67% *vs.* 79%.

Whites With and Without College Degrees

As we've seen, whites tend to be a little less supportive of measures that aim to make it more difficult for dangerous and impulsive individuals to have guns. The July and September 2019 NPR/PBS News-Hour Marist polls looked to see how gender and education affect that.[409] The polls broke out white college grads and *white* non-grads by gender. Let's start with the non-college grads. (See table.)

NPR/PBS				
Whites *without* College Degrees				
	July 2019		Sept. 2019	
	Favor	Oppose	Favor	Oppose
Men	32%	65%	38%	58%
Women	67%	29%	71%	25%
Difference	-35%	+36%	-33%	+33%

White Men and Women without College Degrees

In the July survey, only **32%** of white men *without* a college degree favored a ban on assault weapons, and **65%** opposed a ban. But among **white women without college degrees**, the split was **67%** in favor and **29%** opposed. That was an enormous 35-percentage-point gap in support between white men and white women without college degrees. In the September poll, there was a 33-percentage-point gap in support for a ban between men and women without college degrees.

There was also a large gender gap between white men and women who had college degrees, but it was smaller. In the NPR/PBS/Marist poll in July 2019, white men *with* college degrees favored a ban on the sale of assault weapons **54%** to 45%. White women *with* college degrees favored a ban on the sale of assault weapons **76%** to 24%. That was a 22-percentage- point gap in support and a 21-percentage-point gap in opposition between white men and white women with college degrees.[410]

In the NPR/PBS poll in September 2019, **57%** of white men with college degrees favored a ban on assault weapons, and 41% opposed. Once again, **76%** percent of white women with college degrees favored a ban on assault weapons; this time, only 19% opposed a ban.

NPR/PBS Whites *with* College Degrees				
	July 2019		Sept. 2019	
	Favor	Oppose	Favor	Oppose
Men	54%	45%	57%	41%
Women	76%	24%	76%	19%
Difference	-22%	+21%	-19%	+22%

That's a 19-percentage point gap in support for (and a 22-point gap in opposition to) an assault weapon ban.

White Men Without College Degrees Were the Outliers

There was also a large gap between white men who were and weren't college grads. In July, that gap was also a 22-percent-point gap in support (with a 20-point gap in opposition). In September, the support gap between white men who were and weren't college grads was 19 percentage points (with a 17-point gap in opposition). That makes white males without college degrees the clear outliers.

Polls don't tell us why individuals in a demographic group—in this case, white males who aren't college grads—hold the opinions they do. But there are clear differences between white men and women, and between those with and without college degrees. The core opposition to this measure, and likely to every other measure discussed in this book, lies with white men without college degrees.

Annual Income Over $100,000

Traditionally, high-income individuals have been a stronghold for Republicans, but a supermajority of individuals earning more than $100,000 a year overwhelmingly support a ban on assault weapons.

Favor	Oppose	Polling Dates	Poll
68%	23%	2/22-26/18	Morning Consult
74%	22%	3/29-1/18	Morning Consult
73%	23%	8/2-6/18	Morning Consult
70%	25%	8/5-7/18	Morning Consult
62%	36%	9/2-5/19	ABC/WaPo

Average: **69%** *vs.* **26%**. *Ratio: 2.7 to 1.*

Should We Ban All Semi-Automatics?

Some polls did not ask about "assault weapons." Instead, they asked about banning semi-automatic rifles. The polls in this grouping have their ambiguities, but on the whole, they seem to be asking if we should ban *all* semi-automatic rifles, not just those with "assault weapon" features.

In a poll for USA Today, Suffolk University asked, "Should semi-automatic weapons like the AR-15 be banned in the United States?" This raises its own questions: Would banning semi-automatic weapons "like" the AR-15 ban all semi-automatic rifles? Or would it ban only the rifles with the features associated with "assault weapons"?

AP-NORC asked if respondents supported or opposed, "A nationwide ban on the sale of AR-15 rifles and *similar* semiautomatic weapons?" "Similar semiautomatic weapons" has the same problem as semi-automatics "like" the AR-15. It's unclear if this is asking about a ban on semi-automatics or just those semi-automatics, which, like the AR-15, have "assault weapon" features? The AP-NORC question has the added feature of limiting the ban to the "sale" of semi-automatic weapons, whereas the Suffolk University question ("banned") could be interpreted more broadly.

Three other polls seem more clearly to be asking if the respondent favored a ban of all semi-automatic rifles.

SSRS asked respondents in a "CNN poll" if they favored or opposed, "A ban on the manufacture, sale, and possession of high-powered rifles capable of semi-automatic fire, such as the AR-15?" Some gun rights advocates might object to calling the AR-15 "high-powered," but if we ignore that issue, the question seems to be asking about banning the sale and possession of *all* semi-automatics, with AR-15 rifles used as an example.

Fox asked about: "Banning assault rifles *and semi-automatic weapons?*" [Emphasis added.] Does that include semi-automatic pistols?

Time for a reality check: Would asking about banning all semi-automatic rifles instead of "assault weapons" make enough of a difference to change the outcome of a poll? In its March 3-5, 2018, poll, Quinnipiac University set out to find out. It asked first if respondents favored or opposed a ban on the sale of assault weapons; in a subsequent question, it asked if respondents favored or opposed a ban on the sale of semi-automatic rifles.

The results were clearly different. Respondents favored banning assault weapons **61%** to **35%** but were evenly split on banning semi-automatic rifles, **48%** to **48%**. That strongly suggests poll respondents are capable of distinguishing between a ban on assault rifles *versus* a ban of all semi-automatic rifles.

So, with those caveats, this is how survey participants responded to questions about how they felt about banning semi-automatic rifles:

Favor	*Oppose*	*Polling Dates*	*Polling Dates*	*Question*
49%	49%	10/12-15/17	SSRS/CNN	Possession
57%	39%	2/20-23/18	SSRS/CNN	Possession
63%	29%	2/20-24/18	Suffolk	Ban in US
48%	48%	3/03-05/18	Quinnipiac	Ban sale
56%	42%	3/5-11/18	Gallup	Ban sale
58%	29%	3/14-19/18	AP-NORC	Ban sale
60%	36%	3/18-21/18	Fox News	Ban
62%	38%	1/11-28/19	Ipsos/Reuters	Ban
67%	27%	8/11-13/19	Fox News	Ban

Average: **58%** *vs.* **37%**. *Ratio: 1.5 to 1.*

On average, a majority favored banning semi-automatic rifles altogether, but this issue clearly divides Americans, especially if a ban would apply to gun owners who already own a semi-automatic rifle.[411]

Florida Poll

The Parkland students skewered Florida Senator Marco Rubio during the February 21, 2018, CNN Town Hall for his opposition to banning semi-automatic guns. Later, Rubio complained on Twitter that, "Banning all semi-auto weapons may have been popular with the audience at #CNNTownHall, but it is a position well outside the mainstream."

A Quinnipiac University poll of Floridians,[412] released a week later, on February 28, 2018, put support for a ban at 62%. Only 33%, or one in three Floridians, opposed a ban of semi-automatic weapons.

That poll prompted Tim Elfrink, an investigative reporter with serious chops,[413] to comment:

> Maybe Rubio meant the idea was outside the mainstream of the NRA donors who have spent millions to keep him in office, because new polling out this afternoon makes it clear that Florida voters are very comfortable with completely keeping weapons of war out of civilian hands.[414]

On the release of the poll, Peter A. Brown, assistant director of the Quinnipiac University Poll, noted, "Florida voters—be they young or old, white or black, man or woman—have a common enemy." He was apparently referring to semi-automatic weapons and not to Senator Rubio.

Polling Wrap Up

Average: 68% vs. 26%.	*2.6 to 1*	*Banning Assault Weapons*
Average: 60% vs. 36%.	*1.7 to 1*	*Banning sale of AWs*
Average: 50% vs. 48%	*~1 to 1*	*Ban mfg., sale and possession*
Average: 57% vs. 37%	*1.6 to 1*	*Banning all semi-automatics*

On the whole, Americans favored a ban on assault weapons, and on average, a majority are okay with banning all semi-automatic rifles. But Americans are evenly split on banning *possession* of assault weapons and semi-automatic rifles by those who already own them.

The biggest takeaway may be this: In all but three of these polls, a majority wanted a ban, whether it be of assault weapons or all semi-automatics.

The three outlier polls asked adults, not registered voters, about banning the sale *and possession* of assault weapons or semi-automatic rifles. All three outlier polls were from before the Parkland students revolt startled the country into believing that maybe we really could get our representatives in Congress and in our state legislatures to do something constructive about gun violence. In other words, in retrospect, the three outlier polls did everything possible to get a negative response, short of actually shading the wording of the question.

What We're Getting Instead

At least seven states ban assault weapons: California, New Jersey, Connecticut, Hawaii, Maryland, Massachusetts, and New York.[415] Most of those states also prohibit magazines of more than ten rounds.

That means most states have not banned assault weapons. Take Kentucky, for example. In November 2018, police narrowly averted a mass shooting when they arrested a man outside a manufacturing plant in Springfield, Kentucky. The man had an AR-15-style rifle, modified to fire fully automatically, and seven other guns to "get the job done."[416]

In Kentucky's lower chamber, several Democrats introduced a bill, H.B. 502, that would have, among other things, banned assault weapons. Rep. George Brown Jr., D-Lexington, the sponsor of the legislation, said, "Young people in states across the nation, including Kentucky, are speaking out on the need to be kept safe. This bill listens to their voices and offers solutions to stop gun violence."[417]

The Republican-dominated legislature refused to listen to those voices or to consider the bill. A different bill, H.B. 498, would have raised the minimum age for purchase of an assault rifle. That bill also went nowhere.

Kentucky's Tea Party Governor, Matt Bevin, blamed mass shootings on zombies and on television shows that focus on death.[418] Previously, he had blamed gun violence on children's access to smartphones and on

Photo: Courtesy of Springfield Police Department

psychotropic drugs.[419] He's also repeated the widely discredited theory that blames mass shootings on video games. (If that theory were true, then Japan, where video games are extremely popular among young men, would have a terrific amount of gun carnage; instead, it has almost none.)

In short, Bevin blamed everything and anything except guns and men caught up in our toxic gun culture. In November 2019, voters in the deep-red state voted Bevin out of office.

The Courts

Since the U.S. Supreme Court's 2008 decision in *Heller v. District of Columbia*, in which the Supreme Court interpreted the Second Amendment as creating a carefully circumscribed individual right to keep and bear arms, five (of eleven) U.S. Circuit Courts of Appeals have upheld assault rifle bans.[420]

That unanimity does not guarantee the same result in the Supreme Court. Justice Thomas dissents whenever the Supreme Court declines to review lower court decisions that refused to hold such bans unconstitutional. Justice Kavanaugh, while still a judge in the D.C. Circuit, dissented in *Heller II* (a second appeal to the Court of Appeals in the *Heller* case).

He argued that the District of Columbia's ban on assault rifles was unconstitutional. The Federalist Society and the White House, presumably, got pledges of fealty to the NRA from both Justices Gorsuch and Kavanaugh before President Trump nominated them to the high court.

Only time, therefore, will tell what the Supreme Court will do if and when it takes up the question of assault weapon bans. The appointment of Justices Gorsuch and Kavanaugh, both political partisans, gives those who value guns more than human life reason to think the Supreme Court will be sympathetic to their cause. Conversely, those who value human life over guns have reason to be concerned.

13. Should Teenagers Have Assault Weapons?

Item: When Eric Harris and Dylan Klebold planned the Columbine High School massacre in 1999, they had a problem: Both 17 years old at the time, they weren't old enough to buy guns from a licensed dealer. So, without telling her what they were up to, they arranged for a friend, Robyn Anderson, 18, to help. She accompanied Harris and Klebold to the Tanner Gun Show and purchased a Hi-Point 995 carbine and a 12-gauge Savage-Springfield 67H pump-action shotgun.[421] Anderson was able to buy the guns because she was 18 years old. And because she was 18, it didn't occur to her that this was a really bad idea.

Item: From an early age, Kip Kinkel was a troubled child. He was also interested in firearms. His father initially discouraged this but later enrolled him in a gun safety course and bought him, at age 15, a Ruger .22-caliber semi-automatic rifle and later, a 9x19mm Glock 19 pistol.[422]

In May 1998, Thurston High School in Springfield, Oregon, suspended Kinkel after school authorities learned that he brought a stolen handgun to school and had it in his locker. When his father threatened to enroll him in a military school, Kinkel retrieved his Ruger semi-automatic rifle from his bedroom and ammunition from his parents' bedroom. He went to the kitchen, where his father was seated at the kitchen counter drinking coffee, and shot him in the back of the head. Kinkel dragged his father's body into the bathroom and covered it with a sheet.

When his mother arrived home at about 6:30 p.m., Kinkel met her in the garage. He told her he loved her, then shot her three times in the face, twice in the back of the head, and once in the heart. He dragged her body across the floor and covered it with a sheet.

The next day, Kinkel returned to Thurston High School and began shooting. He killed two students and wounded 25 others.

Item: *Nikolas Cruz, the 19-year-old Parkland, Florida shooter, wasn't old enough to purchase a handgun. Or buy a beer. But no law prevented him from walking into a gun dealer in Florida and buying the AR-15-style semi-automatic rifle he used to kill 17 people and to injure 17 others at Marjory Stoneman Douglas High School.*

Item: *On April 27, 2019, the last day of Passover, John T. Earnest, 19, entered the Chabad of Poway synagogue and began firing a Smith & Wesson Model M&P 15 Sport II semi-automatic rifle. He shot and killed 60-year-old Lori Gilbert-Kaye and wounded Rabbi Yisroel Goldstein, the founding rabbi of the congregation. He then fired into a side room, hitting a man and injuring the man's 8-year-old niece with shrapnel. When Earnest tried to reload, he had trouble, and two congregants rushed him. Earnest fled, ending the incident. According to the complaint filed by federal authorities, 19-year-old Earnest bought the gun from a licensed San Diego firearms dealer, picking it up the day before the shooting.*[423]

Item: *July 28, 2019. Santino William Legan, the shooter at the Gilroy Garlick Festival, was a 19-year-old, armed with WASR-10 semi-automatic rifle with a detachable magazine—an "AK-47 variant"—that he purchased in Nevada three weeks earlier.*[424]

Young people in their late teens and early twenties often experiment with alcohol, drugs, and sex.[425] Science and everyday experience tell us individuals in that age bracket too often fail to appreciate or are too quick to dismiss the potential consequences of risky behaviors.[426] In a commentary piece in The Trace, Dr. Crifasi explained:

> While an 18-year-old's brain is similar to that of a fully mature adult, key cognitive processes continue to develop until age 26. These include impulse control, which can affect an individual's ability to safely and appropriately use a gun.[427]

That's the reason why, not that long ago, all fifty states raised the minimum legal age for drinking alcoholic beverages to 21. As news outlets have widely reported, those laws led to significant reductions in deaths from motor vehicle accidents involving drivers ages 18 to 20.[428]

It's much the same with guns. Research confirms what newspapers tell us: Homicide rates rise sharply in the late teens. They used to peak at age 20, but on this score, there is some good news. In recent years, the number of young people under age 21 committing intentional homicides has declined some.[429] But young people under the age of 21 are still re-sponsible for a startling number of homicides each year. In 2018, for ex-ample, they were responsible for about 12% of the homicides for which the age of the offender was known.[430]

Gun rights advocates argue that young people can vote and serve in the armed forces at age 18, so they should be able to buy a gun. But, as noted above, experience proved those weren't sufficient reasons to let young people under 21 buy alcohol. When we allowed 18-year-olds to drink, too many 18-, 19- and 20-year-olds died. We have also allowed individuals under age 21 to have long guns, including semi-automatics, and the results have been similarly tragic.

Even though young adults are able to vote at age 18, they cannot serve in the U.S. House of Representatives until they're 25.[431] Why? Because with the greater responsibility that serving in Congress represents, we require more maturity.

Actual military service is a more compelling argument. Many who advocate for a higher minimum age at which young people may buy an assault weapon (or any gun) would likely not object to an exception for those who serve in the military. Why? Because those who serve in our military undergo intense training to instill discipline and the habit of thinking about more than themselves. They also operate in a system where discipline is constantly reinforced. Young people who serve in the military also receive training in the proper use of weapons.

That training and discipline may be why we don't have a history of young people in the military, ages 18 to 20, engaging in mass shootings, but we do have a long and sad history of young people under age 21 without military experience engaging in mass shootings and other gun homicides.

The May 1998 Thurston High School and the April 1999 Columbine High School shootings raised the question of whether we want teenagers, who are not in the military, to have pump-action shotguns and semi-au-tomatic rifles, especially assault rifles. The shooting at Stoneman Douglas

High School in Parkland, Florida, raised that question once more. So did several shootings in 2019.

The Issue

Should we allow persons under the age of 21, who are not in the military, to buy and own firearms, including semi-automatic weapons?

Federal gun law largely turns on whether the seller is a federal firearm licensee (FFL) or another seller (generally referred to as a "private" citizen.). FFLs include manufacturers, importers, collectors, and licensed firearm dealers. But for present purposes, we're mainly concerned with licensed dealers.

Licensed Firearm Dealers

Federal law prohibits dealers and other FFLs from selling or transferring a gun or ammunition to someone "the licensee knows or has reasonable cause to believe" is under age 18. There are some exceptions having to do mainly with farm and ranch work and service in the military or National Guard.[432] Putting those exceptions aside, if the would-be buyer is a juvenile (*i.e.,* under age 18),[433] an FLL may not sell him or her a firearm (*any* firearm.) Federal law also prohibits licensed dealers and other FFLs from selling *handguns* and ammunition used exclusively in handguns to persons under age 21.

Federal law does permit dealers to sell or transfer long guns—shot-guns and rifles, including assault rifles—to individuals 18 or older.[434] Dealers may also sell unlimited amounts of ammunition for shotguns and rifles, including assault-style rifles, to those 18 and older. (The Appendix contains a table from the Federal Commission on School Safety that summarizes federal law.)

There is a crucial exception. Federal law does not allow a dealer or other licensee to sell or transfer a firearm in a state where the purchase or possession of the firearm would violate state law or a published ordinance.[435] Thus, a state may impose a higher age limit, *e.g.,* a minimum of age 21 to purchase a long gun, and if it does, federally licensed dealers in the state must comply.

Read together, this means that unless state or local law prohibits the sale, a gun dealer or other FFL may sell a shotgun or rifle and ammuni-tion to anyone 18 or older who is not otherwise disqualified (*e.g.,* because of a felony conviction.). That's why 19-year-old Nikolas Cruz, the deeply troubled Parkland, Florida shooter, was able to buy an AR-15 rifle.

Few states regulate in any meaningful way the age at which teenagers can purchase long guns or assault weapons. Brian Freskos, writing for The Trace, put it this way, "In most states, people can legally buy assault-style weapons before they can drink a beer."[436]

Private Citizens / Non-Federal Firearm Licensees

To recap: Under federal law, it is a crime for a licensed dealer to sell a long gun (*i.e.,* a shotgun or rifle) to a "juvenile," *i.e.,* to someone under age 18. It is also a crime for a dealer to sell a *handgun* or ammunition for a *handgun* to someone he or she knows or has reason to believe is under age 21.[437]

But a seller who is not a licensed gun dealer or other FFL—in the usual parlance, a "private citizen"—may sell, lend, or give a long gun to a child or young adult of *any* age. A private citizen may also sell, lend, or give a handgun to anyone who is a resident of the same state if he or she is at least 18.

Gun rights advocates argue that these exceptions make it possible for a father to lend or give a shotgun or rifle to his son or daughter, and to train him or her in the gun's safe use for hunting or sport shooting. Sim-ilarly, the law allows a parent to give his child a pistol at age 18 and to train him or her in its use for personal protection.

The Kip Kinkel vignette at the beginning of this chapter illustrates this —and highlights what can go wrong. Kip Kinkel used the rifle and a Glock pistol his father purchased for him to kill first his father, then his mother, and finally to stage a school shooting in which he killed two and wounded 25. Admittedly, that's an atypical outcome, but the point is that it was legal for Kinkel's father to buy a semi-automatic rifle and give it to his deeply troubled son.[438]

But even if it made sense to allow a parent to give a pump-action shotgun or a semi-automatic rifle to a deeply disturbed 15-year-old, Congress did not write this loophole narrowly to cover just parents and their kids. The loophole also makes it possible for a gang member or street hoodlum to sell or give an assault rifle or pump-action shotgun to a 15-year-old fellow gang member without violating the law.

Ownership and Possession

The preceding paragraphs discussed the *sale* or *transfer* of handguns and long guns to juveniles, *i.e.,* persons under age 18, and to young adults under age 21. The following paragraphs discuss whether federal law allows *possession* of a handgun or long gun by juveniles and young adults under age 21.

The short version is this: Federal law prohibits a juvenile (someone under age 18 from knowingly possessing a *handgun*, subject to the same narrow exceptions that apply to the sale or transfer of any gun to a juvenile.[439] But there is no federal minimum age for long guns.

That's why, with her parent's permission, it was perfectly legal for a 9-year-old girl to fire a 9mm Uzi carbine at Bullets & Burgers, a firing range in Arizona.[440] When she couldn't handle the gun's kickback, she accidentally shot and killed the trainer. So, legal, but 9-year-olds with Uzis may not be our country's best idea.

Some states have enacted minimum age requirements for the ownership of long guns, ranging from 14 in Minnesota to 21 in Illinois and Hawaii. In Florida, when the Stoneman Douglas High School mass shooting took place, the minimum age for owning a long gun was 18. After that shooting, Florida raised the minimum age to 21.

What We Want

This chapter is about whether we should raise the minimum age at which a young person may buy or possess an assault weapon. But there's an important preliminary question that factors into that discussion: Where does the American public stand on raising the minimum age at which someone may purchase *any* firearm to 21?

Age Limit of 21 for Any Firearm?

Polling since the Las Vegas Strip shooting indicates that Americans overwhelmingly favor raising the minimum age at which someone may buy a gun to 21.

Overall

Registered Voters

Favor	*Oppose*	*Polling Dates*	*Poll*
81%	13%	2/22-26/18	Morning Consult
82%	18%	2/27-28/18	Ipsos-NPR
78%	20%	3/3-5/18	Quinnipiac
77%	17%	3/29-4/1/18	Morning Consult
80%	16%	8/2-6/18	Morning Consult
83%	12%	8/5-7/19	Morning Consult
71%	24%	1/11-28/19	Ipsos/Reuters

*Voters: **79%** vs. **18%**. Ratio: 4.4 to 1.*

Adults

Favor	*Oppose*	*Polling Dates*	*Poll*
71%	27%	2/20-23/18	CNN/SSRS
68%	30%	3/5-11/18	Gallup
72%	25%	3/18-21/18	Fox News
72%	26%	4/8-11/18	ABC/WaPo[441]

*Adults: **73%** to **25%**. Ratio: 2.9 to 1.*

*Combined Averages: **76%** vs. **21%**. Ratio: 3.7 to 1.*

When these polls are averaged, **76%** favored raising the age at which someone may buy a gun to age 21. (For a point of comparison, in an October 2017 Public Policy Polling poll, **77%** disapproved of the job Congress was doing.[442])

As we've seen, registered voters are generally a bit more receptive than "adults" to legislative proposals to deal with our gun violence. (Surveys of "adults" include people who can't, won't or don't vote.) In these polls, on average, **79%** of registered voters *vs.* **72%** of adults favored raising the minimum age to 21. CNN, Gallup and Fox surveyed "adults" and got lower percentages in favor of raising the minimum age.

On the other hand, the ABC News/Washington Post poll broke out results for both adults and registered voters. In an unusual twist, the registered voters in its poll were a little *less* likely to support raising the minimum age at which a person may buy a gun. That may be just the sort of random variability that occurs in polling. Or it may be because 47% of the ABC News/Washington Post poll's sample were gun householders (instead of the expected 35% or so).

On average, **21%** of poll respondents opposed raising to 21 the minimum age at which a Nikolas Cruz or Santino Legan may walk into a gun store and buy a pump-action shotgun, semi-automatic rifle, or assault weapon. (For comparison, in an August 2019 Suffolk/USA Today poll, **19%** agreed with President Trump that the U.S. should take steps to buy Greenland, an autonomous territory of Denmark that emphatically was not for sale.[443]

Republicans

A clear majority of Republicans in these polls favored raising the minimum age for purchasing a gun to age 21. In some polls, Republicans favored this by as much as three-to-one. Although not shown here, even higher percentages of Democrats and Independents supported raising the minimum age.

Favor	Oppose	Polling Dates	Poll [Respondents
61%	38%	2/20-23/18	CNN/SSRS [Adults]
81%	13%	2/22-26/18	Morning Consult
72%	28%	2/27-28/18	Ipsos/NPR [Adults]
63%	36%	3/3-5/18	Quinnipiac
57%	39%	3/18-21/18	Fox News [Adults]
67%	28%	3/29-4/1/18	Morning Consult
55%	43%	4/8-11/18	ABC/Wash. Post [Adults]
72%	24%	8/2-6/18	Morning Consult
63%	34%	1/11-28/19	Ipsos/Reuters

Averages: **66%** *vs.* **31%**. *Ratio: 2.1 to 1.*
Registered Voters: **71%** *vs.* **25%**. *Ratio: 2.8 to 1.*

*Adults: **62%** to **36%**. Ratio: 1.7 to 1.*

On average, 66% of Republicans supported raising the minimum age at which young people may purchase guns to 21, and 31% opposed. That's roughly a two-to-one margin. Among registered voters, the averages were 71% to 25%; among "adults," the averages were 61% to 37%.

Trump 2016 Voters

Like Republicans generally, Trump voters favored raising the minimum age for purchase of a gun to 21. In fact, among Trump voters, those who favored raising the minimum age outnumbered those who opposed almost three-to-one.

Favor	Oppose	Polling Dates	Poll
71%	27%	2/20-23/18	CNN/SSRS
75%	21%	2/22-26/18	Morning Consult
72%	25%	3/18-21/18	Fox News [Adults]
62%	31%	3/28-31/18	Morning Consult
74%	23%	8/2-6/18	Morning Consult

*Averages: **71%** vs. **25%**. Ratio: 2.8 to 1.*

The averages were 71% in favor and 25% opposed, a ratio of about 2.8 to 1. In short, by a wide margin, Trump voters believe we should raise the age at which a young person may buy a gun.

Gun Households

A clear majority of those who live in gun households believe we should require someone to be 21 years old to be able to buy a gun.

Favor	Oppose	Polling Dates	Poll
62%	37%	2/20-23/18	CNN/SSRS[444] [Adults]
63%	35%	3/3-5/18	Fox News [Adults]
69%	29%	3/3-5/18	Quinnipiac
70%	27%	3/29-4/1/18	Morning Consult
69%	27%	8/2-6/18	Morning Consult[445]

*Averages: **67%** vs. **31%**. Ratio: 2.1 to 1.*

Averaging these polls, **67%** in households with guns favored requiring a person to be 21 to purchase a gun, and **31%** opposed. CNN and Fox surveyed adults and found 62% and 63% support. Quinnipiac and Morning Consult surveyed registered voters and found 69% to 70% support.

Education

People at all levels of education favored requiring someone to be at least 21 to buy a gun. Support rose with more education.

No College Degree

Favor	Oppose	Polling Dates	Poll
70%	29%	2/20-23/18	CNN/SSRS [Adults]
80%	11%	2/22-26/18	Morning Consult
81%	19%	2/27-28/18	Ipsos-NPR
70%	27%	3/3-5/18	Quinnipiac [Whites]
67%	29%	3/18-21/18	Fox News [White Adults]
76%	28%	3/29-4/1/18	Morning Consult
72%	26%	4/8-11/18	ABC/WaPo [Adults]
78%	16%	8/2-6/18	Morning Consult

Averages: **74%** vs. **23%**. *Ratio: 3.2 to 1.*

Bachelor Degree

Favor	Oppose	Polling Dates	Poll
75%	24%	2/20-23/18	CNN/SSRS [Adults]
82%	11%	2/22-26/18	Morning Consult
83%	17%	2/27-28/18	Ipsos-NPR
78%	21%	3/3-5/18	Quinnipiac [Whites]
73%	25%	3/18-21/18	Fox News [White Adults]
76%	20%	3/29-4/1/18	Morning Consult
70%	27%	4/8-11/18	ABC/WaPo [Adults]
83%	16%	8/2-6/18	Morning Consult

Averages: **78%** vs. **20%**. *Ratio: 3.9 to 1.*

Postgraduate Education

Favor	Oppose	Polling Dates	Poll
88%	9%	2/22-26/18	Morning Consult
79%	16%	3/29-4/1/18	Morning Consult
78%	20%	4/8-11/18	ABC/WaPo [Adults]
85%	13%	8/2-6/18	Morning Consult

*Averages: **83%** vs. **15%**. Ratio: 5.7 to 1.*

Both those with and without college degrees overwhelmingly favored raising the minimum age for purchasing any gun to 21. But once again, as the level of education rose, so did support for this measure.

Annual Income Over $100,000

Most people earning over $100,000 per year favored raising the age at which someone may buy a firearm to 21.

Favor	Oppose	Polling Dates	Poll
86%	7%	2/22-26/18	Morning Consult
76%	21%	3/29-4/1/18	Morning Consult
80%	19%	8/2-6/18	Morning Consult

*Averages: **81%** vs. **16%**. Ratio: 5 to 1.*

In the three Morning Consult polls that broke out those with annual incomes over $100,000, the averages were 81% in favor and 16% opposed, a ratio of about 5 to 1.

Wrap Up: Age To Buy Any Gun

In all of these demographic categories, supermajorities wanted to raise the minimum age at which a young person may purchase a gun to 21. Among those without four-year college degrees, on average, **74%** supported, and 23% opposed raising the age limit to buy any firearm to 21. Among those with a Bachelor's degree, the averages rose modestly to **78%** in favor, with 20% opposed. Among those with a post-graduate education, the margin in favor was **83%** to 15%. And among those with annual incomes of $100,000 or more, the margin in favor was (on aver-age) **81%** to 16% or about 5 to 1.

Minimum Age for "Assault Rifles"?

Now, we're going to switch topics from *any* firearm to assault weapons. In other words, should lawmakers raise the minimum age for the purchase of an assault weapon to 21?

Overall Poll Results

Morning Consult explored opinion on the following question: Should young people be at least 21 years old before they may buy an assault-style weapon?

Favor	*Oppose*	*Polling Dates*	*Poll*
82%	11%	2/22-26/18	Morning Consult
79%	14%	3/29-4/1/18	Morning Consult
80%	14%	8/2-6/18	Morning Consult

*Averages: **80%** vs. **13%**. Ratio: 6 to 1.*

On average, **80%** favored a minimum age of 21 to buy an assault weapon, and **13%** opposed. The public, in short, doesn't want someone under age 21 to be able to walk—or ride his skateboard—into a gun store and buy an assault-style weapon.

Republicans

In these polls, a clear majority of Republicans favored raising the minimum age to 21 to buy an assault weapon.

Favor	*Oppose*	*Polling Dates*	*Poll*
81%	13%	2/22-26/18	Morning Consult
74%	20%	3/29-4/1/18	Morning Consult
75%	18%	8/2-6/18	Morning Consult

*Averages: **77%** vs. **17%**. Ratio: 4.5 to 1.*

More Republicans (81%) favored this in the immediate aftermath of the Parkland shooting than later, but 74% and 75% are very high levels of support in public opinion polls. (In an Ipsos poll conducted June 14-15, 2018, a roughly similar 75% of the public had an unfavorable impression of North Korea's dictator, Kim Jong-un. Among Republicans, 19% had a favorable impression of the murderous dictator.)

Trump 2016 Voters

Those who voted for Donald Trump in 2016 also wanted our lawmakers to raise the minimum age to buy an assault weapon.

Favor	Oppose	Polling Dates	Poll
78%	14%	2/22-26/18	Morning Consult
71%	21%	3/29-4/1/18	Morning Consult
76%	19%	8/2-6/18	Morning Consult

Averages: **75%** vs. **18%**. *Ratio: 4.2 to 1.*

Gun Households

In the two polls to break out gun households, supermajorities favored raising the minimum age to age 21 to buy an assault weapon.

Favor	Oppose	Polling Dates	Poll
70%	20%	3/28-31/18	Morning Consult
78%	19%	8/2-6/18	Morning Consult

Averages: **74%** vs. **20%**. *Ratio: 3.7 to 1.*

Education

Three Morning Consult polls provided the usual crosstabs by educational attainment:

Polling Dates	< Co. Grad	Col. Grad	Post Grad
2/22-26/18	80%/11%	82%/11%	88%/9%
3/29-4/1/18	78%/14%	79%/15%	88%/10%
8/2-6/18	76%/17%	88%/10%	83%/10%
Averages:	**78%/14%**	**83%/12%**	**86%/10%**

The overall figures fall into the usual stair-step pattern: As educational attainment rises, so does support for restricting access to guns by individuals and groups who shouldn't have them.

Annual Income Over $100,000

Lots of people in the traditionally Republican stronghold of high-income folks want to raise the age at which a young person may buy an assault rifle.

Favor	Oppose	Polling Dates	Poll
86%	7%	2/22-26/18	Morning Consult
80%	16%	3/29-4/1/18	Morning Consult
84%	12%	8/2-6/18	Morning Consult

*Averages: **83%** vs. **12%**. Ratio: 6.9 to 1.*

Sentiment in this group—people with enough disposable income to make campaign contributions—runs almost seven to one in favor.

Polling Wrap Up

Raising the minimum age to purchase/own
(Average: Favor/Oppose)

Demographic:	Any Firearm	Assault Weapon
Overall	**76%/21%**	**80%/13%**
Republicans	66%/31%	77%/17%
Trump Voters	71%/25%	75%/18%
Gun Households	67%/31%	74%/20%
No Bachelor Degree	74%/20%	78%/14%
College Grads	78%/20%	83%/12%
Post Grads	83%/15%	86%/10%
Over $100K	81%/16%	83%/12%

In sum, roughly three quarters (**76%**) of the American public wants Congress and our state legislatures to establish a minimum age of 21 for the purchase of *any* gun. Only 21% opposed.[446]

About two-thirds of Republicans (**66%**) want that as well. Trump voters want the minimum age to buy a gun raised to 21 by **71%** to 25% or about three-to-one. Gun households fell in line at **67%** in favor. Strong majorities at every education level agreed, and as usual, support increased with the amount of education. By about 5 to 1, those making over $100,000 wanted the minimum age raised to 21.

When we change the focus from any gun to assault weapons, **80%** of registered voters (on average) wanted the age limit raised so that young adults under 21 would not be able to buy assault weapons. So did, on average, 77% of Republicans and 75% of Trump voters. On average, 74% of those in gun households also thought we should require someone to be 21 to buy an assault weapon, with only 19% or 20% of those in gun households disagreeing. Among those with incomes of $100,000 or more, support ran at or above 80% or almost seven to one.

And yet Congress—or more accurately, Senator Majority Leader Mitch McConnell and pro-gun, Republican Senators—adamantly refuse to allow a vote on raising the minimum age to buy a long gun, even an assault weapon, to 21.

What We're Getting Instead

After the shooting at the Marjory Stoneman Douglas High School in Parkland, Florida, President Trump repeatedly said we need to raise the age at which young people may purchase guns to 21.[447]

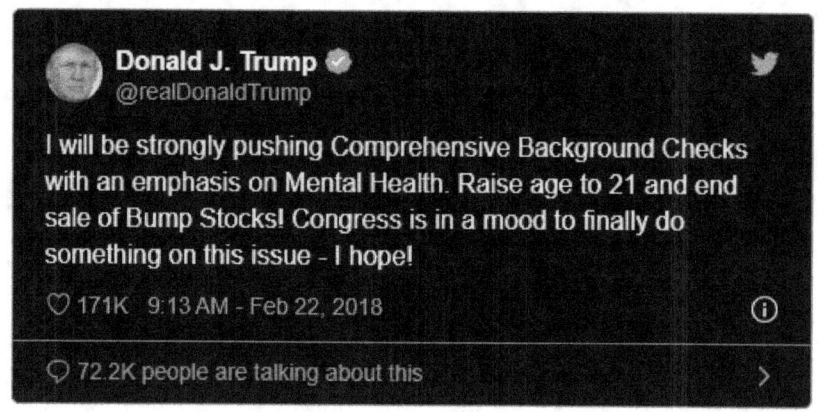

But after NRA representatives met with him privately, Trump walked back his support, saying maybe the courts or the states would take care of the problem.[448]

Mr. Trump may have been referring to Florida, where—under pressure from students and parents—the state legislature passed a package of gun reforms that included raising the minimum age for gun purchases (but

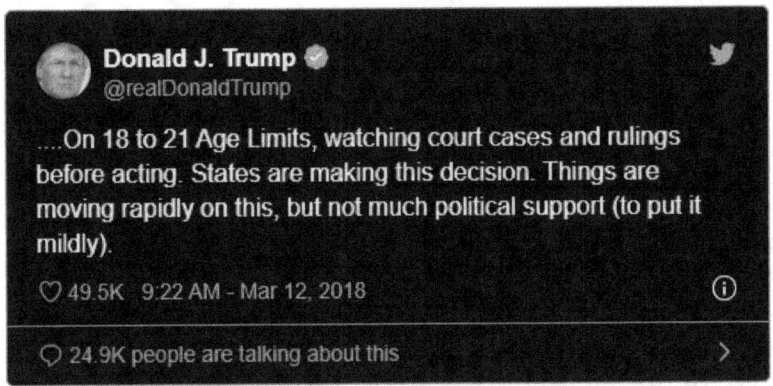

not possession) to 21. The NRA responded by filing suit, challenging the age limit.[449] By the time the courts resolve that litigation, most voters will have long since forgotten Mr. Trump's earlier stance.

After the Parkland shooting, the White House established a commission to study school safety but put Secretary of Education Betsy DeVos in charge of it. The White House also rigged the Commission's charter to make sure it would not recommend measures the NRA opposed. As The Washington Post explained:[450]

> The commission was the White House's effort to show it was responding to the national outrage. At one point, Trump himself suggested he would take on the National Rifle Association and might back new age limits. But he quickly reversed course and, six months later, his commission is echoing the mainstream Republican view that no new laws are needed.

Consistent with its goal of pretending to look for solutions without upsetting the NRA, the Commission's final report, released in December 2018, recommended against minimum-age-to-purchase laws.[451] It noted, almost as an aside, that the *federal* age limit for the purchase of handguns has been effective in reducing gun carnage. The Commission, however, argued that existing research did not demonstrate that state-level minimum-age-laws for long guns or assault weapons would reduce homicides or suicides.[452] That, of course, was just another way of saying: We haven't tried that in any serious way, so there's no evidence that it works. The Commission ignored the fact that we *do* have a lot of evidence for what happens when we *allow* 18-, 19- and 20-year-olds to buy assault weapons.

The Commission pointed out, correctly, that young mass-casualty shooters often get their guns from their parents, other relatives, or friends. Therefore, the Commission argued, the better course was for an unspecified someone to advise parents about the importance of safe storage of their guns. (*See* Chapter 16.) The Commission did not explain why, given the lives at stake, it wouldn't be better to do both—cut off sales to teenagers like Nikolas Cruz *and* tell parents to store their guns safely. Or better still, tell parents they will be held liable for the consequences if their kid uses their gun to kill himself, a sibling, or a classroom full of 6- and 7-year-old kids.

After the Parkland shooting and the Parkland students launched the #NeverAgain campaign, Dick's Sporting Goods, L.L. Bean, and Walmart changed the age at which customers could buy firearms in their stores to 21.

After the Poway synagogue shooting, Senator Dianne Feinstein promised to reintroduce a bill to increase the minimum buying age for semi-automatic rifles to 21. She first introduced the bill after the 2018 Parkland shooting, but Senator Mitch McConnell and his fellow Republicans in the Senate refused to allow that bill to come to the floor for a vote.[453]

Conclusion

Even though, as we've seen, most Americans, including Republicans, want our lawmakers to raise the age limit to buy an assault rifle to age 21, Senator Mitch McConnell and his Republican colleagues in the Senate refused to allow a vote on Senator Feinstein's current bill or any other bill that might reduce gun sales. Evidently, the support Senator McConnell and his fellow Republican senators get from the gun lobby is more im-portant to them than the lives of our children and other loved ones. It's no wonder Senator McConnell calls himself the "Grim Reaper."

14. Should We Ban Large-Capacity Magazines?

Item: When Kip Kinkel, 15, reached the Thurston High school cafeteria in Springfield, Oregon, on May 20, 1998, he began firing. His shooting spree left two students—Ben Walker and Mikael Nickolauson—dead and 25 others wounded. When Kinkel exhausted the rounds in his magazine and had to reload, students rushed and subdued him. If they hadn't, the carnage would have been worse.

Item: In a grocery store parking lot in Tucson, Az., Jared Lee Loughner emptied the contents of his first magazine—33 rounds—into Congresswoman Gabby Gifford and the people surrounding her. When Loughner stopped to reload, he fumbled and dropped the new magazine. A woman, wounded and on the ground, saw Loughner try to reach the magazine and grabbed his hand, preventing him from reaching it. When she did, two men tackled Loughner. The heroics saved lives but would have saved more if the first magazine had fewer rounds.[454]

Item: In the 2014 Seattle Pacific University shooting, a student hid in an office until the shooter, Aaron Ybarra, stopped to reload. The student then ran out of the office, pepper-sprayed Ybarra in the face and wrestled his gun away.[455]

Item: When Travis Reinking, naked except for a green camo jacket, began shooting patrons inside the Waffle House in Nashville, Tenn., a customer, James Shaw Jr., 29, hid behind a swinging door. When Reinking stopped to reload, Shaw rushed out and wrestled the AR-15-style rifle away from Reinking. At that point, Reinking fled. Police credited Shaw with averting further bloodshed.[456]

Item: A court decision narrates: "On the morning of December 14, 2012, in Newtown, Connecticut, a gunman used an AR-15-type Bushmaster rifle and detachable thirty-round magazines to murder twenty first-graders and six adults in the Sandy Hook Elementary School. ... Nine terrified children ran from one of the classrooms *when the gunman paused to reload, while two youngsters successfully hid in a restroom. ... In all, the gunman fired at least 155 rounds of ammunition within five minutes, shooting each of his victims multiple times."*[457]

Item: *Filled with rage against women, Scott Paul Beierle used a Glock 9mm to kill two women and shoot four others during his rampage at the Hot Yoga studio in Tallahassee, Florida.*[458] *When Beierle fired all the rounds in the gun's magazine and had to reload, the one male student rushed him. Beierle pistol-whipped the man, but the man grabbed a broomstick and rushed Beierle again. While Beierle fought the man, the other students in the class escaped, and the incident ended with Beierle killing himself. The death toll in the November 2018 incident would have been higher if Beierle had used a large-capacity magazine.*

High-profile shootings draw attention not only to military-style weapons but also to the large-capacity magazines (LCMs) that make those weapons so lethal. In fact, some argue that it is a mistake to focus on the rifle or pistol; it's the large-capacity magazine, they say, that enables the shooter to fire off so many rounds without stopping to reload.

Those high-profile shootings include some of the country's most horrific mass shootings. Here's a partial list:

- On April 16, 2007, Seung-Hui Cho, an undergraduate student at Virginia Polytechnic Institute and State University in Blacksburg, Virginia, shot 49 people on campus with two semi-automatic pistols, killing 32 and wounding 17. He primarily used a Glock 9 mm with 15-round magazines, but at one site, he also used a Walther .22-caliber with a ten-round magazine. Cho fired at least 170 rounds in nine minutes.[459]

- At the 2012 Sandy Hook Elementary School in Newtown, Connecticut, Adam Lanza used large-capacity magazines to fire upwards of 150 rounds as he slaughtered twenty 6- and 7-year-old kids and six adults.[460]

- In the 2012 Aurora, Colorado theater shooting James Eagan Holmes used, among other weapons, a Smith & Wesson M&P 15 Sport semi-automatic rifle with a 100-round drum magazine to kill 12 and wound 58.[461]

- In the 2016 Pulse nightclub shooting in Orlando, Omar Mateen used a SIG Sauer MCX semi-automatic rifle and a 9mm Glock 17 semi-automatic pistol to kill 49 and wound 53 others. Mateen's rifle had a 30-round magazine, and the pistol had a 17-round magazine.[462]

- In the 2017 Las Vegas strip shooting, some of the magazines the killer used held 100 or more rounds.

- Early on the morning of Sunday, August 4, 2019, in an entertainment zone in Dayton, Ohio, Connor Betts had a one-hundred-round drum in his AR-15-style assault weapon. When he opened fire, his shooting spree lasted only 32 seconds before the police shot and killed him. But in those 32 seconds, Betts was able to kill nine and injure 26 others.[463]

Mother Jones reporters Mark Follman and Gavin Aronsen reviewed the 62 mass shootings between 1982 and 2012 and found that the shoot-ers used large-capacity magazines in 50% of the shootings.[464]

They quoted David Chipman, who served 25 years as a special agent in the Bureau of Alcohol, Tobacco, Firearms, and Explosives, as saying, "It turns a killer into a killing machine." Chipman conceded that banning large-capacity magazines would not prevent gun crimes from happening, but argued that a ban might well reduce the carnage: "Maybe three kids get killed instead of 20."

A team of researchers from Teachers College in Columbia University, the School of Medicine in Quinnipiac University, and the Harvard T.H. Chan School of Public Health collaborated to evaluate the effect of large-capacity magazine bans on the frequency and lethality of mass shootings in the U.S.[465] To do that, they gathered state data from high-fatality shootings from 1990 to 2017. They defined high-fatality mass shootings as those involving six or more fatalities, not counting the per-petrator. They defined large-capacity magazines as those holding more than ten rounds.

They compared high-fatality mass shootings in states that banned LCMs and those that didn't. After crunching the numbers, they found that "LCM bans appear to reduce both the incidence of and the number of people killed in high-fatality mass shootings." More specifically, in states that did not ban LCMs, high-fatality shootings occurred at more than double the rate of states that did ban them. And there were three times as many deaths from high-fatality mass shootings in non-ban than in the states that banned LCMs.

Another very recent and impressively thorough study concluded, "LCM bans also seem to reduce the incidence of fatal mass shootings and the number of fatalities in mass shootings."[466]

The Issue

Should we ban, for civilian use, the manufacture, sale, and possession of large-capacity magazines?

Proponents of a ban on the manufacture, sale, and possession of large-capacity magazines for civilian use argue that assault weapons and large-capacity magazines are part of the sick fantasy that attracts and emboldens school shooters and other high-profile multiple-victim shooters. The Rhode Island Coalition Against Gun Violence put it this way: "High Capacity Magazines are the Accessory of Choice for Mass Killers."[467]

But those who want a ban on large-capacity magazines rely mainly on the argument that banning the sale and possession of large-capacity magazines would reduce the number of persons injured and killed in those high-profile mass casualty shootings. To cite the Rhode Island Coalition Against Gun Violence again: "RI State Law Limits the Rounds Used in Hunting Deer and Ducks. There is NO LIMIT for Weapons Used to Kill People."[468]

Proponents also point to incidents, like those in the introduction to this chapter and elsewhere in this book, in which individuals were able to restrain or drive off the shooter when his magazine emptied, and he needed to reload[469] or were able to use that moment to escape.[470] Cops point out that when a drive-by shooter fires off rounds from the car in which he's a passenger, he fires until he empties the magazine in his gun. If he has a ten-round magazine instead of a thirty-round magazine, maybe the kid at the end of the block doesn't get shot.[471]

Those who argue against a ban insist that an experienced shooter can exchange a magazine so quickly, the magazine limit is illusory.[472]

- "I don't know where liberals got this idea that changing magazines takes five minutes. It takes, at most, a single second. Maybe a second and a half if you really suck at it. A skilled shooter can swap mags in a fraction of a second."[473]

- "And, yes, magazines can be swapped out in a couple of seconds without intense training. If you've never touched a gun in your life, I could show you how to do it, and you could make 2 or 3 second reloads with 5 minutes of practice, assuming you aren't too far below average in terms of physical dexterity."[474]

- "To a well-organized, trained shooter if you arbitrarily made the limit a five-round magazine, it takes only about 2 seconds to change magazines, and a trained shooter can do this so automatically that they hardly notice a mag change."[475]

In other words, the notion of potential victims hiding, escaping, or rushing and subduing a shooter when the shooter stops firing to reload is impossible; it's just another ridiculous failure of "liberals" to understand how guns and large-capacity magazines work.

Scientists have a wry saying to deal with those situations in which their theories say something cannot happen, and yet it does: "If something actually happens," they say, "it's probably not impossible." So too, here. The argument that a shooter can change magazines so quickly that it would be impossible for potential victims to charge the shooter or to escape would be more persuasive if incidents like those recounted at the beginning of this chapter hadn't happened.

Simply put, the argument that paranoid schizophrenics like Jared Loughner and Travis Reinking can change magazines under the most intense pressure of their lives with the same brisk efficiency of "a well-organized, trained shooter" at a shooting range is at odds with the evidence. The same may well be true of kids with attention-deficit/hyperactivity disorder (ADHD), another group some believe may be at risk to become school shooters.[476]

***

Gun zealots also object to prioritizing society's interest in limiting mass murder ahead of the enjoyment they get from shooting an assault weapon with a large-capacity magazine. As one gun rights advocate argued on Quora, doing that "punishes" gun owners "who never do anything wrong with [their weapons]. These people are asking, 'Why am I being punished? Why am I subject to restriction?' Would you say they've done something wrong, to deserve it?"[477] Others echo that sentiment.

That's an argument between those who believe society should not constrain their rights for the safety of others and those who believe that modest limitations on "rights"—or hobbies—to save lives are justified. It's the argument that arose when we required seat belt use, when we required motorcyclists to wear helmets, and when we cracked down on drunk driving. Each time we heard, "Why should I be punished when I've never had an accident?" The answer society landed on was this: Society has the right to take measures that protect its members from injury. Besides, all too often, the injured person shows up at a hospital emergency department without insurance and unable to pay for treatment.

Here's another way to look at the issue:

Late in the afternoon on May 31, 2019, DeWayne Craddock, 40, a long-time employee of Virginia Beach, entered a municipal building with two legally purchased .45 caliber semi-automatic handguns. According to James Cervera, Virginia Beach's police chief, Craddock began firing "indiscriminately." Altogether, he shot twelve fatally and injured at least four more. Craddock equipped at least one of the handguns with large-capacity magazines that enabled him to fire repeatedly before reloading. Police engaged Craddock in an extended gun battle and eventually killed him. During the melee, a bullet hit one of the police officers; only a protective vest spared his life.[478]

Here's the thing: Before that incident, Craddock was a law-abiding, responsible citizen.

The same was apparently true of Ian David Long, 28, the Marine veteran responsible for the Borderline Bar and Grill shooting in Thousand Oaks, California, on November 7, 2018. That incident also claimed twelve victims.[479] Long also used a .45 caliber Glock semi-automatic pistol equipped with large-capacity magazines.

Stephen Paddock, who used hundred-round magazines in the Las Vegas Strip massacre, was another law-abiding citizen before he opened fire from the Mandalay Bay in Las Vegas.[480]

And so on.

If we reframe it a bit, the argument is: Why should law-abiding citizens—like Craddock or Long or Paddock—be denied the right to have large-capacity magazines?

As one gun policy expert points out, we make a mistake if we accept uncritically "the common mantra that law-abiding, licensed firearm owners are not the problem."[481] In fact, in the case of gun homicides, "the killer is frequently, until that moment, a law-abiding firearm owner pulling the trigger on a lawfully held gun."

* * *

Another argument against restrictions on large-capacity magazines insists that there are already too many large-capacity magazines in the hands of gun owners to make any ban effective or even feasible. As someone opposed to limits on LCMs put it on Quora, "People often forget that there is a vast stockpile of arms and ammunition in the US —300 million-odd guns[.]"[482]

Gun owners, according to this argument, are not likely to surrender their magazines if possession were to become illegal. In fact, some "responsible, law-abiding" gun zealots swear they would bury their magazines in their backyards if necessary.[483] In short, when those who want to do something about gun violence argue that we shouldn't allow our country to become a version of Mogadishu in the 1990s, where seemingly every man carried his own assault rifle with a large-capacity magazine, gun zealots counter: "Too late!"

If Congress were to ban the sale, but not the possession, of large-capacity magazines, the experience of the prior ban suggests that it might well take a decade or more before we would see a large drop off in large-capacity magazines being used in mass shootings, cop killings, and other crimes. On the other hand, if Congress and the states don't act, the number of large-capacity magazines in gun owners' hands may continue to increase; in that case, the related carnage will never end and may get even worse.

***

Opponents of a ban also repeat the old NRA canard that gun laws only regulate law-abiding citizens. Criminals, they insist, will somehow always be able to get guns and large-capacity magazines.

It is true that on television shows and in movies, professional killers and sophisticated terrorists *are* always able to buy whatever guns and related paraphernalia they need to pull off their exploits. Perhaps with that in mind, gun zealots argue that even if Congress banned assault weapons and large-capacity magazines, "criminals" would still be able to buy as many AR-15-style rifles and large-capacity magazines as they want on the black market *or somehow*.

Most mass shooters weren't "criminals" before they began firing indiscriminately at strangers. Thus, the unarticulated part of the argument is this: Even if Congress were to ban assault weapons and large-capacity magazines, mentally ill teens using their spending money will always, in some unspecified way, be able to get their hands on assault weapons and large-capacity magazines. So too will paranoid schizophrenics like Jared Lee Loughner, who was so strange and delusional he had trouble buying ammunition at Walmart,[484] or Travis Reinking, who couldn't find his pants.

***

More sophisticated defenders of large-capacity magazines argue that a ban would not reduce the overall crime rate. *See, e.g.*, "Regulating the capacity of magazines doesn't stop crime, it doesn't slow crime down, it doesn't affect it at all."[485] Or this: "[T]here is no evidence that banning 'high capacity' magazines will reduce crime."[486] They bolster this argument with the undeniable fact that the overwhelming majority of gun crimes involve handguns, and that mass shootings are relatively rare events that account for only a very small portion of the overall annual death toll from guns.

The argument shoots down a strawman argument no one is making. Proponents of a ban don't argue that a ban on large-capacity magazines would reduce the overall crime rate (shoplifting, possession of a dime bag of marijuana, etc.). Proponents don't even argue that banning large-capacity magazines would reduce the gun-crime rate.

As already mentioned, proponents of a ban are mainly concerned about mass shootings. They are also concerned but don't mention enough that drug dealers and other hardened criminals should not be better armed than the police. But even that concern does not address the overall gun crime rate, which mainly involves people becoming angry, grabbing a readily available gun, and doing something they likely soon regret.

* * *

In the interest of being complete, opponents of a ban also argue that regulating the size of magazines is completely illogical and arbitrary. To illustrate that point, they offer silly analogies about regulating the size of egg cartons or the bandwidth of computers.

Eccentric Republican Congressman Louis "Louie" Buller Gohmert, Jr. found a way to top even those arguments:

> In fact, I had this discussion with some wonderful, caring Democrats earlier this week on the issue of, well, they said, "surely you could agree to limit the number of rounds in a magazine, couldn't you? How would that be problematic?"
>
> [...]
>
> And I pointed out, well, once you make it ten, then why would you draw the line at ten? What's wrong with nine? Or eleven? And the problem is once you draw that limit; it's kind of like marriage when you say it's not a man and a woman anymore, then why not have three men and one woman, or four women and one man, or why not somebody has a love for an animal?[487]

In other words, opponents of a ban argue that there is no natural definition of "large-capacity." Any limit is necessarily arbitrary.

They also argue that whatever limit legislators set is likely to be reduced by "liberals" and "gun grabbers" to zero. As Congressman Gohmert explained:

> There is no clear place to draw the line once you eliminate the traditional marriage, and it's the same once you start

putting limits on what guns can be used, then it's just really easy to have laws that make them all illegal.[488]

Lawmakers, however, draw arbitrary limits all the time. Why is the speed limit on the expressway 70 mph instead of 68 or 72? And if we set the speed limit at 65 mph, does that guarantee we're eventually going to reduce it to zero?

While not as interesting as Rep. Gohmert's argument, it is worth noting that courts reject on Second Amendment grounds bans that go below ten rounds[489]—negating his "slippery slope" argument—at least with respect to large-capacity magazines. How to define marriage and whether Rep. Gohmert should be in Congress are questions well outside of this book.

Below, we will look to see which side's arguments the public finds more convincing, but first an aside about street crime.

Large-Capacity Magazines and Street Crime

When proponents of a ban on large-capacity magazines argue that those magazines produce more victims in mass shootings, and Second Amendment absolutists argue that a ban would not affect the overall crime rate, the two groups are talking past one another.

To a limited extent, however, large-capacity magazines *do* figure into street crime, especially crimes involving drug dealers and shootings of police officers. Laws banning large-capacity magazines give the police another tool for taking those bad actors off the streets. They may also help reduce the number of police officers shot and killed.[490]

The assault rifle ban, 1994-2004, also banned large-capacity magazines. The ban, however, grandfathered in the millions of magazines already in the hands of gun manufacturers, gun dealers, and gun owners on the ban's effective date. Gun manufacturers, in fact, used the months before September 13, 1994, when the ban became effective, to produce as many LCMs as they could. They also continued to import LCMs, which don't disclose their date of manufacture, and to sell them as preban merchandise.

As a result, on September 13, 2004, when the ban expired, it was only beginning to reduce the availability and illegal use of large-capacity magazines. But despite grandfathered magazines and other problems, it is simply not accurate to say that banning LCM's didn't "affect [crime] at all."

In 2004, when Professor Christopher S. Koper wrote his preliminary analysis of the ban for the Department of Justice, he surveyed the impact of the ban in several states and cities. His conclusions:

- LCMs [Large Capacity Magazines] are used in crime much more often than AWs [Assault Weapons] and accounted for 14% to 26% of guns used in crime before the ban.

- The failure [of the ban] to reduce LCM use was likely due to the immense stock of exempted pre-ban magazines, which has been enhanced by recent imports.

In a 2017 follow up to his 2004 study,[491] Professor Koper attempted, among other things, to get a feel for whether criminals are using assault weapons and large-capacity magazines more now than when the assault ban ended in 2004. This part of his study focused on three cities: Baltimore, Minneapolis, and Richmond. The precise years analyzed varied a bit depending on the years for which data from those cities were available:

- In Baltimore, the percentage of crime guns that were LCM weapons was **48.6%** higher in 2012-2014 than in 2004.

- In Minneapolis, the percentage of crime guns that were LCM weapons was **49.4%** higher in 2012-2014 than in 2006-2007.

- In Richmond, Va., from 2003-2004 to 2008-2009, the increase was **111.5%**.

That's strong evidence that the ban and its end had a meaningful impact on the role of large-capacity magazines in crime.

Professor Koper's 2017 study also found that cop killers used large-capacity magazine-compatible firearms in **41%** of the murders of police in the post-ban years 2009 through 2013, the years covered by his study. The yearly range ran from 35% to 48%.

The Washington Post analyzed data kept by the Virginia State Police. Its reporters found the percentage of crime guns equipped with large-capacity ammunition magazines *declined* after Congress enacted the federal ban.[492] As the stock of grandfathered guns dried up, the percentage reached a low of 10% in 2004. Then, after the ban expired, the percentage climbed steadily. By 2010, the percentage of crime guns equipped with large-capacity ammunition magazines was close to 22%.

Similarly, after the ban ended in 2004, the Los Angeles Police Department's Gun Unit also saw a dramatic increase in the number of large-capacity magazines it recovered. In 2003, the last full year of the ban, the L.A. police recovered **38** large-capacity magazines. In 2004, they recovered **725** large-capacity magazines, a 1,808% increase. In 2005, the number jumped to **940** large-capacity magazines.[493] "Even as crime has declined significantly in the city over the past several years," LAPD Chief Charlie Beck noted, "large-capacity ammunition magazines are still being used by violent street gangs. Common sense restrictions on these magazines would help LAPD officers better protect the public and themselves."

Thus, a subsidiary issue is: Besides discouraging high-profile mass shootings and reducing the number killed and wounded in those incidents, do we want to do what we can to reduce the risks that law enforcement officers face when dealing with drug dealers and other vicious criminals?

Those who want to try to reduce the risks to which law enforcement officers are exposed answer that question one way. Those who believe their "right" to use large-capacity magazines is more important than the lives of law enforcement officers answer that question the other way.

What We Want

Pollsters jumped on the issue of banning large-capacity magazines after the October 1, 2017, Las Vegas Strip mass shooting. They returned to the issue after the February 14, 2018, Parkland, Florida school shooting. Morning Consult also returned to the issue in August 2018 and again in August 2019.

Overall Results

Favor	Oppose	Polling Dates	Poll
72%	20%	10/5-9/17	Morning Consult
64%	34%	10/5-10/17	Quinnipiac
78%	22%	10/10-11/17	Ipsos/NPR
69%	20%	2/15-19/18	Morning Consult
70%	20%	2/20-26/18	Morning Consult
73%	27%	2/27-28/18	Ipsos/NPR
63%	34%	3/3-5/18	Quinnipiac
64%	24%	8/2-6/18	Morning Consult.
67%	32%	9/24-10/7/18	Pew
70%	31%	1/11-28/19	Ipsos/Reuters
73%	20%	8/5-7/19	Morning Consult
58%	38%	8/20-25/19	Suffolk/USA
60%	36%	9/2-5/19	ABC/WaPo
61%	14%	9/5-8/19	NPR/PBS/Marist
70%	30%	9/3-15/19	Pew

*Averages: **67%** vs. **27%**. Ratio: 2.5 to 1.*
*Voters: **67%** vs. **23%**. Ratio: 2.9 to 1.*
*Adults: **68%** vs. **31%**. Ratio: 2.2 to 1.*

Ipsos, Pew and ABC/Washington Post, and Suffolk polled adults; the other polls surveyed registered voters.

On average, **67%** of us favor, and **27%** of us oppose a ban on large-capacity magazines. The poll results vary a bit depending on how many gun owners were in the sample population and on how the polling organization framed the question. But by any measure, the public came down clearly in favor of a ban on large-capacity magazines. (*Note:* The outlier August 2019 USA/Suffolk poll, which showed the lowest level of support, 58%, also had the highest percentage of gun householders of any poll in this book—50%.)

Banning "Possession" Is Less Popular

SSRS, polling for CNN, asked if registered voters favored a ban on the sale *or possession* of "high-capacity or extended ammunition magazines, which allow some guns to shoot more than ten bullets before they need to be reloaded." The question suggested that gun owners would have to give up their existing stock of large-capacity magazines. It also suggested that the cut-off point would be ten rounds. That formulation moved about 5% from "support" to "oppose." (When 5% move from one column to the other, the result is a ten-point difference.)

- In October 2017, **54%** of registered voters favored, and **43%** opposed a ban on the sale *or possession* of high-capacity or extended ammunition magazines, which allow some guns to shoot more than ten bullets before they need to be re-loaded.[494]
- In February 2018, **63%** of registered voters favored, and **34%** opposed a ban on the sale *or possession* of "high-capacity or extended ammunition magazines."[495]

On average, in these two polls, a majority, **59%**, favored a ban on the sale **or possession** of large-capacity magazines, defined as magazines that hold more than ten rounds. That compares with **69%** in the polls that asked only about "banning" large-capacity magazines.

Gender Gap

Men are generally a little more resistant, and women a little more open to measures to deal with our gun violence problem, but on this issue, the disparities are quite large:

Men *Favor/Oppose*	*Women* *Favor/Oppose*	*Polling Dates*	*Poll*
65%/28%	80%/12%	10/5-9/17	Morning Consult
56%/42%	71%/25%	10/5-10/17	Quinnipiac
43%/55%	65%/32%	10/12-15/17	CNN (SSRS)
64%/28%	74%/16%	2/15-19/18	Morning Consult
68%/25%	72%/17%	2/20-26/18	Morning Consult
53%/45%	74%/23%	2/20-23/18	CNN (SSRS)
64%/36%	82%/18%	2/27-28/18	Ipsos-NPR
51%/46%	68%/27%	9/2-5/19	ABC/WaPo
42%/55%	70%/24%	9/5-8/19	NPR/PBS

Average (Men): **57%** *vs.* **39%**. *Ratio: 1.5 to 1.*

Average (Women): **73%** vs. **21%**. *Ratio: 3.4 to 1.*

These polls are inconsistent, but in all but two of them, majorities of both men and women favored banning large-capacity magazines. Women were about 16 percentage points more likely than men to approve a ban.

Republicans

Quite a few polls broke out respondents by political party. Here are the results for Republicans:

Favor	Oppose	Polling Dates	Poll
64%	29%	10/5-9/17	Morning Consult
44%	52%	10/5-10/17	Quinnipiac
69%	31%	10/10-11/17	Ipsos-NPR*
41%	54%	10/12-15/17	CNN (SSRS)*
63%	28%	2/15-19/18	Morning Consult
48%	51%	2/20-23/18	CNN (SSRS)*
60%	32%	2/20-26/18	Morning Consult
59%	41%	2/27-28/18	NPR/Ipsos*
39%	57%	3/3-5/18	Quinnipiac
52%	35%	8/2-6/18	Morning Consult
58%	41%	1/11-28/19	Reuters/Ipsos*
43%	51%	9/2-5/19	ABC/WaPo*
40%	51%	9/5-8/19	NPR/PBS/Marist*

Averages: **52%** vs. **43%**. *Ratio: 1.2 to 1.*
Registered Voters: **54%** vs. **39%**. *Ratio: 1.3 to 1.*
Adults (*): **51%** vs. **46%**. *Ratio: 1.1 to 1.*

These results are inconsistent. Six polls showed clear majorities of Republicans in favor of a ban on large-capacity magazines. But six other polls showed majorities of Republicans opposed to a ban. Results ranged from 64% and 69% in favor in two polls in October 2017 to only 44% and 41% in favor in two other polls in the same month.

SSRS, Quinnipiac, and the ABC/Washington Post polls framed the question in a way that may (at least partially) explain the discrepancy between their polls and the rest. They included a 10-round limitation. Quinnipiac, for example, asked: "60. Do you support or oppose a nationwide ban on the sale of high-capacity ammunition magazines that hold more than ten bullets?" Evidently, some of us might be okay with a limitation on "large-capacity magazines" if the limit were higher. Others oppose any limitation on how many rounds a magazine may hold.

In the six polls that did not attempt to define a large-capacity magazine, respondents (on average) favored a ban 61% to 33%. In the six polls that used a ten-round limit, respondents (on average) opposed a ban, 42% (in favor) to 53% (opposed).

The NPR/PBS NewsHour/Marist poll did not include a 10-round definition of a high-capacity magazine, and yet it also showed very low support for a ban on large-capacity magazines. That poll, however, had an unusually high percentage of gun owners in the sample, creating the possibility that it is a special case.

In short, there is no clear trend among these poll results, but on the whole, support for a ban on large-capacity magazines among Republicans has been eroding. Republicans, moreover, oppose a ban if the limit is set at the usual ten rounds.

Trump 2016 Voters

Favor	Oppose	Polling Dates	Poll
63%	29%	10/5-9/17	Morning Consult
59%	31%	2/15-19/18	Morning Consult
60%	32%	2/20-26/18	Morning Consult
54%	36%	8/2-6/18	Morning Consult.
37%	55%	9/5-8/19	NPR/PBS/Marist

*Averages: **55%** vs. **37%**. Ratio: 1.5 to 1.*

In all of the polls but the last, folks who voted for Donald Trump in the 2016 election favored a ban on large-capacity magazines, although support does seem to have been trending down. (The last poll is the NPR/PBS NewsHour/Marist poll. As we've noted elsewhere, that poll over-weighted gun owners. Forty percent of the Marist sample were gun owners, as opposed to the expected ~22%.)

Here's an odd point of comparison for the **37%** (on average who opposed restricting large-capacity magazines: After the Orlando shooting, candidate Donald Trump accused President Barack Obama of siding with terrorist organizations like ISIS. The accusation was an obvious falsehood, but in a Quinnipiac poll, **37%** of white men and **39%** of gun owners said they believed Trump's bizarre assertion.[496] At the time, the Obama Administration was bombing ISIS and arming its fiercest opponents, the Kurds. (After he became president, Trump gave Turkey the green light to attack our longtime allies, the Kurds, a decision that allowed many ISIS fighters to escape and gave ISIS a chance to regroup.

Gun Households

In most polls since the Las Vegas Strip massacre for which the polling organization has made data on gun households available, a sometimes-slim majority from gun households favored a ban on large-capacity ammunition magazines.

Favor	*Oppose*	*Polling Dates*	*Poll*
63%	32%	10/5-9/17	Morning Consult
52%	45%	10/5-10/17	Quinnipiac
55%	42%	2/20-23/18	CNN (SSRS)[497]
50%	48%	3/3-5/18	Quinnipiac
53%	37%	8/2-6/18	Morning Consult
48%	48%	9/2-5/19	ABC/WaPo
47%	59%	9/5-8/19	NPR/PBS (owners)

Average: ***53%*** *vs.* ***44%***. *Ratio: 1.2 to 1.*

In all but two of these polls, gun householders favored a ban on large-capacity magazines. On average, **53%** of those living in gun households favored, and **42%** opposed a ban on large-capacity magazines. But there is a fairly clear trendline over this period toward less support among those in gun households for a ban on large-capacity magazines.

Education

People with a Bachelor's degree favored banning large-capacity magazines by a much larger margin than those without a college degree, and those with post education or professional degrees were even more supportive.

Polling Dates	Poll	No Deg.	Col. Degree	Post Grad
10/5-9/17	Morn. Consult	68%/22%	78%/15%	78%/15%
2/15-19/18	Morn. Consult	67%/21%	67%/21%	76%/27%
2/20-26/18	Morn. Consult	66%/22%	77%/19%	81%/14%
10/5-10/17	Quinnipiac	58%/38%	67%/31%	--/--
10/12-15/17	CNN/SRRS	50%/47%	64%/34%	--/--
2/20-23/18	CNN/SRRS	58%/39%	75%/23%	--/--
3/3-5/18	Quinnipiac	55%/40%	70%/28%	--/--
8/2-6/18	Morn. Consult	57%/26%	74%/22%	84%/14%
9/2-5/19	ABC-WaPo	55%/41%	69%/28%	74%/21%
9/5-8/19	NPR-PBS	56%/39%	69%/28%	--/--
Average	*(Favor/Opp.)*	**59%/34%**	**71%/25%**	**79%/18%**

Annual Income Over $100,000

Higher-income folks were more supportive of a ban on large-capacity magazines.

Favor	Oppose	Polling Dates	Poll
79%	16%	10/5-9/17	Morning Consult
74%	19%	2/15-19/18	Morning Consult
82%	13%	2/20-26/18	Morning Consult
73%	21%	8/2-6/18	Morning Consult
68%	31%	9/2-5/19	ABC/WaPo

Average: **75%** vs. **20%**. *Ratio: 3.8 to 1.*

Polling Wrap Up

If we average these polls, a super majority of Americans, **67%**, favored a ban on the sale of large-capacity magazines. On average, **26%** opposed a ban. That's 2.5 to 1. (Two polls asked about banning posses-sion and got a lower level of support (-8) and a higher level (+18) level of opposition.)

Women (73% vs. 21%) favored a ban on high-capacity magazines at rates that ran about 16 percentage points higher than men (57% vs. 39%).

Breakouts of Republicans showed highly variable results, but when averaged, a majority of Republicans supported a ban on the sale of large-capacity magazines (Republican adults, 52% vs. 43%; Republican regis-tered voters 54% to 39%. If there is to be a limit, Republicans, appar-ently, would set it at something higher than 10-rounds. Importantly, the trendline among Republicans appears to be toward less support for ban-ning large-capacity magazines and more opposition. The same is gener-ally true of those who voted for Donald Trump in 2016 (55% in favor of a ban LCMs *vs.* 37% opposed.

On average, a majority, **53%**, of those who live in households where there is a gun favored a ban (*vs.* 44% opposed. But here too, the trend appears to be toward less support.

People at every educational level supported a ban on large-capacity magazines, and as usual, support rose with educational level. Among those without a college degree, the split was **59%** in favor and 34% op-posed. Among those with a college degree, the split was **71%** to 25%. Among those with a post-graduate education, the split was a remarkable **79%** to 18%.

The decline in support in the summer of 2019 was largely among white males without college educations. That demographic probably ac-counts for much of the erosion in support among Republicans, Trump supporters, and gun householders.

On average, 75% of those with annual incomes over $100,000 sup-ported a ban, versus only 20% who opposed. That is more than 3 to 1 in favor of banning large-capacity magazines.

What We're Getting Instead

In Congress, Republicans have been willing to offer "thoughts and prayers" to the families of those killed by weapons with large-capacity magazines, but legislation to reduce the carnage wasn't in their thoughts and didn't have a prayer as long as they had enough votes in the Senate to stop it.

The States

Eight states and the District of Columbia have adopted bans on large-capacity magazines.[498] Virginia, where the Virginia Tech and the Virginia Beach shootings occurred, is not—as of this writing—among the states to restrict large-capacity magazines. In fact, just months before the Virginia Beach shooting, Republican legislators blocked a proposal, S.B. 1748, to limit the size of magazines.[499]

After the shooting, Virginia's Democratic governor, Ralph Northam, called the state's legislators into a special session to address mass shootings and gun crime. The Republican-dominated Virginia legislature promptly adjourned the special session without considering a single bill.

A few months later, in the November 2019 election, voters replaced enough Republicans to give Democrats a slim majority in the legislature. In polls, gun violence was the number one issue for Virginia voters.[500]

When the new legislature met, thousands of demonstrators marched on the state capital in an effort to dissuade the legislature from doing what voters elected it to do. Some gun extremists threatened to kill Democratic lawmakers if they passed the measures they campaigned on.[501]

The new legislature passed several gun-violence-prevention bills, which Governor Ralph Northam signed into law on April 10, 2020. But due to defections by a handful of conservative Democratic legislators, the package did not include bans on assault weapons or large-capacity magazines.[502]

The Giffords Law Center tracks states that enact bans on large-capacity magazines. Readers should consult it for up-to-date information. The reader who needs legal advice should consult an attorney familiar with gun legislation.

The Courts

In 2016, Californians overwhelmingly approved a ballot initiative, Proposition 63, that prohibited possession of large-capacity magazines. The ban would have gone into effect July 1, 2017, but a federal judge upheld a challenge to the ban and issued a preliminary injunction barring the law from going into effect.[503]

The District Court held: (i the ban on large-capacity magazines violated the Second Amendment; and (ii the ban also violated the Takings Clause of the Fifth Amendment, which prohibits taking property for public purposes without just compensation. The latter holding applied only to large-capacity magazines already in the hands of gun owners.

On July 17, 2018, in a two-to-one decision, the Ninth Circuit Court of Appeals upheld the lower court's preliminary order, gutting Califor-nia's large-capacity magazine ban.[504] The appellate panel said it found no error in the lower court's preliminary assessment of the evidence and sent the case back to the trial court for further proceedings. Given the narrow grounds for its ruling, the Ninth Circuit designated its decision non-prec-edential, meaning attorneys may not cite it as precedent in other cases.

Due to the court order staying California's ban on large-capacity magazines, the gunman in the Thousand Oaks shooting was able to buy and use a large-capacity magazine in his shooting rampage.[505]

The Ninth Circuit's unpublished decision was at odds with a Second Circuit[506] decision that upheld "the core provisions of the New York and Connecticut laws prohibiting possession of semi-automatic assault weapons and large-capacity magazines."[507] The Second Circuit ruled that the prohibitions did not violate the Second Amendment and were not void for vagueness. It did, however, strike down the provision of New York's law limiting magazines to seven rounds as too restrictive. The "Takings Clause" issue was not before the Second Circuit.

The unpublished Ninth Circuit decision was also at odds with a Third Circuit decision that upheld New Jersey's ban on magazines holding more than ten rounds.[508] The court began its opinion with this statement:

> Today we address whether one of New Jersey's responses to the rise in active and mass shooting incidents in the United States—a law that limits the amount of ammunition that may be held in a single firearm magazine to no more than ten rounds—violates the Second Amendment, the Fifth Amendment's Takings Clause, and the Fourteenth Amendment's Equal Protection Clause. We conclude that it does not.

The court elaborated, "New Jersey's law reasonably fits the state's interest in public safety and does not unconstitutionally burden the Second Amendment's right to self-defense in the home."

In upholding the large-capacity magazine ban against a Second Amendment challenge, the Third Circuit joined the Second Circuit[509]; the Fourth Circuit[510]; the Seventh Circuit[511]; the Ninth Circuit[512]; and the D.C. Circuit.[513] The First Circuit has very recently come to the same conclusion.[514]

That's an impressive lineup, but the Supreme Court may yet take a case raising this issue and rule the other way. Unless and until it does, the governing law in most of the country is this: Bans on magazines holding more than ten rounds do not violate the Second Amendment.

15. Should We Ban Bump Stocks?

Item: *Gun rights activists portray gun ownership as an essential part of freedom. On its website, Slide Fire, the company that pioneered and was the primary manufacturer of bump stocks, described its product in glowing terms under the heading:*[515]

FREEDOM UNLEASHED

Slide Fire proclaimed that its products, "revolutionized recreational shooting by allowing for a whole new method of fire." It bragged that "our stock grants shooters the freedom of controlled rapid fire without compromising the safety of themselves or others around them."

Item: *In preparation for the worst mass shooting in our country's history, Stephen Paddock, 64, attached bump stocks to thirteen of his semi-automatic rifles, effectively converting the rifles into machine guns. He moved those and other guns into a suite on the 32nd floor of the Mandalay Bay hotel. From that vantage point, between 10:05 and 10:15 p.m. on the night of October 1, 2017, Paddock unleashed some of the "freedom" Slide Fire touted. Altogether, Paddock fired at least 1,049 rounds at the concertgoers 32 floors beneath his suite, killing 58 people and leaving 413 with gunshot or shrapnel wounds. Hundreds more sustained injuries fleeing.*[516]

Item: *Bump stock prices on the secondary market soared.*[517]

In the 1920s and early 1930s, the American public reacted with shock at lurid newspaper and newsreel accounts of Prohibition-era gangsters using sawed-off shotguns and Thompson submachine guns—"Tommy guns"—to murder rivals and cops. Congress responded to the public revulsion by enacting the National Firearms Act of 1934, which banned the sale of short-barreled shotguns and machine guns (automatic rifles) to civilians. Those prohibitions remain core prohibitions of federal law. As a result, ATF highly regulates automatic weapons.

"Bump stocks" or "bump fire stocks" are devices that replace the original stationery stock on a semi-automatic rifle, usually an AR- or AK-style rifle. They are designed to harness the rifle's recoil to provide the main impetus for firing the next round. In effect, they turn a semi-automatic weapon into an automatic weapon or, in regulatory terms, into a machine gun like those the National Firearms Act banned.

But unlike automatic weapons, ATF did not regulate bump stocks. As ATF explained in a March 2018 regulatory notice, "Individuals, therefore, may purchase these devices without undergoing a background check or complying with any other federal regulations applicable to firearms."[518] In other words, any felon, fugitive, paranoid schizophrenic, or mass-murderer wannabe could buy one.

Slide Fire Solutions, LP, the original and primary manufacturer of bump stocks, sold the devices online and through retailers. It held mul-tiple patents and aggressively enforced them to keep competitors off the market. As a result, at the time of the Las Vegas Strip shooting, it had only one active competitor. Not surprisingly, Slide Fire made the devices used in the Las Vegas Strip shooting.[519]

Given the number killed and injured in that shooting, there was an immediate call for Congress to ban bump stocks and to take other measures to address mass shootings. Several Congressmen began work on bills to ban the devices.

As we've seen, despite his promises to stand by the NRA, even President Trump called for a ban on the sale of bump stocks.

In Congress, Senator Dianne Feinstein made the first overt move. On October 4, 2017, she introduced legislation to ban bump stocks.[520] Her bill had twenty-four co-sponsors, all Democrats.[521] Even some Re-publican Senators indicated that they might be open to legislation ban-ning bump stocks.

Senate Majority Leader Mitch McConnell, R-Ky., and other Re-publican leaders immediately pushed back, arguing that it was too soon to discuss how to prevent another similar massacre from occurring. Senator McConnell argued that the Senate's priority should not be protecting everyday Americans from gun violence; it should be passing the

Republican tax bill that provided huge tax breaks for very high-income individuals and bg corporations.⁵²²

On October 5, 2017, the NRA issued a statement that opposed legislation but called on the Bureau of Alcohol, Tobacco, Firearms, and Explosives (BATFE or ATF to review whether bump stocks complied with federal law. The statement said:

> In Las Vegas, reports indicate that certain devices were used to modify the firearms involved. ... the National Rifle Association is calling on the Bureau of Alcohol, Tobacco, Firearms and Explosives (BATFE) to immediately review whether these devices comply with federal law. The NRA believes that devices designed to allow semi-automatic rifles to function like fully-automatic rifles should be subject to additional regulations.

The statement was widely seen as a dodge by the NRA to keep Congress from passing legislation addressing gun violence. The NRA and the gun manufacturers it represents may have feared that Congress would do more than ban bump stocks.

Chris Cillizza, CNN's Editor-at-Large, wrote:⁵²³

> Consider first that the NRA is calling on the Bureau of Alcohol, Tobacco, and Firearms (ATF) to handle the bump stock issue. Why does this matter? Because if ATF takes on the issue, it means that Congress doesn't.

In effect, the NRA gave the ATF permission to revise its regulations to regulate the devices. It was a stunning confirmation of the extent to which ATF is a "captive agency" under the control of the NRA.

The move had its intended effect. Action stalled in both the House, where House leadership under Paul Ryan insisted that Congress wait for a regulatory fix, and in the Senate, where Senator McConnell stood in the way.⁵²⁴

In December 2017, the Department of Justice, ATF's parent agency, published an Advance Notice of Proposed Rulemaking.⁵²⁵ Part of the formal regulatory process, the purpose of the notice was to gather information before the agency proposed a new regulation. In this case, the agency sought information about "the nature and scope of the market" for bump stock devices. Instead, interested parties and the public inundated the agency with comments urging the agency to interpret, or not interpret, the existing statues to apply to bump stock devices. The Administrative Procedure Act required the agency to review each comment. The mountain of comments had the effect of bogging down the rulemaking process as ATF slogged through the comments.

That's where things stood when the 2018 Valentine's Day shooting at the Marjory Stoneman Douglas High School in Parkland, Florida, occurred. The Parkland school shooter did not use a bump stock, but his rampage and the response by the Parkland students put every aspect of the gun debate back on the table.

But not in Moran, Texas, where Slide Fire had its operations. In the days immediately after the Parkland school shooting, Slide Fire offered a President's Day Sale on its products with the coupon code "MAGA."[526] For its British readers, The Guardian explained, "That's a salute to the campaign slogan of President Donald Trump, who promised to 'Make America Great Again,' and who has responded to the deadly massacres in the past five months by continuing to oppose any new gun control laws."

In a marketing email announcing the sale, Slide Fire promoted the offer with the tagline, "#HeresToFreedom."

The Issue

Should Congress ban bump stocks and other devices that enable a semi-automatic rifle to fire more-or-less like an automatic rifle or machine gun?

After the Parkland shooting, President Trump signed a memorandum directing the Justice Department and ATF "to dedicate all available resources to complete the review of the comments received, and, as expeditiously as possible, to propose for notice and comment a rule banning all devices that turn legal weapons into machineguns."[527]

After the news media reported Trump's action, the websites of the two manufacturers that sold bump stocks crashed under demand from people wanting to buy the devices before ATF outlawed them. Once again, prices in the secondary market shot up.[528]

ATF posted a Notice of Proposed Rulemaking on March 29, 2018. It proposed a regulation (or "rule") banning bump stocks and similar devices.[529] That opened another comment period, one that extended to June 27, 2018.

As required, in its Notice of Proposed Rulemaking, ATF attempted to assess the economic impact of its proposed regulation. ATF recited that there were two manufacturers of the devices at the time and 2,281 retailers. Despite the seeming exactitude, ATF made clear that the latter figure—2,281 retailers—was just a rough estimate.

Because the agency had not regulated the devices, ATF did not know how many of the devices manufacturers had sold. But based on the information it collected in response to its Advance Notice, ATF estimated that from 2010, when Slide Stock began selling bump stocks, to the end of 2017, manufacturers probably sold between 35,000 and 75,000 bump stocks per year. That meant, in total, they had sold 2.8 to 6 million of the devices. From ATF's discussion of how it arrived at those numbers, it's clear that rough estimate was little more than what engineers and the Army used to call a SWAG ("scientific wild-ass guess").

ATF pointed out that if it banned bump stocks, current owners would be required to destroy, disable, or turn in their devices, thus losing the value of the devices. Slide Fire sold bump stocks at prices ranging between $179 and $425.95. ATF estimated that the total amount spent on these devices from 2012 through 2017 at somewhere between $56 million and $96 million. One comment—which likely came from Slide Fire—estimated sales at $76,195,750. ATF seemed to suggest that the estimate was probably the best available.

If ATF finalized the proposed regulation, Slide Fire and other sellers would also lose future sales of bump stocks. ATF noted, however, that bans by several states reduced the economic impact of the proposed reg-ulation on future sales. At the time, six states had banned the devices—California, Florida, Massachusetts, New Jersey, New York, and Washing-ton. (Since then, additional states have also banned the devices.)

On October 2, 2018, a year and a day after the Las Vegas shooting, President Trump said the regulation banning bump stocks was "two or three weeks" away. The Justice Department, which would know, said it would be months before it finalized the regulation.[530]

And that's where things stood on the anniversary of the Las Vegas Strip massacre. Paul Ryan in the House and Mitch McConnell in the Senate blocked legislation banning the devices, and the proposed regulation remained under review. Gun rights groups were expected to file suit as soon as the regulation issued, arguing that the regulation misconstrued the statute, violated the Second Amendment, and was an unlawful taking of property (the banned bump stocks) without just compensation under the Constitution's "Takings Clause."

Congressional action would have been quicker. It would also have avoided the inevitable litigation arguing that the regulation was contrary to the statute. If congressional legislation included a buy-back program, it would also have avoided a "Takings Clause" challenge. That would have left only a Second Amendment challenge for gun rights groups to pursue.

The New York Post commented that Congress did not have to wait months or years for the slow regulatory process and pointed out that while the regulatory process dragged on, the public remained at risk.[531]

On April 17, 2018, Slide Fire announced it was shutting down.[532] Shortly after that, Slide Fire struck a deal to sell off the remainder of its inventory, citing "rising demand" for bump stocks.[533]

What We Want

Should Congress ban the sale of firearm attachments (*i.e.*, bump stocks and similar devices) that allow semi-automatic rifles to fire at almost the same rate as an automatic weapon?

In summary fashion, here's what polls found:

Overall Results

Favor	Oppose	Target:	Polling Dates	Poll
72%	14%	Adults	10/5/17	YouGov
79%	13%	Voters	10/5-9/17	Morning Consult
73%	25%	Voters	10/5-10/17	Quinnipiac
82%	18%	Voters	10/10-11/17	NPR/Ipsos
51%	46%	Adults	12/3-5/17	CBS/SSRS
76%	16%	Voters	2/15-19/18	Morning Consult
74%	18%	Voters	8/2-6/18	Morning Consult
66%	17%	Adults	12/20/18	YouGov
56%	38%	Adults	2/20-22/18	CBS/SSRS
81%	19%	Adults	2/27-28/18	NPR/Ipsos
70%	17%	Adults	3/14-19/18	AP-NORC

Averages: **71%** *vs.* **22%**. *Ratio: 3.2 to 1.*
Registered voters: **77%** *vs.* **18%**. *Ratio: 4.3 to 1.*
Adults: **66%** *vs.* **25%**. *Ratio: 2.6 to 1.*

On average, about 71% of the American public wanted a ban on bump stocks, and only 23% opposed a ban. That's about 3 to 1 in favor of a ban.

The two CBS News polls, both conducted by SSRS, jump off the page as outliers. They pegged support for banning bump stocks at 51% and 56%, with opposition at 38% and 46%. It is not clear why the SSRS/CBS polls were such extreme outliers—although SSRS polls generally show much less support for gun-violence-prevention measures than other polls.

Republicans

Favor	Oppose	Polling Dates	Poll
61%	23%	10/5/17	YouGov (daily poll)
75%	17%	10/5-9/17	Morning Consult
62%	34%	10/5-10/17	Quinnipiac[534]
77%	23%	10/10-11/17	Ipsos-NPR[535]
51%	46%	12/3-5/17	CBS News/SSRS[536]
71%	21%	2/15-19/18	Morning Consult[537]
51%	41%	2/20-22/18	CBS News/SSRS
73%	27%	2/27-28/18	Ipsos-NPR[538]
63%	27%	8/2-6/18	Morning Consult[539]
54%	28%	12/20/18	YouGov Daily[540]

Averages: **64%** *vs.* **29%**. *Ratio: 2.2 to 1.*

Despite the outlier CBS News/SSRS polls, *on average*, **64%** of Republicans supported, and **29%** opposed a ban.

Trump 2016 Voters

Three Morning Consult polls offered glimpses of where President Trump's supporters stood on bump stocks. Two polls broke out those who voted for Trump in 2016; the third broke out those who approved of the way Trump was handling gun issues.

Favor	Oppose	Polling Dates	Poll
75%	16%	10/5-9/17	Morning Consult
69%	23%	2/15-19/18	Morning Consult
65%	26%	8/2-6/18	Morning Consult

Averages: **70%** *vs.* **22%**. *Ratio: 3.2 to 1.*

On average, **70%** of Trump supporters favored, and **22%** opposed a ban on bump stocks.

Gun Households

Three polls provided crosstabs for those in gun households. Two tapped into public sentiment immediately after the Las Vegas shooting, and the other was more recent.

Favor	Oppose	Polling Dates	Poll
67%	29%	10/5-10/17	Quinnipiac
74%	20%	10/5-9/17	Morning Consult
65%	29%	8/2-6/18	Morning Consult

*Averages: **69%** vs. **26%**. Ratio: 2.7 to 1.*

In households where there wasn't a gun, an even larger majority, 79%, favored a ban; only 11% opposed.

Education

Five polls made available crosstab data that included breakdowns by educational level. Americans at every education level supported a ban on bump stocks, but as usual, support was stronger as education levels rose.

No College Degree

Favor	Oppose	Polling Dates	Poll
75%	17%	10/5-9/17	Morning Consult
70%	27%	10/5-10/17	Quinnipiac [Whites]
73%	17%	2/15-19/18	Morning Consult
78%	22%	2/27-28/18	Ipsos-NPR
68%	20%	8/2-6/18	Morning Consult

*Averages: **73%** vs. **20%**. Ratio: 3.7 to 1.*

Note: Quinnipiac University broke out whites at the various levels of education, perhaps because whites are, on the whole, most resistant to attempts to reduce our gun violence problem.

Bachelor Degree

Favor	Oppose	Polling Dates	Poll
85%	9%	10/5-9/17	Morning Consult
78%	20%	10/5-10/17	Quinnipiac [Whites]
79%	15%	2/15-19/18	Morning Consult
81%	16%	8/2-6/18	Morning Consult
85%	15%	2/27-28/18	Ipsos-NPR

*Averages: **82%** vs. **15%**. Ratio: 5.5 to 1.*

Post Grads

Favor	Oppose	Polling Dates	Poll
85%	9%	10/5-9/17	Morning Consult
86%	8%	2/15-19/18	Morning Consult
84%	13%	8/2-6/18	Morning Consult

Averages: **85%** vs. **10%**. *Ratio: 8.5 to 1.*

In these polls, *on average*, **72%** of those without a college degree favored a ban on bump stocks, and **22%** opposed a ban. Among those with a college degree, **81%** favored a ban, and only **17%** opposed a ban. In the three surveys that broke out those with education beyond a Bachelor's degrees, on average, **85%** supported a ban; only **10%** opposed a ban.

Annual Income Over $100,000

Most poll respondents in the over-$100,000-annual-income bracket believed Congress should ban bump stocks. They outnumbered those who disagreed more than five-to-one.

Favor	Oppose	Polling Dates	Poll
73%	16%	10/5/17	YouGov[541]
84%	10%	10/5-9/17	Morning Consult
82%	12%	2/22-26/18	Morning Consult
81%	15%	8/2-6/18	Morning Consult
80%	16%	12/20/18	YouGov[542]

Averages: **80%** vs. **14%**. *Ratio: 5.7 to 1.*

Polling Wrap Up

In polls since the Las Vegas Strip shooting, the American public supported a ban on bump stocks by more than 3 to 1. Most Americans don't understand why a civilian would want that level of weaponry. And they don't want to see that level of weaponry fall into the hands of gangs, drug dealers, right-wing militias, terrorists, or the mentally ill.

And it's not just the public as a whole. Republicans favored a ban **64%** to 29% or about two to one. Perhaps following President Trump's lead, Trump voters supported a ban on the devices, **70%** to 22%, or more than three to one. Gun householders supported a ban **69%** to 26%, a margin of more than two-to-one.

Voters with and without college degrees strongly supported a ban, with support rising as educational levels rose. Those with post-graduate education—doctors, lawyers, scientists, teachers with master's degrees, and so on—favored banning bump stocks by an enormous **85%** to 10%. Individuals with annual incomes of more than $100,000 favored banning the devices **80%** to 14%—more than five to one.

What We're Getting Instead

On December 18, 2018, the Department of Justice announced that the Acting Attorney General had signed off on the regulation banning bump stocks. The formal notice of the regulation appeared in the Federal Register on December 26, 2018.[543] It gave owners 90 days, or until March 26, 2019, to disable or turn in any bump stocks they owned. Because ATF had no authority to do so, the regulation did not provide compensation to those who turned in their devices.

Publication of the regulation made it unlikely Congress would ad-dress the issue. It also made it certain the courts would have to do so. The Gun Owners of America, a group more radical than the NRA, and some other pro-gun groups immediately filed suit to challenge the regu-lation.[544]

In three of those cases gun owners and gun rights organizations filed suit in the federal district court in D.C. and requested a preliminary injunction preventing the new regulations from going into effect. (A preliminary injunction is an order that preserves the *status quo ante* until the court can hold a trial on the merits. To get a preliminary injunction, a party must show that it will sustain an irrevocable loss unless the court issues a preliminary injunction. It must also show that it is likely to prevail on the merits.)

The District Court denied the requests for a preliminary injunction, announcing its decision in a 65-page opinion on February 25, 2019.[545] On appeal, the U.S. Court of Appeals affirmed in a lengthy two-to-one decision, holding that the plaintiffs had not shown that their claims had a realistic chance of success.[546]

In another challenge to the regulation, a federal District Court in Utah also denied a preliminary injunction, finding that the suit was unlikely to succeed.[547]

In 2019, the Supreme Court denied two emergency petitions from District of Columbia District Court decisions challenging the bump stock ban.

On March 2, 2020, the Supreme Court declined to review the decision from the D.C. Circuit of Appeals.[548] In a statement regarding the denial, Justice Gorsuch sharply criticized the lower court's reasoning, but noted that the decision was preliminary, that other courts of appeals were considering similar challenges to the bump stock regulation, and that the Supreme Court would benefit from the input from those courts. "But," Justice Gorsuch warned, "waiting should not be mistaken for lack of concern."[549]

Apparently, we've not heard the last word from the Supreme Court on this issue.

Meanwhile, on October 23, 2019, the U.S. Court of Claims denied compensation to bump stock owners, citing the longstanding rule that "the government, as the sovereign, has the power to take property that is dangerous, diseased, or used in criminal activities without compensation. Here, ATF acted properly within the confines of the limited federal police power."[550]

When the bump stock regulation went into effect, a reporter in Texas got this statement from Michael Cargill, owner of the Austin-based Central Texas Gun Works: "As a private citizen, I am going to resist. ... We are going to resist, and we are not going to comply."[551]

"I think the president made the wrong decision," Don Spencer, pres-ident of the Oklahoma 2nd Amendment Association, told a reporter for the Tulsa World in Oklahoma. Spencer added, "I think it's something that opens up the possibility for civil war. People are not willing to give up their guns just because it has a certain kind of stock attached to it. This is an attack on Second Amendment rights."[552] (The regulation did not require people to give up their guns, only the detachable stock.)

> "I think the president made the wrong decision. I think it's something that opens up the possibility for civil war. ... This is an attack on Second Amendment rights." Don Spencer, president of the Oklahoma 2nd Amendment Association.

As of this writing, civil war has not broken out over the issue in Oklahoma.

Jeff Kasky, the father of Cameron Kasky, one of the Parkland student leaders, had a different take. He told CNN, "Please don't get confused and think that banning bump stocks solves anything more than just a very, very small Band-aid on a gaping wound."[553]

Some States Have Banned Bump Stocks, But Most Have Not

According to the Giffords site, eight states banned bump stocks in 2018: Connecticut (HB 5542), Delaware (HB 300), Florida (S.B. 7026), Hawaii (S.B. 2046), Maryland (S.B. 707), New Jersey (S.B. 3477), Rhode Island (HB 300), and Washington (S.B. 5992).[554] In 2019, Nevada banned bump stocks when Governor Steve Sisolak (D) signed AB291, the so-called 1 October Bill, into law.[555] The District of Columbia also banned bump stocks. New York S.B. 2448 went further and banned all trigger activators.[556]

Secret Agent Man

In March 2018, Francho Bradley, 59, and Adrianne Jennings, 40, both of Frisco, Texas, apparently became the first in the nation to get themselves arrested for possession of a bump stock.

The arrest occurred in Tewksbury, Massachusetts, when Bradley himself called the police from his truck to say that the surveillance feed in his room in the Residence Inn in Tewksbury went dead. Bradley said he suspected a break-in and requested the police check his room because he left a pistol there. Bradley said he didn't want the pistol to fall into the wrong hands.

When police officers checked his room, they found an AK-47, an AR-15-style rifle with a grenade launcher, a large-capacity shotgun, a bump stock, and numerous rounds of ammunition.⁵⁵⁷ Among other problems, Massachusetts had banned bump stocks.

After getting a search warrant for the room and the couple's car, police officers also found nineteen large-capacity magazines for various guns, dozens of more rounds of ammunition, walkie talkies, tactical vests, and smoke grenades. "It should be noted," police wrote in a report, "that five of the high capacity magazines were affixed to each other by a homemade case. This was con-cerning because it allows an indi-vidual to shoot off all five maga-zines in a short amount of time."

Police also learned that Bradley had gotten parking tickets in Boston near where the March for Our Lives protest was to take place the coming weekend.

Photo courtesy of Tewksbury Police Department.

Police said the parking violations were con-sistent with what they would expect if Bradley was conducting surveil-lance of the area. In other words, his actions were what police would expect if Bradley were planning to use his arsenal to kill demonstrators at the March for our Lives rally.

But not to worry!

Bradley told the police he was on a secret government mission—he just couldn't reveal the agency for which he was working.⁵⁵⁸

As this book was about to be published, Mr. Bradley was still awaiting trial and had not been convicted of any crime. He was expected to have his day in court shortly after the COVID 19 lockdown ended and the courts resumed holding trials.

Conclusion

The American public, Republicans, and gun owners supported legislation banning bump stocks. Despite that, the Republican leadership in Congress thwarted efforts to enact a legislative ban on bump stocks and similar devices. Speaker Paul Ryan, Senate Majority Leader Mitch McConnell, and other pro-gun Congressional leaders flatly refused to allow debate on the floor of Congress or a vote on a law banning bump stocks.

16. Should We Require Gun Owners to Secure Their Guns?

Item: January 31, 2019. In Miami-Dade County, a father changed his child's diaper, and then, leaving a loaded gun on the bed, he went outside to put the diaper in the trash. The toddler picked up the gun, one of several left loaded and unsecured in the home, and shot himself in the stomach. The police charged the father and another man who was in the home with aggravated child abuse, child neglect, and culpable negligence. Police also charged the father, who initially claimed the gunshot was due to a drive-by shooting, with making a false statement.[559]

Item: April 8, 2019. A 4-year-old boy in Paulding County, Georgia, found a loaded, unsecured handgun in the front console of his mother's car and shot his six-year-sister in the head. The girl died two days later. As often happens in such cases, the Sheriff's office declined to file charges against the devastated parents, whose negligent storage of the gun led to their daughter's death. On a Go Fund Me site, the parents presented themselves as devout Christians.[560] Because when Jesus said, "Turn the other cheek," what he actually meant was, "Keep a loaded gun handy at all times."

Item: May 12, 2019. On Mother's Day, Evan Sun, the 4-year-old son of an Ohio state trooper, found his father's unsecured, loaded gun. While playing with it, he shot himself in the head. Rushed to the hospital, he died there from the gunshot wound. The State Highway Patrol identified the trooper and boy's father as Fu Sun of its Toledo post.[561] The Lucas County Common Pleas Court found Sun guilty of negligent homicide.[562]

Item: May 14, 2019. Charles McFarland, 76, put an antique WWII vehicle on display at a University of Tennessee baseball game. He left an unsecured, loaded gun in the vehicle. A mother brought her 8-year-old to the game. When the child explored the antique vehicle, he found the gun. Thinking it was a toy, the child pulled the trigger and shot his mother. Media reports said she was conscious but in critical *condition. Police charged McFarland with reckless endangerment with a deadly weapon.*[563]

Item: *May 15, 2019. According to police Jackson City, Tennessee, Chrisaiah Arrington, a 3-year-old, found a gun in his mother's home and shot himself in the face. Doctors at a nearby hospital declared the child dead. Police charged the mother, Linda Arrington, 25, and her boyfriend, Antonio Dancer, with negligent homicide. Police said it wasn't the first time the toddler found a loaded gun in the home.*[564] *In November 2019, a Madison County Grand Jury indicted the pair on murder and child neglect charges.*[565]

If they find a gun, young children are likely to play with it. That's the takeaway from an experiment involving more than a dozen 6- and 7-year-olds. When the kids "found" a gun placed in the room by the researchers, all but two played with it.[566]

In an earlier experiment involving thirty-one 4- and 5-year-olds, researchers divided the youngsters into two groups. One group received the NRA's Eddie Eagle gun-safety training. The other group went through a behavior modification program involving role-playing and feedback. Both programs were effective in teaching the kids to parrot back the safety messages, but neither affected how the kids reacted when left alone with a gun.[567]

Since those studies appeared in *Pediatrics*, several local television stations have restaged the "real life" situation with unloaded and disabled guns and got the same result. Despite what many parents believe, telling young kids not to play with a gun simply doesn't work.[568]

The results are sad. At least 73 times in 2018, a child under age 12 found a loaded, unsecured gun and shot and killed himself or another child with it. According to a report in USA Today, that number was in line with the totals for the previous five years.[569] (That tally, however, didn't include instances in which a child accidentally shot a parent or other adult.)

In South Carolina, the State Child Fatality Advisory Committee reviews child deaths that are unexplained, suspicious, or criminal in nature. After reviewing child deaths in the state from 2010 to 2017, the Committee reported that **66** of the child deaths it reviewed involved unsecured firearms that led to accidental firearm discharges, homicide, or suicide.[570]

***

As the incidents at the beginning of this chapter suggest, all too often, toddlers and other kids in this country find guns left loaded and unsecured and accidentally kill or injure themselves or someone else while playing with them.

The author of a recent Huffington Post article about accidental shootings by toddlers wielding unsecured firearms began his article this way.[571]

> Somewhere in the U.S. today, a child will find a loaded gun in a home. They won't have to look hard. It will be unlocked and stored in an easily accessible place. The child will pick up the firearm, and soon enough, it will go off exactly like it's supposed to. The bullet will strike a friend, or a sibling, or the child who found the gun in the first place. Someone will be injured or killed.

The fact that so many toddlers can get their hands on unsecured, loaded guns prompted the Brady Campaign's controversial 2016 promotional spot, "Guns Don't Kill People. Toddlers Kill People."[572] The satirical spot went viral.

An article in The Denver Post in 2017 reported, "American toddlers are still shooting people on a weekly basis."[573] Articles in Australia and New Zealand newspapers called these deaths, "The gun massacre America isn't talking about."[574]

The same year, a Lexington, Kentucky newspaper, The Herald-Leader, narrowed the focus to Kentucky. It did a series, "Guns and Kids," about young kids in the state who accidentally shot themselves or someone else with a gun left loaded and unattended by a parent or another adult.[575] The tagline for the series read: "A child shoots himself or another child in Kentucky once every seven weeks, on average."

Child Access Protection Laws

This chapter concerns Child Access Protection (CAP) laws. CAP laws hold gun owners responsible when they don't keep their guns secured, and a child unintentionally shoots himself or someone else. Or uses the gun to commit suicide. Or takes the gun to school and kills or injures classmates and school personnel.

Proponents urge the adoption of CAP laws mainly to protect toddlers and youngsters from finding an adult's loaded gun and accidentally killing or injuring themselves or someone else. But proponents also argue that CAP laws may reduce the number of young people committing suicide. And they note, school shooters under age 18 typically use their parent's or another adult's unsecured gun to kill their classmates and teachers.

Opponents of CAP laws acknowledge that safe storage might save their child's life or the life of some other child but say it's more important to have a loaded gun at hand in case of an intruder. They also argue that adolescents suddenly seized with the idea of committing suicide will choose another means if a gun isn't available. And if their parent's gun isn't available, opponents insist, adolescent shooters will somehow always be able to get a gun and ammunition.

Here's what we know for certain: Gun owners who keep their guns loaded and unsecured are responsible for a remarkable number of toddlers and other children dying each year. Sometimes, they leave a gun where their own toddler or the toddler they're supposed to be watching can find it and accidentally kill a sibling, a playmate, or himself. Other times, the child may be a little older, but the result is the same: The child finds the loaded gun and accidentally kills himself or someone else.

If the child is older still and having a bad day, he or she may find a parent's or stepparent's unsecured gun and use it to commit suicide.[576] Or like Adam Lanza, Kip Kinkel, and Gabriel Ross Parker, he may take his parent's or stepparent's gun to school and use it to kill other students.

Gun rights advocates dismiss accidental shootings and suicides as not part of our country's gun violence problem. They prefer to define gun violence almost exclusively in terms of mass shootings, home intrusions, and inner-city black-on-black violence. But for the rest of us, accidental shootings and youth suicides *are* a part of the overall picture of lives lost due to guns—a particularly sad part.

The NRA and other gun-rights organizations tell their members they need to keep their guns loaded and within easy reach to deal with the ever-present threat of an intruder breaking into their homes.[577] Gun owners, they insist, need to be ready to defend themselves against intruders intent on rape, robbery, or murder. The image that comes to mind for most gun rights' zealots is likely that of a black man, or more recently, a brown-skinned immigrant.

Our children pay a terrible price for that fearmongering.

The Issue

Should we enact Child Access Protection laws, *i.e.*, laws that hold gun owners responsible when they fail to keep their guns safely locked up, and a child finds the gun and accidentally or intentionally kills or injures himself or someone else?

There is no federal Child Access Protection (CAP) law. Nothing in federal law requires gun owners to keep their guns, when not in use, locked in a safe, locked in a gun rack, or stored with a trigger lock. And no federal law imposes penalties, civil or criminal, on gun owners who store their guns negligently—even when a toddler or older child finds a loaded gun and accidentally shoots himself or someone else. Or uses it to commit suicide. Or uses it to kill his classmates and teachers.

At the state level, some states have enacted CAP laws, and others have not. In the states that have, CAP laws vary from state to state and come in a variety of flavors. As of this writing, only one, Massachusetts, actually requires gun owners to lock up their guns when not in use. Most CAP laws simply make gun owners criminally or civilly liable, or both, when they negligently keep a gun unsecured, *and* a child uses it to injure or kill someone (*e.g.,* California, Hawaii, Massachusetts, Minnesota, District of Columbia).

Some states don't have CAP laws but do have older laws that impose penalties for the knowing, intentional, or reckless provision of a gun to a minor below the age specified in the statute. Many of those laws are limited to handguns.

When a child uses a gun left unsecured by the owner to shoot someone, the victims (or their families) sometimes sue the gun owner even in states that do not have CAP laws. When they do, they rely on negligence and traditional tort doctrines. Those doctrines offer numerous defenses and make winning compensation difficult. Depending on how a CAP law is written, it may provide a more definite basis for recovery.

Firearm Deaths and Nonfatal Injuries 2008-2017

The Centers for Disease Control and Prevention (CDC) collects data on gun deaths and nonfatal injuries. Its estimates of non-fatal injuries are problematic, but the best available.[578] The table shows the CDC's fatality and injury counts for the year 2018.

2018 Gun Fatalities and Injuries Among Children					
	Ages 0-4	*Ages 5-9*	*Ages 10-14*	*Ages 15-17*	*Total 0-17*
Deaths	98	70	367	1,194	1,729
Injuries	***	***	***	5,185	6,516[579]

The CDC doesn't collect information on who was holding the gun when it discharged. But from press reports and The Gun Archive, we know that for the youngest age groups, they themselves or another child was usually holding the gun when it fired.

Adolescent Firearm Suicides

And then there are the adolescents who use a parent's or another adult's unsecured gun to commit suicide. CDC reports that there were 683 such firearm suicides in 2007 (1.7 per 100,000), the year before the Supreme Court's *Heller* decision. (That decision discovered in the Second Amendment a right to keep a handgun in the home, unrelated to service in a militia.) Since then, the annual toll has risen steadily, reaching 1,296 teen suicides in 2018 (3.1 per 100,000).[580] (*See* chart, Gun Suicides, Ages 10-19.) Those 1,296 suicides in 2018 amounted to almost 25 young people, ages 10-to-19, who used guns to end their lives every week. The gun usually belonged to a parent or other relative.

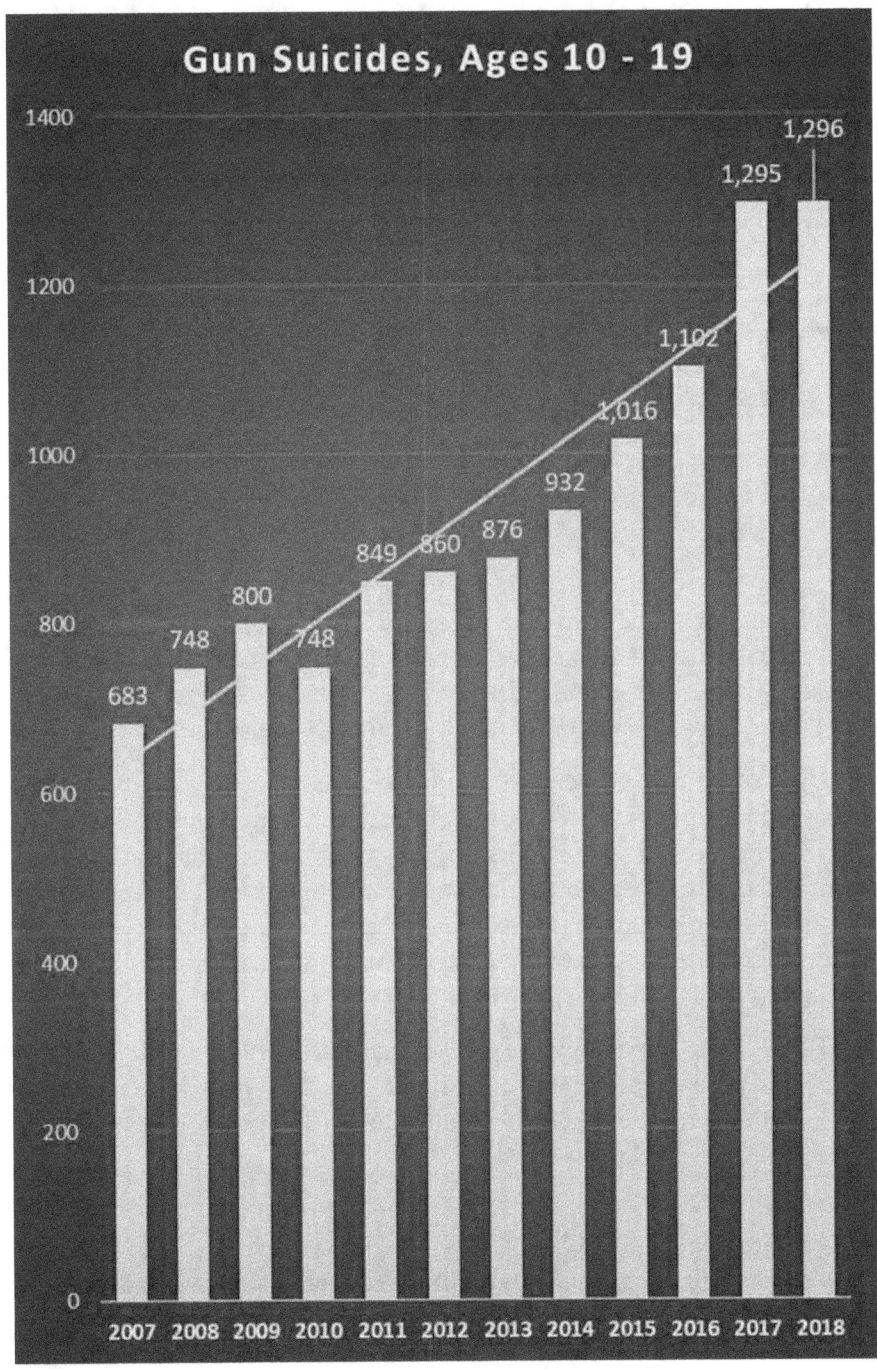

Among non-Hispanic **white males** in that age group, the 2018 rate was **6.93** per 100,000—double the overall national rate for that age group. In the South, where guns are prevalent, the situation was even worse. There, the gun-suicide rate among non-Hispanic white males, ages 10-19, was **12.97**, almost double the national rate for non-Hispanic white males in the same age bracket and quadruple the national rate for that age group.

The breakdown by age is grim:

- Among children ages 10 to 14 years old, the death toll in 2015 was 139 kids dead by firearm suicide; in 2016, it was 160 kids dead; in 2017, it was 185; and in 2018, it was 202.

- Among teens ages 15 to 19, the death toll was even higher. In 2015, some 877 teens died by firearm suicide; in 2016, 942 killed themselves with a gun; in 2017, it was 1,110; and in 2018, it was 1,094.

Despite the slight drop in teens, ages 15 to 19, killing themselves with guns in 2018, the trendlines are worrisome. And worse than that if one focuses on the trendline since 2010, the year the Supreme Court extended the right to keep a handgun in the home to the states.

Household gun ownership is positively associated with the overall (not just firearm) youth-suicide rate.[581] For each ten percentage-point increase in household gun ownership, the youth suicide rate increased by about **27%**.[582] In other words, despite *ipse dixit* statements to the contrary by gun advocates, the data show that for many of these young people, if there were no gun available, the moment would have passed, and the young person would have gone on living.

To be sure, those child suicides constituted only a small part, just over 4.5%, of the more than 24,432 firearm suicides the CDC counted in 2018. But each time a child uses a gun to kill himself or herself, it is a heartbreaking tragedy.

School Shootings

Wall-to-wall news coverage about a teenager who uses a gun to shoot his classmates and teachers holds our attention in a way that a brief news report of a little boy accidentally shooting and killing his sister doesn't. A school shooting also grabs more attention than whispered accounts around the office coffee station about a coworker whose teenager used the coworker's gun to kill himself. But here's something important to remember about school shootings: *Adults who leave their guns and ammunition unsecured supply the guns and ammunition for most school shootings.*

This is something the public has known since the Sandy Hook Elementary School shooting in Newtown, Connecticut. On Friday, December 14, 2012, before fatally shooting twenty 6- and 7-year-olds and six adult staff members, Adam Lanza shot and killed his mother, Nancy Lanza, age 52. Investigators found her body, still in her pajamas, in her bed, with four gunshot wounds to her head. Lanza then took his mother's Bushmaster XM15-E2S rifle and ten magazines, with 30 rounds each, to Sandy Hook Elementary School.

In 2018, Washington Post reporters John Woodrow Cox and Steven Rich examined cases in which youths under age 18 used a parent's or another grownup's firearm in an incident of school gun violence. By their count, children perpetrated at least 145 school shootings from 1999 through 2018. In the 105 cases in which police identified the weapon's source, 80% came from the child's home or from the home of a relative or friend.[583]

In an editorial, The Washington Post put it this way: "Want to prevent school shootings? Lock up guns."[584] The editorial cited the paper's series and concluded that if kids did not have access to family members' guns, two-thirds of school shootings might not have occurred.

Gun violence researchers have drawn the same conclusion. After researching mass shootings during the previous two years, Jillian Peterson and James Densley concluded that perpetrators got their weapons from family members in 80% of school shootings.[585]

In fact, we may be lucky there aren't more school shootings. According to the U.S. Education Department, state authorities recorded 1,600 incidents of gun possession in schools during the 2015-2016 academic year.[586] In Tennessee, which does not have a CAP law, some school districts reported a gun or the threat of a gun at a school nearly once every three days.[587] Presumably, not all of those guns belonged to the parents of those students. But many did.

Child Access Protection laws would not have prevented all of those children from accidentally shooting themselves or someone else. Even in the face of CAP laws, some irresponsible parents will insist on keeping a loaded gun in the house or in their car or purse. For the same reason, CAP laws would not have prevented every one of those adolescent suicides. But CAP laws—especially if accompanied with stiff penalties and awareness campaigns—may well have prevented many of them. And CAP laws may provide society and innocent parents of injured or slain children some small measure of justice.

What We Want

Where does the public stand on CAP laws? Do we want Congress and our state legislatures to enact CAP laws, to avoid children suffering and dying from unsecured guns? Or do we think it's wrong to make gun owners legally responsible when they failed or refused to secure their guns, and as a result, a child died or was injured?

In the Johns Hopkins survey mentioned elsewhere, **74%** of adults said that we *should* require gun owners to lock up the guns in their homes when not in use.[588] That survey was from January 2017, before the late 2017 and early 2018 high-profile mass shootings in Las Vegas, Nevada, and Parkland, Florida.

Morning Consult also included the issue in some of its polls. It asked: "Do you support or oppose—Requiring that all gun owners store their guns in a safe storage unit?" That went further than most CAP laws, which impose liability only if a child finds the gun *and* shoots himself or someone else. Similarly, APM Research Lab asked if respondents favored or opposed, "Mandating that guns are stored with a lock in place."[589]

Overall Results

Favor	Oppose	Dates	Poll
77%	17%	10/5-9/17	Morning Consult[590]
76%	16%	2/22-26/18	Morning Consult[591]
76%	16%	8/2-6/18	Morning Consult[592]
78%	18%	7/16-21/19	APM (SSRS)[593]

Averages: **76%** vs. **16%**. *Ratio: 4.7 to 1.*

As the table shows, among registered voters, those who believe we should require gun owners to store their guns in a safe storage unit outnumber those who disagree more than four-to-one. In fact, a clear majority, 60%, felt "strongly" that we should have a mandatory safe-storage law.

Republicans

In all three polls, Morning Consult broke out how Democrats, Republicans, and Independents stood on requiring gun owners to store their guns safely. Republicans were a little less inclined to support CAP laws than the public in general:

Favor	Oppose	Polling Dates	Poll
70%	26%	10/5-9/17	Morning Consult
73%	21%	2/22-26/18	Morning Consult
69%	25%	8/2-6/18	Morning Consult
68%	26%	7/16-21/19	APM (SSRS)

Averages: **70%** *vs.* **25%** *Ratio: ~3:1*

Even so, Republicans who believe we *should* require gun owners to store their guns in a safe storage unit outnumbered Republicans who don't by three-to-one. (Democrats favored requiring gun owners to secure their guns by even larger margins. *E.g.,* in the October 2017 Morning Consult poll, the margin among Democrats was 85% *vs.* 17%.)

Trump 2016 Voters

Morning Consult broke out 2016 Donald Trump and Hillary Clinton voters. Here are the results for Trump voters:

Favor	Oppose	Polling Dates	Poll
69%	26%	10/5-9/17	Morning Consult
68%	25%	2/22-26/18	Morning Consult
67%	27%	8/2-6/18	Morning Consult

Averages: **68%** *vs.* **26%** *Ratio: 2.6 to 1.*

By more than two-to-one, Trump supporters agree that we should require gun owners to secure their guns. Clinton voters favored CAP laws by much larger margins.

Gun Households

Morning Consult provided crosstab data on gun households for only two of these polls. The results are essentially the same, suggesting little movement in the intervening months on this issue:

Favor	Oppose	Polling Dates	Poll
66%	28%	10/5-9/17	Morning Consult
68%	26%	8/2-6/18	Morning Consult

Averages: **67%** *vs.* **27%** *Ratio: ~2.5:1*

As the table shows, by more than two-to-one, those in gun households believed we should require gun owners to secure their guns.

APM Research Lab broke out: (1) gun owners; (2) those who didn't own a gun but lived in a home where someone else did; and (3) individuals who lived in a home where no one owned a gun. The first group, gun owners, split **66%** to 31% in favor of safe storage (about 2 to 1). The second group, those who lived in gun households but didn't own a gun, favored a safe-storage law by an even more robust **84%** to 14% (6 to 1). And the third group, those who lived in homes where no one owned a gun, showed about the same level of support, **85%** in favor and only 11% opposed to a safe-storage law.

Education

Whether gun owners should leave their guns where kids can get them and use them to kill themselves or others is not a complicated issue. That may be why educational level seems to have only a modest effect on attitudes toward CAP laws.

Less Than College Degree

Favor	Oppose	Polling Dates	Poll
76%	17%	10/5-9/17	Morning Consult
73%	17%	2/22-26/18	Morning Consult
74%	17%	8/2-6/18	Morning Consult

Average: **74%** *favored,* **17%** *opposed. Ratio: 4.4 to 1.*

Bachelor Degree

Favor	Oppose	Polling Dates	Poll
79%	16%	10/5-9/17	Morning Consult
80%	15%	2/22-26/18	Morning Consult
81%	16%	7/16-21/19	APM (SSRS)
80%	14%	8/2-6/18	Morning Consult

*Average: **80%** favored, **15%** opposed. Ratio: >5 to 1.*

Postgraduate

Favor	Oppose	Polling Dates	Poll
79%	15%	10/5-9/17	Morning Consult
81%	14%	2/22-26/18	Morning Consult
77%	17%	8/2-6/18	Morning Consult

*Average: **79%** favored, **15%** opposed. Ratio: >5 to 1.*

APM Research Lab broke out groups by education a little differently. Those with a high school education or less supported requiring gun owners to store their guns safely **73%** to 22%. Among those with at least some college, **83%** were in favor and 16% opposed.

Annual Income Over $100,000

Respondents in the over $100,000-annual-income bracket who believed gun owners should store their guns in a safe storage unit outnumbered those who disagreed almost five-to-one.

Favor	Oppose	Polling Dates	Poll
78%	18%	10/5-9/17	Morning Consult
84%	10%	2/22-26/18	Morning Consult
75%	20%	8/2-6/18	Morning Consult

*Average: **79%** vs. **16%**. Ratio: 4.9 to 1*

Polling Wrap Up

About three-quarters of registered voters believe we should require gun owners to secure their guns when not in use. Republicans believe we *should* require gun owners to lock up their guns by about three-to-one.

Trump supporters also agree that we should require gun owners to secure their guns. On average, Trump supporters split 68% in favor of a law requiring safe storage *vs.* 26% opposed.

People at every educational level say we should require gun owners to secure their guns when not in use. Among those without college degrees, on average, **74%** favored a law to that effect; only 17% opposed. Among those with a Bachelor's degree, on average, **80%** favored CAP laws, and only 15% opposed. The result was essentially the same for those with annual incomes of $100,000 or more: On average, **79%** favored, and only 16% opposed.

But as we discuss in the next section, even though Republicans and these key Republican constituencies support CAP laws, Republican lawmakers in Congress and in many of our state legislatures refuse to consider, let alone enact, laws that hold gun owners who don't secure their guns responsible for the carnage their recklessness makes possible.

What We're Getting Instead

There is no federal Child Access Protection law that makes gun owners responsible when they leave their guns unlocked, and their kid uses it to kill someone. Federal law also does not require gun owners to use a gun storage or safety device when they are not using their guns.

Federal law, however, does make it a criminal offense for a licensed importer, manufacturer, or dealer to sell or transfer a *handgun* unless it provides the buyer or transferee "a secure gun storage or safety device."[594] The federal statute also immunizes a lawful owner of a *handgun* who uses a secure gun storage or safety device from most civil actions based on the criminal or unlawful misuse of the handgun by a third party (*e.g.*, their kid).[595] The federal statute does not apply to long guns.

State Child Access Protection Laws

Except in Massachusetts, state CAP laws do not require gun owners to store their guns safely. Where they exist, state CAP laws make the gun owner's conduct a crime, allow the injured party to sue, or both, *but typically only if* a child finds the gun *and* shoots himself or someone else with it.

The Giffords Law Center has compiled a list of the states that, along with D.C., have enacted child access prevention laws, broken down by whether the law imposes criminal or civil liability and for what.[596] But thirteen of the states on the Giffords site's most comprehensive list penalize "intentional, knowing, or reckless pro-vision" of a handgun to a minor.

When the American Association of Pediatrics (AAP) did a tally in 2016, it identified 18 states that had child access prevention laws, with the ages protected varying from 14 to 18 years old.[597] If we understand CAP laws to be laws that make parents and guardians criminally or civilly liable when they don't lock up their guns *and* a child gets access to the gun and harms someone, then the AAP count, if updated with laws since its tally, would be more accurate.

In 2018, voters in Washington approved voter Initiative 1639, which imposed criminal liability on gun owners who unsafely store guns that are then used by a prohibited person.[598] In 2019, California (S.B. 172), Connecticut (HB 7218), New York (S.B. 245), Delaware (HB 63)[599] and Nevada (AB 291)[600] added CAP laws or strengthened existing CAP laws.

Conclusion

CAP laws protect our children. Together with strong gun laws, they encourage safe gun storage. They reduce the number of children who unintentionally shoot themselves, a playmate, or someone else.[601] They reduce adolescent suicides.[602] CAP laws also reduce the number of kids who carry a gun and threaten other students.[603] Conversely, parents and other adults who do not secure their guns provide four out of five of the guns used in school shootings by youths under age 18.

There is evidence that strong CAP laws also reduce homicides committed by juveniles (individuals under age 18).[604] The researchers noted: "The estimated effect is stronger for whites, as opposed to nonwhites, and is driven by states enforcing a negligent storage standard, the strictest form of CAP legislation."

The public supports CAP laws. In the national polls that addressed CAP laws, on average, 76% were in favor of CAP laws, and only 16% opposed. That was almost five-to-one in favor.

Super majorities of Republicans, Trump voters, and people who live in households where there was a gun supported enactment of CAP laws.

And yet Congress and most of our state legislatures refuse to enact CAP laws. As Supreme Court Justice Elena Kagan asked, albeit in a different context, "Is this how American democracy is supposed to work?"

17. Should We Repeal the Second Amendment and Ban Guns?

Item: On April 28, 1996, at a popular tourist spot in Tasmania, a gunman went on a rampage, using a Colt AR-15 SP1 rifle and 30-round magazines. He killed 20 people in 90 seconds with his first 29 rounds. Altogether, he killed 35 people and wounded 18 more.[605]

Item: In response, Australia and its state governments changed Australia's national and state laws to ban civilian ownership of semi-automatic long guns and pump-action shotguns. They also launched a series of market-price gun buyback programs. In all, Australia destroyed more than one million guns, about a third of the country's estimated gun stock. Among other measures, Australian authorities also prohibited mail and internet gun sales and required registration of all guns. The changes had a profound effect on the country's incidence of mass shootings and gun crime. Among other things, mass shootings came to an abrupt halt.[606]

Item: A follow-up study in 2016 of the impact of Australia's changes in gun regulation noted that the trend of no mass shootings, which began with the ban, continued. "In the 18 years before the ban, there were 13 mass shootings, whereas in the 20 years following the ban, no mass shootings occurred, and the decline in total firearm deaths accelerated."[607]

Item: On March 15, 2019, a shooter in Christchurch, New Zealand, killed 51 Muslims and injured 69 during Friday prayer. The shooter, described in media reports as a white supremacist and part of the Alt-Right, issued a manifesto before the attack. He titled his screed, "The Great Replacement," a reference to the 2011 book *Le Grand Remplacement* by French author Renaud Camus. (The book imagines that nonwhites are conspiring to replace whites of European descent.) In his manifesto, the shooter ranted against nonwhites and immigrants and praised President Trump as "a symbol of renewed white identity and common purpose."

Item: *After the attack, in April 2019, the New Zealand government amended the country's gun law to ban most semi-automatic firearms and some shotguns.*

Item: *In this country, on August 3, 2019, a shooter posted an anti-immigration and white-supremacist manifesto before launching an attack on Mexican Americans and Mexicans in a Walmart in El Paso, Texas. Like the Christchurch shooter's manifesto, the Walmart shooter's screed referred to the right-wing conspiracy theory of The Great Replacement.[608] But unlike Australia and New Zealand, neither Congress nor Texas took steps to prevent similar shootings.[609]*

Individuals and organizations on opposing sides of the gun debate frame gun-violence issues very differently. And as one scholar recently noted, when they do that, they warp the discussion in ways that make it difficult to discuss, let alone agree on solutions.[610]

On one side, there are individuals and organizations who want legislative action to reduce our country's horrific gun-violence problem. They frame the issue of gun-violence prevention in ways that focus on the roughly 40,000 killed by guns each year in this country—and those who are injured, some for life. They tend to focus on school and other mass shootings and on accidental deaths among toddlers.

On the other side, there are individuals and organizations who want legislative action to protect or expand the right to own and carry guns. They frame the issues in ways that favor protecting gun rights and tend to focus on "good guy with a gun" narratives. In doing so, they downplay the lives guns end or disrupt.

And then there are the "Second Amendment people"—Second Amendment absolutists and other fringe gun-rights defenders. As discussed below, they often frame firearm-related issues in a way that reimagines the white male who needs a gun to feel safe or to demonstrate his masculinity as someone who protects everyone from gun confiscation and thus heroically preserves freedom.

These "2A" individuals routinely assert on social media that the folks who advocate measures like those discussed in the preceding chapters are not genuinely concerned about reducing gun deaths and injuries. They scoff at the notion that gun control advocates, or anybody, could be motivated by concern for the people guns kill and injure—or by concerns for others, period. For them, empathy is just another "hoax" liberals dreamt up, like climate change and COVID 19.

Democrats, or liberals, or "gun grabbers," they insist, are actually intent on weakening gun rights and on gun confiscation, as prelude to tyranny. (The "2A people" use words in ways that might astonish the vast majority of Americans. In their posts, the right to bear arms conflates with "freedom," and gun confiscation conflates with "tyranny." Democracy is "mob rule."

Thus, in the 2A view of the world, any proposal to address some aspect of our gun violence is nothing more than the leading edge of a slippery slope leading to gun confiscation and "tyranny." As one such advocate explained, "[A] 'mandatory gun buyback' is nothing but a confiscation with a more politically correct name, and Americans *will not stand* for such tyranny."[611]

What, pray tell, is the ultimate, dastardly goal of gun-violence-prevention advocates? To disarm the population so that the federal government can impose "gun control, nationalized healthcare, universal basic income, and every other idiotic, tyrannical, and wrong-headed idea that the mob thinks is a good plan."[612]

Concern about gun confiscation, however, extends well beyond the "2A" absolutists. A recent, sophisticated poll—the Nationscape project—tapped the opinions of over 110,000 respondents. It found that for Republicans, "don't ban guns" was the second most important issue, just behind "don't impeach Trump."[613]

This might remain a topic for academic studies on framing and agenda building, but for the fact that pro-gun politicians frequently use fear of gun confiscation as the basis for real-world gun policy. Ostensibly, keeping the federal government from wholesale gun confiscation is why we don't have national registration of guns and why the National Tracing Center isn't allowed to put records of gun sales in a database to expedite tracing crime guns. It's also why, or so we're told, the FBI is not allowed to keep information about the background checks it runs, or about the background-check investigations it conducts on suspected terrorists. And it's (supposedly why many states don't have licensing or permit-to-purchase laws.

As discussed in Chapter 3, the Supreme Court's understanding of the Second Amendment changed in 2008. That's when the court's majority ruled in *Heller v. District of Columbia* that the Second Amendment protected an individual right to own a firearm for a lawful purpose, such as the defense of the home—provided the firearm was of the sort in common use at the time and subject to several other qualifications. The *Heller* decision is the law, and given the current make-up of the Supreme Court, it will likely remain so.

As a result, before the federal government or a state could attempt the wholesale confiscation of all guns or all handguns, it would be necessary first to repeal the Second Amendment. The same is true of any compulsory surrender-for-compensation program for all guns or all handguns. That's the case unless one conjures up some dystopian future in which a despotic president ignores the Constitution, Congress and the courts, orders federal agents to seize guns, *and* those agents obey.

This chapter, nonetheless, considers what percentage of Americans, and what percentage of Democrats, want to get rid of the Second Amendment. It also looks at what percentage want to ban all civilian guns or at least all handguns. The ultimate question is: *Is wholesale gun confiscation a likely enough prospect that it should override addressing gun violence and the roughly 40,000 lives it claims in this country each year?*

The Issue

Should we repeal the Second Amendment and confiscate all guns, or all handguns, in civilian hands?

Congress may propose an amendment to the Constitution, *e.g.*, to repeal the Second Amendment, if two-thirds of both houses of Congress concur. The congressional proposal, however, only becomes part of the Constitution if ratified by three-fourths of the states.

For years, something like 90% of Americans have wanted Congress to pass universal background checks, and yet Congress, or at least the Senate, adamantly refuses. Given that Americans cannot get Congress to pass even something as anodyne as that, it is unrealistic to think that Americans would be able to convince Congress to repeal the Second Amendment.

And even if the American public somehow succeeded in getting Congress to propose an amendment repealing the Second Amendment, there is presently no prospect that three-quarters of the states would ratify any such amendment. But let's play along and ask: Do most Americans actually want to repeal the Second Amendment and confiscate guns?

What We Want

Are the "Second Amendment people" correct when they insist that Democrats or liberals want to repeal the Second Amendment and confiscate all civilian guns? Let's start with polls that asked if we should repeal the Second Amendment.

Should We Repeal the Second Amendment?

Favor	Oppose	Polling Dates	Poll
22%	63%	3/29-4/1/18	Morning Consult
17%	79%	4/6-9/18	Quinnipiac
19%	64%	9/2-6/18	Morning Consult

Averages: **19%** *in favor vs.* **69%** *opposed. Ratio: 3.4 against repeal.*

That's not a lot of polling, but most of it is from right after the Parkland shooting and the March for Our Lives, when sentiment for doing something to reduce gun violence was at its recent high point. Nonetheless, since the Las Vegas Strip mass shooting, what polling there is suggests that only about 19%—roughly one in five—favor repeal of the Second Amendment.

Yeah, But What About Democrats?

To hear many gun-rights advocates talk, Democrats are salivating over the prospect of disarming America. But is that true? Do Democrats want to repeal the Second Amendment?

Four polls suggest that, on average, about one in three Democrats favors repeal of the Second Amendment; nearly half of Democrats are opposed, and about 15% haven't made up their minds.

Favor	Oppose	Polling Dates	Poll
36%	45%	3/29-4/1/18	Morning Consult

Favor	Oppose	Polling Dates	Poll
33%	61%	4/6-9/18	Quinnipiac
29%	49%	8/2-6/18	Morning Consult

*Averages: **33%** vs. **52%**. Ratio: 1.4 to 1 against.*

Although about 15% of Democrats were undecided, most of those who did have an opinion *opposed* repealing the Second Amendment. Moreover, the farther away in time from the Marjorie Stoneman Douglas High School shooting, the less support there was among Democrats for repeal. In short, there's not much evidence in these polls that all or even most Democrats want to repeal the Second Amendment.

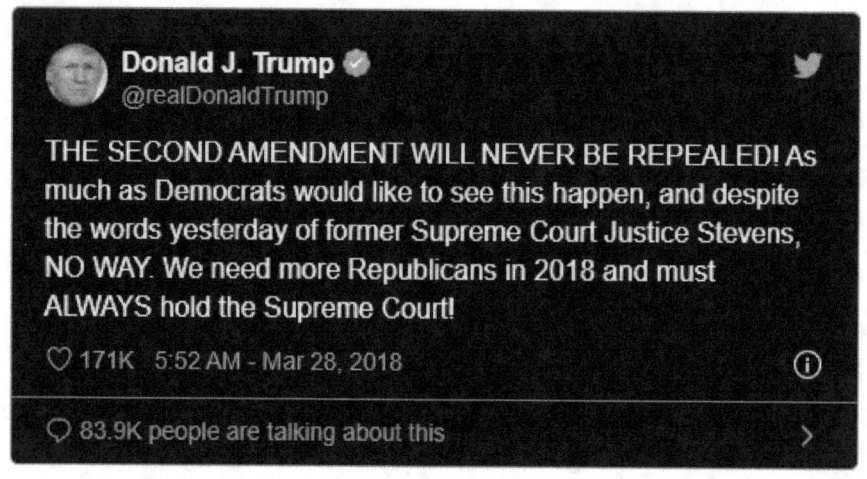

Should We Prevent Americans From Owning Guns?

SSRS, polling for CNN, asked if the public favored or opposed: "Preventing all Americans from owning guns." Ipsos, surveying for NPR, asked the same thing. These polls didn't find much support:

Favor	Oppose	Polling Dates	Poll
25%	71%	10/10-11/17	Ipsos/NPR
11%	86%	10/12-15/17	CNN/SSRS[614]
11%	87%	2/20-23/18	CNN/SSRS[615]

*Averages: **16%** vs. **81%**. Ratio: 5 to 1 against.*

In these polls, Americans were overwhelmingly against banning all civilian guns. That is not a mandate for Congress and the states to repeal the Second Amendment and confiscate all private firearms.

Should There Be A Law Banning Handguns?

In three polls, Gallup asked if there should be a law that bans possession of all handguns (except by the police and other authorized persons).[616] Any such ban would be unconstitutional under *Heller* and *McDon-ald*, so it's not clear why Gallup asked that question, but it did. And so did YouGov, polling for The Economist.

Should be:	*Should not:*	*Polling Dates*	*Poll*
28%	71%	10/5-11/17	Gallup
24%	63%	10/7-10/17	YouGov*
27%	60%	11/12-14/17	YouGov*
27%	60%	2/18-20/18	YouGov*
26%	63%	2/25-27/18	YouGov*
28%	71%	10/1-10/18	Gallup
27%	63%	8/10-13/19	YouGov*
29%	70%	10/1-13/19	Gallup

Averages: **27%** *favored banning handguns,* **65%** *opposed.*
Ratio: 2.4 to 1 against.

*The Economist sponsored these YouGov polls.

As the table indicates, on average, only 27% favored banning all civilian handguns; 65% opposed that.

Polling Wrap Up

In short, only about one in five Americans and one in three Democrats favor repeal of the Second Amendment. Only about one in six Americans and less than one in three Democrats are ready to say "enough" and end all civilian gun ownership. And only about one in four believe we should ban all handguns—the guns used most often in both gun homicides and gun suicides.

What We're Getting Instead

The specter of gun confiscation too often stands in the way of gun registration and other measures intended to rein in gun violence. The "slippery slope" argument provides a convenient cover story for politicians whose campaign accounts are flush with gun industry and gun-rights activists' money.

Politics aside, gun dealers find that raising the specter of gun confiscation is a great way to boost sales. Whenever gun dealers spread rumors that the government is about to ban the sale of assault rifles or some other gun, lots of gun buyers immediately queue up at gun stores to buy whatever the rumors say the government is about to ban. That con never grows old; lots of gun owners always fall for it.

Gun rights groups like the NRA and Gun Owners of America also need that specter. It helps to keep membership up and contributions coming in.

PART THREE: GUNS *vs.* DEMOCRACY

Why do we get the laws the gun lobby wants and not the laws most Americans want?

18. What We Want *vs.* What We're Getting

Opinion polls since the Parkland shooting tell us that Americans don't think Congress is doing a good job. In particular, most Americans don't think Congress is doing enough to deal with gun violence.

In February 2018, shortly after the Parkland shooting, an ABC/Washington Post poll painted a bleak picture: **77%** thought Congress was not doing enough to deal with gun violence; only **19%** thought it was. In a Quinnipiac University poll that month, **75%** said Congress was not doing enough to deal with gun violence; a mere 17% thought it was. An Ipsos/NPR poll asked if Congress needed to do more to address gun violence. Some **78%** said "yes"; only **15%** said "no." (*For perspective:* Some 15% also said the media or the government or somebody adds secret mind-controlling technology to television broadcast signals.[617])

In an April 2018 Quinnipiac University poll, conducted after the March for Our Lives, only **12%** of registered voters said they approved of the way Congress was handling its job. Despite the vicious smears gun-rights dogmatists leveled at the Parkland students, **52%** had a favorable opinion of the students.[618] In a June 2018 Public Policy Polling survey, after it became clear that once again Congress would not act, only **6%** approved of the way Congress was handling its job. In contrast, **54%** approved of the high school students who lead the protests against gun violence across the country.

Gun violence hits black families especially hard. Among them, the congressional approval figures are even bleaker. In the February 2018 Quinnipiac University poll, only **6%** of blacks thought Congress was doing enough to prevent gun violence; **93%** disagreed.[619] In the June 2018

Public Policy Polling survey, only **3%** of African Americans approved of the job Congress was doing.

As the November 2018 mid-terms approached, an "A" rating from the NRA became toxic. The NRA responded by changing its website to hide the ratings it gives politicians. Despite that, in the midterms, voters rejected forty Congressmen with top NRA ratings.[620] Many of the candidates who took their places had "F" ratings from the NRA and campaigned on gun reform.[621]

What about those in the small minority who say Congress is doing enough to reduce gun violence? How do they justify thwarting the will of a super majority of their fellow citizens?

Gun Owners of America is a gun rights organization that prides itself on being even more extreme than the NRA. As public opinion turned ever more starkly against the gun lobby's extremist agenda during 2018, Bob DePino, vice-president of the organization's Vermont chapter, argued that elected officials should ignore polling data. "Public opinion," he said, "should not drive legislation."[622] The notion that legislators should ignore what voters want is a fundamentally undemocratic notion.

Representative Thomas Massie of Kentucky, who chairs the Second Amendment Caucus in the House, went further. He complained that Speaker Paul Ryan and other Republicans in leadership positions in Congress wouldn't ignore what the country wanted and pass pro-gun legislation instead. "Our leadership seems like the sheriff deputies at the Florida shooting," he told a reporter for The Atlantic. "They don't want to go in and take fire, and instead just hope the issue [concern about gun violence] will burn itself out."[623]

In recent years, the public has succeeded in using voter initiatives and referenda to pass gun reform measures that their NRA-cowed legislators were too afraid to enact. In response, the NRA has joined with other rightwing groups to urge states to eliminate voter initiatives and referenda, *i.e.,* to curtail direct democracy.[624]

On Facebook, Twitter, and other social media sites, gun rights zealots routinely refer to democracy as "mob rule." They threaten violence and even civil war if the great majority of Americans (who want most of the proposals discussed in this book) gets its way. In short, the gun lobby and its most extreme supporters simply do not believe in democracy.[625] (*Remember:* There's a big differ-ence between most gun owners and gun-rights extremists. The former don't threaten violence if they don't get their way; the latter do.

What If The Majority Got Its Way?

What if Congress and state legislatures were to enact the gun-violence-prevention laws that most Americans want?

Enact Universal Background Checks?
Averages:90% for **vs.** *8% against.*
Ratio: 12 to 1.

Enact "No Fly, No Buy"?
Averages:84% **vs.** *12%.*
Ratio 7.3 to 1.

Close the "Boyfriend" Loophole?
One poll:66% **vs.** *22%.*
Ratio: 3 to 1.

Pass the Violence Against Women Act?
Recent Poll:73% **vs.** *10%.*
Ratio: 7.3 to 1.

Close the Emergency Restraining Order Loophole?
One poll:68% **vs.** *21%.*
Ratio: 15 to 1.

Enact Violent Misdemeanor Laws?
Averages:85% *vs.10%.*
Ratio: 8.5 to 1.

Enact Red Flag/Extreme Risk Laws?
Averages:79% **vs.** *16%.*
Ratio: 6.2 to 1.

License Gun Owners?
Averages:77% vs.20%. Ratio: 3.9 to 1.

Register Guns?
Average: **75%** vs. **21%**.
Ratio: 3.6 to 1.

Ban Assault Weapons?
Averages: **63%** vs. **32%**.
Ratio: 2 to 1.

Enact an Age Limit of 21 for Any Firearm?
Averages: **76%** vs. **21%**.
Ratio: 3.7 to 1.

Enact an Age Limit of 21 for Assault Weapons?
Averages: **80%** vs. **13%**.
Ratio: 6 to 1.

Ban Large-Capacity Magazines?
Averages: **67%** vs. **27%**.
Ratio: 2.5 to 1.

Ban Bump Stocks?
Averages: **71%** vs. **22%**.
Ratio: 3.2 to 1.

Enact Child Access Protection Laws?
Averages: **76%** vs. **16%**.
Ratio: 4.7 to 1.

That's what most of us want. Let's pull it all altogether.

Altogether, Now!

Universal Background Checks, Gun Owner Licensure, and Tracking Guns

For starters, Congress would require background checks before every gun sale or transfer, not just those sales handled by licensed gun dealers. In short, Congress would close the "private sale" loophole that feeds the black market and makes it easy for criminals, domestic abusers, and other prohibited persons to get guns.

Congress would also authorize the FBI to add known and suspected terrorists to background checks, so that gun dealers know not to sell them guns and explosives. And yes, anyone on that list would have the right to appeal and to challenge the designation in court. In fact, they already do.[626]

Congress or all fifty states would require gun owners to obtain a license to own a gun. To get that license, would-be gun owners would need to go in-person to a law enforcement office. Law enforcement officers would photograph and fingerprint them to make sure they are who they say they are and to make sure they aren't felons, fugitives, or otherwise prohibited from owning a gun. Those requirements would discourage felons and other prohibited persons from playing the "lie and try" game that goes on now at gun stores.

Congress would also require ATF to track every gun sale or transfer. When law enforcement officers find a gun at a crime scene or in possession of someone who has committed a crime, they would be able to identify the last registered owner quickly. Law enforcement and others would also be able to use that tracking data to identify crooked dealers who illegally sell to Mexican drug cartels, black marketeers, and other bad actors.

Universal background checks, licensing gun owners, and tracking gun transactions would not by themselves solve our gun violence problem. We should think of those laws instead as a necessary precondition to bringing our gun violence down to some more manageable level. But it's worth noting that states like Massachusetts, Connecticut, and New York have already enacted most or all of these laws, and they have some of the lowest gun homicide and gun suicide rates in the country. Conversely, states like Alaska, Alabama, Mississippi, and Louisiana have none of these laws, and they have some of the highest gun-homicide and gun-suicide rates in the country.

As I write this, I can almost hear strident gun rights advocates shouting their usual objection. No matter what we do, they insist, criminals will always be able to get guns from the black market, by robbing a gun store, or in some other, unspecified way. Notwithstanding those *ipse dixit* pronouncements, there is plenty of evidence that these laws do make it harder for criminals to get guns.[627] They also reduce homicide and intimate partner homicide rates.[628] In fact, the findings of a very recent study "suggest that laws requiring firearm purchasers to be licensed through a background check process supported by fingerprints and laws banning LCMs are the most effective gun policies for reducing fatal mass shootings."[629]

Moreover, if Congress enacted these laws, it would take away the current option of getting guns from nearby states with weaker laws.

Despite what gun zealots argue, the world is not divided into two groups—law-abiding gun owners and violent criminals. These laws, for example, would make it much harder for a paranoid schizophrenic with no criminal associations to buy a gun and use it to kill whomever the voices inside his head tell him to kill. They would also make it harder for the abusive husband or boyfriend under a restraining order to buy a gun. And when a prohibited person gets a gun anyway, these laws would make it easier to arrest and prosecute him before he kills someone.

Violent Domestic Abuser and Violent Misdemeanor Laws

If we still had a working democracy, we would have laws that not only bar violent domestic abusers from having guns but would require abusers to surrender their guns immediately. We would also authorize law enforcement to remove guns from abusers who don't surrender their guns promptly. And those laws would apply to individuals who physically abuse, stalk, or threaten dating partners.

We would also have laws that more broadly ban individuals convicted of violent misdemeanors from having guns for several years from their last conviction.

Red Flag/Extreme Risk Laws

If a super majority of Americans had their way, more states would have "red flag" or "extreme risk" laws. Those laws allow police and family members—and in a few states, others, such as a school or employer—to petition a court for an order authorizing the police to remove temporarily the guns of an individual who is in crisis, *i.e.*, whose behavior demonstrates that he or she is an imminent danger to himself or others.

Red flag laws would also prevent those individuals from passing a background check.

Research indicates that red flag/extreme risk laws work well in re-ducing gun suicides in the states that have them.[630] They might also pre-vent at least some mass shootings. The good news is that after the Park-land school shooting and the #NeverAgain student protests, several ad-ditional states have enacted red flag laws. But as of this writing, too many states and Congress have not.

Age Limits On Buying A Gun Or An Assault Weapon

Relative to the rest of the population, young people ages 18 to 20 are at high risk of doing all sorts of risky and impulsive things, including engaging in acts of gun violence. Federal law already prohibits licensed gun dealers from selling handguns to individuals in that age group, with certain exceptions for use in farming, ranching, and law enforcement.

If the majority of Americans had their way, Congress and our state legislatures would extend those laws to *all* guns. In other words, we would ban the sale to and possession of *any* firearm by *any* young person under age 21, except those in military service or those who qualify under the existing exceptions pertaining to farming, ranching, and law en-forcement.

If we had majority rule in this country, Congress would ban assault weapons. But if Congress were unwilling or unable to go that far, an even more substantial majority want Congress to ban young people under age 21, who are not serving in the military, from having assault weapons.

Yes, it is true—as Second Amendment absolutists insist—that the differences between an assault weapon and other semi-automatic rifles are, when not used in combat, largely cosmetic. That's because those fea-tures were designed for combat. Guns with those features, however, have a special allure for the sickos who want to die in a blaze of revengeful infamy. In other words, guns with those features deserve special attention because they inspire and embolden those twisted souls to act out their mass-murder fantasies.

Gun rights folks might want to take that last point seriously, because if there really is no meaningful difference between an assault weapon and other semi-automatic rifles, there are plenty of folks who are ready to say,

"Okay, then let's ban all semi-automatic rifles." In the polls that asked that question, on average, 58% were in favor of a ban on *all* semi-automatic rifles. Only a minority, 37%, opposed.

Large-Capacity Magazines

A majority would also ban the large-capacity magazines that make assault weapons and other semi-automatics so deadly. That, by the way, would also impact the semi-automatic pistols that play a much larger role in street crime and in the killing of police officers.

Bump Stocks

A sizable majority of Americans would like Congress and our state legislatures to enact laws banning bump stocks and other devices that allow a semi-automatic weapon to fire as if it were fully automatic. The ATF has banned bump stocks by regulation. Gun rights extremists are challenging the regulation in court, and even if they are unsuccessful, another administration could change or repeal that regulation.

Most Americans do not want to see another tragedy like the Las Vegas Strip massacre, and they certainly don't want to die or lose a loved one in another horrific event like that. But Congress—or more specifically, Republican and other pro-gun Members of Congress—are more interested in protecting gun sales than our loved ones.

Child Access Prevention

And finally, a majority of Americans would have Congress and our state legislatures enact legislation that requires gun owners to secure their firearms, so that toddlers don't find them and shoot themselves, a sibling or playmate. And so that their adolescent child doesn't use the unsecured gun to kill himself or herself. If parents would secure their guns, they would also make it impossible, or at least much harder, for their underage child to become the next school shooter.

Would Those Laws Work?

If implemented, would those laws lead to meaningful reductions in mass shootings, suicides, homicides, or unintentional shootings? A very substantial body of empirical research suggests that they would. But this volume isn't about that. It's about what most Americans want.

The polling data collected in the previous chapters make clear that the American public wants Congress and our state legislatures to give most of these proposals an honest try. Our daily newspapers, radio, and television news reports tell us about congressional failure to enact those proposals—and about the price Americans pay for their refusal.

If Congress and our state legislatures were to enact the laws Americans want, we would find out soon enough if these proposals would bring the firearm carnage in this country down to something like the level that exists in other developed, high-income countries that regulate gun access more tightly.

Driving Away Better The More Educated

It's hardly news to point out that the Republican Party's positions on guns, climate change, immigration, white supremacy, and other issues will likely have important consequences for both the party's and the country's future.

One consequence is that the Republican Party is driving away better educated voters. That's a point driven home by a poll Morning Consult conducted shortly after the shootings in Gilroy, El Paso, and Dayton in late July and August 2019.[631] The poll found that most people believed easy access to guns was an important factor in mass shootings. Some **74%** of Registered Voters felt that way; **21%** somehow didn't think so. *See* Table POL8_8. But the interesting thing wasn't that division, which was what one might have expected. It was the breakout by educational attainment.

Among those without a college education, **71%** thought easy access to guns was a factor in mass shooting, including 49% who thought it was "a lot" to blame. Among those with Bachelor's degrees, **77%** thought easy access to guns was at least partially to blame for mass shootings, including 51% who thought it was "a lot" to blame. And among those with post-graduate degrees, **83%** agreed, with 63% believing easy access to guns was "a lot" to blame. That was a 12 percentage point difference between those with the least education and those with the most.

The poll also asked in substance, but not in these words: *Are Republicans in Congress at least partially to blame for America's high level of mass shootings?* Only **34%** of those without college educations thought so, but **49%** of respondents with Bachelor's degrees believed congressional Republicans were at least partially to blame; and a solid majority, **58%**, of those with post-graduate educations—doctors, lawyers, scientists, teachers with Master degrees, etc.—agreed. That was a **24-point** difference in opinion between America's least educated and most educated.

Similarly, only **39%** of those without Bachelor's degrees thought President Trump was at least partially to blame for the mass shootings during his term in office. That rose to an enormous **77%** among college graduates and to an even higher **83%** among those with postgraduate educations. There was an amazing **44-point** difference in opinion between the country's least and best-educated strata.

Only **36%** of those without college degrees blamed the NRA, at least in part, for mass shootings, but a majority—**52%**—of those with Bachelor degrees believed the NRA bore some of the blame. So did a huge **83%** of those with post-college education. That was a dramatic **47 percentage point** difference between the country's the least and most educated.

Add to those figures the educational breakouts throughout this book, and the impression is inescapable: At least on gun violence, the Republican Party is tying itself in a very significant way to the least educated portion of the population and alienating the better educated. More specifically, the party is tying itself to the non-Hispanic white portion within that demographic. And more precisely still, it is tying itself to the folks within that demographic whose sense of self-worth is tied up with toxic masculinity, racial resentment, nativism, and guns.

Republicans still make up about the same percentage of the U.S. electorate as before Donald Trump ran for president in 2015-2016 (roughly 25% of registered voters). But there has been a dramatic shift in who identifies as a Republican. In October 2019, The Wall Street Journal noted that that the Republican Party was increasingly a party of whites without college educations.[632] It cited these figures to illustrate the point: In 2014, some **49%** of Republican voters were whites without a college degree. By 2018 the percentage of Republicans who were whites without college educations climbed to **59%**. At the same time, Republicans with college degrees declined from **38%** in 2014 to **29%** in 2018. The observation was not a new one.[633]

Is that really the direction the Republican Party, the party of business and the wealthy, wants to go? Is it good for the Republican Party or the country if it increasingly limits itself not just to whites, but to the least educated whites? Is it good for the party or the country if the Republican Party insists on being the party of white supremacy, Evangelicalism, and gun violence in a country that every day becomes better educated, more diverse, less religious, and more fed up with our country's gun carnage?

19. Why Does Congress Refuse What Most Americans Want?

There are at least three popular theories about why pro-gun Members of the U.S. House and Senate and many state legislators ignore what the great majority of Americans want and instead support the legislation advocated by the NRA and other, even more extreme gun rights organizations.

The first theory assumes that Republican politicians act as they do because they want NRA money and support, or at least, don't want to prompt the NRA to work against their re-election. And it's not just the NRA's financial and other support. It's also the financial backing of gun manufacturers, the gun dealers in each state, and the fringe gun-rights organizations. And, yes, those men who show up in our state capitals dressed in military-style fatigues and tactical gear, carrying assault weapons, hoping to intimidate legislators, probably figure into the equation as well.

The second theory posits that Republican politicians are sincere Second Amendment hard-liners—or if you prefer, ideologues—and simply don't care what the country or their constituents want. Or how many people will die as a result of their obduracy.

The third theory argues that there are structural problems in our form of representative democracy that make this problem possible.

Let's look at each theory, beginning with the notion that the gun lobby has bought off Representatives and Senators, or at a minimum, has intimidated them into submission. After that, we'll turn to the theory that pro-gun legislators are sincerely pro-gun and willingly complicit in our nation's gun carnage. Then, we'll briefly discuss the theory that our form of representational democracy no longer functions properly.

Theory 1:
The Gun Advocates in Congress Don't Want to Get on the Wrong Side of the Gun Lobby and its Money

Why do pro-gun members of Congress and state legislators continue, again and again, to vote down, or refuse to allow to come to a vote, the legislation that most Americans—even members of their own party—want?

The conventional answer is that pro-gun politicians don't want to get on the wrong side of the NRA and the gun manufacturers and gun dealers it represents. This is the proverbial carrot-and-stick scenario. The NRA spent an astounding $54,747,518 on behalf of Donald Trump and Congressional candidates in 2016.[634] When the NRA divvies up its campaign war chest, it usually gives larger amounts to those who have earned more favorable ratings from the organization, *e.g.*, by introducing or co-sponsoring bills the NRA wants and by voting the way NRA lobbyists tell them to vote.

According to one analysis, the fifty-six senators who voted in June 2016 against expanding background checks had received a combined total of roughly $36 million from the NRA.[635] That total included all the money they received from the NRA over their careers, both directly and indirectly. It also included the money the NRA spent to defeat their election opponents. Those numbers, however, did not count the amounts spent during the final months of the 2016 campaign. They also did not include money the NRA spent to lobby Congress.

Republican Congressmen who do not bend to the will of the NRA face the risk that the NRA will recruit someone to run against them in the next primary election. They also run the risk that the NRA will pour money into advertising and campaign contributions to help that opponent replace them. That's the stick—or, if you prefer, the gun—the NRA holds to their heads.

Most congressional districts are "safe" districts for one party or the other. In part, that's because Americans have been sorting themselves geographically. It's also due to the extreme gerrymandering of the Republican "REDMAP" campaign after the 2010 census. As part of that effort, Republican-controlled state legislatures crammed as many Democratic-leaning voters into as few districts as possible and drew the borders of other districts with scientific precision to assure the election of as many Republican members of Congress as possible.[636] It's also due, in many states, to the fact Republicans have purged large numbers of Democrats and racial minorities from those eligible to vote, moved voting places away from Democrats and racial minorities, and engaged in other anti-democratic tactics.

For most in Congress, that means the only real threat to their reelection comes not from the other party, but from a challenger in their own party's primary. The people who vote in Republican Party primaries tend to be further to the Right than other Republicans—just as people who vote in Democratic Party primaries tend to be further to the Left than Democrats as a whole. Thus, Members of Congress of both parties must be concerned about appealing to the farther-from-the-center wings of their parties.

But Republican members of Congress face extreme pressure not only from the NRA but from the Koch network of billionaire donors and from other Far Right groups. That's because those groups are quick to "primary" Republicans who don't vote as they want.[637] This combination of the threat of a primary challenger and unlimited spending by PACs and super PACs combine to keep most Republican Congressmen in line with what the NRA, gun manufacturers, and gun dealers want.

Gun manufacturers and gun dealers give large sums to PACs and Super PACs run by the NRA and other pro-gun groups. Like the storm surges pushed ashore by hurricanes, that money floods into election contests, drowning the opposition.

Even so, the power of the NRA and other gun rights groups derives in no small part from the perception that large numbers of voters share the NRA's extreme views. But, as we've seen, polls show that perception is overblown. *Yes,* Americans overwhelmingly support the right Americans also support most of the laws discussed in this book.

In this country, there are noisy, bullying folks opposed to doing anything about our gun violence except to arm themselves. They are quick to show up on Facebook and other social media, where they viciously attack anyone who disagrees with their pro-gun stance. But—as we've seen—they are a small minority, out of step with the rest of the country.

In an off-year election in 2019, Democratic candidates for the Virginia legislature ran on promises to enact legislation to keep guns out of the hands of dangerous and impulsive individuals. Voters in Virginia responded by electing enough Democrats to dominate the Virginia House. In the process, they swept lots of pro-gun Republicans out of office.

Gun rights advocates blamed the electoral defeat on the fact that the NRA was caught up in internal scandals and wasn't able to spend enough money to buy the election. "But for gun control activists," an article in Mother Jones asserted, "this blue wave signifies something bigger: Republicans' allegiance to the gun lobby is eroding their appeal with suburban voters they can't afford to lose."[638]

On January 20, 2020, large numbers of gun-rights advocates, white nationalists, and militia members gathered in Richmond, Virginia. It was the day set aside to honor Martin Luther King, Jr., the civil rights icon murdered by a white supremacist with a gun. But the gun-rights activists weren't there to honor Reverend King's life and legacy. They showed up from all over Appalachia to demonstrate against universal background checks and the other measures the new Democratic majority in the legislature had campaigned on.

Many of the demonstrators dressed in camouflage fatigues and tactical gear. Some called ahead with death threats against the Democratic legislators. In short, this wasn't just a demonstration. It was an attempt to intimidate Democratic legislators into not passing the legislation voters had elected them to enact.

In mid-April, when the direction of the legislative session became clear, armed demonstrators showed up again. When they did, President Trump sent a tweet that seemed to encourage the armed men to take matters into their hands. "LIBERATE VIRGINIA," he told the armed men, "and save your great 2nd Amendment. It is under siege!" Fortunately, there was no significant violence.

By late April 2020, the legislature passed, and Governor Northam signed into law, most of the proposed new gun laws (although some of them emerged from Virginia's legislature in watered-down form). The new laws included comprehensive background checks and a higher age for gun purchases—laws President Trump said he would strongly push for, but came out against when the NRA tugged on his leash.

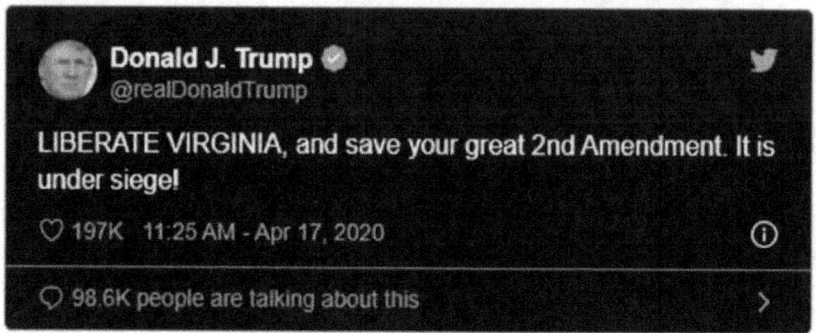

Were the 2018 and 2019 elections just temporary setbacks for the gun-rights hardliners? Or did those elections mark a turning point, signaling that Americans were about to reclaim their democratic institutions from the gun lobby and the armed men who threaten civil war if our elected representatives pass the gun laws most Americans want? That remains to be seen, but both sides do seem to agree on one thing: The election in November 2020 may well reveal if the tide has turned against the gun rights hard-liners and back toward the great majority of Americans.

Theory 2:

The Congressmen Who Push Extreme Gun Laws in Congress Really Are That Extreme

A second, less discussed theory is that the pro-gun Members of Congress may be ideologically committed to a vision of the United States in which everyone is armed to the teeth. There is evidence for this theory too.

In a thought-provoking essay in The Nation,[639] Marilynne Robinson makes the point that the Republicans in Congress *are* gun-rights ideologues. But she hedges, noting that for the most part, it's hard to tell how

Republicans rationalize their pro-gun stance. That's because Republicans don't explain why they ignore what the public wants and vote instead for laws designed to encourage gun sales.

In her view, Republicans in Congress rely on what she refers to as "non-political means" to hang onto power—gutting our campaign finance laws, gerrymandering, voter suppression, initiative nullification, and so on:

> The adamant resistance of Republicans to any attempt to make the public safer from military weapons may well be ideological. [But because] they have resorted to nonpolitical means to hold and assert power, they are never obliged to say what vision of the country or its future can be reconciled with their refusal to even allow debate in Congress on this agonizing problem of gun violence.[640]

We all tend to assume that someone who can get himself or herself elected to Congress must be a responsible, pragmatic individual, even if we don't agree with his or her views. And that used to be the case when Congressional candidates had to win votes from independents and even from the other party to win. But in recent years, in response to the demands of the rightwing billionaires who fund the party, as a result of their own personal beliefs, or both, Republican politicians have taken some pretty extreme positions.

Here's an example:

In June 2016, a heavily armed man with mental health issues entered the Pulse nightclub in Orlando. He killed 50 mostly gay and Hispanic patrons and wounded another 52 individuals. In the days following that tragedy, pro-gun Congressman Thomas Massie (R, Ky.) exhibited on his website an image of himself brandishing an assault rifle. In doing so, Congressman Massie responded to the grim tragedy in Orlando by signaling his solidarity with a mass murderer of gays and Hispanics—or, at least, with the sort of weapon that enabled his murderous rampage.

Massie co-founded and heads the "Second Amendment Caucus," the group of House members who banded together to promote the interests of gun manufacturers, gun dealers, and others who profit from gun violence.

As we've seen, poll after poll show that most Americans want background checks for *all* gun sales, including private sales. Rep. Massie, however, is adamantly opposed. He argues that we should do away with with background checks.

Similarly, polls show that most Americans believe that suspected terrorists on the "No Fly" list should not be able to walk into a gun store and buy a semi-automatic weapon and as much ammunition as they can pay for. Rep. Massie doesn't just disagree. He also argues that suspected terrorists should be able to buy, or make at home, guns that aren't detectable by airport, courthouse and school security systems.

When Stephen Paddock used assault rifles, large-capacity magazines, and bump stocks to kill 58 and wound hundreds more at the Route 91 country music concert in Las Vegas, even the NRA suggested that ATF should revisit its decisions allowing the sale of bump stocks. President Trump, who benefited "bigly" from the $30 million the NRA spent to help get him elected, ordered the ATF to ban bump stocks. Rep. Massie objected that the president was selling out the Second Amendment rights of gun owners.

Rep. Massie has taken money from the NRA, but unlike other pro-gun politicians, he has mainly associated himself with the National Association for Gun Rights and other groups that are even more extreme than the NRA. As I discuss below, he has joined with those organizations in advocating for gun manufacturers' and gun dealers' "right" to sell guns and ammunition to anybody and everybody, no matter the risks that presents to our kids and grandkids, to our teachers and police, and everyone else.

Massie has frequently associated himself with Larry Pratt, the long-time Executive Director of Gun Owners of America—despite Pratt's history of association with racist and anti-Semitic groups.

In 2018, Showtime aired Sacha Baron Cohen's series, *Who is America?* In one segment, Cohen pretended to be an Israeli counter-terrorism expert promoting a "Kinder Guardians" program to arm kids ages three to twelve years old. (Cohen deadpanned that you don't want to give guns to two-year-olds; they're called the "terrible twos" for a reason.) In the segment, Pratt endorsed the "Kinder Guardians" program.

Rep. Massie has also made a number of appearances with Phillip van Cleave, the president of Virginia Citizens Defense League. Van Cleve made an appearance on the same episode of *Who Is America?* Van Cleve was enthusiastic about the (fake Kinder Guardians program. "Yeah, well," he said about arming children ages three to twelve, "I think that would be a good idea."

I don't know if Rep. Massie thinks arming three-year-old children is a good idea, but we know he wants to lower the age for young adults to purchase pistols to at least age 18—never mind that young men age 18 to 21 years old lead the nation in gun homicides.

It's not clear how many in Congress share Representative Massie's guns-no-matter-what-the-cost-to-society stance, but it's worth noting that the Second Amendment Caucus Massie heads in the House claimed thirteen members—all white-male Republicans with extreme rightwing views, most from rural districts. (President Trump chose one of them, Mark Meadows, to be his chief of staff.

Caucus members sponsored or co-sponsored several NRA bills in the 2017-2019 Congress, including a bill to deregulate silencers—like the silencer or "suppressor" used by the shooter in the deadly Virginia Beach attack. At a time when suicides are epidemic among our veterans, caucus members also supported H.R. 1148, The Veteran's Second Amendment Protection Act. If it had become law, HR 1148 would have allowed severely mentally ill and even comatose veterans to buy guns.

Massie and other Second Amendment Caucus members also voted for a bill whose only purpose was to allow severely mentally ill individuals receiving Social Security disability benefits to buy guns.

In short, there's plenty of evidence that at least some Members of Congress are gun rights extremists.

Theory 3:
There Are Structural Problems With Our Form of Representative Democracy

Another theory argues that there are structural problems with our form of representative democracy.

Here's one such problem: The twenty *least* populous states in 2020 had a combined population of roughly **33.8 million** or about **10%** of the U.S. population.⁶⁴¹ By contrast, California had a population of **39.9 million** or about **12%** of the U.S. population.⁶⁴² Each of those twenty low-population states has two senators, or 40 senators altogether. California, which has about 6.2 million more citizens than all twenty low-population states combined, also gets two senators.

Yes, two senators for each state is what the Constitution stipulates. And *yes*, the Founding Fathers wrote the Constitution that way to guarantee that small New England states would be given a larger voice in the Senate.

But the Constitution doesn't guarantee that senators representing 10% of the population should be able to block legislation that 90% of the population, or 90% of registered voters, want. That's the consequence of the Senate filibuster rule, which itself is a relic from a period when Senators invoked the filibuster only in unusual circumstances, *e.g.*, when Congress wanted to curtail racial segregation or make the Southern pastime of lynching blacks a federal crime.

For most of our country's history, filibusters were unusual.⁶⁴³ But today, any controversial bill is likely to face a filibuster. It takes the votes of three-fifths of the Senate to end a filibuster—that's 60 of the Senate's 100 votes. In other words, under current Senate rules, 41 senators can prevent a bill from reaching the floor for a vote on the merits. That means those low-population states representing about 10% of the population have enough senators to block anything from reaching an up-or-down vote if they can get just one more senator to join them.⁶⁴⁴

The inequities of the Constitution's provision awarding two senators to every state carry over into the Electoral College. That's why the candidate who loses the popular vote can become president—as has happened in two of the last five presidential elections, 2000 and 2016. (Put differently, that's why two of our last three presidents won election despite losing the popular vote to the other candidate.⁶⁴⁵)

Allowing unlimited dark money to influence campaigns—the current situation under the *Citizens United* decision—compounds those

those problems.[646] The Republican "Red Map" or extreme gerrymander after the 2010 census, Republican voter-suppression tactics, and Republican efforts to nullify or restrict voter referenda and voter initiatives further compound those problems. The Republican practice of stripping powers from state officials when voters elect a Democrat to their state's executive branch also compound the problem. Combined, those tactics make clear that the Republican leadership, their consultants and funders have launched an all-out attack on democracy in the United States.

In July 2019, an Economist/YouGov poll asked, "How satisfied are you with the way democracy is working in America?" Half of the respondents said they were "Not too satisfied" or "Not at all satisfied."[647]

When asked if democracy was the best form of government, a surprising **15%** disagreed. Almost as worrisome, **14%** said they didn't know what they thought. The poll didn't ask those who disagreed what form of government they thought was better.[648]

All Three Theories May Be Correct

As the discussion above indicates, there is substantial evidence to support all three views. That suggests they may all be correct, at least to some extent.

Some Congressmen *do* vote for extreme, NRA-backed bills because they would rather take the NRA's money than risk its ire and that of other, even more extreme gun-rights groups.

Some in Congress sponsor and push extreme pro-gun legislation because they are far outside the mainstream. Congressman Thomas Massie (R., Ky, who demonstrated his fealty to the gun lobby by posing with an assault weapon after the Orlando massacre, certainly falls into that category.

And there are structural problems that politicians, political consultants, and organizations like the NRA leverage to make our country serve the interests of the gun industry. They do so at a terrible cost in lives disrupted and lost.

20. What Can We Do?

What can we do if Congress refuses to pass the legislation most Americans want?

Senate Majority Leader Mitch McConnell is famous for not letting bills go to the Senate floor for a vote. That way, Republican Senators don't have to go on record as opposing legislation most Americans want, but special interest groups oppose What, realistically, can we do if "Senator No" refuses to allow the Senate to vote on gun-violence-prevention bills?

What, in other words, can we do if our democracy no longer works for our kids and us, but works instead for gun manufacturers, gun dealers, and gun-wielding criminals?

Don't Despair and Say, "Nothing Can Be Done."

First and foremost, we can refuse to lose hope. We can refuse to say, *No matter what we do, nothing will happen.*

"This world-weary prediction of inaction is pernicious," ProPublica's Alec MacGillis wrote in a mini-essay on Twitter.[649] "It demoralizes those who are actually motivated to fight against gun violence. And it lets off the hook those who are opposed to reform." MacGillis added: "The NRA's influence depends heavily on the PERCEPTION of its power. By building up the gun lobby as an indomitable force, pessimistic liberals are playing directly into its hands."

Inspiration, fortunately, is not hard to come by. The remarkable level of mass shootings in late 2017 and early 2018 prompted David Hogg, Emma González, Cameron Kasky, and their fellow high school students at Marjory Stoneman Douglas High School in Parkland, Florida to take a stand.

They, in turn, inspired fellow students around the country and their parents to take to the streets, demanding action. And, as we've already noted, they got action: Even if the Republican-controlled 115th Congress (2017-2018 steadfastly refused to act, the states, including some states with Republican Governors, enacted over fifty new gun-violence-prevention laws in 2018.

And then the November 2018 midterms replaced many Congressmen with "A" ratings from the NRA with new faces—many with "F" ratings from the NRA. True, control of the Senate did not change hands; Senator McConnell retains control. But he's deeply unpopular and up for election in 2020. It's not enough for "Murder Turtle" to trend on social media when he blocks gun-violence-prevention legislation. Those who disagree with his policies, can contribute to his opponent's campaign.

After the shootings in Gilroy, El Paso, Dayton, and Odessa-Midland, some retail giants took a few timid steps. Walmart, Kroger, Target, Walgreen, CVS, and other retailers asked customers not to carry guns into their stores. Walmart also announced that it would stop selling certain types of ammunition and would discontinue sales of handguns in Alaska. You can encourage those retailers and other retailers to do more.

What else can we do?

Don't Shy Away Just Because The Issue Is Controversial

As we have seen, gun-violence-prevention legislation is controversial mainly in the abstract; there is widespread agreement on the particulars. But the belligerence and invective that strident gun rights advocates bring to any gun-violence-prevention discussion makes the issue seem terribly controversial. Their venom makes many unwilling to engage on the issue, at least on social media, where gun rights advocates are often brutally aggressive.

When the Parkland student leaders stood up and spoke out, right-wing media responded by spreading vicious lies and conspiracy theories about them. They claimed that the student leaders, like David Hogg, were "crisis actors" flown in and coached by anti-gun groups. Emma González, they said, was a communist with ties to Cuba, who had ripped up a copy of the U.S. Constitution. And so on.[650]

Encouraged by the propaganda, strident gun enthusiasts responded with death threats against David Hogg, Emma González, and the other student leaders. "Even now when people come up to us quietly to say thank you," Ms. González wrote in an opinion piece for The New York Times, "you never know if they're trying to shoot [us] at close range."[651] She added: "I am personally deathly afraid of them, and I know, from traveling the country during the summer for the Road to Change tour, that many of the people who disagree with us mean it when they say that they only want to talk if we're standing on the other end of their AR-15s."

It couldn't have been any consolation for those young people at the time, but at year-end, the fact-checking organization PolitiFact singled out the conspiracy theories and smears directed at the Parkland student leaders as the 2018 "lie of the year." PolitiFact said, "In another year of lament about the lack of truth in politics, the attacks against Parkland's students stand out because of their sheer vitriol."[652]

By more than a two-to-one margin, however, Republicans thought that critics of the Parkland students treated the students fairly.[653]

So, yes, some folks will bring hatefulness, conspiracy theories, lies, and even threats to the conversation. And, yes, if you decide to make this an issue around the Thanksgiving dinner table, things could get testy. But even if the holiday dinner is not the right forum, there are plenty of other opportunities to discuss these issues. Gun extremists need to know they aren't in the majority, and that their views don't represent those of most gun owners.

Stay Informed

Sign up for the gun violence newsletter The Trace. Visit the Brady Campaign, Giffords, Everytown for Gun Safety, or Moms Demand Action for Gun Sense in America websites. Sign up for their newsletters and bulletins. And while you're there, make a donation. Better still, if you can afford it, sign up for regular monthly donations.

Vote!

What's more important to us—guns or our kids? High-capacity gun magazines or high-performing schools? And what kind of country do we want? Do we want our country to be like Mogadishu in the 1990s, where every male seemed to have an assault weapon or an RPG? Or do we want to be the country that was once the envy of the world?

We make those choices at the polls when we vote for or against pro-gun House and Senate candidates. We also make those choices when we vote for or against pro-gun state legislators.

And to be blunt, we also make those choices when we don't register to vote and when we don't bother to go to the polls. In the 2016 presidential election, only 56% of the voting-age population cast ballots.[654] The United States placed 28th in voter turnout among the thirty-six Organization for Economic Cooperation and Development (OECD nations. The average among OECD nations was 75%.[655] The 2018 election set a record high for midterm voter participation. For the first time, over 100 million—probably 118 million—voted.[656] But according to the Election Project, that represented only 50% of eligible voters.[657]

Here's the point: When we don't register to vote or don't bother to vote, we tell our kids, "Your lives just aren't worth it."

The choices we've made have put too many corrupt, craven, and ideologically extreme men and women in Congress and in our state legislatures. Those choices frighten our children and should embarrass all of us.

If you're not registered to vote, register. If you think you're registered to vote but haven't voted in a while, double-check your registration—especially if your election official is a Republican. In recent years, Republican election officials have developed the anti-democratic habit of purging people, especially people of color, from the voter rolls before elections.

Learn where your Representative, Senator, and state legislators stand on gun-violence-prevention legislation. And then vote for candidates who want to do something constructive about our horrific gun violence.

Get Involved

If there is a local gun violence advocacy group in your area, join and get involved. The next time there is a rally or vigil in your area, show up. If your Representative or Senator or state legislator holds a constituent meeting, attend and ask what he or she is doing on the issues discussed in this book.

Communicate With Your Legislators

Write your Congressman, Senator, and state legislators and let them know that you expect them to support and vote for gun-violence-prevention legislation. Follow up with a call when a specific piece of legislation is pending.

If you don't know what to say, ask the people at Giffords or the Brady Campaign for help. Or, better still, don't worry about how to phrase your message. Just call and speak as you would to your neighbor. Or, if you can't call, write. Or, if none of that works for you, send them a copy of this book.

If you can, donate to the campaign of a Representative or Senator or state legislator who is willing to push for gun-violence-prevention legislation. Or volunteer to help with his or her campaign.

It's time we join with the Parkland students and their supporters around the country and tell our representatives in Congress and in our state legislatures, "Stop taking NRA money. Vote for strong laws to rein in our gun violence, or we'll find someone else to represent us, someone who actually cares about our kids."

Conclusion

"Congress could pass gun-control legislation, if it were a functioning institution. But in this matter above all, we have learned that even overwhelming public opinion counts for nothing."[658]

Pro-gun politicians refuse to enact or even consider the legislation the majority of Americans want. In fact, they refuse to enact or even consider legislation that the majority of Republicans, supporters of President Trump, and gun owners want.

Sadly, a book like this—*i.e.*, about the chasm between the laws Americans want and what Republicans in Congress are willing to legislate—could be written about any number of issues.[659] As one observer noted, Congress has become a "cruel parody of representative democracy."[660]

Consider, for example, healthcare. Polls in 2017 showed that the American public wanted the Affordable Care Act ("Obamacare") improved, not abandoned, and yet congressional Republicans were determined to repeal it. They were willing to repeal the healthcare law even though that meant tens of millions of Americans would lose their health insurance, and some would die. Only a courageous vote by the late Senator John McCain, terminally ill at the time, saved it.

A book like this could also be written about climate change and the environment. The American public accepts the scientific consensus that climate change is real and caused by human activity. Unlike Mr. Trump, most of us don't believe that climate change is a decades-long "hoax," in which all of the world's climate scientists are co-conspirators.[661] And yet Republicans in Congress, beholden to or afraid of the Koch network of billionaire donors, make sure we don't move away from fossil fuels or do anything else to forestall the looming planetary disaster.

Instead, the Trump Administration is selling off our wilderness areas to mining companies and has appointed a coal-industry lobbyist to head the EPA. Under President Trump, the EPA has lifted many protections against pollution of our air and water. It's just a matter of time until studies show that those changes have led to cancers, birth defects, or other health problems.

The Trump Administration is backing efforts by industry to build petrochemical plants along the Ohio River. That threatens to create a new "Cancer Valley" in the Appalachian Ohio River Valley, similar to the petrochemical "Cancer Alley" in Louisiana and Texas. No polls show that people in that region want to die from cancer, or see their children or grandchildren die from cancer, so that foreign petrochemical com-panies can make bigger profits.

A book like this could also be written on immigration, Deferred Action for Childhood Arrivals ("DACA"), and the "dreamers."[662] (For anyone not following the issue, DACA is a program created by the Obama administration in 2012 to protect from deportation undocumented individuals who were brought to the United States as children by their parents. Most of them only know the United States as their home and dream of becoming citizens and contributing to our country. Only kids with clean records are eligible.

Public Policy Polling noted that something that "really does bring together Americans across the political spectrum is support for DACA." In its poll, 74% of voters thought undocumented children brought to the U.S. by their parents and raised in the country should be allowed to stay and apply for citizenship. Only 18% thought we should deport the DACA kids to countries they never knew, ruining their lives and depriving our country of their talents and contributions.

There was no tidal wave of support among the public or voters for separating families and putting asylum seekers and immigrants in cages or in concentration camps. Polls did not show that the American public wanted immigration officials to ignore allegations of sexual abuse of de-tainees. Polls did not show that most Americans wanted ill detainees to be ignored and left to die. And yet, that's what President Trump and congressional Republicans gave us.

A book like this could be written about income and wealth inequality. The American public didn't demand that we add trillions of dollars to the national debt to pay for tax cuts for big corporations and billionaires. And yet, that's what Republican officeholders gave us.

Guns are simply a special case. In no other area is the gulf between what the public wants and what Republicans in Congress are willing to legislate so large and so longstanding.

Such wide disparities across so many issues between what majorities in this country want and what Senator Mitch McConnell —"Senator No"—and his fellow Republican lawmakers are willing to allow to come to a vote, let alone be enacted into law, calls into question whether we still have a functioning democracy.

Writing in The New Yorker, columnist Osita Nwanevu argued:

> The American political divide rests not between the two halves of a deeply divided public but, rather, between a significant majority of the American population and a conservative minority that is both disproportionately empowered by our political institutions and incorrigibly opposed to democratic policies.[663]

That divide is exceptionally sharp in the Senate, where small-population, rural, conservative states are overrepresented, and the filibuster gives them veto power over what most Americans want Congress to do.

It's also at play in the Electoral College, where that disproportionate representation made George W. Bush president, even though Al Gore won the popular vote. The Electoral College also made Donald J. Trump president, even though Hillary Clinton won the popular vote by almost three million votes. Voters in large, populous states like California and New York cast votes in Senate and presidential elections that count for only a small fraction of what a vote cast in Alaska or Wyoming does.

In the 2014 midterm election, Republican candidates for the U.S. Senate won 24,631,488 votes to the 20,875,493 votes won by their Democratic opponents, an advantage of about 3.75 million votes. Given that, one would expect Republicans to pick up some seats. In fact, Republicans won 24 races, and Democrats won only 12. Put differently, Republicans won 50.7% of the vote but won twice as many seats as Democrats.

In the 2016 election, voters cast 3.9 million more votes nationwide for Democratic senatorial candidates than for Republican candidates—just a little larger than the Republican margin in 2014. And yet 21 Republican senate candidates won election versus only 12 Democratic candidates—almost the same result as in 2014. In Alaska, the winning Republican senatorial candidate got 111,382 votes; in California, the winning Democratic candidate got over 5.25 million votes.

In 2018, Democratic candidates racked up 40,558,262 votes for the U.S. Senate. That was nine million more votes than their Republican opponents, who garnered 31,490,026 votes. In percentages, Democrats got 55% of the vote, and Republicans got 43%. Given that, one might be forgiven for supposing that Democrats picked up seats in the Senate. In fact, despite the shellacking they took at the polls, Republicans *gained* three seats in the Senate.

In short, neither the presidency nor the U.S. Senate any longer reflect the majority of voters in this country. And that's even before the effects of Republican voter suppression and dark money are reckoned with.

Law Professor Tim Wu came to the same conclusion in a New York Times opinion piece entitled "The Oppression of the Supermajority."[664] The article's subheading captures the gist of his thesis: "The defining political fact of our time is not polarization. It's the thwarting of a largely unified public." He argues that respect for democracy implies that supermajorities of the population should usually get the legislation they ask for.

Hopes and Dreams

Our kids and grandkids have hopes and dreams. They don't want a loser with an assault weapon or pump-action shotgun to extinguish their futures.

No matter how many times pro-gun legislators make rote promises of "thoughts and prayers," they simply don't care about the hopes and dreams of our children. Or about our kids' fears and concerns. They couldn't, or they wouldn't stand in the way of legislation to deal with guns and gun violence.

Although our kids' and grandkids' lives are on the line, pro-gun legislators sneer that our high schoolers are not old enough to have an opinion worth hearing. They accuse our kids of being "crisis actors." They tell them to shut up. And to duck and cover.

That's not how a functioning democracy works.

Clifford Young is the President of US Ipsos Public Affairs, one of the organizations whose polls I've cited frequently in this book. Referring to the consensus on specific gun-violence-prevention measures, he wrote:[665]

> With this kind of broad consensus, there really is no excuse not to provide reasonable and efficacious solutions to this problem. ... **Such a rift between public opinion and its leaders never ends well for the leaders**. [Emphasis added.]

The adamant refusal by pro-gun members of Congress to permit enactment of the legislation most of us want may be good for gun manufacturers' and gun dealers' bottom lines. And it may be good for those legislators' re-election campaign funds. But to state the obvious, it's not good for the kids who go to school each day wondering if today is the day a classmate or former classmate will gun them down. It's also not good for the women shot by domestic abusers, often along with their kids. It's not good for the toddlers who find unloaded and unsecured guns and kill or maim themselves or someone else. And it's not good for the roughly 24,000 who will turn their guns on themselves each year—or for the shattered families they leave behind.

When our legislators cynically reject what most Americans—even supermajorities of Americans—want, it's also not good for democracy. Year after year, our representatives in Congress and in our state legislatures ignore what the great majority of Americans want. That breeds cynicism and undermines Americans' faith in our government, in our political processes, and in democracy itself. Already, too many Americans excuse themselves from voting with the complaint, "Why bother? Nothing will change."

That notion—"nothing can be done"—is one with poisonous consequences for democracy. It's also demonstrably false. After a disturbed former student went on a killing rampage at their school, students at Marjory Stoneman Douglas High School in Parkland, Florida, refused to follow the well-established rituals. They refused to say, as so many others had, "nothing can be done." Instead, they stood up and said, "Never again!" They bluntly told politicians to pass gun legislation or be replaced.

Galvanized by their courage, millions marched in support of their stance. And state legislators, or at least some of them, responded to the public pressure. As we've seen, in the months that followed, state legislatures passed dozens of new laws aimed at various aspects of our gun violence problem. In the November 2018 midterms, voters cast out forty Congressmen with top NRA ratings.[666] Many of the candidates who took their places had "F" ratings from the NRA and campaigned on gun reform. Congress, states, and philanthropists have put up fresh money for gun violence research. At the same time, investigative reports have revealed longstanding patterns of self-dealing and self-enrichment by NRA executives and board members, prompting investigations and lawsuits.

In 2019, the effort continued. Some 32 states and the District of Columbia passed a total of 137 bills regulating gun access.[667] Despite super PACs and dark money, gerrymandering, voter suppression efforts, and initiative nullification, we still have the power of the ballot box. If we don't lose heart, we can replace even more of those in Congress and in our state legislatures who refuse to protect our kids and grandkids, who refuse to protect abused spouses and dating partners, and who refuse to protect toddlers. We can elect instead men and women who promise to put our family members' lives ahead of gun industry profits and gun-industry campaign contributions.

And if we do that, we just may save our democracy.

APPENDICES

Federal Age Limits for Possession, Sale, and Purchase

Chart from: Federal Commission on School Safety

	Long Guns	Handguns
Minimum Age of Possession	None	18, with exceptions
Licensed Sellers (FFLs)	FFLs prohibited from selling or delivering long guns/ammunition to individuals younger than 18	FFLs prohibited from selling or delivering handguns/ammunition to individuals younger than 21
Unlicensed Seller	May sell a long gun to a person of any age	May sell a handgun to a resident of their own state as long as the buyer is at least 18

The Gun Policy Polls

Brief Overview

The polls listed below provided the data on where U.S. adults and registered voters stand on the legislative proposals that are the subject of Chapters 4-17. Some of these polls covered only one or two of those issues and appeared only once or twice in those chapters. Others covered several proposals and appeared more frequently. For more details on these and the other polls cited in the text, see the next appendix. In this table, "N" is the number of respondents who participated in the poll. "Gun HH" refers to households in which there is a gun.

Adults/ Voters	N =	Phone? Online?	Gun HH?	Polling Dates	Poll
Adults	1,001	Phone		6/20-23/16	ABC/WaPo
Adults	808	Phone		2/15-18/18	ABC/WaPo
Adults Voters	1,002 865	Phone	47%	4/8-11/18	ABC/WaPo
Adults Voters	1,003 877	Phone	46%	9/2-5/19	ABC/WaPo
Adults	1,009	Phone	37%	7/16-21/19	APM (SSRS)

GUNS, POLLS, and DEMOCRACY

Adults/ Voters	N =	Phone? Online?	Gun HH?	Polling Dates Dates	Poll
Adults	1,122	Hybrid	38%	3/14-19/18	AP-NORC
Adults	1,063	Hybrid	35%	3/14-18/19	AP-NORC
Adults	1,120	Phone	_	12/3-5/17	CBS/SSRS
Adults	1,012	Phone	_	2/20-22/18	CBS/SSRS
Adults	1,001	Phone	_	6/16-19/16	CNN/ORC
Adults	1,010	Phone	_	10/12-15/17	CNN/SSRS
Voters	894				
Adults	1,016	Phone	_	2/20-23/18	CNN/SSRS
Voters	1,014	Phone	_	3/18-21/18	Fox News
Voters	1,013	Phone	_	8/11-13/19	Fox News
Adults	1,028	Phone	43%	10/5-11/17	Gallup
Adults	767	Phone		3/5-11/18	Gallup
Adults	1,019	Phone	46%	10/1-10/18	Gallup
Adults	2,291	Phone		8/15-30/18	Gallup
"A"	1,099				
Adults	1,526	Phone	_	10/1-13/19	Gallup
Adults	1,006	Online	_	10/10-11/17	Ipsos/NPR
Adults	1,005	Online	_	2/27-28/18	Ipsos/NPR
Adults	6,813	Online	41%	1/11-28/19	Ipsos/Reuters
Adults	803	Phone	46%	3/2-5/18	Monmouth
Adults	800	Phone	44%	8/16-20/19	Monmouth

Adults/ Voters	N =	Phone? Online?	Gun HH?	Polling Dates Dates	Poll
Voters	1,996	Online	38%	10/5-9/17	Morning Consult
Voters	1,989	Online	_	2/15-19/18	Morning Consult
Voters	1,992	Online	41%	2/22-26/18	Morning Consult
Voters	1,997	Online	40%	3/29-4/1/18	Morning Consult
Voters	1,994	Online	39%	8/2-6/18	Morning Consult
Voters	1,960	Online	36%	8/5-7/19	Morning Consult
Adults	1,011	Phone	47%	4/10-13/18	NPR/PBS
Voters	827				
Adults	880	Phone	_	2/5-11/19	NPR/PBS
Voters	772				
Adults	1,346	Phone	_	7/15-19/19	NPR/PBS
Voters	1,175				
Adults	1,317	Phone	_	9/5-8/19	NPR/PBS
Voters	1,160		_		
Adults	1,000	Phone	46%	8/10-14/19	NBC/WSJ
Voters	834				
Adults	3,930	Online	_	3/13-27/17	Pew
Adults	10,683	Online	_	9/24-10/7/18	Pew
Adults Some Qs.	9,895 4,954	Online	_	9/3-15/19	Pew
Voters	4,151	Hybrid	_	12/6-7/16	PPP
Voters	846	Hybrid	_	3/23-25/18	PPP

Adults/Voters	N =	Phone? Online?	Gun HH?	Polling Dates	Poll
Voters	679	Hybrid	_	6/8-10/18	PPP
Voters	1,610	Phone	_	6/21-27/16	Quinnipiac
Voters	1,482	Phone	46%	10/5-10/17	Quinnipiac
Voters	1,577	Phone	45%	11/7-13/17	Quinnipiac
Voters	1,230	Phone	_	12/13-18/17	Quinnipiac
Voters	1,249	Phone	_	2/16-19/18	Quinnipiac
Voters	1,122	Phone	44%	3/3-5/18	Quinnipiac
Voters	1,181	Phone	47%	4/6-9/18	Quinnipiac
Voters	1,120	Phone	44%	1/9-13/19	Quinnipiac
Voters	1,209	Phone	_	3/1-3/19	Quinnipiac
Voters	1,078	Phone	41%	5/16-20/19	Quinnipiac
Voters	1,422	Phone	_	8/21-26/19	Quinnipiac
Voters	1,000	Phone	44%	2/20-24/18	Suffolk/USA
Voters	1,000	Phone	50%	8/20-25/19	Suffolk/USA
Adults	1,000	Online	_	7/24-25/14	Huff Post
Adults	3,310	Online	_	10/5/17	YouGov
Adults	1,500	Online	_	2/25-27/18	Economist
Voters	1,296				
Adults	2,595	Online	_	12/20/18	YouGov (Daily)
Adults	17,391	Online	_	4/8/19	YouGov (Daily)

YouGov conducted the Economist and Huffington Post polls. Marist conducted the NPR/PBS polls.

REED

The Gun Policy Polls With More Detail

ABC/Washington Post

The ABC News/Washington Post polls were conducted by landline and cellular telephone in English and Spanish, among a random national sample of adults. Langer Research Associates of New York, N.Y., conducted these surveys, with sampling, data collection, and tabulation by SSRS of Media, Pa. N = number of respondents.

Archive: https://www.washingtonpost.com/wp-stat/polls /postpollarchive.html.

ABC/Washington Post Poll, Aug. 16-20, 2017. N = 1,014 adults. Margin of error ± 3.5 points, including design effects. [Public's opinions of white supremacists; no gun questions.] Gregory Holyk, ABC News (June 28, 2016) (with link to poll results). Langer Research.

ABC/Washington Post Poll, Feb. 15-18, 2018. N = 808 adults nationwide. Margin of error, including design effects ± 4. [No data on gun ownership.]. See details on the survey's methodology here. (Feb. 15-18, 2018), adults (February 20, 2018).

ABC/Washington Post Poll, Apr. 8-11, 2018. N = 1,002 adults nationwide. Margin of error, including design effects ± 3.5. N = 865 registered voters. Margin of error ± 4 points. [Gun household? Yes: 47%; No: 52%.]

ABC/Washington Post Poll, Sept. 2-5, 2019. . N = 1,003 adults nationwide. Margin of ± 3.5 percentage points for the full sample, including design effects. .

See: Mike DeBonis and Emily Guskin, , *The Washington Post (released* Sept. 9, 2019).

See: Gary Langer, , *ABC News* (Sept. 10, 2019).

American Psychological Association

Stress in America 2019: Stress over election, health care and mass shootings (Nov. 5, 2019). . The Harris Poll conducted this year's survey on behalf of APA from Aug. 1 to Sept. 3, 2019. N = 3,617 adults. Because the sample is based on those who were invited and agreed to participate in research panels, no estimates of theoretical sampling error can be calculated. Interviews in English and Spanish. Data were weighted to reflect the 2018 Current Population Survey by the U.S. Census Bureau.

See also: Andrea Diaz, *CNN* (Oct. 30, 2018). The survey was conducted among 3,459 people 18 and older. It also included interviews with 300 teenagers ages 15 to 17. The survey measures attitudes and perceptions of stress.

AMP Research Lab (SSRS)

AMP Research Labs, July 16-21, 2019, *released* **Aug. 20 and Oct. 2, 2019.** SSRS of Glen Mills, Pennsylvania, conducted live phone interviews of 1,009 adults for AMP Research Lab. The margin of error for total respondents was ± 3.42% at the 95% confidence level. Design effects associated with weighting were included in the calculation of this margin of error.

AMP released the results in three separate packages: APM Survey: Americans' Views On Key Gun Policies, (Aug. 20, 2019); (Oct. 2, 2019); (Oct. 2, 2019).

The APM Research Lab conducted this survey jointly with two partners: , a reporting collaboration of 10 public radio stations covering the role of guns in American life, and American Public Media's initiative to foster new conversations about mental health.

Part One: What do Americans think of "red flag" or ERPO laws?

AMP Research Labs, July 16-21, 2019, *released* **Aug. 20, 2019.** . . [Includes data on how many own guns.]

Guns & America:

Part Two: Knowledge of gun-related deaths

APM Survey: Americans' views on key gun policies, Part 2:, July 16 to 21, 2019, *released* **Oct. 2, 2019.** N = 1,009 U.S. adults. Overall margin of error is ± 3.4 percentage points. [Only one-quarter of Americans are aware that suicides are the leading type of gun-related deaths in the United States.]

Part 3: Mandating that guns be stored with locks in place

APM Survey, July 16-21, 2019 *released* **Oct. 2, 2019.** N = 1,009 U.S. adults age 18 or older. Overall margin of error is ± 3.4 percentage points.

AMP Research Labs, July 16-21, 2019, *released* **Aug. 20 and Oct. 2, 2019,** (Oct. 2, 2019).

AP-NORC

Conducted by The Associated Press-NORC Center for Public Affairs Research with funding from The Associated Press and NORC at the University of Chicago.

AP-NORC Center Poll, Mar. 14-19, 2018. Data Summary. N = 1,122 adults. Margin of error: ± 4.2 percentage points at the 95% confidence level among all adults. AP-NORC did not publish cross tab data.

AP-NORC Center Poll, Mar. 14-18, 2019. . N = 1,063 adults. Margin of error: ± 4.1 percentage points at the 95% confidence level among all adults. AP-NORC did not publish cross tab data. [Gun owner, gun household data.]

See also: **Gun Laws and Public Safety,** AP-NORC, Mar. 2019, , .

CBS News (SSRS

SSRS of Glen Mills, PA, conducted data collection on behalf of CBS News. SSRS conducted interviews in English and Spanish using live phone interviewers and weighted responses to reflect U.S. Census figures on demographic variables. The error due to sampling for results based on the entire sample could be ± 4%. The error for subgroups may be higher. The margin of error includes the effects of standard weighting procedures, which enlarge sampling error slightly.

CBS News Poll, June 13-14, 2016, *released* **Jun. 15, 2016.** Gauging Americans' views on Orlando mass shooting (Jun. 15, 2016).

See: Anthony Salvanto, Fred Backus, Sarah Dutton, and Jennifer De Pinto, , CBS News (June 15, 2016).

CBS News Poll, Dec. 3-5, 2017, *released* **Dec. 11, 2017**. . N = 1,120 adults nationwide. Margin of error ± 4. (party-affiliation only). Telephone interviews in English and Spanish using live interviewers. The data were weighted to reflect U.S. Census figures on demographic variables.

See: Jennifer De Pinto, Fred Backus, Kabir Khanna, and Anthony Salvanto, (Dec. 11, 2017).

CBS News Poll, Feb. 20-22, 2018, *released* **Feb. 23, 2018**. . N = 1,012 adults nationwide. Phone interviews in English and Spanish. Margin of error ± 4. [No crosstabs.]

See: CBS News Poll: , CBS News (Feb. 23, 2018).

CNN/ORC and CNN/SSRS

CNN/ORC International, June 16-19, 2016, *released* **June 20, 2016**. . N = 1,001 adults by telephone. The margin of sampling error for results based on the total sample is ± 3 percentage points. The sample also includes 891 interviews of registered voters with a margin of error of ± 3.5 percentage points. The sample also includes 891 interviews among registered voters (± 3.5 percentage points). [Crosstabs]

See also: Jennifer Agiesta, , CNN Politics (Jun. 21, 2016); Jennifer Agiesta and Tom LoBianco, , CNN (June 20, 2016). [Crosstabs]

CNN SRSS, Oct. 12-15, 2017, *released* **Oct. 17, 2017**. . . N = 1,010 Adults. Live telephone interviews in English and Spanish. SSRS conducted the study for CNN. The margin of sampling error for total respondents is ± 3.5 at the 95% confidence level. For the sample of 894 registered voters, it is ± 3.8 percentage points. *See also:* Jennifer Agiesta, CNN (Oct. 17, 2017).

CNN SRSS, Feb. 20-23, 2018, *released* **Feb. 25, 2018**. . N = 1,016 adults by telephone. Results for the full sample have a margin of sampling error of ± 3.7 percentage points; it is larger for subgroups. SSRS, Trump-Guns, Table 849. The margin of sampling error for total respondents is ± 3.7 at the 95% confidence level.

See also: Jennifer Agiesta, CNN (Feb. 25, 2018).

Eliott C. McLaughlin, CNN (Feb. 28, 2018).

SSRS Archive: https://ssrs.com/tag/cnn-poll-conducted-by-ssrs/

Fox News

The Fox News Polls below were conducted under the joint direction of Anderson Robbins Research (D) and Shaw & Company Research (R). *Note: In 2019, the firm Anderson Robbins Research changed its name to Beacon Research; the Fox News bipartisan polling team remained unchanged.*

Landline and cellphone telephone numbers were randomly selected for inclusion in the survey using a probability proportionate to size method, which means phone numbers for each state are proportional to the number of voters in each state.

Fox News, Mar. 18-21, 2018, *released* **Mar. 25, 2018**. Dana Blanton, , Fox News (Mar. 25, 2018). N = 1,014 registered voters. Results based on the full sample have a margin of sampling error of ± 3 percentage points. landline and cellphone interviews with 1,014 randomly chosen registered voters nationwide.

See: Dana Blanton, , Fox News (Mar. 25, 2018).

Fox News, Aug. 11-13, 2019, *released* **Aug. 14, 2019**. Dana Blanton, , Fox News. N = 1,013 registered voters. Results based on the full sample have a margin of sampling error of ± 3 percentage points. [Gun Ownership/Gun HH asked but not shown.]

Fox poll archive:

https://www.foxnews.com/category/columns/fox-news-poll

Gallup

Gallup conducts interviews with respondents on landline and cellular phones, with interviews conducted in Spanish for respondents who are primarily Spanish-speaking.

Lydia Saad, ,"Gallup's Guide to U.S. Public Opinion on Guns," Gallup Blog (Aug. 5, 2019) (Overview of Gallup polls on gun-related issues).

Gallup Poll, Oct. 5-11, 2017, *released* **Oct. 16, 2017.** , N = 1,028 adults. For results based on the total sample of national adults, the margin of sampling error is ± 4 percentage points at the 95% confidence level.

See also: Megan Brenan, "Support for Stricter Gun Laws Edges Up in U.S." Gallup conducted this poll Oct. 5-11, 2017, *released* Oct. 16, 2017.

See also: Lydia Saad, "Americans Widely Support Tighter Regulations on Gun Sales," Gallup (Oct. 17, 2017).

Gallup Poll, Mar. 5–11, 2018, *released* **Mar. 15, 2018**. "Americans' Views on Measures to Prevent Mass School Shootings (Trends)," Gallup News Service (Mar. 15, 2018). N = 1,515 adults (limited questions). For results based on the total sample of national adults, the margin of error is ± 3 percentage points at the 95% confidence level. Gallup asked a random sub-sample of 767 adults a favor/oppose list of questions. The margin of sampling error was ± 5 percentage points at the 95% confidence level. All reported mar-gins of sampling error include computed design effects for weighting. [No data on % of gun owners or gun households.]

See also: Frank Newport, "Broad Agreement on Most Ideas to Curb School Shootings," Gallup (Mar. 15, 2018) (Same poll with data for additional questions).

Gallup Poll, Oct. 1-10, 2018, *released* **Oct. 17, 2018**. "Gallup Poll Social Series: Crime [Data]." N = 1,019 adults, ages 18+, living in all 50 U.S. states and the District of Columbia. For results based on this sample of national adults, the margin of sampling error is ±4 percentage points at the 95% confidence level.

See: RJ Reinhart, "Six in 10 Americans Support Stricter Gun Laws," Gallup News (Oct. 17, 2018).

Gallup Poll, Aug. 15-30, 2019, *released* **Sept. 10, 11 & 13, 2019**. August Wave 2, Final Topline, Timberline: 937008, JT: 315, Princeton Job #: 19-08-015. N = 2,291 adults. Telephone interviews. Margin of sampling error is ±3 percentage points at the 95% confidence level. For results based on the sample of 1,099 national adults in Form A, the margin of sampling error is ±4 percentage points. For results based on the sample of 1,192 national adults in Form B, the margins of sampling error are ±3 percentage points.

See also: Megan Brenan, "Nearly Half in U.S. Fear Being the Victim of a Mass Shooting," Gallup News Service (Sept. 10, 2019)

See also: Lydia Saad, "More Blaming Extremism, Heated Rhetoric for Mass Shootings," Gallup News Service (Sept. 11, 2019).

See also: Jeffrey M. Jones, "Americans' Views of NRA Become Less Positive," Gallup News Service (Sept. 13, 2019).

Gallup, "In Depth: Guns," Gallup historical trends, Gallup News Service (Sept. 28, 2019). [Gun in home? Yes = 37% in 2019.]

Justin McCarthy, "64% of Americans Want Stricter Laws on Gun Sales," Gallup News Service (Nov. 4, 2019).

Johns Hopkins Center for Gun Policy and Research

Colleen L. Barry, Daniel W. Webster, Elizabeth Stone, Cassandra K. Crifasi, Jon S. Vernick, and Emma E. McGinty, "Public Support for Gun Violence Prevention Policies Among Gun Owners and Non–Gun Owners in 2017," *American Journal of Public Health* (June 6, 2018). Conducted **Jan. 2-16, 2017**, the survey used NORC's AmeriSpeaks online panel (N = 2,124). The probability-based panel was designed to be representative of the US population and used random-digit dialing and address-based sampling.

Ipsos

Ipsos for NPR, Oct. 10-11, 2017, *released* **Oct. 11, 2017.** "Majority of Americans Hold Incorrect Assumptions about Guns." (Data Tables). N = roughly 1,006 adults interviewed online in English. The poll has a credibility interval of ± 3.5 percentage points for all respondents. [In the sample, 26% personally owned a gun, 74% did not. Also, 29% lived in a household where someone else owned a gun; 71% did not.]

See: Clifford Young, Julia Clark, Mallory Newall, "Majority of Americans Hold Incorrect Assumptions about Guns," Ipsos poll on behalf of NPR (Oct. 13, 2017).

See also: Max Greenwood, "Poll: 82 percent support a ban on bump stocks," *The Hill* (Oct. 13, 2017).

Ipsos/NPR, Feb. 27-28, 2018, *released* **Feb. 28, 2018**. Ipsos/NPR poll: "Majority of Americans support policies aimed to keep guns out of hands of dangerous individuals." N = roughly 1,005 adults age 18+ from the continental U.S., Alaska, and Hawaii, interviewed online in English. The poll has a credibility interval of ± 3.5 percentage points for all respond-ents. [No gun ownership data]

See: Chris Jackson and Mallory Newall, Ipsos/NPR poll: "Majority of Americans support policies aimed to keep guns out of hands of danger-ous individuals" (Feb. 28, 2018).

See: Asma Khalid, "NPR Poll: After Parkland, Number of Americans Who Want Gun Restrictions Grows" [Heard on <u>Morning Edition</u>] (Mar. 2, 2018)

Ipsos for Reuters, Jan. 11-28, 2019, *released* **Feb. 8, 2019**. Reuters/Ipsos Data: "American Perceptions on Gun Control." (Data Tables) N = 6,813 adults. The Reuters/Ipsos poll was conducted online in English. It has a credibility interval, a measure of precision, of ± 2 percentage points. [In the sample, 28% personally owned a gun; 72% did not. Also, 17% lived in a household where someone <u>else</u> owned a gun; 83% did not. Total gun households = 41%.]

See: Chris Kahn, "Americans support gun control, but doubt lawmakers will act:" Reuters/Ipsos poll," *Reuters* (Feb. 8, 2019).

Ipsos for USA Today, Aug. 5-6, 2019, *released* **Aug. 6. 2019**. (Data Ta-ble) N = 1,004 adults. Interviewed online in English. The poll has a credibility interval of plus or minus 3.5 percentage points for all respondents.

See: Chris Jackson and Mallory Newall, "Americans Are Divided On Who Is Responsible For Mass Shootings," Ipsos (Aug. 6, 2019). (Data Tables).

Ipsos for Reuters, Jan. 11-28, 2019, *released* **Feb. 8, 2019**). "American Perceptions on Gun Control." (Toplines) (Data Tables) N = 6,813 adults. Interviewed online in English. The poll has a credibility interval of plus or minus 1.4 percentage points for all respondents.

Monmouth

Monmouth University Polling Institute in West Long Branch, NJ, con-ducted these polls by telephone.

Monmouth University Poll, "Gun Owners Divided on Gun Policy; Parkland Students Having an Impact," **March 2-5, 2018**, *released* **March 8, 2018**. N = 803 adults. The results in this release have a margin of error of ± 3.5 percent. [One-third (34%) reported currently owning firearms, and 7% reported being members of the NRA.] (Crosstabs) The Mon-mouth poll reached only 803 adults and had a very high percentage of gun householders (46%). (Q. 21—database)

Monmouth University Poll, "National: Public Divided On Assault Weapons Policy," **Aug. 16-20, 2019**, *released* **Sept. 9, 2019**. N = 800 adults. Telephone. Margin of error of ± 3.5 percentage points. [One-third of American adults (34%) report currently owning firearms, and 7% re-port being members of the NRA.]

Morning Consult

Morning Consults conducted the interviews for these polls online. It weighted the data were to approximate a target sample of Registered Vot-ers based on age, race/ethnicity, gender, educational attainment, and re-gion.

Morning Consult, Oct. 5-9, 2017, *released* **Oct. 17, 2017**. "Morning Con-sult National Tracking Poll #171004." N = 1,996 Registered Voters. In-terviews conducted online. The data were weighted to approximate a tar-get sample of registered voters based on age, race/ethnicity, gender, ed-ucational attainment, and region. Results from the full survey had a mar-gin of error of ± 2 percentage points. [Gun household? Yes, 38%; No, 62%; Clinton voters 27%, No 73%; Trump voters 53%, No 47%.] *See also:* Steven Shepard, "Poll: Majority backs stricter gun control laws after Vegas shooting," Politico PlayBook (Oct. 11, 2017).

Morning Consult, Feb. 15-19, 2018, *released* **Feb. 28, 2018**. "Morning Consult National Tracking Poll #180211." N = 1,989 Registered Voters. Results from the full survey have a margin of error of ± 2 percentage points. [Gun household? Yes 40%, No 60%.]

Morning Consult, **Feb. 22-26, 2018**. "National Tracking Poll #180217." N = 1,992 Registered Voters. Results from the full survey have a margin of error of ± 2 percentage points. [Gun household? Yes 41%, No 59%.]

See also: Steven Shepard, "Gun control support surges in polls," Politico Playbook (Feb. 28, 2018.

Morning Consult, Mar. 29-Apr. 1, 2018. "Morning Consult National Tracking Poll #180339." N = 1,997 Registered Voters. Results from the full survey have a margin of error of ± 2 percentage points. Interviews conducted online. Morn-ing Consult weighted the data to approximate a target sample of registered vot-ers based on age, race/ethnicity, gender, educational attainment, and region. [Gun household? Yes, 40%, No 60%.]

Morning Consult, Aug. 2-6, 2018. "Morning Consult National Tracking Poll #180805." N = 1,994 Registered Voters. Results from the full survey have a margin of error of ± 2 percentage points Interviews con-ducted online. Morning Consult weighted the data to approximate a tar-get sample of registered voters based on age, race/ethnicity, gender, ed-ucational attainment, and region. [Gun household? Registered Voters: Yes, 39%, No, 61%.]

Morning Consult, Aug. 5-7, 2019. "Morning Consult National Tracking Poll #190816." N = 1,960. Registered Voters. Results from the full survey have a margin of error of ± 2 percentage points. [Gun house-hold? Registered Voters: Yes, 36%, No, 64%.]

National Public Radio/PBS NewsHour (Marist)

The Marist Poll sponsored in partnership with NPR and PBS NewsHour. Live telephone interviews.

NPR/PBS NewsHour/Marist Poll, Oct. 15-17, 2017. (Data Tables N =1,09 3adults. Results were statistically significant within ±3. percentage points.[This poll addressed none of the issues covered by this book; just general sentiment questions.]

NPR/PBS NewsHour/Marist Poll, April 10-13, 2018. (Data Tables N = 1,011 adults. Results are statistically significant within ±3.6 percent-age points (and higher for subsets. N = 827 registered voters. The results for this subset are statistically significant within ±3.9 percentage points. There are 345 gun owners. The results for this subset were
ıtage points. The

error for samples increased for cross tabulations.

Gun owners: 37% of adults and 40% of registered voters. Table, p. 2. Gun Households: 45% of adults and 47% of voters.] [This poll asked about gun issues but didn't ask the question discussed in this volume.]

NPR/PBS NewsHour/Marist Poll, Feb. 5-11, 2019, *released* Feb. 11, 2019. N = 880 adults. (Data Tables). N = 722 registered voters. (Data Tables). Results are statistically significant within ±3.9 percentage points (and higher for subsets). There are 314 gun owners. The results for this subset are statistically significant within ±6.5 percentage points. [37% of adults and 40% of registered voters in the sample were gun owners.]

See: Domenico Montanaro, "Poll: A Year After Parkland, Urgency For New Gun Restrictions Declines," NPR (Feb. 14, 2019).

NPR/PBS NewsHour/Marist Poll, July 15-17, 2019, *released* **July 23, 2019**. (Data Tables). N = 1,346 adults. Phone with live callers. Margin of error of ± 3.5 percentage points. The survey reached 1,175 registered voters and has a margin of error for that group of ± 3.7 percentage points.

See also: Marist Poll, "NPR/PBS NewsHour/Marist Poll Results & Analysis." (July 23, 2019).

NPR/PBS NewsHour/Marist Poll, Aug. 14-19, 2019, *released* **Aug. 23, 2019**. [Aug. 14-19, 2019 poll had no gun questions at all.]

NPR/PBS NewsHour/Marist Poll, Sept. 5-8, 2019, *released* **Sept. 10, 2019**. (Data Tables) N = 1,317 adults. Results are statistically significant within ± 3.6 percentage points. N = 1,160 registered voters. The results for this subset are statistically significant within ±3.8 percentage points. There are 514 gun owners for a margin of error of ± 5.8 percentage points. [In the sample, 40% of Adults and 42% of registered voters were gun owners.]

See also: Domenico Montanaro, "Poll: Most Americans Want To See Congress Pass Gun Restrictions," NPR (Sept. 10, 2019). (Crosstabs)

NPR/PBS NewsHour/Marist Poll, Dec. 9-11, 2019, *released* **Dec. 10, 2019**. (Data Tables). N = 1,744 adults. Results are statistically significant within ± 3.5 percentage points. N = 1,508 registered voters. The results for this subset are statistically significant within ± 3.7 percentage points. Interviews in English by telephone using live interviewers. [No data on gun ownership or gun households.]

NBC/Wall Street Journal

Hart Research Associates (D) and Public Opinion Strategies (R) conducted these NBC/Wall Street Journal polls.

NBC News/Wall Street Journal Poll, Oct. 23-26, 2017. (Data Tables) N = 900 Adults. The margin of error for 900 interviews among Adults is ±3.27%. The margin of error for 753 interviews among Registered Voters is ±3.57%. Interviews on landlines and cell phones. [47% of the sample lived in gun households. 48% did not.] [Gun ownership was the only relevant gun question.]

See: "NBC News/Wall Street Journal Survey," Hart Research Associates/Public Opinion Strategies, Study #17409 (Oct. 23-26, 2017);

See also: Mark Murray, "Trump's Approval Rating Drops to Lowest Level Yet in New NBC News/WSJ Poll," NBC News (Oct. 29, 2017).

NBC News/Wall Street Journal Poll, Mar. 10-14, 2018. Data Tables. N = 1,100 Adults. The overall margin of error was ± 3.0 percentage points. Interviews on landlines and cell phones. [47% of the sample lived in gun households. 50% did not.] [Gun ownership was the only relevant gun question.]

See: "Hart Research Associates/Public Opinion Strategies Study #18164, March 2018, Social Trends Survey NBC News/Wall Street Journal Survey." Data Tables. Interviews: 1100 Adults. March 10-14, 2018. The margin of error for 1100 interviews among Adults is ± 2.95%. The margin of error for 930 interviews among Registered Voters is ± 3.21%.

See also: Janet Hook, "Democrats Regain Double-Digit Advantage Over GOP in Voter Sentiment Poll," *Wall Street Journal* (Mar. 18, 2018).

See also: Mark Murray, "Democrats hold double-digit lead for 2018 midterm elections," NBC News (Mar. 18, 2018).

Carrie Dann, "A majority of Americans are ready to protest. Here's what's got them fired up," NBC News (March 30, 2018).

NBC News/Wall Street Journal Poll. April 8-11, 2018. "Tax Overhaul Remains Unpopular" (April 8-11). The margin of error for 900 interviews among Adults is ± 3.27%. The margin of error for 720 interviews among Registered Voters is ±3.65%. Interviews on landlines and cell phones.

[44% of the sample lived in gun households; 51% did not. No other gun questions relevant.] [Gun household and More/Less Strict Qs only]

See: "April 2018 NBC News/Wall Street Journal Survey," Hart Research Associates/Public Opinion Strategies Study #18233.

See also: Janet Hook, "Updated April 16, 2018 Tax Overhaul Remains Unpopular, Poll Shows," *Wall Street Journal* (Apr. 16, 2018).

NBC News/Wall Street Journal Poll, Aug. 10-14, 2019. "Half of Americans Disapprove of Trump's Response to Mass Shootings." N = 1,000 adults nationwide. Margin of error ± 3.1. Study # 19305. Data Table. [46% of the sample lived in a household where someone owned a gun. 49% lived in homes where no one owned a gun.]

See: Hart Research Associates/Public Opinion Strategies, Study #19305, "August 2019 Social Trends Monitor NBC News/Wall Street Journal Survey."

See also: Ken Thomas, "Half of Americans Disapprove of Trump's Response to Mass Shootings," *Wall Street Journal* (Aug. 18, 2019).

Pew Research Center

The American Trends Panel (ATP), created by Pew Research Center, is a nationally representative panel of randomly selected U.S. adults. Panel-ists participate via self-administered web surveys. Panelists who do not have internet access at home are provided with a tablet and wireless internet connection.

Pew Research Center, March 13-27 and **April 4-18, 2017**, *released* **June 22, 2017**. Full Report and Topline. N = 3,930 U.S. adults, including 1,269 gun owners, using the Pew Research Center's American Trends Panel. Combined Final Topline, Wave 25: March 13—27, 2017; Wave 26: April 4 —18, 2017. [Full report, Chart, p. 16: 30% currently own a gun; 40% live in a gun household.]

See: Kim Parker, Juliana Menasce Horowitz, Ruth Igielnik, Baxter Oli-phant and Anna Brown, "America's Complex Relationship with Guns: An in-depth look at the attitudes and experiences of U.S. adults," Pew Research Center (June 22, 2017).

See also: Baxter Oliphant, "Bipartisan support for some gun proposals, Stark partisan divisions on many others," Pew Research Center, FacTank (June 23, 2017).

Pew Research Center, American Trends Panel, Wave 38, Sept. 24-Oct. 7, 2018, "Gun Policy Remains Divisive, But Several Proposals Still Draw Bipartisan Support." Final Topline. N = 10,683. Forms 2 and 3 only, N = 5,307. The margin of sampling error for the full sample of 10,683 is ± 1.5 percentage points. The module of questions about gun attitudes was asked of half of the respondents (5,307) with a margin of sampling error of ± 2.1 percentage points.

Pew Research Center, American Trends Panel, Wave 53, Final Topline, **Sept. 3-15, 2019**. N = 9,895. The margin of sampling error for the full sample of 9,895 respondents was ± 1.5 percentage points. [Gun ownership not disclosed.]

See also: Pew, "In a Politically Polarized World, Sharp Divides in Both Political Coalitions" (Dec. 17, 2019) (about political divides within and between parties; mentions gun policy.)

Public Policy Polling

PPP surveys are conducted through automated telephone interviews. This poll was not paid for or authorized by any campaign or political organization In these polls, 80% of participants, selected through a list based sample, responded via the phone, while 20% of respondents who did not have landlines conducted the survey over the internet through an opt-in internet panel.

Public Policy Polling, March 27-30, 2013, *released* Apr. 2, 2013. "Democrats and Republicans differ on conspiracy theory beliefs." N = 1,247 registered voters. The margin of error for the overall sample is ± 2.8%.

Public Policy Polling, Dec. 6-7, 2016, *released* **Dec. 9, 2016.** "Trump Remains Unpopular; Voters Prefer Obama on SCOTUS Pick." N = 1,224 registered voters. The margin of error was ± 2.8%.

Public Policy Polling, Aug. 18—21, 2017. *released* **Aug. 23, 2017.** "Trump Holds Steady After Charlottesville; Supporters Think Whites, Christians Face Discrimination." N = 887 registered voters. The margin of error was ± 3.3%.

Public Policy Polling, Oct. 27-29, 2017, *released* **Oct. 31, 2017**. "Support For Impeachment At Record High," PPP_Release_Na-tional_103117.pdf. N = 572 registered voters. The margin of error was ± 4.1%.

Public Policy Polling, Dec. 11-12, 2017, *released* **Dec.19, 2017**. "Only Trump Voters Care About Merry Christmas/Happy Holidays Debate." N = 862 registered voters. The margin of error was ± 3.3%.

Public Policy Polling, Mar. 23-25, 2018, *released* **Mar. 27, 2018**. "Voters Like High School Gun Protesters; Don't Like NRA," N = 846 registered voters. The margin of error was ± 3.4%. Public Policy Polling, "Voters Like High School Gun Protesters; Don't Like NRA" (Mar. 27, 2018).

Public Policy Polling, June 8-10, 2018, *released* **June 13, 2018**. "Tax Reform Still Not Helping GOP; Dems Lead House Ballot By 6." N = 679 registered voters. The margin of error was ± 3.8%. [No Gun ownership question.]

PRRI

PRRI, American Values Survey, Aug. 22-Sept. 15, 2019. N = 2,527 Adults. Toplines. Final Presentation (Dec. 2019). Interviews were conducted both online using a self-administered design and by telephone using live interviewers. All interviews were conducted among participants in AmeriSpeak, a probability-based panel designed to be representative of the national U.S. adult population run by NORC at the University of Chicago. [No gun questions.]

See also: PRRI Staff, "Fractured Nation, Widening Partisan Polarization And Key Issues In 2020 Presidential Elections," PRRI (Oct. 20, 2019), pp. 31—31).

Quinnipiac University

Quinnipiac uses gold-standard surveys using random digit dialing with live interviewers calling landlines and cell phones. Surveys are conducted in English or Spanish dependent on respondent preference with live in-terviewers calling landlines and cell phones.

Quinnipiac University, June 21-27, 2016, *released* **June 30, 2016**. "Overwhelming Support For No-Fly, No-Buy Gun Law, Quinnipiac

University National Poll Finds; Support For Background Checks Tops 90 Percent Again." N = 1,610 registered voters nationwide with a margin of error of ± 2.4 percentage points. [Crosstabs] [No data on gun owner-ship or gun householders, but does have breakouts of how gun house-holders feel about issues.]

Quinnipiac University, Oct. 5-10, 2017, *released* **Oct. 12, 2017**. "U.S. Voter Support For Gun Control At All-Time High, Quinnipiac Univer-sity National Poll Finds; Trump Helped Texas, Florida, Not Puerto Rico, Voters Say." N = 1,482 voters nationwide with a margin of error of ± 3 percentage points, including the design effect. [Crosstabs] [No data on gun ownership or gun householders, but does have breakouts of how gun householders feel about issues.]

Quinnipiac University, Nov. 7-13, 2017, *released* **Nov. 15, 2017**. "Latest Massacre Drives Gun Control Support To New High, Quinnipiac Uni-versity National Poll Finds; Voters Reject GOP Tax Plan 2-1." N = 1,577 voters nationwide with a margin of error of ± 3 percentage points, in-cluding the design effect. [Crosstabs] [No data on gun ownership or gun householders, but does have breakouts of how gun householders feel about issues.]

Quinnipiac University, Dec. 13-18, 2017, *released* **Dec. 20, 2017**. Quin-nipiac University, "Americans Have Little Hope For World Peace In 2018, Quinnipiac University National Poll Finds; 'Merry Christmas' Is Bogus Issue, Voters Say 4-1," Dec. 13 - 18, 2017, *released* Dec. 20, 2017). N = 1,230 voters. Margin of error of ± 3.3 percentage points, including the design effect. Live interviewers call landlines and cell phones.

Quinnipiac University, Feb. 16-19, 2018, *released* **Feb. 20, 2018**. "U.S. Support For Gun Control Tops 2-1, Highest Ever, Quinnipiac University National Poll Finds; Let Dreamers Stay, 80 Percent Of Voters Say." N = 1,249 voters nationwide with a margin of error of ± 3.4%, including the design effect. [Crosstabs] [No data on gun ownership or gun HHs, but does breakout how gun HHs feel about issues.]

Quinnipiac University, Feb. 23-26, 2018, *released* **Feb. 28, 2018**. "Flor-ida Voters Oppose Teachers With Guns, Quinnipiac University Poll Finds; Support For Assault Weapon' Ban Almost 2-1," https://poll.qu.edu/florida/release-detail?ReleaseID= 2524. N = 1,156

Florida voters with a margin of error of ± 3.6%, including the design effect. [Crosstabs] [Florida only]

Quinnipiac University, March 3-5, *released* **March 6, 2018.** "U.S. Vot-ers Oppose Trump Emergency Powers On Wall 2-1 Quinnipiac Univer-sity National Poll Finds; 86% Back Democrats' Bill On Gun Background Checks." N = 1,122 voters nationwide with a margin of error of ± 3.5%, including the design effect. [Crosstabs] [No data on gun ownership or gun householders, but does have breakouts of how gun householders feel about issues.] [Crosstabs]

Quinnipiac University, April 6-9, 2018, *released* **April 11, 2018.** "Trade War With China Is Bad, U.S. Voters Say 3-1, Quinnipiac University National Poll Finds; Voters Support National Guard, But Not The Wall." N = 1,181 voters nationwide with a margin of error of ± 3.4 percentage points, including the design effect. [Crosstabs] [No data on gun owner-ship or gun householders, but does have breakouts of how gun house-holders feel about issues.]

Quinnipiac University, Jan. 9-13, 2019, *released* **Jan. 14, 2019.** "U.S. Voters Back Dem Plan To Reopen Government 2-1, Quinnipiac Univer-sity National Poll Finds; More U.S. Voters Say Trump Tv Address Was Misleading." N = 1,209 voters nationwide with a margin of error of ± 3.3 percentage points, including the design effect. [Crosstabs] [No data on gun ownership or gun householders, but does have breakouts of how gun householders feel about issues.]

Quinnipiac University, Mar. 1-3, 2019, *released* **Mar. 5, 2019**. "64 Per-cent Of U.S. Voters Say Trump Committed A Crime Quinnipiac University National Poll Finds; President Gets Mixed Grades For North Ko-rea." N = 1,120 voters nationwide with a margin of error of ± 3.4 per-centage points, including the design effect. [Crosstabs] [No gun questions. Mainly about President Trump.]

Quinnipiac University, May 16-20, 2019, *released* **May 22, 2019**. "U.S. Voter Support For Abortion Is High, Quinnipiac University National Poll Finds; 94 Percent Back Universal Gun Background Checks." N = 1,078 voters nationwide with a margin of error of ± 3.7 percentage points, including the design effect. [Crosstabs] [No data on gun owner-ship or gun householders, but does have breakouts of how gun house-holders feel about issues.]

Quinnipiac University, July 17-20, 2019, *released* **July 26, 2019.** "Ohio Voters Oppose Fetal Heartbeat Abortion Ban Quinnipiac University Poll Finds; 90 Percent Support Universal Gun Background Checks." N = 1,431 **Ohio** voters with a margin of error of ± 3.2 percentage points, including the design effect. [Crosstabs]

Quinnipiac University, Aug. 21-26, 2019, *released* **Aug. 29, 2019.** "Majority Of Voters Say Climate Change Is An Emergency Quinnipiac University Poll Finds; 72% Say Congress Needs To Act To Reduce Gun Violence." N = 1,422 self-identified registered voters nationwide with a margin of error of ± 3.1 percentage points, including the design effect. [Crosstabs]. [No data on gun ownership or gun households.]

Social Sphere

A new national poll of young Americans (14- to 29- years-old) finds that school shootings are the most concerning issue when they think about the future of America and that voting-age respondents are likely to carry these concerns into voting booths in the midterm elections. The survey also found broad support for stricter gun laws, even among gun owners.

The comprehensive study, released in two parts and directed by John Della Volpe, CEO of SocialSphere and Director of Polling at the Harvard Kennedy School Institute of Politics, began in June 2018 with six focus groups and town meetings with young Americans in Atlanta, Columbus and Los Angeles.

Social Sphere, September 4-24, 2018, *released on several dates in late* **2018.** N = 2,235 U.S. 14- to 29-year-olds. Online and Telephone (English and Spanish) with NORC at the University of Chicago's AmeriSpeak Panel Margin of Error: ± 2.83 percent at the 95% confidence level Funded by The Joyce Foundation. https://www.socialsphere.com/data-insight.

Social Sphere, "In Advance of Midterms, New National Poll Finds Young Voters Rank School Shootings as Most Important Issue for America's Future," *Cision* (Oct. 22, 2018).

Suffolk University/USA Today

These polls used live telephone interviews of households where respondents indicated they were registered to vote.

Suffolk University/USA Today, Feb. 20-24, 2018, *released* **Feb. 27, 2018.** "Suffolk University/USA Today Poll Shows Strong Support for Gun Controls but Little Faith that Congress Will Act." N = 1,000 voters. The margin of error is ± 3 percentage points at a 95 percent level of confidence. [Data Tables] [Marginals] [Gun households Yes: 44% No: 53%.]

Suffolk University/USA Today, Aug. 20 - 25, 2019, *released* **Aug. 9, 2019.** "Poll: 90% of Registered Voters Want Firearms Background Checks." [Data Tables] [Marginals] N = 1,000 voters using live telephone interviews. The margin of error is ± 3 percentage points at a 95 percent level of confidence. [Gun households yes 50%, no 46%.]

YouGov

YouGov polls are administered online to an "opt-in" panel, *i.e.,* to individuals who volunteer to serve as YouGov panelists. And except in its daily polls, YouGov typically poses a large number of questions in each poll. In return, it gets an awful lot of non-answers—perhaps as a result of fatigue or flagging interest on the part of respondents or perhaps simply because it offers that option.

Whatever the reason, the "don't know" or "no opinion" responses in the YouGov polls are so large as to bring down substantially both the numbers of those who support and those who oppose most of the gun-violence-prevention proposals discussed here. Some of its polls showed sup-port as much as 20 percentage points below what other polls taken around the same time showed.

There may be another problem hiding in the YouGov data: Some of those who volunteered may have done so because they are strongly op-posed to gun-violence-prevention measures and wanted to tip the scales in that direction.

There's another issue with including the sponsored YouGov polls. Those polls typically gives respondents a "don't know" or other "no response" option. Although respondents are always able to say they "don't know" or refuse to answer, most polls don't volunteer that option. The result is that when YouGov polls on gun issues (and probably on other contro-versial issues) get far more no-response answers than other polls. That reduces the percentages of both those who support and those oppose whatever policy proposal the poll asks about. That makes the YouGov sponsored poll results not readily comparable with other polls (not apples-to-apples in the usual metaphor). The non-responsive answers, however, seem to reduce the percentages who "sup-port" any gun-violence-prevention proposals more than the percentages who "oppose" those proposals. That suggests that support for gun-violence-prevention measures may be softer than other polls suggest.

As a result, I've left the usual YouGov polls out except where there were few or no other polls. But I've included the results from YouGov "daily" polls. Those polls draw from such a large number of respondents, they overwhelm the special pleaders.

The same phenomenon isn't evident when YouGov asks purely factual questions—*e.g., Do you personally own a gun? If so, how many guns do you own?* With that in mind, I've also included the YouGov polls on personal and household gun ownership. I do that because YouGov has collected quite a lot of data on those topics and because its data are consistent with the largest (and therefore, presumably, the most accurate) polls.

YouGov Polls

YouGov uses samples selected from its online opt-in panel to match the demographics and other characteristics of the adult U.S. population. Its polls are administered on-line.

YouGov/Huffington Post Poll, July 24-25, 2014, *released* **July 26, 2014.** "Poll Results: Domestic Violence and Gun Control" (Toplines) (July 26, 2014). N = 1,000 adults. The margin of error is ± 4.7%. Data Tables.

See also: Katie Jagel, "Poll Results: Domestic Violence and Gun Control," YouGov.com (July 26, 2014).

2017

Daily Poll:
YouGov, Daily Poll, Oct 5, 2017. N = 3,310 adults. [Bump stock Question]

Other YouGov Polls:

HuffPost/YouGov poll, Oct. 2-3, 2017. N = 1,000 adults/U.S. citizens. Margin of error: ± 4.2% (adjusted for weighting). Data Tables.

The Economist/YouGov Poll, Oct. 7-10, 2017. N = 1,500 adult citizens. Data Tables.

See also: Kathy Frankovic, "Even 43% of gun owners want bump stocks banned completely," YouGov (Oct. 13, 2017).

The Economist/YouGov Poll, Nov. 12-14, 2017. N = 1,500 adult citizens. Toplines. Data Tables.

CBS News—Guns (YouGov, Dec. 5-11, 2017. N = 2,073 Adults. Toplines and Data Tables. Margin of error ± 2.7%.

2018

Respondents were selected from YouGov's **opt-in Internet panel** using sample matching. A random sample (stratified by gender, age, race, edu-cation, and region) was selected from the 2014 American Community Study. Voter registration was imputed from the November 2014 Current Population Survey Registration and Voting Supplement.

The Economist/YouGov Poll, Feb. 25-27, 2018. Toplines. Data Tables. N = 1,500 Adults. 1,296 Registered voters. Margin of error: ± 3.2% (adjusted for weighting): Adults ± 2.9% Registered voters: ± 2.9%. Web-based interviews.

The Economist/YouGov Poll, Mar. 4-6, 2018. Toplines. Data Tables. N = 1,500 Adults. Registered voters: 1,310. Margin of error: ± 3.3% (adjusted for weighting) Registered voters: ± 2.9%.

The Economist/YouGov Poll, Mar. 25-27, 2018. Toplines. Data Tables. N = 1,500 (Adults); 1330 (Registered voters). Margin of error: ± 3.4% (adjusted for weighting); ± 2.8% (Registered voters). Web-based interviews.

The Economist/YouGov Poll, July 29-31, 2018. Toplines. Data Ta-bles. N = 1,500 adult citizens. 1,222 (Registered voters). Margin of error (adjusted for weighting): ± 2.8%; Registered voters: ± 2.9%.

The Economist/YouGov Poll, Nov. 4-6, 2018. Toplines. Data Tables. N = 1,500 Adults. N = 1,290 Registered voters. Margin of error ± 3% Adults (adjusted for weighting); ± 2.8% (Registered voters) [Q. 33 - per-sonal gun ownership. No other relevant gun questions.]

The Economist/YouGov Poll, Nov. 11-13, 2018. Toplines. Data Tables. N = 1,500 Adults; 1,284 Registered Voters. Margin of error ± 3% Adults and ± 2.9% Registered voters (adjusted for weighting). Web-based interviews. [Gun ownership question.] [No questions on gun policy.]

YouGov, Daily Poll, **Dec. 20, 2018.** N = 2,595 Adults.

2019

2019 Daily Polls:

YouGov, Daily, **Mar. 21, 2019.** N = 1,372 adults surveyed. ("Would you support or oppose a national ban on all military-style semi-automatic weapons in the US?" 57% favored, 31%opposed, 11% Don't Know).

YouGov, Daily, **April 8, 2019. N = 17,391** US adults were questioned on Apr. 8, 2019. Results are weighted to be representative of the US population. (Violence Against Women Act question).

Other 2019 Polls:

The Economist/YouGov Poll, Mar. 17-19, 2019. Toplines. Data Tables. N = 1,500 Adult citizens. Web-based interviews.

The Economist/YouGov Poll, April 13-16, 2019. N = 1500 Adult citizens. Web-based interviews. Toplines. Tables.

See also: Kathy Frankovic, "20 years after Columbine, Americans find schools less safe," YouGov.com (Apr. 18, 2019). (Q. 3. How satisfied are you with the way democracy is working in America? Q. 4. Do you agree or disagree with the following statement: Democracy is the best form of government.)

The Economist/YouGov Poll, July 27-30, 2019. Toplines. Sample 1500 US Adult citizens Conducted July 27 - 30, 2019 Margin of Error ± 2.6%.

The Economist/YouGov Poll, Aug. 3-6, 2019. N = 1,500 adult citizens. Toplines. Data Tables. N = 1,161 Registered voters. Margin of error ± 2.6% (adjusted for weighting) ± 2.9% (Registered voters)

See: Kathy Frankovic, "After Ohio and Texas mass shootings, Democrats turn focus to gun control" (Aug. 8, 2019).

HuffPost/YouGov, Mass shootings, Aug. 5-6, 2019. N = 1,000 US adult citizens. Margin of error: ± 3.3% (adjusted for weighting). Data Tables.

See: Ariel Edwards-Levy, "Most Americans Favor An Assault Weapons Ban," *HuffPost* (Aug. 8, 2019, updated Aug. 9, 2019).

The Economist/YouGov Poll, Aug. 10-13, 2019. Toplines. Data Tables. N = 1,500 adults. 1,127 Registered Voters. Margin of error (Adults) ± 2.6% (adjusted for weighting); Registered voters = ± 3%.

The Gun Ownership Polls

Sorted by percentage of Gun Households

How Many In Each Poll Owned a Gun or Lived in a Gun Household?

Expected personal gun ownership: ~22%.
Expected Gun Households: 33%-40%.

Gun Owner?	Gun Household?		Polling Dates	Poll
	Yes	No		
26%	–	–	10/10-11/17	Ipsos
37%	–	–	2/5-11/19	NPR/PBS (Adults)
40%	–	–	2/5-11/19	NPR/PBS (Voters)
40%	–	–	9/5-8/19	NPR/PBS (Adults)
42%	–	–	9/5-8/19	NPR/PBS (Voters)
24%	30%	52%	8/3-6/19	Economist/YouGov
20%	34%	55%	3/4-6/18	Economist/YouGov
20%	34%	55%	3/25-27/18	Economist/YouGov
24%	34%	53%	2/18-20/18	Economist/YouGov
–	35%	62%	3/14-18/19	AP-NORC
–	36%	64%	8/5-7/19	Morning Consult
22%	36%	55%	3/17-19/19	Economist/YouGov
22%	36%	55%	10/2-3/17	Huff Post
22%	36%	54%	11/12-14/17	Economist/YouGov
21%	37%	56%	8/10-13/19	Economist/YouGov
22%	37%	55%	2/25-27/18	Economist/YouGov
22%	37%	54%	7/29-31/19	Economist/YouGov
22%	37%	51%	9/14-17/19	Economist/YouGov

Gun Owner?	Gun Household?		Polling Dates	Poll
	Yes	No		
23%	37%	53%	4/13-16/19	Economist/YouGov
29%	37%	60%	7/16-21/19	APM (SSRS)
–	38%	62%	10/5-9/17	Morning Consult
–	38%	59%	3/14-19/18	AP-NORC
–	39%	61%	8/2-6/18	Morning Consult
–	40%	60%	3/29-4/1/18	Morning Consult
15%	40%	60%	12/5-11/17	CBS/YouGov
24%	40%	52%	11/4-6/18	Economist/YouGov
29%	40%	58%	10/1-13/19	Gallup**
–	41%	-	2/16-19/17	Quinnipiac
–	41%	-	2/23-26/18	Quinnipiac
–	41%	59%	2/22-26/18	Morning Consult
–	41%	-	5/16-20/18	Quinnipiac
24%	41%	51%	11/11-13/18	Economist/YouGov
28%	41%	59%	1/11-28/19	Ipsos/Reuters
29%	43%	56%	10/5-11/17	Gallup**
–	44%	53%	2/20-24/18	Suffolk/USA
–	44%	-	3/3-5/18	Quinnipiac
–	44%	51%	4/8-11/18	NBC/WSJ
–	44%	-	1/9-13/19	Quinnipiac
34%	44%	51%	8/16-20/19	Monmouth
–	45%	-	11/7-13/17	Quinnipiac
–	46%	-	105-10/17	Quinnipiac
–	46%	49%	8/10-14/19	NBC/WSJ
–	46%	53%	9/2-5/19	ABC/WaPo
31%	46%	53%	10/1-10/18	Gallup**
34%	46%	47%	3/2-5/19	Monmouth
–	47%	48%	10/23-26/17	NBC/WSJ
–	47%	50%	3/10-14/18	NBC/WSJ
–	47%	–	4/6-9/18	Quinnipiac

Gun Owner?	*Gun Household?*		*Polling Dates*	*Poll*
	Yes	No		
–	47%	53%	4/10-13/18	NPR/PBS
–	47%	52%	4/8-11/18	ABC/WaPo
–	50%	46%	8/20-25/19	Suffolk/USA

Quinnipiac University graciously provided the share data used for its polls.

*YouGov conducted the Economist and Huffington polls.
** Based on national adults.

Chronological Order
Gun Owner/Household %

Averages: Gun Households: **43%**. *Range: 35% - 50%.*

Gun Owner?	Gun Household?		Polling Dates	Poll
	Yes	No		
–	41%	–	2/16-19/17	Quinnipiac
22%	36%	55%	10/2-3/17	Huff Post
–	38%	62%	10/5-9/17	Morning Consult
–	46%	–	10/5-10/17	Quinnipiac
29%	43%	56%	10/5-11/17	Gallup**
–	–	–	10/10-11/17	Ipsos/NPR
–	47%	48%	10/23-26/17	NBC/WSJ
–	45%	–	11/7-13/17	Quinnipiac
22%	36%	54%	11/12-14/17	YouGov
15%	40%	60%	12/5-11/17	CBS/YouGov
–	41%		2/23-26/18	Quinnipiac
–	41%	59%	2/22-26/18	Morning Consult
22%	37%	55%	2/25-27/18	YouGov
24%	34%	53%	2/18-20/18	Economist
–	44%	53%	2/20-24/18	Suffolk/USA
–	44%		3/3-5/18	Quinnipiac
20%	34%	55%	3/4-6/18	YouGov
–	47%	50%	3/10-14/18	NBC/WSJ
–	38%	59%	3/14-19/18	AP-NORC
20%	34%	55%	3/25-27/18	YouGov
–	40%	60%	3/29-4/1/18	Morning Consult
–	47%		4/6-9/18	Quinnipiac
–	44%	51%	4/8-11/18	NBC/WSJ
–	47%	52%	4/8-11/18	ABC/WaPo
–	47%	53%	4/10-13/18	NPR/PBS
–	41%		5/16-20/18	Quinnipiac

Gun Owner?	Gun Household?		Polling Dates	Poll
	Yes	No		
–	39%	61%	8/2-6/18	Morning Consult
31%	46%	53%	10/1-10/18	Gallup
24%	40%	52%	11/4-6/18	YouGov
24%	41%	51%	11/11-13/18	YouGov
–	44%		1/9-13/19	Quinnipiac
28%	41%	59%	1/11-28/19	Ipsos/Reuters
	–	–	2/5-11/19	NPR/PBS (Adults)
40%	–	–	2/5-11/19	NPR/PBS (Voters)
34%	46%	47%	3/2-5/19	Monmouth
–	35%	62%	3/14-18/19	AP-NORC
22%	36%	55%	3/17-19/19	YouGov
23%	37%	53%	4/13-16/19	YouGov
29%	37%	60%	7/16-21/19	APM (SSRS)
22%	37%	54%	7/29-31/19	YouGov
24%	30%	52%	8/3-6/19	YouGov
–	36%	64%	8/5-7/19	Morning Consult
21%	37%	56%	8/10-13/19	YouGov
–	46%	49%	8/10-14/19	NBC/WSJ
34%	44%	51%	8/16-20/19	Monmouth
–	50%	46%	8/20-25/19	Suffolk/USA
–	46%	53%	9/2-5/19	ABC/WaPo
40%	–	–	9/5-8/19	NPR/PBS (Adults)
42%	–	–	9/5-8/19	NPR/PBS (Voters)
22%	37%	51%	9/14-17/19	YouGov
29%	40%	58%	10/1-13/19	Gallup

Except where otherwise indicated, The Economist sponsored the YouGov polls listed above.
** Based on national adults.

Gun Owner/Household % Arranged By Poll

Gun Owner?	Gun Household?		Polling Dates	Poll
	Yes	No		
–	47%	52%	4/8-11/18	ABC/WaPo
–	46%	53%	9/2-5/19	ABC/WaPo
29%	37%	60%	7/16-21/19	APM (SSRS)
–	35%	62%	3/14-18/19	AP-NORC
–	38%	59%	3/14-19/18	AP-NORC
15%	40%	60%	12/5-11/17	CBS/YouGov
22%	36%	54%	11/12-14/17	YouGov
24%	34%	53%	2/18-20/18	YouGov
22%	37%	55%	2/25-27/18	YouGov
20%	34%	55%	3/4-6/18	YouGov
20%	34%	55%	3/25-27/18	YouGov
24%	40%	52%	11/4-6/18	YouGov
24%	41%	51%	11/11-13/18	YouGov
22%	36%	55%	3/17-19/19	YouGov
23%	37%	53%	4/13-16/19	YouGov
22%	37%	54%	7/29-31/19	YouGov
24%	30%	52%	8/3-6/19	YouGov
21%	37%	56%	8/10-13/19	YouGov
22%	37%	51%	9/14-17/19	YouGov
29%	43%	56%	10/5-11/17	Gallup
31%	46%	53%	10/1-10/18	Gallup
29%	40%	58%	10/1-13/19	Gallup
26%	–	–	10/10-11/17	Ipsos
28%	41%	59%	1/11-28/19	Ipsos/Reuters
34%	46%	47%	3/2-5/19	Monmouth
34%	44%	51%	8/16-20/19	Monmouth
–	40%	60%	3/29-4/1/18	Morning Consult
–	38%	62%	10/5-9/17	Morning Consult
–	41%	59%	2/22-26/18	Morning Consult
–	39%	61%	8/2-6/18	Morning Consult

Gun Owner?	Gun Household? Yes	No	Polling Dates	Poll
–	36%	64%	8/5-7/19	Morning Consult
–	47%	48%	10/23-26/17	NBC/WSJ
–	47%	50%	3/10-14/18	NBC/WSJ
–	44%	51%	4/8-11/18	NBC/WSJ
–	46%	49%	8/10-14/19	NBC/WSJ
–	47%	53%	4/10-13/18	NPR/PBS
40%	–	–	2/5-11/19	NPR/PBS (V)
37%	–	–	2/5-11/19	NPR/PBS (A)
42%	–	–	9/5-8/19	NPR/PBS (V)
40%	–	–	9/5-8/19	NPR/PBS (A)
–	41%	–	2/16-19/17	Quinnipiac
–	46%	–	10/5-10/17	Quinnipiac
–	45%	–	11/7-13/17	Quinnipiac
–	41%	–	2/23-26/18	Quinnipiac
–	44%	–	3/3-5/18	Quinnipiac
–	47%	–	4/6-9/18	Quinnipiac
–	41%	–	5/16-20/18	Quinnipiac
–	44%	–	1/9-13/19	Quinnipiac
–	44%	53%	2/20-24/18	Suffolk/USA
–	50%	46%	8/20-25/19	Suffolk/USA
22%	36%	55%	10/2-3/17	Huff Post/YouGov

Except where otherwise indicated, The Economist sponsored the YouGov polls listed above.

How Many Guns Do Gun Owners Own?

Some YouGov polls simply broke out gun owners who owned fewer than ten guns and gun owners who owned ten or more guns.

1-9	>10	Dates	Sponsor/Pollster
94%	5%	11/12-14/17	Economist/YouGov
95%	6%	2/18-20/18	Economist/YouGov
96%	4%	3/25-27/18	Economist/YouGov
94%	6%	7/29-31/19	Economist/YouGov
95%	6%	2/18-20/18	Economist/YouGov
95%	5%	Averages	

Gun Owners by No. of Guns

(Polls in Which Those With 90-100 Guns Are Broken Out)

Other YouGov polls divided gun owners into the percentages who owned 1-10 guns, those who owned 11-50 guns, and those who owned 90-100 guns.

1-10 Guns	11-50 Guns	**90-100 Guns**	Polling Dates	Sponsor/Pollster
91%	8%	1%	2/25-27/18	Economist/YouGov
91%	9%	0%	3/4-6/18	Economist/YouGov
92%	7%	1%	4/13-16/19	Economist/YouGov

Note: These are percentages of gun owners, not of the population as a whole.

The Economist/YouGov Polls
and the Percentage of Adults Who Live in Households with 10+ Guns

Several Economist/YouGov polls asked gun householders how many guns there were in their homes.

Gun HHs	1-10 Guns	>10 Guns	% of Adults	Polling Dates	Sponsor/Pollster
36%	94%	5%	1.8%	11/12-4/17	Economist/YouGov
37%	91%	9%	3.3%	2/25-27/18	Economist/YouGov
34%	91%	9%	3.1%	3/4-6/18	Economist/YouGov
34%	96%	4%	1.4%	3/25-27/18	Economist/YouGov
37%	92%	8%	3.0%	4/13-16/19	Economist/YouGov
37%	94%	6%	2.2%	7/29-31/19	Economist/YouGov
36%	93%	7%	~2.5%	*Averages*	

The first column indicates the percentage of respondents who lived in a household in which someone owned a gun. The second and third columns are the percentages *of that number* who lived in households with the specified range of guns. The fourth column (% of Adults) shows the per-centage of all adults who live in homes where there were more than ten guns.

Endnotes

1 J.Baxter Oliphant, "Bipartisan support for some gun proposals, Stark partisan divisions on many others," Pew Research Center, *FacTank*, June 23, 2017.

2 Quinnipiac University, March 1-3, 2019, released March 5, 2019, "64 Percent Of U.S. Voters Say Trump Committed A Crime, Quinnipiac University National Poll Finds; President Gets Mixed Grades For North Korea."

3 Domenico Montanaro, "Poll: Most Americans Want To See Congress Pass Gun Restrictions," NPR (*All Things Considered*), September 10, 2019.

4 Nate Cohn and Margot Sanger-Katz, "On Guns, Public Opinion and Public Policy Often Diverge," *The New York Times*, August 10, 2019.

5 For some easy-to-follow charts showing how Congressional Representatives and Senators, individually and by party, have voted on gun issues, *see*: Danielle Kurtzleben, "CHART: How Have Your Members Of Congress Voted On Gun Bills?" NPR, February 19, 2018

6 Alicia Samuels, "Gun owners and non-gun owners agree on many gun safety proposals," *The Hub*, Johns Hopkins University, May 17, 2018.

7 Clifford Young, "When it comes to guns, Americans use common sense; their political leaders don't," *The Hill*, March 27, 2018.

8 Bill Bishop with statistician Robert Cushing, THE BIG SORT: Why the Clustering of Like-Minded America Is Tearing Us Apart (Boston: Houghton Mifflin, 2008).

9 *See, e.g.*, B. Kalesan, M.D. Villarreal, K.M. Keyes, *et al.*, "Gun ownership and social gun culture," *Injury Prevention* 2016;**22**:216-220. For discussion, see Francie Diep, "The latest survey of American gun-owners looks at the culture they live in," *Pacific Standard*, June 30, 2015.

10 This conclusion is based on the totality of the data discussed in this book but see, *e.g.,* the Ipsos/Reuters poll from January 2019, in which just 7% agreed that "Gun ownership should have no or very few restrictions." Q. PV20-V9. Ipsos for Reuters, January 11-28, 2019, released February 8, 2019. "Reuters/Ipsos Data: American Perceptions on Gun Control," Toplines, Data Tables.

11 In that sense, this volume updates chapter 13 of Thomas Gabor, CONFRONTING GUN VIOLENCE IN AMERICA (Springer Nature/Palgrave Macmillan, 2016). which made the same point using earlier polls.

12 Public Law 115–8, 131 Stat.15 (February 2, 2017). *See:* Jessica Taylor, "House Votes to Overturn Obama Rule Restricting Gun Sales to the Severely Mentally Ill," NPR, February 2, 2017; Ashley Kilough and Ted Barrett, "Trump signs bill nixing Obama-era guns rule," CNN, February 28, 2017.

13 H.R.. 1181 (March 3, 2017).

14 Nicholas Nehamas and David Smiley, "Florida school shooter's AR-15 may have jammed, saving lives, report says," *Miami Herald*, February 27, 2018.

15 Stoneman Douglas students Julia Cordover, Jonathan Blank, Carson Abt, Ariana Klein, Justin Gruber, and Sam Zeif spoke during the televised meeting.

16 Isabella Gomez and Amanda Jackson, "Women's March organizers are planning a national student walkout to protest gun violence, "CNN; "ENOUGH: National School Walkout," *The Action Network*.

17 "March for Our Lives," February 18, 2018; Kelly-Leigh Cooper, "In Florida aftermath, US students say 'Never Again.'" BBC; Lam, Katherine, "Florida school shooting survivors plan march demanding end to gun violence," *Fox News*, Feb-ruary 18, 2018.

18 Melissa Herrman and David R. Jones, "How Democrats won the House," CBS News, November 7, 2018; "Mid-term elections: Democrats win House in set back for Trump," BBC News, November 7, 2018 ("Tuesday's vote was seen as a referendum on a polarizing president, even though he is not up for re-election till 2020."); Zack Stanton, Steven Shepard and Ruairí Arrieta-Kenna, "How Demo-crats Won Over Older Voters—And Flipped the House,"*Politico Magazine*, November 13, 2018 (citing health insurance).

19 Associated Press, "The Latest: West Texas residents grieve at prayer vigil," September 1, 2019.

20 Nate Silver, "The Polls Are All Right," *Five Thirty Eight*, ABC News, May 30, 2018.

21 See "YouGov" in the Appendix for a fuller discussion.

22 According to a thoughtful answer on Quora, US Census data indicate that "8.5% of the income-earning, non-student population makes 100K+ per year, and 91.5% of the same population makes less." *See:* John Grumbine, Response to "What percent of Americans make more than $100,000?" Quora, updated July 5, 2018, citing US Census Data, American Community Survey, Public Use Microdata Sample.

23 Census Bureau, "Quick Facts, Population Estimates, July 1, 2019 (Education)"; Census Bureau, Selected Social Characteristics In the United States, American Community Survey, 2018: ACS 5-Year Estimates, Data Profiles, Table ID: DO02.

24 Angela Stroud, GOOD GUYS WITH GUNS: The Appeal and Consequences of Concealed Carry (Chapel Hill: University of North Carolina Press with Jennifer Carlson, CITIZEN PROTECTORS: The Politics of Gunsinan Age of Decline (New York: Oxford University Press, 2015. See also: Angela Stroud, Good Guys With Guns: Hegemonic Masculinity and Concealed Handguns, *Gender & Society*, February 21, 2012.

25 Sadly, to a large extent, that's because the news media treat shootings by whites of other whites, especially white kids, as events that merit hours on end of coverage, and shootings by blacks of other blacks as events that don't deserve as much coverage.

26 See, *e.g.,* Susan Spillane, Meredith S. Shiels, Ana F. Best, Emily A. Haozous, *et al.*, "Trends in Alcohol-Induced Deaths in the United States, 2000-2016," JAMA *NetwOpen.* 2020;3(2e1921451.doi:10.1001/jamanetworkopen.2019.2145(February 21, 2020(Women are catching up with men; Yana C. Vierboom, "Trends in alcohol-related mortality by educational attainment in the U.S., 2000-2017." Population Research Policy Review.2020Feb;39(1:77-97. doi:10.1007/s111 13-019-09527-0. Epub 2019 April 5. See also the papers by Case and Deaton cited below.

27 Paola Scommegna, "Opioid Overdose Epidemic Hits Hardest for the Least Educated," PRB, January 10, 2018; Jessica Y. Ho, "The Contribution of Drug Overdose to Educational Gradients in Life Expectancy in the United States, 1992-2011," *Demography* 54, no.3 (2017:1175-1202. Vice Chairman's Staff of the Joint Economic Committee, "The Numbers Behind the Opioid Crisis (at the request of Senator Mike Lee," November 2017.

28 Anne Case and Angus Deaton, DEATHS OF DESPAIR AND THE FUTURE OF CAPITALISM (Princeton and Oxford: Princeton University Press, 2020. Angus Deaton won the Nobel Prize for economics in 2015. For a review, *see:* Zachary Siegel, "Capitalism Is Killing Us," *The Nation,* April 23, 2020; Atul Gawande, "The Blight, How our economy has created an epidemic of despair," *The New Yorker,* March 23, 2020, pp.59-63; or David Canning, "Reversing the rise in mid-life mortality," *Science,* vol. 367, issue 6485, p.1433. DOI:10.1126/science. aba3036.

Professors Case and Deaton developed their thesis in two papers written for other economists: Anne Case and Angus Keaton, "Rising morbidity and mortality in mid-life among white non-Hispanic Americans in the 21st century," PNAS, December 8, 2015, 112(4915078-15083; first published November 2, 2015 .https://doi.org/10.1073/pnas.1518393112; and Anne Case and Angus Deaton, "Mortality and morbidity in the 21st century," Brookings Papers on Economic Activity, Spring 2017, p. 97-467.

29 Peter M. Aronow and Benjamin T. Miller, "Policy misperceptions and support for gun control legislation," *The Lancet,* vol. 387, No. 1001 (January 16, 2016), p. 223.

30 Brady McCombs, "Utah man accused of threatening to kill members of Congress," *The Washington Post*, June 6, 2019; Associated Press,"Utah Man Accused of Threatening to Kill Members of Congress," *The New York Times*, June 6, 2019; Emily Singer, "Trump Supporter Arrested For Threatening To Kill Members Of Congress," *The National Memo*, June 7, 2019.

31 Then candidate Donald Trump put the expression" Second Amendment people" into our national lexicon when he suggested that if Hillary Clinton were elected, she would be able to appoint federal judge and Supreme Court justices and "there will be nothing you can do about it"—unless, maybe,the "Second Amendment people"could. The statement was widely interpreted to mean that guns-rights advocates should kill Ms. Clinton if she won. *See, e.g.:* Nick Corasaniti and Maggie Haberman, "Donald Trump Suggests 'Second Amendment People' Could Act Against Hillary Clinton," *The New York Times*, August 9, 2016; Eliza Collins, "Trump suggests '2nd Amendment people' could stop Clinton," *USA Today*, August 9, 2016; Jeremy Diamond and Stephen Collinson, "Donald Trump's 'Second Amendment' gun advocates could deal with Hillary Clinton," CNN, August 10, 2016.

32 Hillary Rodham Clinton, WHAT HAPPENED (New York: Simon Schuster 2017, pp. 398-406.

33 Alex Yablon and Daniel Nass, "U.S. Gun Death Rate Hit 20-Year High in 2017, CDC Data Shows," *The Trace*, December 10, 2018, drawing on CDC's WONDER public health data base rather than an official pronouncement from the agency; Sarah Mervosh, "Nearly 40,000 People Died From Guns in U.S. Last Year, Highest in 50 Years," *The New York Times*, December 18, 2018.

34 See Rodrigo F. Alban, Miriam Nuño, Daniel R. Margulies, "Weaker state guns laws secondary to firearms," *J. of Surgical Research*, Vol. 221 (January 2018), pp. 135-142.

35 Erin Grinshteyn and David Hemenway, "Violent death rates in the US compared to those of the other high-income countries, 2015," *Preventive Medicine*, Vol. 123 (June2019), pp. 20-26. https://doi.org/10.1016/j.ypmed.2019.02.026. Available *online* February 26, 2019. German Lopez, who follows gun violence among other issues, provides what may be the best available recent journalistic analysis. See German Lopez, "America Is One of 6 Countries That Make Up More Than Half of Gun Deaths Worldwide," *Vox*, August 29, 2018.

36 Global Burden of Disease 2016 Injury Collaborators, "Global Mortality From Firearms, 990-2016, "JAMA.2018;320(8:792-814.doi:10.1001/jama.2018.10060, corrected on August 28, 2018. The chart uses CDC age-adjusted firearm fatality data from WISQARS for 2016 for the United States.

37 The Human Development Index, 2016.

38 Robert Steinbrook,"Interstate Association of State Firearm Laws With Suicide and Homicide," *JAMA Intern. Med.* 2018.178(5):701.doi:10.1001/jama internmed.2018. 0200.

39 Its crude firearm rate, 3.4, was also the lowest in the nation. Centers for Disease Control and Prevention, National Center for Health Statistics, Underlying Cause of Death 1999-2018 in the CDC WONDER Online Database, released in 2020. Data are from the Multiple Cause of Death Files, 1999-2018, compiled from data provided by 57vital statistics jurisdictions through the Vital Statistics Cooperative Program.

40 Mississippi's crude rate was 22.4 firearm fatalities per 100,000.

41 Gun Violence Archive, as of October 5, 2020.

42 B. Kalesan, M.A.Vyliparambil, Y. Zuo, *et al.*, "Cross-sectional study of loss of life expectancy at different ages related to firearm deaths among black and white Americans," *BMJ Evidence-Based Medicine* (December 4, 2018. Doi: 10.1136/bmj-ebm- 2018-111103. *See:* Alexi Cohan, "Study: Gun violence driving down African-American life expectancy,"*Boston Herald*, December 5, 2018.

43 S.A. Spitzer, D.Vail, LTennakoon, *et al.*, "2019 Readmission risk and costs of firearm injuries in the United States, 2010-2015," PLoSONE14(1:e0209896. https://doi.org/10.1371/journal.pone.0209896.

44 Erin Renee Morgan, Anthony Gomez, Ali Rowhani-Rahbar, "Firearm Ownership, Storage Practices, and Suicide Risk Factors in Washington State, 2013–2016," *American Journal of Public Health*, 108, no. 7 (July 1, 2018: pp. 882.

45 Maya Rossin-Slater, Molly Schnell, Hannes Schwandt, *et. al.*, "Local Exposure to School Shootings and Youth Antidepressant Use," NBER Working Paper No. 26563, December 2019. See also: *The Trace*, December 21, 2019.

46 Erika Christakis, "Active-Shooter Drills Are Tragically Misguided," *The Atlantic*, March 2019, pp. 10-12. Ms. Christakis reported on a12-year-old writing a heartbreaking "last letter" to his parents during what was a drill.

47 Kristin Lam, "Major teacher unions call for schools to stop 'psychologically distressing' active shooter drills," *USA Today*, February 1, 2020. *See also*: Max Londberg, "Ohio children feel traumatized by some active shooter drills. Do students need them?" *Cincinnati Enquirer*, February 24, 2020.

48 APA, Stress in America™ Survey, "Generation Z Stressed About Issues in the News but Least Likely to Vote," American Psychological Association, October 30, 2018. See also: Andrea Diaz, "Generation Z reported the most mental health problems, problems, and gun violence is the biggest stressor," CNN, October 30, 2018. The survey included 459 people (18 and older as well as interviews with 300 teenagers (ages

15 to 17). It measured attitudes and perception of stress to identify the leading sources of stress among the general public.

49 Della Volpe and his team conducted focus groups of 14- to 29-year-olds in multiple cities—Atlanta, Chicago, Columbus, L.A. and Parkland, Fla. They then polled 2,235 people from the same age group. SocialSphere,"In Advance of Midterms, New National Poll Finds Young Voters Rank School Shootings as Most Important Issue for America's Future," *Cision,* October 22, 2018.

50 In the poll, 68% of American sages 14 to 29 said school shootings are the most important issue facing the U.S. *The Trace,* January 12, 2019; Mike Allen, "School shootings are this generation's 9/11," *Axios AM,* January 8, 2019.

51 Steve Levine, "School shootings have united Gen Z and young millennials," *Axios,* January 8, 2019.

52 *Idem.*

53 "Audience members ran for cover during a performance of 'Fiddler on the Roof,'" *The Trace,* November 16, 2018; Christina Tkacik, Sarah Meehan and Lillian Reed, "Drunk man shouts 'Heil Hitler, Heil Trump,' does Nazi salute during Baltimore performance of 'Fiddler on the Roof,'" The Baltimore Sun, November 16, 2018.

54 Michael Wilson, "There Was No Gunfire in Times Square. But the Panic Was Still Real," *The New York Times,* August 8, 2019.

55 Ipsos, "Majority of Americans Hold Incorrect Assumptions about Guns," October 11, 2017.

56 AMP Research Labs, July 16-21, 2019, released October 2, 2019, "Americans' Views On Key Gun Policies, Part 2: Knowledge of gun-related deaths."

57 Ipsos, "Majority of Americans Hold Incorrect Assumptions about Guns," October 11, 2017.

58 NPR/PBS NewsHour/MaristPoll, February 5-11, 2019. See: Domenico Montanaro,"Poll: A Year After Parkland, Urgency For New Gun Restrictions Declines,"NPR, February 14, 2019. Data Tables.

59 Mark Joslyn and Donald P. Haider-Markel, "Motivated Innumeracy: Estimating the Size of the Gun Owner Population and Its Consequences for Opposition to Gun Restrictions," *Politics & Policy,* November 20, 2018. https://doi.org/10.1111/polp.12276. See: AAAS, "Most people overestimate total number of US gun owners," Eureka Alert!, December 10, 2018; Mark Joslyn and Donald P. Haider-Markel, "Americans vastly overestimate the number of gun owners," *The Washington Post,* May 7, 2018. Dr. Joslyn has expanded this discussion in his just published book: Mark R. Joslyn, THE GUN GAP: The Influence of Gun Ownership on Political Behavior and Attitudes. New York Oxford University Press 2020.

60 Emily Swanson, "Major survey shows gun owner ship declining," Associated Press, March 9, 2015.

61 Tom W. Smith, Faith Laken, and Jaesok Son, "Gun Ownership in the United States: Measurement Issues and Trends," NORC at the University of Chicago, GSS Methodological Report No. 123, January 2014, revised October 2015.

62 Deborah Azrael, Lisa Hepburn, David Hemenway, et al., "The Stock and Flow of U.S. Firearms: Results from the 2015 National Firearms Survey," RSF: *The Russell Sage Foundation Journal of the Social Sciences,* Vol. 3, No. 5 (October 2017: 38–57. https://doi.org/10.7758/RSF.2017.3.5.02. *See:* Kate Masters, "Why a New Survey From Harvard and Northeastern Is the Most Authoritative Assessment of American Gun Ownership in 20 Years," *The Trace,* September 19, 2016.

63 *Idem.,* at p. 42, "The Gun Stock," col. 2.

64 Most of the public opinion polls reported in this book involve 800 to 1,500 respondents.

65 Ipsos/NPR poll, October 10-11, 2017, released October 11, 2017, "Majority of Americans Hold Incorrect Assumptions about Guns."

66 Ipsos/Reuter Poll, January 11-28, 2019 [Toplines].

67 AMP Research Labs, July 16-21, 2019, released August 20, 2019. "Americans' Views On Key Gun Policies: Opinions on 'red flag' laws," August 20, 2019.

68 Monmouth University Poll, "Gun Owners Divided on Gun Policy; Parkland Students Having an Impact," March 2-5, 2019, released March 8, 2019. Monmouth University Poll, "National: Public Divided On Assault Weapons Policy," August 16-20, 2019, released September 9, 2019.

69 Among the respondents in the 2018 NPR/PBS sample, 37% of adults and 40% of registered voters said they were gun owners. NPR/PBS News-Hour/Marist Poll, April 10-13, 2018. Table, p. 2. That probably tells us more about the representativeness of the poll's sampling than it does about the actual percentage of gun owners.

70 General Social Survey, 2018, Civil Liberties, "Does respondent have gun in the home?" "Yes"/ "No"/ "Total."

71 Emily Swanson, "Major survey shows gun ownership declining," Associated Press, March 9, 2015.

72 "Behavioral Risk Factor Surveillance System," Wikipedia

73 Catherine A. Okoro, David E. Nelson, James A. Mercy, et al., "Prevalence of Household Firearms and Firearm-Storage Practices in the 50 states and the District of Columbia. "Findings From the Behavioral Risk Factor Surveillance System," 2002, vol.

116, No. 3 *Pediatrics* (September 2005).

74 Quinnipiac University graciously provided the author with unpublished gun household share data.

75 The "Yes" percentage is the sum of those who personally owned a gun and those who said someone else in the household did.

76 NPR/PBS NewsHour/Marist Poll, September 5-8, 2019, released September 10, 2019 [Data Tables].

77 Suffolk University/USA Today, August 20-25, 2019, released August 29, 2019. "Poll: 90% of Registered Voters Want Firearms Background Checks." [Marginals, Tables]

78 For more details on these and the other commercial polls cited in this book, please refer to the Appendix.

79 Ipsos, "Majority of Americans Hold Incorrect Assumptions about Guns," October 11, 2017. For discussion, see Danielle Kurtzleben, "Poll: Majorities of Both Parties Favor Increased Gun Restrictions," NPR *Morning Edition*, October 13, 2017.

80 Nate Silver, "Party Identity in a Gun Cabinet," *The New York Times*, December 18, 2012.

81 The 2017 Ipsos/NPR poll mentioned above asked, "Do you personally own a gun?" Some 34% of Republicans said they did. Only 20% of Democrats did.

82 "Southern Strategy," Wikipedia.

83 Bindu Kalesan, Marcos D. Villarreal, Katherine M. Keyes, *et al.*, "Gun ownership and social gun culture," *Injury Prevention* 2016;22:216-220.

84 "Firearm death rates in the United States by state," Wikipedia

85 Debora Azrael, Lisa Hepburn, David Hemenway, Matthew Miller, "The Stock and Flow of U.S. Firearms: Results from the 2015 National Firearms Survey," *RSF: The Russell Sage Foundation Journal of the Social Sciences*, Vol. 3, No. 5, pp. 38–57, October 2017. https://doi.org/10.7758/RSF.2017.3.5.02 ("The Stock and Flow").

86 General Social Survey, Civil Liberties, "household gun ownership."

87 GSS Data Explorer, Trends, Civil Liberties, "Does Respondent have a gun in home?" NORC. The percentage of Americans, age 25 or older, without a high school diploma has been declining steadily. It was about 76% in 1940. By 2018, it was 10%. So, over time, this demographic—people with less than a high school education—has become both smaller and less well armed. U.S. Census Bureau, "America's Education: Population 5 and Over by Educational Attainment," December 14, 2017. U.S. Census Bureau, "Educational Attainment in the United States: 2018," February 21, 2019.

88 GSS Data Explorer, Trends, Civil Liberties, "Does Respondent have a gun in in home?" NORC.

89 Robert Seltzer, Doctors Against Handgun Injury, "After September 11, A Rise in Gun Sales," *The New York Times,* December 5, 2001 (sales increased by 21% percent and may have been greater in New York; Richard Fabrizio, "Gun sales rise, then level off, after 9/11," Seacoast-online.com, February 10, 2002, updated January 31, 2011.

90 Jeffrey M. Jones, "Men, Married, Southerners Most Likely to Be Gun Owners," Gallup, February 1, 2013.

91 Kim Parker, Juliana Menasce Horowitz, Ruth Igielnik, *et al.,* "America's Complex Relationship with Guns," survey of U.S. adults conducted March 13-27 and April 4- 18, 2017.

92 "The Stock and Flow," at p. 44. According to a report from the Small Arms Survey June 2018, American citizens possessed a total of 393 million guns. If correct, that meant there were 120.5 firearms per 100 residents. Firearm possession in the U.S. is uncertain because federal law prohibits the ATF from maintaining a central registry of firearms possessed by private owners.

93 "Stock and Flow," *op cit.,* at p. 43.

94 Lois Beckett, "Meet America's Gun Super-Owners—With An Average of 17 Firearms Each," *The Trace,* September 20, 2016. Ms. Beckett writes for The Guardian, but the article grew out of a partnership with The Trace.

95 ATF, "Fact Sheet--Facts and Figures for Fiscal Year 2017," May 2018.

96 Jeremy Adam Smith, "Why Are White Men Stockpiling Guns?" *Scientific American,* "Observations" blog, March 14, 2018, collects and discusses the available research. For more depth, see: Jennifer Carlson, CITIZEN PRO-TECTORS: The Everyday Politics of Guns in an Age of Decline (New York: Oxford University Press, 2015; Angela Stroud, GOOD GUYS WITH GUNS: The Appeal and Consequences of Concealed Carry (Chapel Hill University of North Carolina Press, 2016.)

97 *Idem.*

98 Amanda Marcotte, "How the Gun Industry Preys on Paranoid, Insecure Men Like Elliot Rodger," *AlterNet,* May 22, 2014.

99 Wolfgang Stroebe, N. Pontus Leander, Arie W. Kruglanski, "Is It a Dangerous World Out There? The Motivational Bases of American Gun Ownership," *Personality and Social Psychology Bulletin,* June 8, 2017.

100 Perhaps not authoritative but colorful: David Neiwert, "Cohen's Warning about a 'Peaceful Transition' After the 2020 Election Reminds Us: The Authoritarianism Tide Is High," *Daily Kos,* March 4, 2019.

101 "Militia Organizations in the United States," Wikipedia. See also: Kyle Mantyla,

Rick Joyner, "Christians Need to Establish Militias in Preparation for the Coming Civil War," *Right Wing Watch*, September 3, 2019.

102 David Neiwert, "Cohen's Warning about a 'Peaceful Transition' After the 2020 Reminds Us: The Authoritarianism Tide Is High," *op. cit.*

103 J.J. MacNab, "Sovereign' Citizen Kane," *Intelligence Report*, Issue 139, *Southern Poverty Law Center*, Fall 2010.

104 Bob Paudert as-told-to Alex Yablon, "My Son Was Murdered in the Line of Duty by Right-Wing Extremists. Trump Should Focus on the Threat Posed by Sovereign Citizens.'" *The Trace*, February 15, 2017; Parkin, William S., and Joshua D. Freilich, Steven M. Chermak, Jeff Gruenewald. 2016. "Background Report: Criminal Justice & Military Deaths at the Hands of Extremists," START College Park, MD: START, Novem-ber 2016; Jessica Rivinius, "Sovereign citizen movement perceived as top terroris threat; New study assesses top threats, preparedness among law enforcement," START, July 30, 2014; Carter,David, and Steve Chermak, Jeremy Carter, Jack Drew. "Understanding Law Enforcement Intelligence Processes," Report to theOffice of University Programs, Science and Technology Directorate, U.S. Department of Homeland Security. College Park, MD: START, 2014.

105 Google "white supremacist + meth + guns" for additional reports of arrests for this combination.

106 The Southern Poverty Law Center tracks these groups.

107 Ipsos, "Majority of Americans Hold Incorrect Assumptions about Guns," October 11, 2017.

108 Democratic presidential debate, June 27, 2019, "More Democratic candidates declared gun reform a priority during the second night of the party's opening 2020 debate," *The Trace, Daily Bulletin*, June 28, 2019.

109 Kate C. Prickett, Carmen Gutierrez, Soudeep Deb, "Family Firearm Ownership and Firearm-related Mortality Among Young Children: 1976- 2016," *Pediatrics* (January 28, 2019). For discussion, see: Shilpa J. Patel, Monika K. Goyal, Kavita Parikh, "'Smart' Choices': Shared Decision-making in Firearm Storage and Personalized Firearms," *Pediatrics* (January 28, 2019); *The Trace, Daily Bulletin*, January 28, 2019.

110 *Idem.*

111 Anthony A. Bragga and Philip J. Cook, "TheAssociationof Firearm Caliber with Likelihood of Death from Gunshot Injury in Criminal Assaults," *JAMA Netw. Open* 018;1(3):e180833. For discussion, see: Margot Ne Sanger-Katz and Quoctrung Bui, "People Kill People. But the Bullets Seem to Matter," *The New York Times*, March 27, 2019.

112 For brief overview, see the excellent article by David Heath, Elise Hansen and A.

J. Willingham, "How an 'ugly,' 'unwanted weapon became the most popular rifle in America," CNN, December 4, 2017. See also: "AR-15 style rifle," Wikipedia. For more depth, see: Tom Diaz, MAKING A KILLING: The Business of Guns in America (Thew Press, March 1 ,2000); Tom Diaz, THE LAST GUN: How Changes in the Gun Industry Are Killing Americans and What It Will Take to Stop It (The New Press, 2013); C.J. Chivers, THE GUN (Simon & Schuster, October 12, 2010) (about the AK-47 and its variants).

113 "Cleveland Elementary School shooting, Stockton," Wikipedia.

114 "Slaughter in a School Yard," Time, January 30, 1989.

115 Heath, Hansen and Willingham, *op. cit.*, citing ATF data.

116 *Idem.*

117 See, e.g., "Gun control debates create gun production booms, government data show," *The Washington Post*, February 23, 2018.

118 David Heath, Elise Hansen and A.J. Willingham, "How an 'ugly,' unwanted weapon became the most popular rifle in America," CNN, December 14, 2017.

119 "The Stock and Flow" at pp. 42-43.

120 John R. Lott, "Concealed Carry Permit Holders Across the United States:" (July 18, 2017) .https://ssrn.com/abstract=3004915 or http://dx. doi org/10.2139/ssrn. 3004915.

121 Violence Policy Center, "Concealed Carry Killers."

122 Carl T. Bogus, "Was Slavery a Factor in the Second Amendment?" *The New York Times*, May 24, 2018.

123 Constitution, Art. 1, Sec. 8, Clauses 15 and 16.

124 *Idem.*

125 Constitution, Art. 2, Section 2, Clause 1.

126 This account draws from Carl T. Bogus, "The Hidden History of the Second Amendment," 31 *U.C. Davis Law Review* No. 2 (Spring 1998, 309-408. See also: Thom Hartmann, "The Second Amendment Was Ratified to Preserve Slavery," Truth-out, January15, 2013; Stephanie Mencimer, "Whitewashing the Second Amendment," *Mother Jones*, March 20, 2008.

127 Some Second Amendment absolutists insist on social media that but for the Second Amendment, the American colonies might well have lost their war for indepen-dence, nd therefore that we might still be living under British rule. Individuals who hold that view may find it consternating to learn that the states did not ratify the Second Amendment until a decade after the British surrender at Yorktown. Slavery a Factor in the Second Amendment?" *The New York Times*, May 24, 2018.

128 Colin Woodward, AMERICAN NATIONS: A History Of The Eleven Rival Regional Cultures Of North America (New York: Viking, 2011), Ch. 10.

129 Article I, section 8, Clause 15.

130 Bruce Blay, Quora," Do you think that civilians will shoot other Americans if there's an assault weapons ban?" Answered September 4, 2019.

131 Rick Scheff, Quora, Answered Oct 11, 2015.

132 Monmouth University Poll, "Gun Owners Divided on Gun Policy, Parkland Students Having an Impact," March 2-5, 2018, released March 8, 2018.

133 *United States v. Miller,* 307 U.S. 174 (1939). The Supreme Court cited and followed Miller in a footnote in *Lewis v. United States,* 445 U.S. 55 (1980.).

134 *District of Columbia v. Heller,* 554 U.S. 570 (2008).

135 Michael E. Miller, "'The War of Races': How a hateful ideology echoes through American history," *The Washington Post,* December 27, 2019. Charles Law, THE DAY FREEDOM DIED: The Colfax Massacre, the Supreme Court, and the Betrayal of Reconstruction (Henry Holt and Co., 2008).

136 Quoting *Gibbons v. Ogden,* 22 U.S., 9 Wheat. 1, 211 (1824).

137 During the Civil Rights struggle of the 1960s, southern politlicians claimed they were defending "states' rights." What they meant, but preferred not to spell out explicitly, was the states' right, recognized in *Cruikshank,* to deny black citizens the protections enshrined in the Bill of Rights without interference from the federal government.

138 As long as the Court interpreted the Second Amendment as protecting only the States' right to have a "well regulated militia," the question didn't come up.

139 *McDonald v. City of Chicago,* 561 U.S. 742 (2010. Importantly, the court did not strike down the ordinances on the grounds that they required gun registration.

140 Juliana Keeping, "Man accidentally shoots self in genitals, is arrested in Oklahoma City," NewsOK.com, July 17, 2012; Meg Alexander, "Man shoots himself in genitals," KFOR News 4, July 16, 2012.

141 *Yasmeen Daniel v. Armslist, LLC,* Wis. Sup. Ct., Case No. 2017-AP-344 (April 30, 2019). See also: Connor Simpson, "Wisconsin Shooter Wasn't Allowed to Possess Firearms," *The Atlantic,* October 21, 2012; Azana Spa Shootings, Wikipedia.

142 Todd Richmond, "Wisconsin Court Says Gun Site Not Liable in Spa Shooting," Associated Press, April 30, 2019.

143 *Yasmeen Daniel v. Armslist, LLC, et al.,* No. 19-153, *cert. denied,* _ U.S. _ (November. 25, 2019).

144 Public Policy Polling, "Voters Like High School Gun Protesters; Don't Like NRA," March 27, 2018

145 .Paul J. Weber, Jake Bleiberg, and Michael Balsamo, "Texas shooter got gun at private sale; denied in 2014 check," Associated Press, September 3, 2019.

146 Alcohol, Tobacco, Firearms and Explosives, "Best Practices: Transfers of

Firearms by Private Sellers," ATF Pamphlet 5300.21, January 2013.

147 Matthew Miller, Lisa Hepburn, Deborah Azrael, "Firearm Acquisition Without Background Checks: Results of a National Survey," *Annals of Internal Medicine* (February 21, 2017).

148 Pub. L. 103–159, 107 Stat. 1536, enacted November. 30, 1993.

149 "Gun Show Loophole," Wikipedia.

150 "Licensed" here refers to federally licensed firearms dealers.145 Paul J. Weber, Jake Bleiberg, and Michael Balsamo, "Texas shooter got gun at private sale; denied in 2014 check," Associated Press, September 3, 2019.

151 "Private sale" refers to a sale by and/or a purchase from a non-federally-licensed firearms dealer.

152 Scott Glover, "One gun's path to destruction," CNN, March 21, 2019; Scott Glover, "Unlicensed dealers provide a flow of weapons to those who shouldn't have them, CNN investigation finds," CNN, March 25, 2019.

153 Technically, the federal law applies to all "federal firearm licensees" or "FFLs." FFLs include manufacturers, importers, dealers and collectors. For simplicity, the text refers to dealers, who handle most sales to retail customers.

154 See: 18 U.S.C. § 922(a)(1)(A).

155 See: 18 U.S.C. § 922(g).

156 See: 18 U.S.C. § 922(d).

157 See: 18 U.S.C. § 922(a)(5).

158 Siegel M., and C. Boine, "What Are the Most Effective Policies in Gun Homicides?" Rockefeller Institute of Government (2019.) https://bit.ly/2YPAz7P (collecting citations to studies that reached this conclusion).

159 L. K. Lee, E.W .Fleegler, C.Farrell, *et al.*, "Firearm Laws and Firearm Homicides: A Systematic Review." *JAMA Intern Med.* 2017 Jan 1;177(1): 106-119. doi: 10.1001/jamainternmed.2016.7051.

160 Bindu Kalesan, Matthew E Mobily, Olivia Keiser, *et al.*, "Firearm legislation and firearm mortality in the USA: a cross-sectional, State-level study," *The Lancet.* 387, 10030:1847–1855 (April 2016). doi:10.1016/S0140-6736, 1501026-0.

161 See: Patrick McGreevy, "Gun owners stockpile ammo before new California background check law begins," *The Los Angeles Times,* June 9, 2019.

162 Webster D.W., Vernick J.S., Bulzacchelli, M.T. "Effects of a gun dealer's change in sales practices on the supply of guns to criminals," *J. Urban Health.* 2006 Sep;83(5:778-87.doi:10.1007/s11524-006-9073-2. PMID: 16937-085; PMCID: PMC 2438583. See also: J.S. Vernick, D.W. Webster, M.T. Bulzacchelli, *et al.*, "Regulation of firearm dealers in the United States: an analysis of State law and opportunities for

improvement," *J. Law Med Ethics*. 2006 Winter; 34(4):7 65-75.

163 Amanda Ripley, "Ignoring Virginia Tech," *Time*, April 15, 2018. 164 United States of America v. Christopher Henderson *et al.*, Case: 1:18 -- 00284. Document #:1 Filed: 05/09/18..

165 Jason Meisner, "3 men charged with trafficking dozens of guns bought over Armslist.com to Chicago gang members," *Chicago Tribune*, May 15, 2018; Jason Meisner, "Guns bought in Kentucky and resold in Chicago linked to three homicides: prosecutors," *Chicago Tribune*, May 22, 2018; Associated Press, "Guns allegedly trafficked from Kentucky bought online by 3," *Louisville Courier Journal*, May 16, 2018. Facebook has since banned gun sales, but now sellers advertise a gun accessory, such as a holster, for what a gun would cost. Individuals unable to buy a gun legally understand that the Facebook ad is actually an ad for a gun.

166 Margot Sanger-Katz, "Support for Gun Control Seems Strong. But It May Be Softer Than It Looks," Upshot, *The New York Times*, March 24, 2018.

167 Megan Brenan, "Ten Takeaways About Americans' Views of Guns," Gallup, May 2, 2018.

168 Frank Newport, "American Public Opinion, Terrorism and Guns," *Gallup Blog*, June 13, 2016.

169 Anthony Salvanto, Fred Backus, Sarah Dutton and Jennifer D. Pinto, "Gauging Americans' Views on Orlando Mass Shooting," CBS News, June 15, 2016.

170 *Idem.*, Q.28. "Do you support or oppose requiring a criminal background check of every person who wants to buy a firearm?"

171 The "evidence" for the child-sex ring was this: John Podesta was Hillary Clinton's 2016 campaign manager. One night during campaign, Podesta's brother emailed him, inviting Podesta to have supper with him and his family. Podesta accepted and said he would stop on the way and get pizza.

172 Quinnipiac University Poll Find Support For 'Assault Weapon' Ban Almost 2-1," February 28, 2018.

173 Tim Elfrink, "Florida Voters Heavily Back Assault Weapons Ban, Oppose Armed Teachers," *Miami New Times*, February 28, 2018.

174 Dana Blanton, "Fox News Poll: Voters favor gun measures, doubt Congress will act," Fox News, March 25, 2018.

175 Quinnipiac University, July 17–20, 2019, released July 26, 2019. "Ohio Voters Oppose Fetal Heartbeat Abortion Ban, Quinnipiac University Poll Finds; 90 Percent Support Universal Gun Background Checks."

176 Langer Research, "Six in 10 Fear a Mass Shooting; Most Think Gun Laws Can Help," ABC News/Washington Post Poll, September 9, 2019.

177 Quora, "What percentage of Americans make more than $100,000 a year?" Answer

GUNS, POLLS, and DEMOCRACY

by John Grumbine, July 5, 2018.

178 Public Policy Polling, "Trump Holds Steady After Charlottesville; Supporters Think Whites, Christians Face Discrimination," August 23, 2017.

179 Public Policy Polling, "Conspiracy Theory Poll Results," April 2, 2013.

180 Public Policy Polling, "Tax Reform Still Not Helping GOP; Dems Lead House Ballot By 6," June 8-10, 2018. A clear majority, 82%, did not think we should punish our close ally and trading partner to the north for something that happened in 1812. But even that 82% is not as high as the majorities that favor comprehensive background checks.

181 Rebecca Shabad, "Why more than 100 gun control proposals in Congress since 2011 have failed," CBS News, June 20, 2016; Ed O'Keefe and Philip Rucker, "Gun-control overhaul is defeated in Senate," *The Washington Post*, April 17, 2013.

182 Jonathan Weisman, "Senate Blocks Drive for Gun Control," *The New York Times*, April 17, 2013.

183 *Idem*.

184 *See, e.g.*, Adam Nagourney, Ian Lovett and Richard Pérez-Peña, "San Bernardino Shooting Kills at Least 14; Two Suspects Are Dead," *The New York Times*, December 2, 2015.

185 See: 159 *Cong. Rec.* S 2699—S2729, S. 2729-2744, April 17, 2013. *See:* Kelsey Snell and Karoun Demirjian, "Senate rejects gun control amendments offered following San Bernardino shooting," Power Post, *The Washington Post*, December 3, 2015; Burgess Everett and Seung Min Kim, "Gun measures fail in Senate," CNN, December 3, 2015.

186 See: 162 *Cong. Rec.* S4335, S4350, S4353, June 20, 2016. See also: Jennifer Steinhauer, "Senate Rejects 4 Measures to Control Gun Sales," *The New York Times*, June 20, 2016; Amber Phillips, "The Senate voted on 4 popular gun control proposals Mon-day. Here's why none of them passed," *The Washington Post*, June 20, 2016.

187 Carl Hulse, "Three Separate, Equal and Dysfunctional Branches of Government," *The New York Times*, June 23, 2016; David M. Herszenhorn and Emmarie Huetteman, "Democrats End Sit-In After 25 Hours, Drawing Attention to Gun Control," *The New York Times*, June 23, 2016 ("Mr. Ryan said he's 'not going to allow stunts like this to stop us from carrying out the people's business.'"); Editorial Board, "Paul Ryan takes the coward's way out again," *Star-Ledger*, January 6, 2017 ("The Democrats staged a protest. The Speaker, apparently with a straight face, called it a 'threat to democracy.'")

188 18 U.S.C. § 922(d)(2) and (g)(2). The law defines a "fugitive means any person

who has fled from any State to avoid prosecution for a crime or to avoid giving testimony in any criminal proceeding."

189 OIG/DOJ, "Audit of the Handling of Firearms Purchase Denials Through the National Instant Criminal Background Check System," Audit Div. 16 - 32, September 2016. In its most recent annual report, the FBI said that since inception, the NICS has denied a total of 184,988 sales to fugitives, with 13,597 of those denials in 2018. Department of Justice, Federal Bureau of Investigation, Criminal Justice Infor-mation Services Division, National Instant Criminal Background Check System, NICS Section, 2018 Operations Report.

190 Eric Levitz, "Trump Administration Gave 500,000 Fugitives the Right to Buy Guns," *New York Magazine*, Intelligencer, October 17, 2017; Sari Horwitz, "Tens of thousands with outstanding warrants purged from back-ground check database for gun purchases," *The Washington Post*, November. 22, 2017; Sari Horwitz, "FBI remove thousands of wanted fugitives from gun control database," *The Independent*, November 23, 2017; Rhonda Cook, "Trump Administration change allows some facing arrest to buy guns," *Atlanta Journal-Constitution*, October 10, 2017.

191 Quinnipiac University, "U.S. Voters Oppose Trump Emergency Powers on Wall, Quinnipiac University Poll Finds; 86% Back Democrats' Bill On Gun Background Checks," March 6, 2019. ("25. As you may know, the U.S. House of Representatives has passed a bill that would require background checks on all gun sales, including those at gun shows and through online retailers. Do you support or oppose this bill?")

192 Quinnipiac University, August 21-26, 2019, released August 29, 2019, "Majority Of Voters Say Climate Change Is An Emergency Quinnipiac University Poll Finds; 72% Say Congress Needs To Act To Reduce Gun Violence."

193 Nikki Carvajal and Paul LeBlanc, "Trump on guns: '"We do have a lot of background checks right now,'" CNN, August 18, 2019; Matthew Vann, "Trump appears to back away from stronger gun sale background checks," *ABC News*, Aug 19, 2019; Elaina Plott, "Trump's Phone Calls with Wayne LaPierre Reveal NRA's Influence," *The Atlantic*, August 20, 2019; Matthew Daly, Trump threatens to veto gun bills pushed by Democrats," AP, February 26, 2019; Brooke Seipel, "White House threatens to veto background check bills," *The Hill*, February 25, 2019; Mike DeBonis, "House pushes ahead on gun control, backs expansion of background checks," *The Washington Post*, February 27, 2019.

194 "President Trump has pumped the breaks on gun reforms," *The Trace, Daily Bulletin*, August 21, 2019.

195 *The Trace, Daily Bulletin*, July 29, 2018.

196 Ryan Tarinelli, Associated Press, "Nevada governor signs gun background check law," 2 KUTV, February 17, 2019.

197 Joshua Panas, "Governor signs universal background check bill into law," KOB4, March 8, 2019.

198 Allison Anderman, "Gun Law Trend Watch 2019 Year-End Review," Giffords Law Center, December 18, 2019.199 "Governor Northam Signs Historic Gun Safety Legislation into Law," April 10, 2020.

200 Giffords Law Center, "Background Checks, Summary of State Law."

201 *Rucho v. Common Cause*, 588 U.S. _, _ (June 27, 2019 (Kagan, J., dissenting).

202 Staff, Intelligence Report: The Year in Hate and Extremism, Southern Law Center, Spring 2016, p. 8; United States Attorney's Office, N.D. Georgia, "Men Sentenced for Conspiracy to Use Weapons of Mass Destruction," August 28, 2015.

203 Matt Zapotosky, "Feds: White supremacists plotted to attack synagogues, black churches," *The Washington Post*, November 10, 2015; Mark Bowes and Bill McKelway, "Federal, state weapons investigations lead to five local arrests," *Richmond Times-Dispatch*, November 10, 2015.

204 Jeannie Roberts, "Investigation into Arkansas-based white supremacist group leads to dozens of arrests, authorities say," *Arkansas Democrat Gazette*, October 12, 2017; "Multiple White Supremacist Gang Members among 54 Defendants Charged in RICO Indictment," Department of Justice, Office of Public Affairs, February 12, 2019.

205 Isabel Rosales "39 suspected gang members charged in major drug, gun trafficking investigation in Pasco," *ABC Action News*, WFTS Tampa Bay, November 15, 2018, updated November 16, 2018.

206 "More Than 40 Defendants Linked to Notorious White Supremacist Street Gang Indicted," U.S. Attorney, S.D. Georgia, November 19, 2018; "All 43 defendants in Operation Vanilla Gorilla now convicted of drug, firearms crimes," U.S. Attorney, S. D. Georgia, July 17, 2019.

207 THV11 Digital, "54 white supremacists arrested for multiple violent crimes in Russellville," THV11 Ark., February 12, 2019.

208 Erin Donaghue, "Racially-motivated violent extremists elevated 'national threat priority,' FBI director says," CBS News, February 5, 2020.

209 This description is based on "Terrorist Screening Database," Wikipedia.

210 Russell Berman, "Could Congress Have Stopped Omar Mateen From Getting His Guns?" *The Atlantic*, June 14, 2016; "Orlando Nightclub Shooting," Wikipedia. The FBI removed Mateen from the Terrorist Screening Data Base investigation. He was therefore no longer identified in the TSDB as a suspected terrorist when he purchased the guns used in the Pulse nightclub.

211 Del Quentin Wilber, "Omar Mateen was taken off a terrorist watch-list, but keeping

him on it wouldn't have stopped him from buying guns," *Los Angeles Times,* June 12, 2016.212 The table and related information appear in a letter from Diana C. Maurer, Director, Homeland Security and Justice Issues, Government Accountability Office, to Senator Diane Feinstein, captioned, "Update on Firearm and Explosives Background Checks Involving Terrorist Watchlist Records," March 7, 2016.

213 See: 18 U.S. Code § 921(a)(22).

214 PEW, "America's Complex Relationship with Guns: An in-depth look at the attitudes and experiences of U.S. adults," June 22, 2017. Polling dates: March 13-27 and April 4-18, 2017.

215 Langer Research, "Vast Support for a Watch-List Gun Ban; Clinton Prevails in Response to Orlando" ("Americans overwhelmingly support barring barring gun purchases by individuals on the FBI's terrorist watch list—the FBI's terrorist watch list—an initiative that has thus far failed in Congress."

216 Some polling organizations, *e.g.,* Pew, do not make crosstab data available.

217 Democrats favored this 85% to 15%, and Independents 83% to 6%. By the slimmest of margins, Republicans were more enthusiastic about this than anyone.

218 For comparison, in this poll, 13% of Republicans said they thought, "Hillary Clinton is connected to a child sex ring being run out of a pizzeria in Washington DC."

219 *See, e.g.,* Kelsey Snell and Karoun Demirjian, "Senate rejects gun control amendments offered following San Bernardino shooting," Power Post, *The Washington Post,* December 3, 2015; Burgess Everett and Seung Min Kim, "Gun measures fail in Senate," *Politico,* December 3, 2015.

220 *Congressional Record,* 114th Cong., 1st Sess., v. 161, No. 75 (December 3, 2015, pp. S8346-47.

221 Jennifer Steinhauer, "Senate Rejects 4 Measures to Control Gun Sales," *The New York Times,* June 20, 2016; *Congressional Record,* S4335-S4353 (June 20, 2016.

222 See: 18 U.S.C. 925A.

223 Jordain Carney, "Senators introduce bill to block terrorists.

224 Jordain Carney, "Schumer: Trump caved to NRA on gun control," *The Hill,* February 22, 2018.

225 William Vitka, "Md. man gets almost 50 years for murder of ex-girlfriend in Southeast," WTOP, July 20, 2018; Keith L. Alexander, "Man convicted in murder of his ex-girlfriend, a church youth minister," *The Washington Post,* May 8, 2018; Lindsay Watts, "Ex-boyfriend charged with DC woman's murder had restraining order filed against him," FOX 5, June 21, 2016.

226 Jennifer Mascia, "Once Every 16 Hours, an American Woman Is Fatally Shot by a

Current or Former Romantic Partner," *The Trace*, February 9, 2016 ("The tally comes amid States' uneven attempts to plug loopholes in federal laws meant to keep guns out of abusers' hands."); Associated Press, Data Set, 2016. 227 S.B. Sorenson and R.A. Schut, "Nonfatal gun use in intimate partner violence: A systematic review of the literature," *Trauma Violence and Abuse*, Vol: 19 issue: 4, page(s): 431-442, first published online: September 14, 2016, print issue published October 1, 2018; David Hemenway, PRIVATE GUNS, PUBLIC HEALTH, New Ed. (Ann Arbor: University of Michigan Press, 2017), p.331.DOI:10.3998/mpub. 9725179.

228 Emma E. Fridel and James Alan Fox, "Gender Differences in Patterns and Trends in U.S. Homicide, 1976–2017," *Violence and Gender*, Vol. 6, No. 1, published online March 11, 2019. https://doi.org/10.1089/vio. 2019.0005. For discussion, see: Khalida Sarwari, "Domestic Violence Homicides Appear to be on the Rise. Are Guns The Reason?" *News*, Northwestern University, April 8, 2019; *The Trace, Daily Bulletin*, April 10, 2019.

229 Public Law 104-208 (1996).

230 18 U.S.C. 922(g)(8).

231 18 U.S.C. 922(g)(9).

232 18 U.S.C. 922(g)(1)(g)."It shall be unlawful for any person (1), who has been convicted in any court of a crime punishable by imprisonment for a term exceeding one year ..."

233 Samantha Bee, "Close the Boyfriend Loophole," *Full Frontal*, Act 2, November 1, 2017.

234 Associated Press, FBI Supplemental Data, Homicide Data Set, 2016; Ryan J.Foley, "States taking action to keep guns out of abusers' hands," *Associated Press News*, February 6, 2016.

235 This is purely hypothetical. In real life, it is unlikely ATF agents would intervene in this circumstance.

236 See: 8 U.S.C. 923(g)(8), possession of firearm by someone who is the subject of a domestic violence restraining order.

237 18 U.S.C. 923(g)(8)(A).

238 18 U.S.C. 923(g)(8)(B).

239 18 U.S.C. 923(g)(8)(C)(i) and (ii).

240 18 U.S.C. 921(a)(32).

241 Susan Davis, "House Passes Bill Protecting Domestic Abuse victims; GOP Split Over Gun Restrictions," National Public Radio, *Morning Edition*, April 4, 2019.

242 YouGov Survey, April 8, 2019. (YouGov questioned 17,391 U.S. adults electronically on April 8, 2019.

243 *The Trace, The Daily Bulletin,* April 5, 2019.

244 Giffords LawC enter, http://lawcenter.giffords.org/gun-laws/policy-areas/who-can-have-a-gun/domestic-violence-firearms/#federal.ra.

245 Katie Zezima, "States move to restrict domestic abusers from carrying guns," *The Washington Post,* September 21, 2017. Nationwide, 27 states have passed laws curtailing access to guns by people convicted of domestic violence offenses or subject to protective orders, according to Everytown. Of those, 17 states have laws in place requiring them to relinquish their guns; Sarah Hansell, "Guns and Domestic Violence:Oregon's Loophole," *Street Roots,* April 12, 2017.

246 The sexual harassment allegations against Ohio's male legislators are beyond the scope of this book. *But see:* Julie Carr Smyth, A.P., "Rep. Bill Seitz Cleared In Sexual Harassment Investigation," *U.S. News,* June 15, 2018 (Rep. Seitz's long-time law firm conducted the investigation that cleared him. *See also:* Laura A. Bischoff, "Ohio senators to undergo sexual harassment training," *Dayton Daily News,* Oct 17, 2017.

247 Why Ohio's Republican legislators thought it important to protect men who physically abuse women with whom they have only business or social relationships is well outside the scope of this book.

248 Sarah Hansell, "Guns and Domestic Violence: Oregon's Loophole," *Street Roots,* April 12, 2017.

249 Allison Anderman, "Gun Law Trend Watch 2019 Year-End Review," Giffords Law Center, December 18, 2019.

250 Cal. A.B. 164, amending Section 29825 of the Penal Code, October 11, 2019.

251 Arkansas H.B. 1851 amending Arkansas Code § 9-15-207(b), April 1, 2019.

252 Louisiana HB 279, enrolled Act 427, 2019.

253 New Mexico S.B. 328, April 4, 2019.

254 Robert Nott, "New Law targets guns in cases of domestic violence," *Santa Fe New Mexican,* April 4, 2019.

255 House Bi ll 2013, eff. Jun 10, 2019: Chapter 201, 2019 Laws.

256 Connor Radnovich, "Two hearings on major gun bills draw hundreds to Oregon Capitol," *Salem Statesman Journal,* April 2, 2019.

257 Substitute House Bill1 786, Chapter 245, Laws of 2019, 66th Legislature 2019 Regular Session, Protection, No-Contact, And Restraining Orders--Firearms And Weapons, effective July 28, 2019.

258 April M. Zeoli and Jennifer K. Paruk, "Potential to prevent mass shootings through domestic violence firearm restrictions," *Criminology & Public Policy,* online December 16, 2019, and the literature reviewed by the authors.

https://doi.org/ 10.1111/1745-9133.12475. See also: *The Trace, The Canon,* January 25, 2020.

259 Judith Retana, "Police: Protection order filed just days before fatal shooting," WDTN.com, July 21, 2019, updated July23,2019; Jade Marshall and Christina Schaefer, WKEF/WRGT Staff, "Woman killed in double shooting at Family Dollar filed protection order just days before," Fox 28 WKEF/WRGT, July 21, 2019.

260 Pierce County settles law suit stemming from 2015 fatal shooting of woman by her husband, *Seattle Times/Tacoma News Tribune,* December 26, 2019; Jack Brown, "Hours before couple shot dead, deputies brought restraining order," *Seattle Times,* April 18, 2015, updated April 20, 2015; Alexis Krell, "Prairie Ridge woman got protection order hours before husband killed her," *The News Tribune,* April 19, 2015, updated April 20, 2015.

261 For readability, I use the gender-specific nouns and pronouns that usually apply. The same principles apply if the abuser is female. They also apply if the relationship is not the usual male-female relationship.

262 Poco Kernsmith and Sarah W. Craun, "Predictors of Weapon Use in Domestic Violence Incidents Reported to Law Enforcement," *Journal Of Family Violence* 23, 589-596, 2008.

263 Quinnipiac University, March3-5, 2018, "U.S. Voters Oppose Trump Emergency Powers On Wall 2-1 Quinnipiac University National Poll Finds; 86% Back Democrats' Bill On Gun Background Checks."

264 YouGov does not survey randomly selected individuals by phone. Instead, it uses standing panels of people who volunteer to be panelists, and it obtains their views online. YouGov then makes statistical adjustments in an attempt to reproduce what a random sample should look like. Given its methodology, this book does not generally use YouGov polls, but does so here because there are so few polls on this issue.

265 Katie Jagel, "Poll Results: Domestic Violence and Guns," YouGov/Huffington Post, July 26, 2014.

266 Laura Kiesel, "Don't Blame Mental Illness for Mass Shootings; Blame Men," *Politico,* January 17, 2018.

267 In a different poll, when asked which racial group faces the most discrimination in our country today, a similar 21% said "white people." When asked who they would rather be president, Barack Obama or Jefferson Davis, 21% said they preferred Jefferson Davis. (Jefferson Davis was the pro-slavery president of the Confederacy.) See: Public Policy Polling, August 18-21, 2017 [press release and data]. Just to be clear: That doesn't necessarily mean the 21% who objected to protecting abused partners

were the same 21% who endorsed racist statements. But it would be interesting to know how big the overlap between misogyny and racism is.

268 Colleen L. Barry, Daniel W. Webster, Elizabeth Stone, *et al.*, "Public Support for Gun Violence Prevention Policies Among Gun Owners and Non–Gun Owners in 2017," *American Journal Of Public Health,* June 6, 2018.

269 Melissa Jeltsen, "The NRA Wants To Solve Domestic Violence By Arming Victims. It Probably Won't Work," *Huffington Post,* July 15, 2017; Evan Defilippis, "Having a Gun in the House Doesn't Make a Woman Safer," *The Atlantic,* February 23, 2014; Claire Landsbaum, "NRA Ad Claims 'Real Women's Empowerment' Is Owning a Gun," *The Cut,* July 13, 2016 ("the NRA suggests we arm every single woman."); Shannon Watts, "Buy More Guns or Get Punched by the NRA's Clenched Fist of Truth," *Medium,* July 1, 2017 ("The gun lobby's leadership is getting desperate. They see the same polls we do—they know that the positions they advocate for are not popular with the public. So, what they lack in facts, they try to make up for in fear.").

264 YouGov does not survey randomly selected individuals by phone. Instead, it uses standing panels of people who volunteer to be panelists, and it obtains heir views online. YouGov then makes statistical adjustments in an attempt to reproduce what a random sample should look like. Given its methodology, this book generally does not use YouGov polls, but does so here due to the paucity of polling on this issue.

265 Katie Jagel, "Poll Results: Domestic Violence and Guns," YouGov/ *Huffington Post,* July 26, 2014.

266 Laura Kiesel, "Don't Blame Mental Illness for Mass Shootings; Blame Men," *Politico,* January 17, 2018.

267 In a different poll, when asked which racial group faces the most discrimination in our country today, a similar 21% said "white people." When asked who they would rather be president, Barack Obama or Jefferson Davis, 21% said they preferred Jefferson Davis. (Jefferson Davis was the pro-slavery president of the Confederacy. See: Public Policy Polling, August 18-21, 2017 [press release and data]. Just to be clear: That does not necessarily mean the 21% who objected to protecting abused partners were the same 21% who endorsed racist statements. But it would be interesting to know how big the overlap between misogyny and racism is.

268 Colleen L. Barry, Daniel W. Webster, Elizabeth Stone, *et al.*, "Public Support for Gun Violence Prevention Policies Among Gun Owners and Non–Gun Owners in 2017," *American Journal Of Public Health,* June 6, 2018.

269 Melissa Jeltsen, "The NRA Wants To Solve Domestic Violence By Arming Victims. It Probably Won't Work," *Huffington Post,* July15, 2017; Evan Defilippis, "Having a Gun in the House Doesn't Make a Woman Safer," *The Atlantic,* February 23,

2014; Claire Landsbaum, "NRA Ad Claims' Real Women's Empowerment' Is Owning a Gun," *The Cut,* July 13, 2016 ("the NRA suggests we arm every single woman."); Shannon Watts, "Buy More Guns or Get Punched by the NRA's Clenched Fist of Truth," *Medium,* July 1,2017 ("The gun lobby's leadership is getting desperate. They see the same polls we do—they know that the positions they advocate for are not popular with the public. So, what they lack in facts, they try to make up for in fear.").

270 *The Trace, Daily Bulletin,* September 3, 2019.

271 John Koziol, "Prosecutors cite history of road rage in man charged in shooting," *New Hampshire Union Leader,* June 16, 2019.

272 Nora Biette-Timmons, "More People Are Pulling Guns During Road-Rage Incidents," *The Trace,* August 10, 2017.

273 Jeffrey W. Swanson, Nancy A. Sampson, Maria V. Petukhova, *et al.,* "Guns, Impulsive Angry Behavior, and Mental Disorders: Results from the National Comorbidity Survey Replication," NCS-R, 33 *Behav. Sci. L.* 199, 209, 2015.

274 G J. Wintemute, M.A. Wright, C.M. Drake, *et al.,* "Subsequent criminal activity among violent misdemeanants who seek to purchase handguns: risk factors and effectiveness of denying handgun purchase." JAMA.2001;285(8: 1019–26.

275 *See:* 18 U.S.C.§ 922(d(1 ("sell or otherwise dispose of" a firearm or ammunition to; § 922(g)(1) ("to ship or transport in interstate or foreign commerce, or possess in or affecting commerce, any firearm or ammunition; or to receive any firearm or ammunition which has been shipped or transported in inter-state or foreign commerce"; § 922(n) for a person under indictment for a crime punishable by more than a year in prison to ship or transport or receive a firearm or ammunition in interstate or foreign commerce.

276 See, *e.g.,* C. C. Branas, S. Han , D.J. Wiebe, "Alcohol use and firearm violence." *Epidemiol Rev.* 2016;38(1:32–45; J.A. Ladapo, M. N. Elliott, D.E. Kanouse, *et al.,* Firearm ownership and acquisition among parents with risk factors for self-harm or other violence," *Academy of Pediatrics* 2016; 16:742-749; G. J. Wintemute,"Alcohol misuse, firearm violence perpetration, and public policy in the United States," *Preventive Medicine,* vol. 79, October 2015, pp. 15-21.

277 Jeffrey W. Swanson, Nancy A. Sampson, Maria V. Petukhova, *et al.,* "Guns, Impulsive Angry Behavior, and Mental Disorders: Results from the National Comorbidity Survey Replication," NCS-R, 33 *Behav. Sci. L.* 199, 209, 2015.

278 The Center for Responsive Politics. https://www.opense-crets.org/pacs/pacgot.php?cycle=2020&cmte=C00053553, and National Rifle Association filings with the Federal Election Commission.

279 C.K. Crifasi, M. Merrill-Francis, A. McCourt, *et al.,* "Association between

Firearm Laws and Homicide in Urban Counties," Journal of Urban Health: Bulletin of the New York Academy of Medicine, May 21, 2018. DOI: 10.1007/s11524-018-0273-3, PMID: 29785569.

280 Thomas P. Kapsidelis, AFTER VIRGINIA TECH: Guns, Safety, and Healing in the Era of Mass Shootings, University of Virginia Press, 2019; Virginia Tech Shooting, Wikipedia.

281 Alex Yablon, "The Legal Way to Seize Guns From Dangerous People," *The Trace*, March 9, 2018, updated March 13, 2018; Michael Martinez, "California lawmakers push 'gun violence restraining order' after mass killing," Fox 13 Now, Salt Lake City, Utah, May 28, 2014.

282 Jennifer Mascia, "In the Years Since the Isla Vista Shooting, the Incel Subculture Continues to Inspire Gunmen," *The Trace, Daily Bulletin*, May 23, 2019 ("When easy access to guns mixes with violent misogyny.")

283 WFTS Digital Staff, "Man surrenders AR-15 after threat of mass shooting at St. Pete Steak 'n Shake: Records," ABC Action News, WFTS, July 20, 2019; *The Trace*, Daily Bulletin, July 23, 2019.

284 Reis Thebault, "GOP lawmakers wore pearls while gun violence victims testified. Activists were outraged," *The Washington Post*, March 6, 2019; Alex Sundby, "Gun control advocate criticizes Republicans for wearing pearl necklaces during hearing," CBS News, March 6, 2019; Luke O'Neil, "Republicans seem to mock gun violence vic-tims by wearing pearls as they testify," *The Guardian*, March 6, 2019.

285 For a discussion of the links between animal abuse, domestic abuse and firearms, see: Randall Lockwood, Frank R Ascione, CRUELTY TO ANIMALS AND INTERPERSONAL VIOLENCE: Readings In Research And Application, West Lafayette: Purdue University Press, 1998; Deborah Doherty and Jennie Hornosty, "Exploring the Links: Firearms, Family Violence and Animal Abuse in Rural Communities," Final Research Report to The Canada Firearms Centre, Royal Canadian Canadian Mounted Police, Public Safety Canada, 2008; and the body of scholarly research citing those works.

286 Tim Elfrink, "Nikolas Cruz, Who Was Too Disturbed to Carry a Backpack, Legally Bought AR-15," *Miami New Times*, February 15, 2018; Connie Ogle, Nicholas Nehamas and David Ovalle, "Florida school shooting suspect was ex-student who was flagged as threat," *Miami Herald*, February 14, 2018, updated February 15, 2018.

287 KFLY News, "Bizarre behavior no impediment to gun purchases by man accused of killing Lafayette police officer," www.KFLY.com, May 26, 2018.

288 "Nashville Waffle House Shooting," Wikipedia.

289 Emanuella Grinberg, "The Waffle House shooting suspect thought Taylor Swift was stalking him and showed other signs of delusion," CNN, April 23, 2018.

290 Christopher Mele, "Naked Gunman Kills 4 in Nashville Waffle House Shooting, Police Say," *The New York Times*, April 22, 2018.

291 Amir Vera, "Waffle House shooter was once arrested by Secret Service for trespassing near White House," CNN, April 22, 2018; Jess Bidgood, "What Is a Sovereign Citizen?" *The New York Times*, April 23, 2018.

292 Alan Blinder, "Waffle House Shooting: Police Say Suspect Is in Custody." *The New York Times*, April 23, 2018; Dave Boucher, "Waffle House Shooting: Suspect Travis Reinking previously arrested outside White House," *USA Today*, April 22, 2018.

293 Dave Boucher, "Waffle House shooting: Suspect Travis Reinking previously arrested outside White House," *USA Today*, April 22, 2018; Doug Criss, "The Waffle House shooting suspect had his guns taken away—twice," CNN, April 23, 2018.

294 *Idem.*

295 *Boucher, op cit.* (n. 293).

296 Rafael Olmeda, "Man charged with felony won't give up guns. New law letscops put him behind bars," *Sun Sentinel*, April 9, 2018; "Florida police confiscate guns for the first time under state's new gun-control laws," *The Blaze*, March 19, 2018 ("The man told officers he 'was being targeted and burglarized by the Federal Bureau of Investigation and a 1 neighbor who lives in [his] building,' the judge wrote in his order. '[He] could not describe the neighbor but stated that the neighbor [can] "shape shift, he can change heights and I'm not sure where he comes from and 'to be honest, he looks like Osama Bin Laden.'" He also told officers that he had to turn off the electrical breakers because they are electrocuting me through my legs.'"

297 Michael E. Miller, "Idaho shooting suspect's 'hypersexual' Martian manifesto is a window into an unraveling mind," *The Washington Post*, March 9, 2016.

298 The media calls these laws "red flag" laws; the NRA and legislators call them "extreme risk" laws. Both labels refer to the same thing.

299 In California, employers may also seek red flag orders. Some states have debated allowing schools to seek red flag orders as well.

300 Ben Myers, "Why didn't bizarre behavior block man accused in Lafayette police officer's death from buying a gun?" The Acadiana Advocate, May 26, 2018.

301 Jose Niño, "Red Flag Gun Confiscation Laws Won't Stop Shootings," National Association of Gun Rights, August 15, 2019.

302 See, *e.g.,* Evan Defilippis, Devin Hughes, "The GOP's favorite gun 'academic' is a fraud; The journalistic quest for neutrality has led to asacrifice of intellectual integrity," *Think Progress*, Aug 12, 2016; Cydney Hargis, "The Washington Post gave discredited gun researcher John Lott a platform to push repeatedly disproven nonsense," *Media Matters*, July 8, 2019; Meg Kelly, "Do 98 percent of mass public shootings happen in

gun-free zones?" Fact Checker, *The Washington Post*, May 10, 2018.

303 Rep. Thomas Massie and John R. Lott, Jr., "'Red Flag' Laws Are the Wrong Solution to Mass Shootings," National Association of Gun Rights, October 4, 2019.

304 Deborah M. Stone, Thomas R. Simon, Katherine A. Fowler, *et al.*, "Vital Signs: Trends in State Suicide Rates--United States, 1999–2016 and Circumstances Contributing to Suicide - 27 States, 2015," *Morbidity and Mortality Weekly Report* 2018;67:617–62. DOI: http://dx.doi.org/10.15585/mmwr.mm 67722a1.

305 Roxanne Roberts, "Suicide is desperate. It is hostile. It is tragic. But mostly, it is a bloody mess," *The Washington Post*, May 19, 1996, reprinted June 2018.

306 Colleen L. Barry, Daniel W. Webster, Elizabeth Stone, Cassandra K. Crifasi, Jon S. Vernick, and Emma E. McGinty, "Public Support for Gun Violence Prevention Policies Among Gun Owners and Non–Gun Owners in 2017," *American Journal of Public Health*, June 6, 2018.

307 The AMP survey, conducted by SSRS, asked two questions. One inquired about family-initiated extreme risk protection orders and the other about police-initiated orders. The table uses the figures for family-initiated orders. The corresponding percentages for police-initiated orders were 60% in favor and 37% opposed.

308 Langer Research, "Six in 10 Fear a Mass Shooting; Most Think Gun Laws Can Help," ABC News/Washington Post Poll, September 9, 2019, p. 3.

309 See, *e.g.*, Kim Parker, Juliana Menasce Horowitz, Ruth Igielnik, Baxter Oliphant and Anna Brown, "America's Complex Relationship with Guns: An in-depth look at the attitudes and experiences of U.S. adults," Pew Research Center, June 22, 2017, Ch. 1. "The Demographics of Gun Ownership."310 For a more extensive and nuanced discussion, see: Angela Stroud, GOOD GUYS WITH GUNS: The Appeal and Consequences of Concealed Carry (Chapel Hill: University of North Carolina Press, 2016).

311 Michael Livingston, "More States 'red flag' laws to keep guns away from people per-ceived as threats," T*he Los Angeles Times*, May 14, 2018.

312 Every Town for Gun Safety, "ICYMI: NRA Voices Support for Red Flag Laws," March 20, 2018.

313 See, *e.g.*, Beth Reinhard, Katie Zezima, Tom Hamburger, and Carol D. Leonnig, "NRA money flowed to board members amid allegedly lavish spending by top officials and vendors," *The Washington Post*, June 9, 2019; Danny Hakim, "At the N.R.A., A Cash Machine Sputtering," *The New York Times*, May 14, 2019; Mike Spies, "Secrecy, Self-Dealing, and Greed at the N.R.A.," *The New Yorker*, April 17, 2019. Daniel Nass,"An Illustrated Guide to the NRA's Lavish Spending and Cozy Deals: How vendors and executives are bleeding the gun group dry," *The Trace*, May 31, 2019.

314 Michael Livingston, "More States approving 'red flag' laws to keep guns away from people perceived as threats," *Los Angeles Times*, May 14, 2018.

315 See, *e.g.*, Alastair Jamieson, Betsy DeVos Cites Grizzly Bears During Guns-in-Schools Debate, NBC News, January 18, 2017 ("potential grizzlies").

316 Ashley Killough, "Graham, Blumenthal unveil their own gun restraining order bill," CNN, March 8, 2018.

317 Ashley Killough, "Both Florida US senators want States to adopt gun restraining order laws," CNN, March 7, 2018.

318 Connecticut, CONN. GEN. STAT. § 29-38c, 1999; Indiana, IND. CODE ANN. § 35-47-14, 2006; California, CAL. PENAL CODE § 18100, 2016; Washington, R.C.W. 7.94.010, Initiative Measure No. 1491, approved November 8, 2016; and Oregon, 2017 OR S.B. 719 (Governor signed August 15, 2017).

319 Sean Campbell and Alex Yablon, "Red Flag Laws: Where the Bills Stand in Each State," *The Trace*, March 29, 2018, updated July 20, 2018; Grace Segers, "What are 'red flag' laws, and which states have implemented them?" CBS News, updated August 9, 2019.

320 N.Y. S.B. 2451. See: Laura Ly, "New York's governor, joined by Nancy Pelosi, signs 'red flag' gun protection law," CNN, February 25, 2019.

321 John Aguilar and Anna Staver, "Gov. Polis signs hard-fought Colorado red-flag gun measure into law," *The Denver Post*, April 12, 2019; *The Trace, The Canon*, April 13, 2019.

322 "The Colorado GOP tried to recall a Democrat who sponsored a new 'red flag' law," *The Trace, Daily Bulletin*, May 16, 2019.

323 Public Law 289. Indiana H.B. 1651, LegiScan. See also: "2019 Passed State Firearm Legislation," American Gun Owners Alliance.

324 S.B. 5027, Washington State Legislature (signed into law on May 7, 2019, effective July 28, 2019).

325 "Governor Sisolak Signs Controversial Gun Bill Into Law," KTVN, May 29, 2019; *The Trace*, June 16, 2019.

326 Kevin Dayton, "Ige signs 'red flag' gun bill," *Star Advertiser*, June 28, 2019; "More Democratic candidates declared gun reform a priority during the second night of the party's opening 2020 debate," *The Trace, Daily Bulletin*, June 28, 2019; Kevin Dayton, "'Red Flag' Gun Law Signed by Hawaii Governor," Governing (Tribune News Service), July 1, 2019.

327 *The Trace, Daily Bulletin*, October 14, 2019; Bryan Anderson," You'll only be able to buy one gun a month in California under new law," *Sacramento Bee*, October 11, 2019.

328 Christina Maxouris, "New Mexico's governor signed a red flag gun measure into law and urged sheriffs to enforce it or resign," CNN, updated February 26, 2020.

329 Virginia Legislative System, Senate Bill 240 and House Bill 674.

330 "D.C. B22-0588 and B23-028," The Trace, July 29, 2018. Dick Uliano, "DC votes to join Md., other states with 'red flag' gun laws," WTOP, November 28, 2018; Fox 5 DC Staff, "DC Council passes 'Red Flag' law unanimously," Fox 5 DC, December 18, 2018; Peter Hermann, Dana Hedgpeth, and Justin Jouvenal, "D.C. Council approves 'red flag' gun seizure law," *The Washington Post*, December 18, 2018.

331 *See:* Sean Campbell and Alex Yablon, "Red Flag Laws: Where the Bills Stand in Each State," *The Trace*, updated January 10, 2019. Office of Attorney General, "DC's Red Flag Law: Removing Guns From Potentially Dangerous Persons."

332 Matt Pearce, Jenny Jarvie and Molly Hennessy-Fiske," With graduation just days away, Texas school becomes latest casualty—10 dead, 10 wounded in latest campus shooting," *Los Angeles Times*, May 19, 2018.

333 Associated Press, "Texas Republicans squelch 'red flag' gun law prospects," This Is Money.Co.UK, August 5, 2018.

334 Alex Yablon, "Texans Are More Supportive of Gun Reform Than You Might Think," *The Trace, Daily Bulletin*, August 13, 2019.

335 Kelly Fisher, "Marshall County shooting suspect's identity confirmed, will be tried as an adult," *The Tennessean*, February 16, 2018, updated Feb-ruary18, 2018; Mike Stunson, Morgan Eads And KarlaWard, "Two killed, 18 others injured in Kentucky high school shooting," *Lexington Herald Leader*, January 23, 2018, updated January 24, 2018; Stephanie Ingersoll and Darcy Costello, "As Marshall County preps for school, suspected shooter appears in court," *Louisville Courier Journal*, August 3, 2018.

336 Maira Ansari, "Indiana's 'red flag' gun law getting national attention," WAVE 3, February 26, 2018.

337 Jeremy Pelzer, "Gov. Mike DeWine pushes for 'red-flag' law allowing courts to confiscate guns," April2 9,2019; Randy Ludlow, Gatehouse Media Ohio, "DeWine preparing 'red flag' proposal to remove guns from some,"Akron Beacon Journal / Ohio. com, April 29, 2019.

338 *The Trace, Daily Bulletin*, August 7, 2019.

339 Jeffrey W. Swanson, Michael A. Norko, Hsiu-Ju Lin, *et al.,* "Implementation and Effectiveness of Connecticut's Risk-Based Gun Removal Law: Does It Prevent Suicides?" 80 *Law And Contemporary Problems* 179-208, 2017; Aaron J. Kivisto and Peter Lee Phalen, "Effects of Risk-Based Firearm Seizure Laws in Connecticut and Indiana on Suicide Rates, 1981–2015," *Psychiatry Online* June 1, 2018.

340 "Trump appears to be gauging whether he can get away with defying the NRA," *The Trace, Daily Bulletin*, August 9, 2019; Josh Dawsey and Seung Min Kim,

"Trump's openness to extensive background checks for gun buys draws warning from NRA," *The Washington Post,* August 8, 2019; Sheryl Gay Stoltberg, Maggie Haberman, and Jonathan Martin, "Trump Weighs New Stance on Guns as Pressure Mounts After Shootings," *The New York Times,* August 8, 2019.

341 Michael McDevitt, "Ex-cop shot himself to death with gun he'd turned into police years earlier," *Chicago Sun-Times,* August 20, 2018.

342 "A former Illinois police officer killed himself using an old service pistol he was supposed to have surrendered," *The Trace,* August 22, 2018.

343 This summary and the summary of gun registration laws draw heavily from the Gifford Law Center, supplemented by other sources.

344 *See, e.g.,* Kate Masters, Banned From Owning Guns, "Many 'Lie and Try' to Buy Them Anyway. Few Are Punished for the Crime," *The Trace,* May 9, 2016; Joe Davidson, "Lying to buy a gun? Don't worry about the feds. Prosecutions are almost nonexistent," *The Washington Post,* September 11, 2018; Editorial Board, "Lie on a firearms background form? What have you got to lose?" *The Chicago Tribune,* September 18, 2018; Jose Pagliery, "Gun form liars may go onto commit gun crimes, internal ATF research suggests," *CNN Investigates,* December 21, 2018.

345 For a better explanation, see: "Fact Sheet: Permit-To-Purchase for Handguns, Why Handgun Purchaser Licensing Laws Are Necessary," Center for Gun Policy, and Research, John Hopkins Bloomberg School of Public Health, March 2015.

346 Evan Defilippis and Devin Hughes, "How This Piece of Paper Fights Gun Crimes and Saves Lives," *The Trace,* July 7, 2015, updated October 2, 2015.

347 See: 18 U.S.C. § 922(t)(3).

348 See: ATF Office of Enforcement Programs and Services, Permanent Brady Permit Chart, updated March 3-10, 2020.

349 Giffords Law Center, "States that Require Permits for Private Purchasers after Background Checks."

350 German Lopez, "I looked for a state that's taking gun violence seriously. I found Massachusetts," *Vox,* November 13, 2018; *The Trace,* December 1, 2018.

351 D.W. Webster, A.D. McCourt, C.K. Crifasi, *et al.*, "Evidence concerning the regulation of firearms design, sale, and carrying on fatal mass shootings in the United States," *Criminology Public Policy.* 2020;19:171–212. https://doi.org/10.-1111/1745-9133.12487.

352 Colleen L. Barry, Daniel W. Webster, Elizabeth Stone, *et al.*, "Public Support for Gun Violence Prevention Policies Among Gun Owners and Non–Gun Owners in 2017," *American Journal of Public Health,* June 6, 2018. For a discussion, *see:* Michelle Mark, "How gun owners really feel about gun control," *Business Insider,* May 24, 2018.

353 Alex Yablon and Daniel Nass, "ATF data reveals potential gun trafficking hubs," *The Trace,* October 24, 2019.

355 18 U.S.C. § 926(a(3).

354 Fact Sheet, National Tracing Center. Bureau of Alcohol, Tobacco and Firearms at https://www.atf.gov/resource-center/fact-sheet/fact sheet national traci-ng center.

356 ATF, Fact Sheet, National Tracing Center, May 2019.

357 Public Law 99-308, 100 Stat. 449 (May 19, 1986).

358 18 U.S.C. § 921(a)(21) and (22.)

359 18 U.S.C. § 923(e.

360 18 U.S.C. § 923(f)(4).

361 FOPA, Pub. L. 99-308, § 106, amending 18 U.S.C. § 926(a))(3).

362 FOPA, Pub. L. 99-308, § 106, amending 18 U.S.C. § 926(a)(3).

363 FOPA, Pub. L. 99-308, § 106, amending 18 U.S.C. § 926(g))(4).

364 See, e.g., Frank Miniter, "The ATF Shows Off Its Gun-Sale Record Mess--Why? Come In And See," *Forbes*, Marsh 28, 2016; Dan Friedman,"The ATF's Nonsensical Non-Searchable Gun Databases, Explained," *The Trace*, August 24, 2016; "Agency crippled by weak laws, paltry budgets and Congressional restrictions," Center for Public Integrity, February 11, 2013, updated January 6, 2016; Alan Berlow, "How the NRA Hobbled the ATF, Rules pushed by gun lobby and its allies in Congress have left the agency unable to enforce the law," *Mother Jones*, February 11, 2013.

365 Ipsos for NPR, "Majority of Americans Hold Incorrect Assump-tions about Guns," October 11, 2017, Q. 6(b.

366 Pew Research Center, 2018 Pew Research Center's American Trends Panel, Wave 38, Final Topline, September 24-October 7, 2018.

367 Gallup, "Guns," October 5-10, 2017.

368 Monmouth University Polling Institute, "Gun Owners Divided on Gun Policy; Parkland Students Having an Impact," March 8, 2018. [Cross Tabs].

369 Monmouth University Polling Institute, "Gun Owners Divided on Gun Policy; Parkland Students Having an Impact," March 8, 2018. [Cross Tabs, Q.21]. The Monmouth poll reached only 803 adults and had a very high percentage of gun householders, 46%, perhaps explaining why it is such an outlier.

370 Here's an apples-to-oranges comparison for that 21%: In 2019, after hearing the evidence, a judge and jury found beyond a reasonable doubt that Roger Stone, Jr., obstructed a Congressional inquiry (into Russian interference with the 2016 election, made false statements, made false statements, and tampered with a witness. In a YouGov daily poll on February 21, 2020, some 21% thought President Trump should pardon Stone, his longtime buddy.

371 Monmouth University Polling Institute, "Gun Owners Divided on Gun Policy; Parkland Students Having an Impact," March 8, 2018 [Cross Tabs].

372 See: Giffords Law Center, "Registration, Summary of State Law," accessed March 6, 2020; "Guns to Carry, State Laws by State," *The Complete Guide*.

373 Nikolas Kristof, "New Zealand Shows the U.S. What Leadership Looks Like," *The New York Times*, March 20, 2019.

374 David Moye, "Florida Shooting Survivor Suggests Calling AR-15 Rifles 'Marco Rubios,'" *Huffington Post*, February 23, 2018 ("They're both 'so easy to buy,' she said.").

375 William Cummings and Bart Jansen, "Why the AR-15 keeps appearing at America's deadliest mass shootings," *USA Today*, February 14, 2018, updated February 15, 2018.

376 Natasha Singer, "The Most Wanted Gun in America," *The New York Times*, February 2, 2013.

377 Editorial Board, "The Deadly Fantasy of Assault Weapons," *The New York Times*, December 28, 2012; Emma Gray, "Bushmaster Violence," The Blog, *Huffington Post*, December 17, 2012, updated December 6, 2017.

378 Sandy Hook Elementary School shooting, Wikipedia.

379 Compiled by the Stanford Geospatial Center and Stanford Libraries and USA Today. See: William Cummings and Bart Jansen, "Why the AR-15 keeps appearing at America's deadliest mass shootings," *USA Today*, February 14, 2018, updated February 15, 2018.

380 See, *e.g.*, Lucinda Holt and Manny Fernandez, "Death Toll in West Texas Shooting Climbs to 7," *The New York Times*, September 1, 2019; Emily Shapiro and Bill Hutchinson," 7 killed, 22 injured as alleged mass shooting suspect targets more than 15 locations in Odessa, Texas: Police," ABC News, September 1, 2019.

381 Paul J. Weber, Jake Bleiberg and Michael Balsamo, "Texas shooter got gun at private sale; denied in 2014 check," Associated Press, September 3, 2019.

382 Spencer Kimball, "'It was a hate crime': One dead, three injured in synagogue shooting in San Diego area," CNBC, April 27, 2019, updated April 28, 2019. "The manufacturer designed the rifle to circumvent California's assault weapon ban." *The Trace, Daily Bulletin*, June 25, 2019.

383 Deanna Paul and Katie Mettler, "Shooting at California synagogue leaves 1 dead, 3 injured in what mayor calls a 'hate crime' that 'will not stand,'" *The Washington Post*, April 27, 2019; Jamiles Lartey, "San Diego synagogue shooting: one dead and three injured," *The Guardian*, April 27, 2019.

384 Avi Selk, Mark Berman and Joel Achenbach, *The Washington Post*, "Documents detail the Pittsburgh synagogue massacre and name the dead," *The Inquirer*, philly.com, October 28, 2018.

385 Crandon Shooting, Wikipedia; William Cummings and Bart Jansen, "Why the

AR-15 keeps appearing at America's deadliest mass shootings," *USA Today*, February 14, 2018.

386 Gina Liu and Douglas J. Wiebe, "A Time-Series Analysis of Firearm Purchasing After Mass Shooting Events in the United States," JAMA 2019;JAMA Netw Open.2019 Apr 5; 2(4):e191736. doi: 10.1001/jamanetworkopen.2019.1736.

387 "Assault Weapon," Wikipedia.

388 "Flash Suppressor," Wikipedia.

389 "Barrel shroud," Wikipedia.

390 "Assault Rifle," Wikipedia, under the heading, "Distinction from Assault Weapons"; but see "Assault Weapon," Wikipedia.

391 There is no universally agreed upon definition of an "assault rifle." See, *e.g.*, Jaeah Lee, Mark Follman and Gavin Aronsen, "More Than Half of Mass Shooters Used Assault Weapons and High-Capacity Magazines," *Mother Jones*, February 27, 2013; Christopher Ingraham, Wonkblog, "Assault rifles are becoming mass shooters' weapon of choice," *The Washington Post*, June 12, 2016.

392 Christopher S. Koper, University of Pennsylvania, 2004, "An Updated Assessment of the Federal Assault Weapns Ban: Impacts on Gun Markets and Gun Violence, 1994-2003," Report to the National Institute of Justice, United States Department of Justice, June 2004.

393 John Donohue and Theodora Boulouta, "That Assault Weapon Ban? It Really Did Work," *The New York Times*, September 4, 2019; Mark Gius, 2018,"The effects of state and Federal gun control laws on school shootings," *Applied Economics Letter*s, 25:5, 317-320, first published online April 19, 2017. Louis Klaveras, RAMPAGE NATION (Amherst, N.Y.: Prometheus Books, 2016); Elzerie de Jager, Eric Goralnick; Justin C. McCarty; *et al.*, "Lethality of Civilian Active Shooter Incidents With and Without Semiautomatic Rifles in the United States," September 11, 2018, JAMA 2018;320(10):1034-1035. Doi:10.1001/jama. 2018.11- 009.

394 Kravitz-Wirtz N, Pallin R, Miller M, *et al,* "Firearm ownership and acquisition in California: findings from the 2018 California Safety and Well-being Survey," *Injury Prevention*, published online December 5, 2019. For a summary, see: Newsroom, "2018 California Safety and Wellbeing Survey details firearm ownership in the state," U.C. Davis Health, November 11, 2018.

395 Alex Yablon, "Most Californians Who Own 'Assault Rifles' Have 10+ Guns," *The Trace, Data,* November. 12, 2018.

396 Louis Klaveras, RAMPAGE NATION (Amherst, N.Y.: Prometheus Books, 2016). See also: Christopher Ingraham, "It's time to bring back the assault weapons ban, gun violence experts say," *The Washington Post,* Wonk Blog, February 15, 2018.

397 Mark Gius, "The impact of state and federal assault weapons bans on public mass shootings," Applied Economics Letters, 22:4, 281-284 (2015); Mark Gius, "The effects of state and Federal gun control laws on school shootings," Applied Economics Letters, 25:5,317-320 (Online April 19, 2017, in print. (2018); Elzerie de Jager, Eric Goralnick, Justin C. McCarty; *et al.*, "Lethality of Civilian Active Shooter Incidents With and Without Semiautomatic Rifles in the United States," Septem-ber 11, 2018, JAMA.2018; 320(10:1034-1035. For a lay discussion, see: Lois Beckett, "Shootings with semi-automatic rifles more deadly than handguns, study says," *The Guardian*, September 11, 2018.

398 Mark Bowden, BLACK HAWK DOWN (New York: Atlantic Monthly Press, 1999) ("Mogadishu was like the post apocalyptic world of Mel Gibson's Mad Max movies, a world ruled by roving gangs of armed thugs.")

399 NBC/Wall Street Journal Survey, Study # 19305. Some 46% of respondents lived in households where someone owned a gun. That was well above the expected range of 33% - 40%..

400 Monmouth University Poll, "National: Public Divided On Assault Weapons Policy," August 16-20, 2019, released September 9, 2019. Note: 34% of the re-spondents in this poll said they personally owned a gun. The expected percentage was about 22% or maybe 25%. This poll's results may be skewed by the large percentage of gun owners who were respondents.

401 Gallup also asked half the sample one version of this question and the other half an easier-to-follow version. The easier-to-follow version. got much higher "Favor" responses. The table averages the responses. One wonders, however, if the responses to the second question, which was more readily understandable, were better reflected what respondents thought they were "for" or "against." Megan Brenan, "Nearly Half in U.S. Fear Being the Victim of a Mass Shooting," Gallup, September 10, 2019.

402 Gallup and SSRS generally get the lowest "support" and the highest "oppose" numbers. It's possible not all of the lower level of support and higher level of opposition here is due to how they framed the question. That may be due in part to how they select respondents or other factors.

403 Mike DeBonis and Emily Guskin, "Americans of both parties overwhelmingly support 'red flag' laws, expanded background checks for gun buyers," Washington Post-ABC News poll finds," *The Washington Post*, September 9, 2019. [Cross Tabs].

404 Among those who lived in households where there were no guns, 79% favored a ban; only 13% opposed.

405 Among those who lived in households where there were no guns, 75% favored a ban; only 14% opposed.

406 Among those who lived in households where there were no guns, 77% favored a ban; only 15% opposed.

407 The percentages are for gun owners rather than gun householders.

408 Among individuals in households in which no one owned a gun, 70% favored a ban; 27% opposed. Langer Research, "Six in 10 Fear a Mass Shooting; Most Think Gun Laws Can Help," ABC News/Washington Post Poll, September 9, 2019, p. 3.

409 NPR/PBS NewsHour/Marist Poll, September 5–8, 2019, released September 10, 2019 [Data Tables].

410 The September 2019 ABC/Washington Post poll also broke out white men and women who were and weren't college graduates. Only 30% of white males who were not four-year-college graduates supported a ban on assault rifles; 64% opposed. In sharp contrast, white women who were not college grads split 58% in favor and 37% opposed to a ban, for a 28 percentage-point gap in support. Among white male college graduates, support was 59%, opposition 39%. Among white female college-graduates, 67% supported a ban and 37% were opposed, for a gap in support of eight percentage points. This adds support to the observation above that white men without college degrees are outliers.

411 Here are more data points on banning semiautomatic rifles: A Baldwin Wallace University poll of Ohioans released March 26, 2019, asked: "Q4: Would you support or oppose a statewide ban on the manufacture, sale, and possession of high-powered rifles capable of semi-automatic fire, such as the AR-15?" 56% of Ohioans supported and 25% opposed such a ban.

412 "Florida Voters Oppose Teachers With Guns, Quinnipiac University Poll Finds; Support For 'Assault Weapon' Ban Almost 2-1," Quinnipiac University, February 28, 2018. https://poll.qu.edu/florida/release-de-tail?Release ID=2524.

413 Elfrink won the George Polk Award and was a finalist for the Goldsmith Prize for Investigative Reporting.

414 Martin Vassolo and David Smiley, "Most Florida voters favor assault-weapons ban, oppose guns in classrooms, polls say," *Miami Herald,* February 28, 2018; Tim Elfrink, "Here Are the Florida Republicans Who Just Blocked Bans on Assault Weapons, Bump Stocks," *Miami New Times,* February 27, 2018.

415 This list is from the Giffords Law Center: Cal. Penal Code §§ 16350, 16790, 16890, 30500-31115; Conn. Gen. Stat. §§ 53-202a—53-202; DC Code Ann. §§ 7-2501.01(3A, 7-2502.02(a(6, 7-2505.01, 7-2505.02(a), (c); Haw. Rev. Stat. Ann. § 134-1, 134-4, 134-8; Md. Code Ann., Crim. Law §§ 4-301 - 4-306; Md. Code Ann., Crim. Law §§ 4-301 - 4-306; Md. Code Ann., Pub. Safety § 5-101(r; Mass. Gen. Laws ch. 140, §§ 121, 122, 123, 131M; N.J. Stat. Ann. §§ 2C:39-1w, 2C:39-5, 2C:58-5, 2C:58-12, 2C:58-13; N.Y. Penal Law §§ 265.00(22), 265.02(7), 265.10, 400.00 (16-a).

416 Thomas Novelly, "Police: Thwarted Kentucky mass shooter had fully auto AR-15, 7 other guns," *Louisville Courier Journal,* November 20, 2018, updated November 21, 2018.

417 WKYT Staff, "Gun control bill introduced to Ky. House," WKYT, February 26, 2018.

418 Chris Mills Rodrigo, "Kentucky governor blames mass shootings in part on zombie shows," *The Hill,* November. 14, 2018. Thomas Novelly, "Do zombie shows lead to mass shootings? Matt Bevin thinks so," *Louisville Courier Journal,* November. 13, 2018, updated, November. 16, 2018.

419 Mandy McLaren, "Gov. Matt Bevin Blames School Shootings on Cell phones," *Louisville Courier Journal,* June 26, 2018.

420 *Heller v. District of Columbia,* 670 F.3d 1244, 1262-64 (D.C. Cir. 2011) [*Heller II*], upholding D.C.'s assault weapon ban; *Friedman v. City of Highland Park,* 784 F.3d 406 (7th Cir. 2015), upholding city's assault weapons ban; *Wilson v. Cook County,* _ F.3d _ (7th Cir. August 29, 2019) (per curiam), declining to revisit *Friedman; New York State Rifle & Pistol Association, Inc. v. Cuomo,* 804 F.3d 242, 263-64 (2d Cir. 2015), upholding New York and Connecticut's assault weapon bans; *Kolbe v. Hogan,* 849 F.3d 114, 138 (4th Cir. 2017) (*en banc*), upholding Maryland assault A weapon ban; *Worman v. Healey,* 922 F.3d 26 (1st Cir. April 26, 2019) (upholding Massachusetts's assault rifle ban. See: Meagan Flynn and Fred Barbash, "Does the Second Amendment really protect assault weapons? Four courts have said no," *The Washington Post,* February 22, 2018 (predating the First Circuit's decision in *Worman.*

421 At the gun show, Ms. Anderson made the purchase from a private seller, not a licensed dealer. If she had bought the guns from a licensed dealer, the purchase would have been an illegal straw purchase. But because she purchased the guns in a private sale, the transaction was legal.

422 "The Killer at Thurston High: Who Is Kip Kinkel?" Frontline. PBS, "Thurston High School Shooting," Wikipedia.

423 Kristina Davis,"Not guilty plea entered for alleged synagogue shooter on 109 federal charges,"*San Diego Union Tribune,* May 14, 2019; "Poway synagogue shooting," Wikipedia.

424 Richard Winton and Patrick McGreevy, "Gilroy Garlic Festival gunman used a rifle banned in California, officials say," July 29, 2019.

425 This hardly needs a citation, but check out CDC, "Youth Risk Be-havior Surveillance--United States," 2017, MMWR 67:8, June 15, 2018. If you are a parent, it will give you plenty to worry about.

426 See, e.g., Thomas A. Loughran, Joan A. Reid, Megan Eileen Collins, and Edward P. Mulvey, "Effect of Gun Carrying on Perceptions of Risk Among Adolescent Offenders," *American Journal of Public Health,* online: January 21, 2016.

427 Cassandra Crifasi, "More States Should Raisethe Ageto Buy Firearms; Semi-

automatic rifles deserve additional scrutiny," *The Trace,* February 1, 2019.

428 P. M. O'Malley, A. C. Wagenaar, "Effects of minimum drinking age laws on alcohol use, related behaviors and traffic crash involvement among American youth: 1976-1987," *Journal of Studies on Alcohol.* 1991;52:478-429 K. A. Vittes, J. S. Vernick, D. W. Webster, "Legal status and source of offenders' firearms in states with the least stringent criteria for gun ownership," *Injury Preventio*n 2012.

430 Compare the Bureau of Justice Statistics, "Homicide Trends in the U.S. 2012," at http://bjs.ojp.usdoj.gov/content/homicide/teens.cfm, with the FBI gov/explporer/national/united-states/shr, with Crime Data Explorer," Offense Characteristics in the United States for 2018," at https://crime-data-explorer.fr.cloud.gov/explorer/national/united-states/shr.

431 Constitution, Art. 1, sec. 2, para. 2. The minimum age to serve in the Senate is thirty. Constitution, Art. 1, sec. 3, para. 3.

432 18 U.S.C. 922(b), (x)(1).

433 18 U.S.C. 922((x)(5).

434 18 U.S.C. 922(b)(1).

435 18 U.S.C 922(b)(2). An ordinance is generally a law enacted by a city. "Published ordinance" has a tortured meaning, but the gist is, for an ordinance to be considered "published," "the Attorney General of the United States must recognize the ordinance as valid and include it in a publication sent to dealers.

436 Brian Freskos, "Here's Why American Teenagers Can Buy AR-15s," *The Trace,* Rounds, February 2018; Roberto A. Ferdman and Christo-pher Ingraham, "In 30 states, a child can still legally own a rifle or shotgun," Wonkblog, *The Washington Post,* August, 27, 2014.

437 18 U.S.C. § 922(x)(1).

438 On the other hand, it was almost certainly against the law for Mr. Kinkel to buy a handgun from a licensed dealer as a straw purchaser for a 15-year-old. It was also against the law for Kip Kinkel to have the handgun.

439 18 U.S.C. § 922(b), (x)(2).

440 Steve Almasy, Anne Claire Stapleton and Ray Sanchez, "Child firing Uzi at Az.shooting range accidentally kills instructor, police say," CNN, August 28, 2014.

441 ABC News/Washington Post Poll, April 8-11, 2018. Among registered voters, the spread was 69% in favor and 28% opposed.

442 Public Policy Polling, "Support For Impeachment At Record High," 4 Q. 31, October 27-29, 2017.

443 Suffolk University/USA Today, August 20-25, 2019, released August 29, 2019, "Poll: 90% of Registered Voters Want Firearm Background Checks."[Marginals, Tables].

444 In the CNN/SSR Ssurvey, in households without guns,a more robust 80% favored

raising the minimum age to 21; only 10% opposed.

445 In this Morning Consult poll, in house holds without guns,87% favored requiring a person to be 21 to buy a gun; only 9% opposed.

446 To put the 21% in context: In a Suffolk/USA Today poll in March 2018, 19% rejected the unanimous conclusion of US intelligence agencies and said they did not believe Russia made a serious attempt to meddle in the 2016 election. On the other hand, 68.5% acknowledged that it did.

447 See, *e.g.*, Jordyn Phelps, "Trump calls for raising minimum age to buy all guns to 21," ABC News, February 28, 2018.

448 Jill Colvin, AP, "Trump backs off call for raising minimum age to buy gun," *The Denver Post*, March 11, 2018; Jack Crowe, "White House Backs Away from Increasing Age Restrictions on Gun Purchases," *National Review*, March 12, 2018.

449 Dan Sweeney, "Florida House sends Stoneman Douglas gun and school bill to Gov. Scott," *The Sun Sentinel*, March 7, 2018

450 Laura Meckler, "School safety commission poised to oppose new age limits on gun buys," *The Washington Post*, September 12, 2018.

451 "Final Report Of The Federal Commission On School Safety," presented to the President of The United States, Part 1, Ch. 10, pp. 85-88, December 18, 2018.

452 Long guns and assault rifles are infrequently used in child and teen suicides.

453 Jordain Carney, "Feinstein to introduce bill raising age to purchase assault weapons after California shooting," *The Hill*, April 29, 2019; *The Trace, Canon*, May 5, 2019. See: S.66, To Regulate assault weapons, 116th Cong (2019- 2020).

454 Sam Quinones and Nicole Santa Cruz, "Crowd Members Took Gunman Down," *Los Angeles Times*, 39 7 January 9, 2011. For a slightly different version, see: Lanae Erickson Hatalsky and Hayden Thomas, "How High Is Our Capacity for Carnage? It's time for a federal ban on high-capacity magazines," US News.com, November 30, 2017.

455 Associated Press, "Man convicted in Seattle Pacific University shooting that killed student, "Fox News, November 16, 2016; Chris D'Angelo,"Video Shows Student's Heroic Takedown Of Gunman During Seattle Pacific University Shooting," *Huffington Post*, June 15, 2016; Mike Carter, "Dramatic video shows hero disarming shooter at Seattle Pacific University in 2014," *Seattle Times*, June 14, 2016, updated November 15, 2016. The incident did not involve a large-capacity magazine.

456 Christopher Mele and Jacey Fortin, "Man Sought in Waffle House Shooting Had Been Arrested Near White House," *The New York Times*, April 22, 2018.

457 *Kolbe v. Hogan*, 859 F.3d 114 (4th Cir. 2017 (King, J.).

458 "Tallahassee shooting," Wikipedia and sources collected there; Steve Hendrix, "He always hated women. Then he decided to kill them, " *The Washington Post*, June 7, 2019

(discussing Beierle's links to the "incel"—involuntary celibacy—movement.

459 Reed Williams and Shawna Morrison, "Police: No motive found," *The Roanoke Times*, May 2, 2014.

460 "Sandy Hook Elementary School shooting," Wikipedia.

461 David A. Fahrenthold, "Colorado shooting spree could have been worse; shooter's gun jammed, official says," *The WashingtonPost*, July 22, 2012;"Rifle failure that stopped yet more Batman carnage," *Daily Express*, July 23, 2012; "2012 Aurora shooting," Wikipedia.

462 Bart Jansen, "Weapons gunman used in Orlando shooting are high-capacity, common," *USA Today*, June 14, 2016.

463 Kevin Williams, Hannah Knowles, Hannah Natanson and Peter Whoriskey, "Gunman killed sister, eight others in second deadly U.S. mass shooting in 24 hours" *The Washington Post*, August 4, 2019.

464 Mark Follman and Gavin Aronsen, "'A Killing Machine': Half of All Mass Shooters Used High-Capacity Magazines," *Mother Jones*, January 30 2013, "Magazines holding more than 10 rounds were used in 31 of the 62 mass shootings we investigated." See also: Griff Witte, "As mass shootings rise, experts say high-capacity magazines should be the focus," *The Washington Post*, August 18, 2019.

465 Louis Klarevas, Andrew Conner, David Hemenway, "The Effect of Large-Capacity Magazine Bans on High-Fatality Mass Shootings, 1990–2017," A*merican Journal of Public Health* 109, no.12, December1,2019, pp. 1754-1761. https://doi. org/10.2105/AJPH.2019.305311. PMID:31622147.464. Louis Klarevas, Andrew Conner, David Hemenway, "The Effect of Large-Capacity Magazine Bans on High-Fatality Mass Shootings, 1990–2017," *American Journal of Public Health* 109, no. 12, December 1, 2019: pp.754-1761. https://doi.org/10.2105/AJPH.2019.305311. PMID: 31622147.

466 D.W. Webster, A.D. McCourt, C.K. Crifasi, *et al.*, "Evidence concerning the regulation of firearms design, sale, and carrying on fatal mass shootings in the United States," *Criminology and Public Policy*. 2020;19:171–212.https://doi.org/10.1111/1745- 9133.12487.

467 Rhode Island Coalition Against Violence, High Capacity Magazines are the Accessory of Choice for Mass Killers, https://www.ricagv.org/ban-high-capacity-magazines/.

468 *Idem.*

469 See the incidents at the beginning of this chapter.1.

470 In a recent decision, *Association of New Jersey Rifle And Pistol Clubs, Inc.. v. Attorney General New Jersey*, No. 18-3170 (3rd Cir. December 5, 2018), the court cited several examples, including an incident during the Naval Yard shooting, where the shooter tried to kill a woman, was out of ammunition, left to reload, and returned. By then, she found a

new hiding spot and ultimately survived The court also mentioned the 2012 Newton shooting, describing an escape while the shooter reloaded.

471 Mark Follman and Gavin Aronsen, "'A Killing Machine': Half of All Mass Shooters Used High-Capacity Magazines," *Mother Jones,* January 30, 2013.

472 See, *e.g.*, the responses on Quora to the question, "Why does there seem to be so much resistance to a ban on high capacity magazines in the US?"

473 Chris Bast, "2nd Amendment Absolutist," responding on Quora to the question, "Why does there seem to be so much resistance to a ban on high capacity magazines in the US?" Answered June 15, 2016.

474 Paul Harding, responding on Quora to the question, "Why does there seem to be so much resistance to a ban on high capacity magazines in the US?" Updated July 2, 2016.

475 Shannon McRee, Gun Owner, Shooter, Vocal 2A Advocate responding on Quora to the question, "Why does there seem to be so much resistance to a ban on high capacity magazines in the US?" Answered July 24, 2017.

476 C. S. Allely, P. Wilson, H. Minnis, *et al.*, 2017, "Violence is Rare in Autism: When It Does Occur, Is It Sometimes Extreme?" *The Journal of Psychology*, 151:1, DOI: 0.1080/00223980.2016.1175998. There is no evidence that people with ADHD or Autism Spectrum Disorder are more violent than people at large, but rare instances have occurred.

477 Jason Dusek, responding on Quora to the question, "Why does there seem to be so much resistance to a ban on high capacity magazines in the US?" December 28, 2018.

478 Scott Calvert, Zusha Elinson and Sadie Gurman, "Virginia Beach Shooting Leaves at Least 12 Dead," Wall Street Journal, May 31, 2019; Michael E. Miller, Lynh Bui and Julie Zauzmer, "DeWayne Craddock, a long-time Virginia Beach employee, identified as shooter who killed 12 in city building," The Washington Post, June 1, 2019; Bill Hutchinson, "Gunman used security pass, two .45-caliber guns to kill 12 people at Virginia Beach municipal building ," ABC News, June 1, 2019.

479 "Thousand Oaks Shooting," Wikipedia0.

480 "Stephen Paddock," Wikipedia

481 Philip Alpers, "If lawful firearm owners cause most gun deaths, what can we do?" *The Conversation,* October 6, 2015.

482 Jason Dusek, San Francisco Tech Person, responding to the question, "Why does there seem to be so much resistance to a ban on high capacity magazines in the US?" Quora, Answered December 30, 2018.

483 Polls haven't addressed the issue, but I suspect many gun-violence-prevention advocates would be satisfied if gun owners of that persuasion would bury

their large-capacity magazines in their backyards, preferably where no mentally unbalanced teenager knows their location.

484 Dan Barry, "Looking Behind the Mug-Shot Grin," *The New York Times,* January 15, 2011. ISSN 0362-4331; NBC, msnbc.com and news services, "Loughner's parents 'devastated,' 'hurting,'" MSNBC; "Jared Lee Loughner," Wikipedia.

485 C. Caves, Law enforcement, firearms instructor, SWAT Sniper, responding onQuora to the question, "Why does there seem to be so much resistance to a ban on high capacity magazines in the US?" Updated March 6, 2018.

486 Chris Bast, 2nd Amendment Absolutist, responding on Quora to the question, "Why does there seem to be so much resistance to a ban on high capacity magazines in the US?" Answered Jun 15, 2016

487 Kyle Mantyla, "Congressman Louie Gohmert opposes gun control because gay marriage leads to bestiality," *Right Wing Watch,* April 2, 2013.

488 *Idem.*

489 See, *e.g., New York State Rifle And Pistol Association Inc LLC v. Gerald J. Gill, in his official capacity as Chief of Police for the Town of Lancaster, New York,* Nos. 14–36–cv (2d Cir. 2015).

490 Michael Hiltzik, "Assault guns are not just about mass shootings—they're also a big factor in attacks on police and other crimes," Los Angeles Times, October 9, 2017.

491 Christopher S. Koper, William D. Johnson, Jordan L. Nichols, *et al.,* "Criminal Use of Assault Weapons and High-Capacity Semiautomatic Firearms: An Updated Examination of Local and National Sources," *J. Urban of Health,* 2018 95:313-321. DOI: 10.1007/s11 524-017-0205-7, October 2, 2017.

492 David S. Fallis and James V. Grimaldi, "Virginia Data Show Drop in Criminal Firepower During Assault Gun Ban," *The Washington Post,* January 23, 2011; "About the Project: The Hidden Life of Guns," *The Washington Post,* January 22, 2011.

493 Citizens Crime Commission of New York City, "NYC & LA City Councils Introduce Rezo for Federal Ban on Large Capacity Ammunition Magazines," March 2, 2011.

494 CNN, SSRS Poll, October 12-15, 2017, Q. 9.

495 CNN, SSRS Poll, February 20-23, 2018, Q. 21.

496 Quinnipiac University, June 21-27,2016, released June 30, 2016. "Overwhelming Suppot For No-Fly, No-Buy Gun Law, Quinnipiac University National Poll Finds; Support For Background Checks Tops 90 Percent Again," Q. 54.

497 In the CNN, SSRS Poll, February 20-23, 2018, 71% from non-gun households favored and 26% opposed.

498 Cal. Penal Code § 16740 (ten rounds); Colo. Rev. Stat. § 18-12-301(2)(a)(I) (fifteen

rounds); Conn. Gen. Stat. § 53-202w7 (ten rounds); D.C.Code§ 7-2506.01(b) (ten rounds;Haw. Rev. Stat. § 134-8(c) (ten rounds); Md. Code Ann., Crim. Law § 4-305(b) (ten rounds); Mass. Gen. Laws Ch. 140 §§ 121, 131M (ten rounds); N.J. Stat. Ann. 2C:39-1 (y)2C:39-3(j) (ten rounds); N.Y. Penal Law § 265.00(23) (ten rounds; 13 Vt. Stat. Ann. 4021(e)(1)(A, B)(ten rounds for a "long gun" and fifteen rounds for a "handgun").

499 Robert McCartney, "In January, the Virginia GOP killed bill to ban sales of large-capacity magazines," *The Washington Post,* June 1, 2019.

500 The media have covered this saga extensively, but Matt Cohen offers a nice recap in his article, "Bullets vs. Ballots," *Mother Jones,* January/February 2020, pp. 11-13.

501 See, e.g., Gregory S. Schneider and Laura Vozzella, "Prospect of gun control in Virginia draws threats, promise of armed protest," *The Washington Post,* January 5, 2020.

502 On February 17, 2020, four Democrats joined with Republican legislators in the Senate Judiciary Committee, to defeat the bill that would have banned assault rifles and LCMs in Virginia. Timothy Williams, "Virginia Legislature Turns Down Ban on Military-Style Weapons," *The New York Times,* February 17, 2020.

503 See:*Duncanv.Becerra,* 265 F.Supp.3d 1106 (S.D. Cal. 2017).

504 V*irginia Duncan et al. v. Xavier Becerra,* No. 17-56081 (9th Cir. July 17, 2018) (Not for publication).

505 William Cummings, "Court blocked law that would have made posses-sion of magazine in Thousand Oaks illegal," *USA Today,* November 8, 2018, updated November 11, 2018.

506 In the federal system, there are eleven numbered circuits plus the important District of Columbia Circuit.

507 *New York State Rifle And Pistol Association Inc LLC v. Gerald J. Gill, in his official capacity as Chief of Police for the Town of Lancaster, New York,* Nos. 14–36–cv (2d Cir. October 19, 2015).

508 *Association of New Jersey Rifle And Pistol Clubs, Inc. v. Attorney General New Jersey,* No. 18-3170, 910 F3d 106 (3rd Cir. 2018).

509 *N.Y. State Rifle & Pistol Association, Inc. v. Cuomo,* 804 F.3d 242, 263-64 (2d Cir. 2015 (upholding New York and Connecticut's ten-round limit).

510 *Kolbe v. Hogan,* 849 F.3d114, 138 (4th Cir. 2017) (*en banc*), upholding Maryland's ten round limit.

511 *Friedman v. City of Highland Park,* 784 F.3d 406, 411-12 (7th Cir. 2015), upholding city's ten-round limit; *Wilson v. Cook County,* _ F.3d _ (7th Cir., August 29, 2019) (de-lining to revisit Friedman).

512 *Fyock v. City of Sunnyvale,* 779 F.3d 991, 1000 (9th Cir. 2015 (upholding city's ten-round limit.

513 *Heller v. District of Columbia,* 670 F.3d 1244, 1262-64 (D.C. Cir. 2011) [*Heller I*] (up-holding D.C.'s ten round limit).

514 *Workman v. Healey,* 922 F.3d 26 (1st Cir. 2019) (upholding Massachusetts ten-round limit).

515 Slide Fire, LP, website, https://slidefire.com/company/.

516 Joseph Lombardo, Sheriff, "LVMPD Criminal Investigative Report of the 1 October Mass Casualty Shooting," LVMPD Event Number 171001-3519, Las Vegas Metropolitan Police Department, August 3, 2018; and "The Las Vegas Mass Shooter Had 13 Rifles Outfitted with Bump Stocks. He Used Them to Fire 1,049 Rounds," *The Trace*, August 3, 2018; and "2017 Las Vegas Shooting," Wikipedia.

517 Jonathan Berr, "Bump stock prices soar ahead of potential federal ban," CBS MoneyWatch, February 22, 2018; Michael Smith and Polly Mosendz, "The Making of a Millionaire and a Massacre," *Bloomberg Business Week*, October 11, 2017.

518 ATF, "Notice of Proposed Rulemaking, Bump Stock Type Devices," 83 FR 13442 (March 29, 2018) ("Notice").

519 Notice, *op cit.*, 83 FR 13443.

520 S.1916 - Automatic Gunfire Prevention Act, 115th Congress (2017 - 2018).

521 Ali Rogin, "Sen. Feinstein introducing bill to ban bump stocks after Vegas shooting," ABC News, October 4, 2017.

522 *Idem*.

523 Chris Cillizza, CNN Editor-at-large, "The NRA's strategic ploy on bump stocks," CNN, October 6, 2017.

524 See, *e.g.*, Russell Berman, "Why a Congressional Ban on Bump Stocks Is Unlikely," *The Atlantic*, October 19, 2017; Rebecca Shabad,"Proposed bans on bump stocks have stalled in Congress," CBS News, November. 6, 2017.

525 Department of Justice, Bureau of Alcohol, Tobacco, Firearms, and Explosives, ATF, Application of the Definition of Machinegun to "Bump Fire" Stocks and Other Similar Devices, Advance notice of proposed rulemaking; request for comments [DocketNo.2017R–22] RIN 1140–AA52, 82 F.R.60929, December 26, 2017 ("Advance Notice").

526 Lois Beckett, "Rapid fire rifle device on special offer in salute to Trump, 'Bump stock' used by Las Vegas shooter in promotional tie in with presidential campaign slogan," *The Guardian*, February18, 2018; "'Bump Stock' Manufacturer Offers Special 'MAGA' Coupon For President's Day," *Crooks and Liars*, February 21, 2018.

527 President Donald J. Trump, "Application of the Definition of Machinegun to 'Bump Fire' Stocks and Other Similar Devices," Memorandum for the Attorney General, February 20, 2018, 83 FR 7949 (February 23, 2018.) With its usual problems with spelling and terminology, the President's memorandum referred to the Department's "Advance Notice" of proposed rulemaking as an "Advanced Notice."

528 Jonathan Berr, "Bump stock prices soar ahead of potential federal ban," CBS *Money Watch*, February 22, 2018.

GUNS, POLLS, and DEMOCRACY

529 Department Of Justice, Bureau of Alcohol, Tobacco, Firearms, and Explosives, Notice of Proposed Rulemaking,[Docket No. 2017R–22; AG Order No. 4132– 2018] RIN 1140–AA52 Bump-Stock-Type Devices, 83 F.R. 13442 (March 29, 2018).530 Betsy Klein and Laura Jarrett, "Trump says ban on 'bump stocks' coming," CNN, October 2, 2018.

531 Editorial Board, "Takeaways of the failure to ban bump stocks," New York Post, March 7, 2018.532 Aaron Smith, "Bump stock maker Slide Fire will stop taking orders and is shutting down its website," Money. CNN.com, April 17, 2018; Associated Press, "Largest maker of bump stocks will stop accepting orders," The Los Angeles Times, April 18, 2018.

533 "What else to know this week," *The Trace,* July 28, 2018. ("RW Arms bragged on its website,"STOCKS. STOCKED. Our warehouse is loaded with bump stocks from Slide Fire and Bump Fire Systems.")

534 In Quinnipiac's October poll, 82% of Democrats favored and only 17% opposed a ban on bump stocks.

535 In the Ipsos-NPR poll, October 10–11, 2017, Democrats split 88% to 12%.536 In the CBS poll, Democrats split 52% in favor and 46% oppose—figures that are simply not credible when compared with other available data. No explanation is apparent.

537 In the February 15-19, 2018 Morning Consult poll, 51% of Republicans felt "strongly" that there should be a ban.

538 In the Ipsos-NPR poll conducted February 27-28, 2018, 92% of Demo-crats wanted a ban on bump stocks; only 8% opposed.

539 In the Morning Consult poll in August 2018, 86% of Democrats favored a ban; only 9% opposed.

540 YouGov, Daily Poll, December 20, 2018. (Democrats favored the ban 85% to 6%.).

541 YouGov, Daily Poll, October 5, 2017 (Family income > $80,000.

542 YouGov, Daily Poll, December 20, 2018 ("The Trump administration recently banned bump stocks, the firearm attachments that allow semi-automatic weapons to fire like machine guns. Bump stock owners will be required to either destroy them or surrender them to the Bureau of Alcohol, Tobacco, Firearms and Explosives. Do you agree or disagree with the decision to ban them?")

543 ATF, Final Rule, 82 FR 66514-66554 (December 26, 2018).

544 Morgan Gstalter, "Pro-gun group sues Trump administration over bump stock ban," The Hill, December 27, 2018. See also: Firearms Policy Coalition v. Acting Attorney General Whitaker et al., discussed on the Firearms Policy Coalition's website.

545 *Damien Guedes et al. v. Bureau of Alcohol, Tobacco and Firearms,* D. D.C., Civil Action

No. 18-cv-2988 DFF (Dabney Friedrich, D.J.)

546 *Damien Guedes, et al. v. Bureau Of Alcohol, Tobacco, Firearms And Explosives*, No. 19-5042, consolidated with 19-5044 (D.C. Cir. April 1, 2019) (per curiam).

547 Jessica Miller, "Federal judge denies a Utah gun enthusiast's attempt to halt the ban on bump stocks," *The Salt Lake City Tribune*, March 18, 2019.

548 *Damien Guedes, et al. v. Bureau of Alcohol, Tobacco, Firearms and Explosives, et al.*, No. 19-296, *cert. denied*, 589 U.S. _ (2020).

549 *Damien Guedes, et al. v. Bureau of Alcohol, Tobacco, Firearms and Explosives, et al.*, No. 19-296, *cert. denied*, 589 U.S. _ (March 2, 2020) (Statement by Gorsuch. J.).

550 *The Modern Sportsman, LLC. v. The United States*, U.S. Court of Claims, Case No.19-449 (October 23, 2019). See also: Asher Stockler, "'Bump Stock Owners Forced To Destroy Devices Can't Get Compensation From Feds, Judge Says," *Newsweek*, October 25, 2019; *The Trace, Daily Bulletin*, October 28, 2019.

551 Nicole Cobler, "Banning bump stocks is one thing, prying them from owners' hands is another," *Dallas News*, October 17, 2017

552 Kelly Bostian, "'Possibility for Civil War': Owners Not Interested in turning bump stocks over to government," *Tulsa World*, December 20, 2018.

553 Amy Russo, "Parkland Father Calls Bump Stock Ban A 'Small Band-Aid on a Glaring Wound," *Huffington Post*, March 26, 2019.

554 Giffords Law Center, Gun Law Trend Watch, 2018 Mid-Year Review. See also: "What else to know this week," *The Trace*, July 28, 2018.

555 Governor Sisolak Signs Controversial Gun Bill Into Law, KTVN, May 29, 2019, June 14, 2019; *The Trace*, June 16, 2019.

556 Allison Alderman, "Gun Law Trend Watch 2019, Year-End Review," Giffords Law Center, December 18, 2019.

557 Tewksbury Police Department report, 18-12740-AR, March 25, 2018; Tewksbury Police press releases, "Joint Release: Two Held Without Bail in Connection with Possession of Weapons and Ammunition in Tewksbury," March 3, 2018; "Two Arrested on Weapons Charges," March 25, 2018; O'Ryan Johnson, "Texas duo become first in nation charged under bump stock ban," *Boston Herald*, March 26, 2018.

558 Robert Mills, "UPDATE: Texas man facing Tewksbury weapons charges said he was on classified government mission," Lowell Sun, March 26, 2018; Crime Sider Staff, "Cops: Man arrested with weapons cache, bump stock claimed secret government mission," CBS/AP, March 28, 2018. Adrianne Jennings later plead guilty to reduced charges in exchange for agreeing to cooperate in the prosecution of her common law husband. Robert Mills, "Wife in gun cache case cooperates," October 27, 2018.

559 Charles Rabin, "Toddler shot himself while dad was throwing out a diaper, cops say. 2 men charged," Miami Herald, February 1, 2019; Tom Porter, "Florida Father Arrested After Toddler Shoots Himself In Stomach In Miami-Dade Property: Police," Newsweek, February 2, 2019; Fred Grimm, "Florida's tepid gun storage law leads to bloody carnage among kids," South Florida Sun Sentinel, March 22, 2019. 560 Jeff Truesdell, "Girl, 6, Killed When Little Brother Grabs Gun From Center Console and Shoots Her Accidentally; Millie Drew Kelly died two days after the shooting," People, April, 15, 2019; "A 4-year-old Georgia boy fatally shot his 6-year-old sister," sister," The Trace, Daily Bulletin, April 12, 20190561 Associated Press, "4-year-old dies after finding gun from dad, an Ohio statet rooper," WLWT, May 14, 2019; The Trace, Daily Bulletin, May 15, 2019.

562 WTVG, "Ohio State Trooper found guilty in gun death of 4-year-old son, 2019, updated May 15, 2019; The Trace, Daily Bulletin, May 16, 2018.

563 WREG Staff and Luke Jones, "Man charged after 8-year-old accidentally shot mother at Millington baseball game," WREG Channel 3, News, May 14, 2019, updated May 15, 2019; The Trace, Daily Bulletin, May 16, 2019.

564 Adam Friedman, "Police: 3-year-old boy finds gun and kills himself; mother and roommate charged with homicide," Jackson Sun, May 14, 2019; Associated Press, "Police: Tennessee toddler found gun, fatally shot self," WREG Channel 3 News, May 15, 2019.

565 "Cassandra Stephenson, "Mother, roommate indicted on murder and child neglect charges after 3-year-old found gun, killed himself," *Jackson Sun*, November 4, 2019.

566 "Children are likely to play with a gun if they find one," The Trace, December 6, 2018, citing Kate Masters, "The NRA Says 'Eddie Eagle,' Not New Laws, Is the Way to Keep Curious Kids Away from Unsecured Guns," The Trace, April 12, 2016. Discusses: Brian J. Gatheridge, Raymond G. Miltenberger, Daniel F. Huneke, et al., "Comparison of Two Programs to Teach Firearm Injury Prevention Skills to 6- and 7-Year-Old Children," Pediatrics, vol. 114, No. 3, September 1, 2004.

567 Michael B. Himle, Raymond G. Miltenberger, Brian J. Gatheridge, et al., "An Evaluation of Two Procedures for Training Skills to Prevent Gun Play in Children," Pediatrics, vol. 113, No. 1, January 2004.

568 See, e.g., ABC News, "What Young Kids Do With Guns When Parents Aren't Around," January 31, 2014. Diane Sawyer, "Young Guns," 20/20, January 31, 2014; Bradley Blackburn, "Kids and guns: What happens when a child finds a gun? An experiment at Cook Children's Medical Center in Fort Worth placed kids in a room with hidden guns," WFAA, November 14, 2018; Cheryl Holly, "Gun safety programs for kids make parents feel safe having guns at home. But they don't work," NBC News, Think, June 18, 2018.

569 Nick Penzenstadler, "A toddler found a handgun and fatally shot himself. His case is one of at least 73 accidental child deaths involving a gun in 2018," USA Today, March 19, 2019.

570 State Child Fatality Advisory Committee, "SFY 2018 Report, July 2017 – June 2018." For discussion, see Anna Lee, "Unsecured guns were used in dozens of child deaths in SC in recent years, report says," *The Greenville News*, June 28, 2019; "A quarter of sudden deaths of children in South Carolina involve unsecured firearms," *The Trace, Daily Bulletin*, July 1, 2019.

571 Nick Wing, "8 Children Are Accidentally Shot Every Day With Unsecured Firearms In The Home," *Huffington Post*, August 8, 2018.

572 For more information, see: EndFamilyFire.org

573 Christopher Ingraham, "American toddlers are still shooting people on a weekly basis this year," *The Denver Post*, September 30, 2017; Walter Einenkel, "For the last 3 years, toddlers have been shooting themselves and others on a weekly basis," *Daily Kos*, June 8, 2018.

574 Venessa Brown, "The gun massacre America isn't talking about," New Zealand *Herald*, June 25, 2017.

575 John Cheeves and Marcus Dorsey, "Guns and Kids," *Herald Leader*, July 21, 2017, updated August 14, 2018.

576 Researchers use a reasonable but somewhat arbitrary cut-off when counting suicides: A child who kills himself or herself must be at least 10 years old to be considered a suicide.

577 See, *e.g.,* Alex Yablon, "Gun safes work. But most gun owners don't use them," *The Washington Post*, June 4, 2018.

578 Sean Campbell, Daniel Nass, and Mai Nguyen, "The CDC Says Gun Injuries Are on the Rise. But There Are Big Problems With Its Data," *The Trace*, October 4, 2018; Sean Campbell, Daniel Nass and Mai Nguyen, "The CDC Is Publishing Unreliable Data On Gun Injuries. People Are Using It Anyway," *Five Thirty Eight*, October 4, 2018; Sean Campbell and Daniel Nass, "How One Hospital Dramatically Skewed the CDC's Estimate of Nonfatal Gun Injuries," *The Trace, Daily Bulletin*, August 13, 2019.

579 These figures are from the CDC WISQARS database. The CDC did not publish estimates of the number of children in certain age groups who visited Emergency Departments with nonfatal gunshot wounds because its sample size was too small to estimate the numbers injured accurately.

580 Sally C. Curtin, Melonie Heron, Arialdi M. Minino, *et al.*, "Recent Increases in Injury Mortality Among Children and Adolescents Aged 10-19 Years in the United States: 1999-2016," National Vital Statistics Reports, Vol. 67, No. 4, June 1, 2018, Table 2. See also: Fowler, 2017, *supra.*

581 Kathleen A. Fowler, Linda L. Dahlberg, Ph.D., Tadese Haileyesus, M.S., Carmen

Gutierrez, M.A., Sarah Bacon, Ph.D., "Children Firearm Injuries in the Unit-ed States," Pediatrics, 2017;140(1)e20163486, July 2017. 582 Anita Knopov, Rebecca J. Sherman, Julia R. Raifman, *et al.*, "Household Gun Ownership and Youth Suicide Rates at the State Level, 2005-2015," *American Journal of Preventive Medicine,* vol. 56, Issue 3 (March 2019), pp. 335-342.

583 John Woodrow Cox and Steven Rich, "'The gun's not in the closet,'" *The Washington Post,* August 1, 2018; *The Trace,* August 5, 2018; Sean Rossman, "Children are killing themselves more and more with guns," *USA Today,* June 19, 2017, citing: Katherine A. Fowler, Linda L. Dahlberg, Tadese Haileyesus, *et al.,* "Children Firearm Injuries in the United States," *Pediatrics,* 2017;140(1)e2016 3486, July 2017.

584 Editorial Board, "Want to prevent school shootings? Lock up guns," *The Washington Post,* August 21, 2018.

585 Jillian Peterson and James Densley, "Op-Ed: We have studied every mass shooting since 1966. Here's what we've learned about the shooters," *The Los Angles Times,* August 4, 2019.

586 National Center for Education Statistics, "Indicatorm 14: Students Carry-ing Weapons on School Property and Anywhere and Students' Access to Firearms," Youth Risk Behavior Survey, updated March 2018.

587 Dave Broucher, "Special report: In Tennessee, a gun or threat is reported at school every 3 days," *Nashville Tennessean,* October 6, 2018, updated October 7, 2018.

588 Colleen L. Barry, Daniel W. Webster, Elizabeth Stone, et al., "Public Support for Gun Violence Prevention Policies Among Gun Owners and Non–Gun Owners in 2017," *American Journal Of Public Health*, June 6, 2018.

589 APM Survey, July 16-21, 2019.

590 Morning Consult, National Tracking Poll #171004, October 5-9, 2017, released, October 17, 2017, Table POL6_16; Steven Shepard, "Poll: Majority backs stricter gun control laws after Vegas shooting," *Politico PlayBook,* October 11, 2017.

591 Morning Consult, National Tracking Poll #180217, February 22-26, 2018, 42 Table POL7_15.

592 Morning Consult, National Tracking Poll #180805, August 2-6, 2018, Table, POL15_13.

593 AMP Research Labs, July 16-21, 2019, released August 20 and October 2, 2019, "Part 3: Mandating that guns be stored with locks in place," October 2, 2019.

594 18 U.S.C. § 922(z)(1).

595 18 U.S.C. § 922(z)(3).
596 Giffords Law Center, Child Access Laws.
597 American Association of Pediatrics, State Advocacy Focus, "Safe Storage of Firearms."
598 Allison Anderman, "Year-End Trendwatch: 2019 Was a Record Year for Gun Safety," December 19, 2019.
599 Alexis Arnold, "New Delaware Law Requires Safe Storage of Firearms," *Huff Post*, June 7, 2019.
600 "[Nevada] Governor Sisolak Signs Controversial Gun Bill Into Law," KTVN, May 29, 2019, June 14, 2019; *The Trace, Daily Bulletin,* June 11, 2019.
601 D.W. Webster and M. Starnes, "Reexamining the association between child access prevention gun laws and unintentional shooting deaths of children," *Pediatrics*.2000;106(6):1466–1469; L. Hepburn, D.Azrael, M. Miller, *et al.,* "The effect of child access prevention laws on unintentional child firearm fatalities, 1979–2000." *J. Trauma*.2006; 61(2):423–428; Azad HA, Monuteaux MC, Rees C Aetal., "Child Access Prevention Firearm Laws and Firearm Fatalities Among Children Aged 0 to 14 Years, 1991-2016.."*JAMAPediatrics*.2020;174(5):463–469.Doi:10.1001/jama-pediatrics.2019.6227.
602 D.W. Webster, J.S. Vernick, A.M. Zeoli, *et al.,* "Association between youth-focused firearm laws and youth suicides," JAMA.2004;292(5):594–601. PMID:15292085. DOI: 10.1001/jama.292.5.594; Joseph A. Simonetti, Ali Rowhani-Rahbar, Brianna Mills, "State Firearm Legislation and Nonfatal Firearm Injuries," AJPH, online July 9, 2015; Kate C. Prickett, Alexa Martin-Storey, and Robert Crosnoe, "State Firearm Laws, Firearm Ownership, and Safety Practices Among Families of Preschool-Aged Children," *Am J. Public Health.* 2014 June; 104(6:1080–1086.PMCID: PMC 4061995, PMID: 24825210, online June 2014.
603 D. Mark Anderson and Joseph J. Sabia, "Child Access Prevention laws, Youth Gun Carrying, and School Shootings," Discussion Paper No. 9830, Institute for the Study of Labor, IZA, Bonn, Germany, March 2016.
604 D. Mark Anderson, Joseph J. Sabia, and Erdal Tekin, "Child Access Pre-vention Laws and Juvenile Firearm-Related Homicides," NBER Working Papers 25209, National Bureau of Economic Research, Inc., 2018; D. Mark Anderson, Joseph J. Sabia, and Erdal Tekin, "Child Access Prevention Laws and Juvenile Firearm-Related Homicides," September 2019.
605 "2019 El Paso Shooting." Wikipedia.
606 S. Chapman, P. Alpers, K. Agho, M. Jones, "2006: Australia's 1996 gun law reforms: faster falls in firearm deaths, firearm suicides, and a decade without

mass shootings," Injury Prevention 12:365–372; S. Chapman, P. Alpers, K. Agho, et al., "Australia's 1996 gun law reforms: faster falls in firearm deaths," Injury Preven-tion 2015;21:355-3621 July 19, 2016. Simon Chapman, Philip Alpers, Michael Jones, "Association Between Gun Law Reforms and Intentional Firearm Deaths in Australia, 1979-2013," JAMA.2016; 316(3):291-299.doi:10.1001/jama. 2016.8752.

607 Simon Chapman, Philip Alpers, Michael Jones, "Association Between Gun Law Reforms and Intentional Firearm Deaths in Australia, 1979-2013," JAMA. 2016; 316(3):291-99. doi: 10.1001/jama.2016.8752.2

608 When Camus wrote The Great Replacement, he focused on France specifically and more broadly, on Europe. The Alt Right has generalized his theory into a white-genocide conspiracy theory. See: "Great Replacement," Wikipedia.

609 Belief in the basic premises of "the Great Replacement" conspiracy theory is not limited to mass shooters or the Alt Right. In its October 2019 report on that year's American Values Survey, PRRI found that 63% of Republicans believed that "immigrants are invading our country and replacing our cultural and ethnic background." Among Republicans who relied on Fox News as their primary news source, that figure rose to 78%. PRRI Staff, "Fractured Nation, Widening Partisan Polarization And Key Issues In 2020 Presidential Elections," PRRI, October 20, 2019, pp. 31-31.

610 Melissa K. Merry, WARPED NARRATIVES, Distortion in the framing of Gun Policy, Ann Arbor: University of Michigan Press, 2020.

611 Andrew T. Post, responding on Quora to the question, "Would Americans actually shoot cops or government officials if there was a mandatory gun buy-back?" Answered December 3.

612 *Idem.* Some of those other "idiotic, tyrannical, and wrongheaded ideas," I suspect, are unpolluted water and air and measures to mitigate the coming climate change disaster.

613 Lynn Vavreck, John Sides, and Chris Tausa Novitch, "What Is High Priority for Voters? In Both Parties, It's Impeachment," *The New York Times,* December 5, 2019.

614 CNN SRSS, "Rel. 10B Trump, Guns," October 12-15, 2017, released October 17, 2017. CNN October 2017. See: Jennifer Agiesta, "CNN poll: Trump approval steady, but more say he's leading in the wrong direction," CNN, October 17, 2017.

615 CNN SRSS, February 20-23, 2018. CNN Poll was conducted by SSRS February 20-23. See: Jennifer Agiesta, "CNN Poll: Seven in 10 favor tighter gun laws in wake of Parkland shooting."

616 Gallup Poll, March 5-11, 2018, released March 15, 2018. "Americans' Views on Measures to Prevent Mass School Shootings, Trends," Gallup News Service, March 15, 2018.

617 Public Policy Polling, "Democrats and Republicans differ on conspiracy theory

beliefs," April 2, 2013, Q.16. (Unfortunately, there's no way to know how much overlap there is between the two groups of 15%.).

618 Quinnipiac University, April 11, 2018, released April 11, 2018. "Trade War With China Is Bad, U.S. Voters Say 3-1, Quinnipiac University National Poll Finds; Voters Support National Guard, But Not The Wall." Q.2, Unfavorable opinion of Congress Q.41, 52% favorable impression of the Parkland student leaders, 33% unfavorable, and 13% hadn't heard enough about the students to have an opinion.

619 In the same poll, a scant 3% of Democrats thought Congress was doing enough; 95% said it was not.

620 Maggie Astor and Karl Russell, "After Parkland, a New Surge in State Gun Control Laws," *The New York Times*, December 14, 2018, citing Giffords. See also: "State legislatures passed 69 gun violence prevention laws this year, versus 9 that relaxed restrictions," *The Trace*, December 14, 2018; Melissa Block, "2018 Brought A Tectonic Shift In The Gun Control Movement, Advocates Say," NPR, Morning Edition, December 26, 2018; German Lopez, "The 2018 midterm elections may have exposed a shift on gun control," *Vox*, November. 7, 2018.

621 Philip Bump, "The NRA appears to pull old lawmaker grades from its website," *The Washington Post*, June 12, 2018; "NRA Tacitly Admits its Brand Is Toxic, Pulls Down NRA Grades Because 'Our Enemies Were Using That,'" Everytown for Gun Safety, June 13, 2018; Philip Bump, "A leading gun-control group just released nine years of NRA grades for politicians," *The Washington Post*, June 20, 2018.

622 Peter Hirschfeld, "Poll Shows Widespread Support For New Gun Laws," Vermont Public Radio, July 23, 2018.

623 Elaina Plott, "'I Think We Have a Leadership Problem': Growing numbers of congressional Republicans are pressing for action on guns," *The Atlantic*, March 16, 2018.

624 Alex Yablon, "The NRA Steps Into the Fight Against Direct Democracy," *The Trace*, July 2, 2019.

625 On a junior high civics test, it would be important to say that our government is a republic or representative democracy, not an Athenian or pure democracy. But common usage describes countries that have free and fair elections, free speech, a free press, and the rule of law as "democracies" or "liberal democracies," as opposed to authoritarian nations that don't have honest elections, a free press, and the rule of law.

626 18 U.S.C. § 925(c).

627 See, *e.g.,* D.W. Webster, J.S. Vernick, L.M. Hepburn, "Relationship between licensing, registration, and other gun sales laws and the source State of crime guns," *Injury Prevention* 2001;7:184-189; D. Webster, C.K Crifasi, J. S. Vernick, "Effects of the

repeal of Missouri's handgun purchaser licensing law on homicides," *J. Urban Health* 2014 April 91(2):293-302. doi: 10.1007/s11524- 014-9865-8; Erratum in *J Urban Health* 2014 June; 91(3):598-601; K.E. Rudolph, E.A. Stuart, J. S. Vernick, *et al.*, "Association between Connecticut's permit-to-purchase handgun law and homicides," *Am J Public Health.* 2015; 105(8):e49–e54.628.

628 See e.g., C.K. Crifasi, M. Merrill-Francis, A. McCourt, *et al.*, "Association between Firearm Laws and Homicide in Urban Counties," *J Urban Health.* 2018, June 9:5(3):383-390. doi:10.1007/s11524-018-0273-3; A.M. Zeoli, A. McCourt, S. Buggs, *et al.*, "Analysis of the Strength of Legal Firearms Restrictions for Perpetrators of Domestic Violence and Their Association With Intimate Partner Homicide," *Am J.Epidemiology,* 2018 July 1;187(7): 1449-1455.

629 D. W. Webster, A. D. McCourt, C.K. Crifasi, *et al.*, "Evidence concerning the regulation of firearms design, sale, and carryingon fatal mass shootings in the United States," *Criminology & Public Policy.* 2020;19:171–212. https://doi.org/10.1111/1745- 9133.12487.

630 See, *e.g.*, Jeffrey W. Swanson, *et al.*, "Implementation and Effectiveness of Connecticut's Risk-Based Gun Removal La Does It Prevent Suicides?" 80 *Law And Contemporary Problems* 179-208, 2017; Aaron J. Kivisto and Peter Lee Phalen, "Effects of Risk-Based Firearm Seizure Laws in Connecticut and Indiana on Suicide Rates, 1981–2015," *Psychiatry Online,* June 1, 2018.

631 Morning Consult, August 2-6, 2018, National Tracking Poll #190816. August 5-7, 2019.

632 Aaron Zitner and Alex Leary, "Trump Leans on a Changed GOP for Support," Wall Street Journal, October 18, 2019 online and October 19, 2019 in print.

633 Alec Tyson, "The 2018 midterm vote: Divisions by race, gender, education," Pew Research Center Fact Tank., November. 8, 2018; CNN, Exit Polls,2018.

634 Mike Spies and Ashley Balcerzak, "The NRA Placed Big Bets on the 2016 Election, and Won Almost All of Them," Open Secrets.org, November 9, 2016; Russ Choma and Andy Kroll, "The NRA Raised a Record Amount of Money in 2016," *Mother Jones,* January 4, 2018.

635 Kira Lerner, "These 23 GOP Senators Voted Against Background Checks," June 21, 2016.

636 David Daley, RAT F**KED. The True Story Behind The Secret Plan to Steal America's Democracy (New York: Liveright/Norton 2016).

637 Jane Mayer, DARK MONEY: The Hidden History of the Billionaires Behind the Rise of the Radical Right (Doubleday/Penguin Random House LL. 2016).

638 Matt Cohen, "Bullets vs. Ballots," Mother Jones, Jan/February 2020, pp. 11 - 13.

639 Marilynne Robinson, "This Cruel Parody of Representation," *The Nation,* January

29/February 5, 2018, pp. 24-27.

640 *Idem.*

641 World Population Review, "US States - Ranked by Population 2019."

642 Idem.

643 "Filibuster," Wikipedia, collecting cites at notes 57-59.

644 Under current rules, budget reconciliation bills are not subject to filibuster. 645 States also award electors on a winner-take-all basis, which contributes to the problem. When Donald Trump won Wisconsin and Michigan in 2016 by one percent of the popular vote, for example, he got all of those states' votes in the Electoral College. Nothing in the Constitution requires that.

646 Citizens United v. Federal Election Comm'n, 558 U.S. 310 (2010).

647 The Economist/YouGov Poll, July 27-30, 2019. [Toplines] Only 11% said they were "Very satisfied" and 29% pronounced themselves "Somewhat satisfied."

648 In the Economist/YouGov poll, 10% strongly agreed and 20% somewhat agreed that the president should govern without much interference from Congress or the courts. See Q.14. In an August 2017 ABC/Washington Post poll, 10% expressed support for the Alt-Right. See Q. 5. Along the same line, 9% said it was acceptable to hold Neo-Nazi and white supremacist views. See Q.7. Among men, Republicans and strong conservatives 13% felt that Neo-Nazi and white supremacist views were acceptable. Among those who strongly approved of President.Trump's work in office, 17% said Neo-Nazi and white supremacist views were acceptable. A suspiciously large 13% of strong Trump supporters claimed not to have an opinion (sug-gesting that many of them approved of Neo-Nazi or white-supremacist views, but didn't want to say so. See: Langer Research Associates, "Trump Approval Is Low But Steady; On Charlottesville, Lower Still," ABC/Washington Post, February 17, 2018.

649 Alec MacGillis, Mini-Essay on Twitter, February 17, 2018.

650 See, *e.g.,* Michael M. Grynbaum, "Right-Wing Media Uses Parkland Shooting as Conspiracy Fodder," *The New York Times,* February 20, 2018; Jason Wilson, "How right wingers have attacked Parkland students with lies, hoaxes and smears," *The Guardian,* March 26, 2019, collecting links; Craig Timberg and Drew Harwell, "We studied thousands of anonymous posts about the Parkland attack--and found a conspiracy in the making," *The Washington Post,* February 27, 2018; Tina Nguyen, "'Give Me A Break': How The Far Right Is Smearing School-Shooting Survivors," *Vanity Fair,* February 21, 2018.

651 Emma González, "A Young Activist's Advice: Vote, Shave Your Head and Cry Whenever You Need To," *The New York Times,* October 5, 2018.

652 Angie Drobnic Holan, Amy Sherman, "PolitiFact's Lie of the Year: Online smear

machine tries to take down Parkland students," PolitiFact, December 11,2 018; Melina Delkic, "Here's the Fake News About the Florida School Shooting, Debunked," *Newsweek,* February 22, 2018; Brett Clarkson, "The 'online smear machine" that called Parkland students 'crisis actors' is PolitiFact's Lie of the Year," South *Florida Sun Sentinel,* December 11, 2018.

653 Quinnipiac University, April 6-9, released April 11, 2018, Q. 44.

654 United States Election Project, "2018 November General Election: Turn-out Rates," updated December 14, 2018.

655 Drew Desilver, "U.S. trails most developed countries in voter turn out," Pew Research Center, May 21, 2018. "OECD" refers to the Organization for Economic Cooperation and Development and its thirty-six member countries. Those countries are the usual benchmark for comparisons with other advanced democratic nations.

656 Grace Segers, "Record voter turnout in 2018 midterm elections," CBS News, November.7, 2018.

657 United States Election Project, "2018 November General Election Turnout Rates," updated December 14, 2018.

658 Marilynne Robinson, "This Cruel Parody of Representation," *The Nation,* pp. 23 *et seq.,* January 29/February 5, 2018, pp. 23-27.

659 Tim Wu, "The Oppression of the Supermajority," *The New York Times,* March 5, 2019

660 Marilynne Robinson, "This Cruel Parody of Representation," *The Nation,* pp. 23 et seq., January 29/February 5, 2018, pp. 24-27.

661 Quinnipiac University, "Two-Thirds Of U.S. Voters Take Climate Personally, Quinnipiac University National Poll Finds; Opposition To The Wall Hits New High,"Q. 63, April 5, 2017. In this poll, taken March 30-April 3, 2017, some 76% rejected the notion that climate change is a hoax"; only 19% thought it was

662 Public Policy Polling, 2018 Shaping Up Big For Democrats, September 28, 2017.

663 Osita Nwanevu, "The 2020 Presidential Hopefuls and the Politics of Consensus," *The New Yorker,* March 24, 2019. See also: Michael Gordon, "The US is being run by a government that no longer represents the people," *Business Insider,* December 7, 2019.

664 Tim Wu, "The Oppression of the Supermajority," *The New York Times,* March 5, 2019.

665 Clifford Young, "When it comes to guns, Americans use common sense, their political leaders don't." The Hill, March 27, 2018.

666 Maggie Astor and Karl Russell, "After Parkland, a New Surge in State Gun Control Laws," *The New York Times,* December 14, 2018, citing a Giffords Report. See also: "State legislatures passed 69 gun violence prevention laws this year, versus 9 that relaxed.

restrictions," *The Trace*, December 14, 2018; Melissa Block, "2018 Brought A 'Tectonic Shift' In The Gun Control Movement, Advocates Say," NPR, Morning Edition, December 26, 2018; German Lopez, "The 2018 midterm elections may have exposed a shift on gun control," *Vox*, November. 7, 2018

667 Allison Anderman, "Gun Law Trend Watch 2019 Year-End Review," Giffords Law Center, December 18, 2019. See also: Asher Stockler, "Since Parkland Shooting, States Have Enacted 137 Measures To Restrict Gun Access And Reduce Gun Violence, Analysis shows," *Newsweek*, December 19, 2019.

Selected Bibliography

Case, Anne and Deaton, Angus. *Deaths of Despair and the Future of Capitalism.* Princeton and Oxford: Princeton University Press, 2020.

Carlson, Jennifer. *Citizen-Protectors: The Everyday Politics of Guns in an Age of Decline.* Oxford University Press, 2015.

Cook, Philip J. and Kristin A. Goss. *The Gun Debate: What Everyone Needs To Know.* New York: Oxford University Press, 2014.

Daley, D. *Ratf**ked: The True Story Behind the Secret Plan to Steal America's Democracy.* Liveright Publishing Corporation, A Division of W.W. Norton, 2016.

DeBrabander, Firmin. *Do Guns Make Us Free? Democracy and the Armed Society.* New Haven: Yale Unversity Press Books, 2015.

Diaz, Tom. *Making a Killing: The Business of Guns in America.* New Press, 1999.

———. *The Last Gun: How Changes in the Gun Industry Are Killing Americans and What It Will Take to Stop It.* New Press, 2013.

Gabor, Thomas. *Confronting Gun Violence in America.* 1st ed. Palgrave Macmillan, 2016.

Hemenway, David. *Private Guns, Public Health, New Ed.* Ann Arbor, MI: University of Michigan Press, 2017.

Hogg, David, and Lauren Hogg, *#NEVER AGAIN, A New Generation*

Draws the Line. New York: Random House, 2018.

Joslyn, Mark R. *The Gun Gap: The Influence of Gun Ownership on Political Behavior and Attitudes.* New York: Oxford University Press 2020.

King, Stephen. *Guns.* Philtrum Press (Kindle Single), 2013.

Klarevas, L. *Rampage Nation: Securing America from Mass Shootings.* Prometheus Books, 2016.

Lane, Charles. *The Day Freedom Died: The Colfax Massacre, The Supreme Court, and the Betrayal of Reconstruction.* New York: Henry Holt & Co., 2008.

Larson, Erik. *Lethal Passage: How The Travels Of A Single Handgun Expose the Roots of America's Gun Crisis.* Crown Publishers Inc., 1994.

Merry, Melissa K. *Wapred Narratives, Distortion in the Framing of Gun Policy.* Ann Arbor: University of Michigan Press Press, 2020.

Piketty, Thomas (translated by Arthur Goldhammer). *CAPITAL in the Twenty-First Century.* Cambridge, MA: The Belknap Press of Harvard University, 2014.

———. *Captial And Ideology.* Cambridge, MA: The Belknap Press of Harvard University, 2020.

Stroud, Angela. *Good Guys with Guns: The Appeal and Consequences of Concealed Carry.* Chapel Hill: The University of North Carolina Press, 2016.

Stiglitz, Joseph E. *The Price Of Inequality: How Today's Divided Society Endangers Our Future.* New York: W.W. Norton, 2013.

Webster, Daniel W. and Jon S. Vernick, eds., *Reducing Gun Violence in America.* Baltimore: The Johns Hopkins University Press, 2013.

***

Alban, Rodrigo F., Miriam Nuño, Ara Ko, Galinos Barmparas, Azaria V. Lewis, and Daniel R. Margulies. "Weaker Gun State Laws Are Associated with Higher Rates of Suicide Secondary to Firearms." *Journal of Surgical Research* 221 (January 1, 2018): 135–42.

Azrael, Deborah, Lisa Hepburn, David Hemenway, and Matthew Miller. "The Stock and Flow of U.S. Firearms: Results from the 2015 National Firearms Survey." *RSF: The Russell Sage Foundation Journal of the Social*

Sciences 3, no. 5 (October 1, 2017): 38–57.

Barry, Colleen L, Daniel W. Webster. Elizabeth Stone, Cassandra K Crifasi, Jon S Vernick, and Emma E McGinty. "Public Support for Gun Violence Prevention Policies Among Gun Owners and Non–Gun Owners in 2017." *American Journal of Public Health* 108, no. 7 (May 17, 2018): 878–81.

Joslyn, Mark, and Donald P Haider-Markel. "Americans Vastly Overestimate the Number of Gun Owners." *The Washington Post*, May 07, 2018.

Joslyn, Mark R., and Donald P Haider-Markel. "Motivated Innumeracy: Estimating the Size of the Gun Owner Population and Its Consequences for Opposition to Gun Restrictions." *Politics & Policy* 46, no. 6 (2018): 827–50.

Kalesan, Bindu, Matthew E Mobily, Olivia Keiser, Jeffrey A Fagan, and Sandro Galea. "Firearm Legislation and Firearm Mortality in the USA: A Cross-Sectional, State-Level Study." *The Lancet* 387, no. 10030 (April 30, 2016): 1847–55.

Kalesan, Bindu, Marcos D Villarreal, Katherine M Keyes, and Sandro Galea. "Gun Ownership and Social Gun Culture." *Injury Prevention* 22, no. 3 (June 1, 2016): 216–20.

Kalesan, Bindu, Mrithyunjay A Vyliparambil, Yi Zuo, Jeffrey J Siracuse, Jeffrey A. Fagan, Charles C Branas, and Sandro Galea. "Cross-Sectional Study of Loss of Life Expectancy at Different Ages Related to Firearm Deaths among Black and White Americans." *BMJ Evidence-Based Medicine* 24, no. 2 (April 1, 2019): 55–58.

Stroebe, Wolfgang, N. Pontus Leander, and Arie W Kruglanski. "Is It a Motivational Bases Dangerous World Out There? The Motivational Bases of American Gun Ownership. T*he Personality and Social Psychology Bulletin* 43, no. 8 (June 8, 2017): 1071–85.

Stroud, Angela. "Good Guys With Guns: Hegemonic Masculinity and Concealed Handguns." *Gender & Society* 26, no. 2 (February 21, 2012): 216–38.

Wintemute, Garen J. "Alcohol Misuse, Firearm Violence Perpetration, and Public Policy in the United States." *Preventive Medicine* 79 (2015): 15–21.

Wintemute, Garen J, Mona A Wright, Christiana M Drake, and James J Beaumont. "Subsequent Criminal Activity Among Violent Misdemeanants Who Seek to Purchase Handguns Risk Factors and Effec-tiveness of Denying Handgun Purchase." *JAMA* 285, no. 8 (February 28, 2001): 1019–26.

Zeoli, April M.,and Jennifer K Paruk. "Potential to Prevent Mass Shootings through Domestic Violence Firearm Restrictions." *Criminology & Public Policy* 19, no. 1(February 1 ,2020): 129–45.

Index

#HeresToFreedom, 244
#NeverAgain, 14, 83, 115, 152, 218, 290, 310
accidental shootings, 259, 260
Advance Notice, 243, 245
alcohol, 128, 131, 203
Anderman, Allison, 142
Armslist, 73, 74, 75, 76, 79, 80
Armslist.com, 79, 80
assault weapon, 9, 55, 56, 57, 59, 66, 70, 105, 164, 174, 179, 180, 181, 183, 184, 185, 186, 187, 188, 189, 190, 192, 194, 195, 196, 197, 198, 199, 201, 204, 206, 207, 209, 213, 214, 216, 218, 221, 222, 224, 226, 229, 239, 287, 290, 291, 305, 309, 314
  Ator, Seth, 74, 79, 177
attention deficit/hyperactivity disorder
  ADHD, 223
Azana Spa, 73, 76
Bachelor degrees, 51, 87
barrel shroud, 179
Barry, Colleen L., 9, 124, 144, 161, 332
Betts, Connor, 221
black market, 80, 167, 226, 288, 289
Bowers, Robert, 177
boyfriend loophole, 112
Bradley, Francho, 253, 255
Brady Handgun Violence Prevention Act of 1993, 76
Brown, Joshua D., 198, 200, 339
bump stocks, 241, 242, 243, 245, 246, 247, 248, 249, 250, 251, 253, 254, 255, 291, 332
CAP laws, 260, 261, 262, 267, 268, 269, 271, 272, 273

Captive agency, 243
Cargill, Michael, 252
Centers for Disease Control and Prevention
  CDC, 262
Child Access Protection, 261, 267
CAP laws, 260, 261, 272, 287
Chipman, David, 221
Cillizza, Chris, 243
civil war, 99, 253, 285
Clinton, Hillary, 23, 81, 171, 268, 269
Colbert, Tavares Donnell, 73, 76, 77, 167
Columbine High School, 35, 202, 204
Congress, 3, 5, 12, 35, 60, 75, 78, 84, 90, 98, 101, 102, 104, 108, 109, 112, 117, 121, 135, 149, 152, 156, 164, 166, 174, 175, 179, 181, 204, 208, 215, 216, 225, 226, 230, 241, 242, 243, 245, 246, 250, 251, 255, 267, 271, 273, 284, 285, 286, 288, 289, 290, 291, 296, 299, 300, 302, 306, 3(10, 311, 313, 315, 316, 344, 367
Cox, John Woodrow, 149, 266
Craddock, DeWayne, 224, 225
Crifasi, Cassandra K., 332
Cruz, Nikolas, 13, 137, 138, 155, 158, 176, 177, 183, 203, 206, 209, 218
Debnam, Dale, 74
Democrats, 3, 14, 17, 37, 48, 54, 74, 81, 91, 93, 104, 200, 209, 242, 268, 278, 280, 339
DePino, Bob, 285
domestic violence restraining order,
  DVRC   116, 120

Eddie Eagle, 258
Education Department, 266
Elfrink, Tim, 83, 137, 138, 198
Every Town for Gun Safety Everytown, 78
ex parte, 110, 120, 151
Expungement, 131
Farook, Syed Rizwan, 91, 178
fear-mongering, 168, 261
Federal Bureau of Investigation FBI, 76
federal firearm licensee, 205
Feinstein, Diane, 242
flash suppressor, 179
Fox News, 15, 83, 84, 85, 86, 87, 88, 145, 147, 188, 197, 198, 208, 209, 210, 211, 323, 330
Gallup, 49, 50, 81, 186, 187, 331
Giffords Law Center, 94, 114, 124, 142, 160, 238
González, Emma, 13, 306, 307, 308
Goodloe, Stephanie, 107, 109
gun grabbers, 228
gun households, 18, 86, 103, 133, 171, 172, 210, 216, 235, 248, 269
gun lobby, 3, 13, 14, 90, 93, 121, 125, 135, 152, 282, 285, 304, 306
gun mortality, 78
gun owners, 2, 3, 5, 8, 9, 41, 49, 51, 80, 86, 90, 101, 122, 124, 136, 141, 158, 159, 160, 161, 164, 167, 182, 228, 232, 239, 255, 260, 261, 267, 268, 269, 270, 271, 273, 288, 291, 311, 367
Gun Owners of America, 251, 285, 304
gun show loophole, 76
Haider-Markel, Donald P., 41, 42, 43, 47, 360
handgun, 54, 55, 78, 98, 129, 140, 164, 203, 206, 207, 271
Haughton, Radcliffe, 73
Hogg, David, 13, 306, 307, 308
Holmes, James Eagan, 178, 220
Howard, Ian, 138, 139, 155
Independents, 3, 74, 209, 268

Internet loophole, 76
intimate partner, 108, 110, 111, 112, 115, 289
intimate partners, 78, 79
Jennings, Adrianne, 253
Johns Hopkins, 124, 144, 145, 267, 332, 367
juvenile, 205, 207
Kasky, Cameron, 253
Kasky, Jeff, 253
Kaufman, Elinore J., 32
Kelley, Devin, 178
Kinkel, Kip, 202, 206, 219
Klaveras, Louis, 181
Koper, Christopher, 229, 230
Lanza, Adam, 90, 178, 220, 266
large-capacity magazines, 9, 220, 221, 222, 225, 226, 227, 228, 229, 230, 231, 232, 233, 236, 237, 238, 239, 254, 291
Las Vegas Strip, 11, 12, 81, 89, 122, 132, 145, 168, 173, 184, 208, 230, 242, 246, 250, 291
Las Vegas Strip massacre, 89, 132, 168, 184, 208, 246, 291
Lautenberg Amendment, 108, 116
lie and try, 158, 159, 288
long guns, 57, 59, 182, 205, 206, 207, 272
Loughner, Jared, 219, 223, 226
Malik, Tashfeen, 91, 178
Malloy, Tim, 1
March for Our Lives, 14, 74, 151, 171, 255, 284
Marjory Stoneman Douglas High School, 74, 83, 137, 152, 178, 203, 216, 244, 306, 315
Massie, Rep. Thomas, 285, 300, 304
Mateen, Omar, 91, 98, 178, 221
McConnell, Mitch, 152, 242, 243, 246, 255, 306, 307, 313
Mogadishu, 183, 225, 309
Morning Consult, 15, 45, 84, 85, 86, 87, 88, 89, 101, 102, 103, 132, 133, 134, 168, 169, 170, 171, 172, 173,

184, 187, 188, 189, 190, 191, 193, 194, 196, 208, 209, 210, 211, 212, 213, 214, 215, 231, 232, 233, 234, 235, 236, 247, 248, 249, 250, 267, 268, 269, 270, 271, 278, 279, 323, 324, 334, 335, 350, 352, 353, 354 Mother Jones, 221

National Firearms Act of 1934, 65, 241, 242

National Instant Criminal Background
  Check System
    NCIS, 74, 75, 98
  No Fly, 98, 100, 101, 102, 103, 104, 105
  NRA, 10, 54, 75, 99, 105, 125, 140, 149, 150, 152, 167, 181, 198, 217, 226, 243, 251, 258, 261, 285, 296, 297, 302, 304, 306, 307, 310, 316, 340

Nwanevu, Osita, 313
Orlando, 91, 178, 221, 300, 305, 328
outlier, 248
Paddock, Stephen, 12, 178, 225, 241
Parker, Gabriel Ross, 339 *Parkland, Florida*, 13, 74, 83, 105, 137, 143, 151, 176, 203, 205, 206, 216, 230, 244, 267, 306, 315 permit-to-purchase, 77, 158, 160 Peterson, Tyler, 178
Pew Research Center, 51, 101, 338, 339, 367
President Trump, 90, 105, 151, 152, 216, 245, 246, 251
Private sales, 73
Proposition 63, 239
Public Policy Polling
  PPP, 74, 81, 84, 101, 102, 185, 187, 190, 208, 284, 324, 339, 340
published ordinance, 205
Pulse, 91, 98, 104, 221, 300
  Purdy, Edward, 56
Qui........ University, 219, 223, 226

red flag, 2, 136, 137, 138, 140, 141, 142, 143, 144, 147, 149, 150, 151, 1 2, 153, 154, 155, 156, 290

Reinking, Travis, 139, 140, 155, 157,

Quinnipiac, 1, 81, 122, 132, 185, 197, 198, 284, 341, 342, 343, 367

Republicans, 3, 5, 8, 12, 15, 18, 37, 54, 74, 75, 84, 85, 90, 91, 102, 103, 104, 105, 122, 133, 135, 137, 171, 172, 173, 189, 190, 196, 209, 210, 213, 214, 215, 216, 233, 234, 248, 251, 255, 268, 273, 339

Rhode Island Coalition Against Gun Violence, 222
Rich, Steven, 266
rituals, 316
Road to Change, 308
Ryan, Paul, 91, 104, 243, 246, 255, 285
San Bernardino, 91, 104, 178
school shooting, 13, 151, 155, 206, 231, 244, 266, 290
Seattle Pacific University, 219 Second Amendment, 3, 8, 9, 14, 62, 66, 95, 121, 125, 143, 228, 239, 240, 246, 253, 278, 285, 290, 302
Seung-Hui, Cho, 220
Silver, Nate, 48
sky is blue, 74
Slide Fire, 241, 242, 244, 245, 246
Steinbrook, Robert, 32
Stoneman Douglas High School, 13, 14, 105, 143, 152, 176, 183, 205, 207 street crime, 57, 228, 291 substance abuse, 131
Takings Clause, 239, 240 Terrorist Screening
TSDB, 97

Terrorist Screening Center, 97
thoughts and prayers, 238, 314
Thurston High School, 203, 204, 219
Tree of Life Synagogue, 177
Trump, Donald, 12, 15, 23, 36, 81, 85, 86, 90, 102, 103, 105, 133, 135, 171, 172, 173, 190, 210, 214, 215, 216, 217, 234, 244, 245, 248, 251, 268, 269, 271, 273, 311, 312, 329, 339, 340, 341, 342
Trump voters, 81, 85, 90, 103, 133, 135, 171, 172, 173, 210, 215, 216, 251, 268, 273

violent domestic abuse conviction, 108
Violent Misdemeanor, 131, 289
Violent Misdemeanor Law, 289
Virginia Beach, 224, 238
Waffle House, 139, 140, 157, 219
Webster, Daniel W., 332
Wu, Timothy, 314
Yablon, Alex, 182
Ybarra, Aaron, 219
Zawahri, John, 178

Acknowledgments

The author owes a debt of gratitude to the polling organizations that routinely publish the results of their polls, especially those that provide cross-tabulated data. He also wishes to acknowledge the gracious re-sponses he received from those organizations to his queries and in one case his request for additional data. He hopes that this book will encourage researchers to mine that data in greater than is presently the case. He also hopes that the polling companies will take seriously his suggestion that they should adjust their samples to account for the number of gun owners.

The author is also grateful to the many publishers who gave permission to use brief quotes from their publications. The same is true of the indi-viduals who gave permission to quote their responses on Quora, even though they knew the author did not share their views.

Special thanks to Sue Rohan and Yolande Marsden for proofreading. The author is grateful to the Covington Writers Group and to his usual circle of beta readers. You know who you are.

And, of course, many thanks to my wife, Beth. Over the three years of research and writing that went in to this book, new waves of polls and new books and studies arrived seemingly with the frequency of waves crashing on a beach. When that happened, Beth had to listen to my complaints that this project was becoming too big and that I was about to give up on it.

The Author

Gary Reed draws on his extensive legal experience in his writing. He practiced law in a large law firm and later in an in-house capacity. Throughout his career, he handled complex litigation across the country.

The essential skills a litigator must have are the ability to absorb large amounts of material, some of which will be conflicting, draw conclusions objectively, and then explain the material to others—a judge, a jury, or mediator. Or quite often, to corporate management or a regulator. Mr. Reed's goal in writing this book was to apply those hard-won skills to the challenging topic of gun-violence-prevention policy.

Mr. Reed's father took him hunting and fishing and tried to instill in him an interest in hunting and fishing. Even before he was old enough for high school, Mr. Reed learned to shoot and had his own twelve-gauge shot-gun and a .22 rifle. But he never developed his father's interest in hunting or fishing. Neither he nor his father had any interest in guns outside of hunting.

Mr. Reed is the author of two novels, THINGS COULD GET UGLY and A FATAL CELL PHONE VIDEO.

www.ingramcontent.com/pod-product-compliance
Lightning Source LLC
Chambersburg PA
CBHW071347210526
45465CB00001B/8